BUAD 311

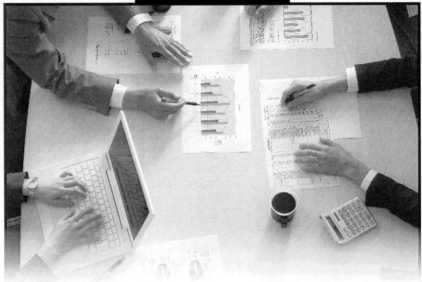

OPERATIONS
MANAGEMENT

University of Southern California | Marshall School of Business

Selected materials from

Matching Supply with Demand: An Introduction to Operations Management, Second Edition

GERARD CACHON
University of Pennsylvania

CHRISTIAN TERWIESCH
University of Pennsylvania

Operations and Supply Chain Management, Thirteenth Edition

F. ROBERT JACOBS
Indiana University/Bloomington

RICHARD B. CHASE
University of Southern California

Case Studies

HARVARD BUSINESS PUBLISHING

 **Learning Solutions**

Boston   Burr Ridge, IL   Dubuque, IA   New York   San Francisco
Bangkok   Bogotá   Caracas   Lisbon   London   Madrid
Mexico City   Milan   New Delhi   Seoul   Singapore   Sydney   Taipei   Toronto

D1401962

BUAD 311
OPERATIONS MANAGEMENT
UNIVERSITY OF SOUTHERN CALIFORNIA | MARSHALL SCHOOL OF BUSINESS

5 6 7 8 9 0 DIG DIG 12

ISBN-13: 978-0-697-79527-4
ISBN-10: 0-697-79527-6

Learning Solutions Manager: Terri Harvey
Production Editor: Jessica Portz
Cover Photo: Businesspeople at a table © Indeed/Getty Images
Cover Design: Fairfax Hutter
Printer/Binder: Digital Impressions

Brief Contents

Table of Contents

Chapter 1

The Process View of the Organization

Matching supply and demand would be easy if business processes would be instantaneous and could immediately create any amount of supply to meet demand. Understanding the questions of "Why are business processes not instantaneous?" and "What constrains processes from creating more supply?" is thereby at the heart of operations management. To answer these questions, we need to take a detailed look at how business processes actually work. In this chapter, we introduce some concepts fundamental to process analysis. The key idea of the chapter is that it is not sufficient for a firm to create great products and services; the firm also must design and improve its business processes that supply its products and services.

To get more familiar with the process view of a firm, we now take a detailed look behind the scenes of a particular operation, namely the Department of Interventional Radiology at Presbyterian Hospital in Philadelphia.

1.1 Presbyterian Hospital in Philadelphia

Interventional radiology is a subspecialty field of radiology that uses advanced imaging techniques such as real-time X-rays, ultrasound, computed tomography, and magnetic resonance imaging to perform minimally invasive procedures.

Over the past decade, interventional radiology procedures have begun to replace an increasing number of standard "open surgical procedures" for a number of reasons. Instead of being performed in an operating room, interventional radiology procedures are performed in an angiography suite (see Figure 1.1). Although highly specialized, these rooms are less expensive to operate than conventional operating rooms. Interventional procedures are often safer and have dramatically shorter recovery times compared to traditional surgery. Also, an interventional radiologist is often able to treat diseases such as advanced liver cancer that cannot be helped by standard surgery.

Although we may not have been in the interventional radiology unit, many, if not most, of us have been in a radiology department of a hospital at some point in our life. From the perspective of the patient, the following steps need to take place before the patient can go home or return to his or her hospital unit. In process analysis, we refer to these steps as *activities*:

- Registration of the patient.
- Initial consultation with a doctor; signature of the consent form.

FIGURE 1.1
Example of a Procedure in an Interventional Radiology Unit

Reprinted with permission of Arrow International, Inc.

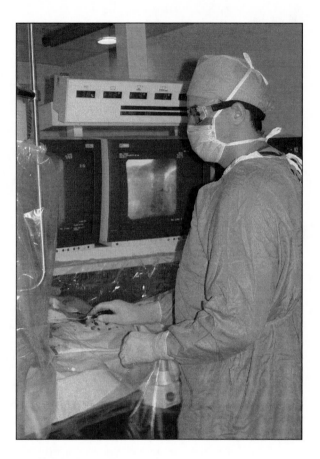

- Preparation for the procedure.
- The actual procedure.
- Removal of all equipment.
- Recovery in an area outside the angiography suite.
- Consultation with the doctor.

Figure 1.2 includes a graphical representation of these steps, called a *Gantt diagram* (named after the 19th century industrialist Henry Gantt). It provides several useful pieces of information.

First, the Gantt chart allows us to see the process steps and their durations, which are also called *activity times.* The duration simply corresponds to the length of the corresponding bars. Second, the Gantt diagram also illustrates the dependence between the various process activities. For example, the consultation with the doctor can only occur once the patient has arrived and been registered. In contrast, the preparation of the angiography suite can proceed in parallel to the initial consultation.

You might have come across Gantt charts in the context of project management. Unlike process analysis, project management is typically concerned with the completion of one single project. The most well-known concept of project management is the *critical path.* The critical path is composed of all those activities that—if delayed—would lead to a delay in the overall completion time of the project, or—in this case—the time the patient has completed his or her stay in the radiology unit.

In addition to the eight steps described in the Gantt chart of Figure 1.2, most of us associate another activity with hospital care: waiting. Strictly speaking, waiting is not really

FIGURE 1.2
Gantt Chart Summarizing the Activities for Interventional Radiology

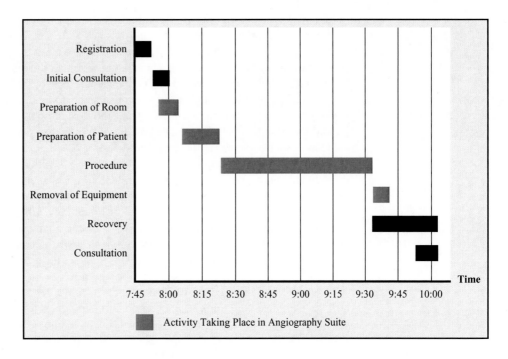

an activity, as it does not add any value to the process. However, waiting is nevertheless relevant. It is annoying for the patient and can complicate matters for the hospital unit. For this reason, waiting times take an important role in operations management. Figure 1.3 shows the actual durations of the activities for a patient arriving at 12:30, as well as the time the patient needs to wait before being moved to the angiography suite.

FIGURE 1.3
Gantt Chart Summarizing the Activities for a Patient Arriving at 12:30

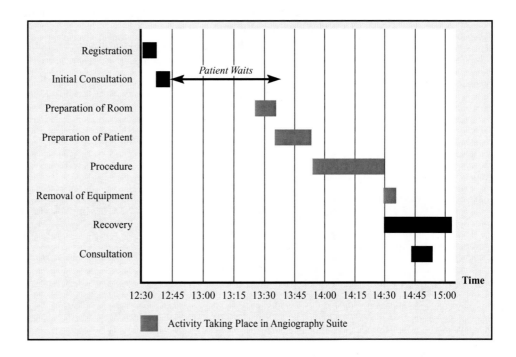

But why is there waiting time? Waiting is—to stay in the medical language for the moment—a symptom of supply–demand mismatch. If supply would be unlimited, our visit to the hospital would be reduced to the duration of the activities outlined in Figure 1.2 (the critical path). Imagine visiting a hospital in which all the nurses, technicians, doctors, and hospital administrators would just care for you!

Given that few of us are in a position to receive the undivided attention of an entire hospital unit, it is important that we not only take the egocentric perspective of the patient, but look at the hospital operations more broadly. From the perspective of the hospital, there are many patients "flowing" through the process.

The people and the equipment necessary to support the interventional radiology process deal with many patients, not just one. We refer to these elements of the process as the *process resources.* Consider, for example, the perspective of the nurse and how she/he spends her/his time in the department of interventional radiology. Obviously, radiology from the viewpoint of the nurse is not an exceptional event, but a rather repetitive endeavor. Some of the nurse's work involves direct interaction with the patient; other work—while required for the patient—is invisible to the patient. This includes the preparation of the angiography suite and various aspects of medical record keeping.

Given this repetitive nature of work, the nurse as well as the doctors, technicians, and hospital administrators think of interventional radiology as a process, not a project. Over the course of the day, they see many patients come and go. Many hospitals, including the Presbyterian Hospital in Philadelphia, have a "patient log" that summarizes at what times patients arrive at the unit. This patient log provides a picture of demand on the corresponding day. The patient log for December 2, is summarized by Table 1.1.

Many of these arrivals were probably scheduled some time in advance. Our analysis here focuses on what happens to the patient once he/she has arrived in the interventional radiology unit. A separate analysis could be performed, looking at the process starting with a request for diagnostics up to the arrival of the patient.

Given that the resources in the interventional radiology unit have to care for 11 patients on December 2, they basically need to complete the work according to 11 Gantt charts of the type outlined in Figure 1.2. This—in turn—can lead to waiting times. Waiting times arise when several patients are "competing" for the same limited resource, which is illustrated by the following two examples.

First, observe that the critical path for a typical patient takes about 2 hours. Note further that we want to care for 11 patients over a 10-hour workday. Consequently, we will have to take care of several patients at once. This would not be a problem if we had unlimited resources, nurses, doctors, space in the angiography suites, and so forth. However,

TABLE 1.1
Patient Log on December 2

Number	Patient Name	Arrival Time	Room Assignment
1		7:35	Main room
2		7:45	
3		8:10	
4		9:30	Main room
5		10:15	Main room
6		10:30	Main room
7		11:05	
8		12:35	Main room
9		14:30	Main room
10		14:35	
11		14:40	

FIGURE 1.4
Time Patient Spent in the Interventional Radiology Unit (for Patients Treated in Main Room Only), Including Room Preparation Time

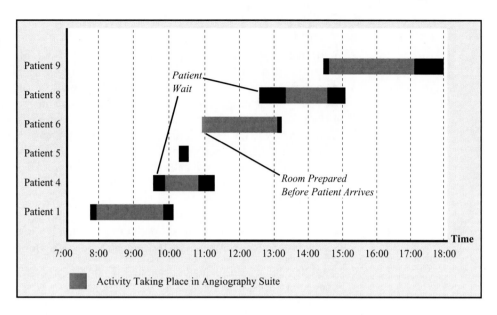

Activity Taking Place in Angiography Suite

given the resources that we have, if the Gantt charts of two patients are requesting the same resource simultaneously, waiting times result. For example, the second patient might require the initial consultation with the doctor at a time when the doctor is in the middle of the procedure for patient 1. Note also that patients 1, 4, 5, 6, 8, and 9 are assigned to the same room (the unit has a main room and a second room used for simpler cases), and thus they are also potentially competing for the same resource.

A second source of waiting time lies in the unpredictable nature of many of the activities. Some patients will take much longer in the actual procedure than others. For example, patient 1 spent 1:50 hours in the procedure, while patient 9 was in the procedure for 2:30 hours (see Figure 1.4). As an extreme case, consider patient 5, who refused to sign the consent form and left the process after only 15 minutes.

Such uncertainty is undesirable for resources, as it leaves them "flooded" with work at some moments in the day and "starved" for work at other moments. Figure 1.5 summarizes at what moments in time the angiography suite was used on December 2.

By now, we have established two views to the interventional radiology:

• The view of the patient for whom the idealized stay is summarized by Figure 1.2. Mismatches between supply and demand from the patient's perspective mean having a unit of demand (i.e., the patient) wait for a unit of supply (a resource).

• The view of the resources (summarized by Figure 1.5), which experience demand–supply mismatches when they are sometimes "flooded" with work, followed by periods of no work.

As these two perspectives are ultimately two sides of the same coin, we are interested in bringing these two views together. This is the fundamental idea of process analysis.

FIGURE 1.5
Usage of the Main Room

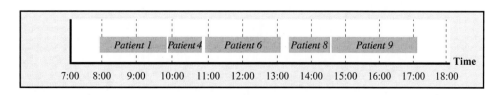

1.2 Three Measures of Process Performance

At the most aggregate level, a process can be thought of as a "black box" that uses *resources* (labor and capital) to transform *inputs* (undiagnosed patients, raw materials, unserved customers) into *outputs* (diagnosed patients, finished goods, served customers). This is shown in Figure 1.6. Chapter 2 explains the details of constructing figures like Figure 1.6, which are called *process flow diagrams*. When analyzing the processes that lead to the supply of goods and services, we first define our unit of analysis.

In the case of the interventional radiology unit, we choose patients as our *flow unit*. Choosing the flow unit is typically determined by the type of product or service the supply process is dealing with; for example, vehicles in an auto plant, travelers for an airline, or gallons of beer in a brewery.

As suggested by the term, flow units flow through the process, starting as input and later leaving the process as output. With the appropriate flow unit defined, we next can evaluate a process based on three fundamental process performance measures:

• The number of flow units contained within the process is called the *inventory* (in a production setting, it is referred to as *work in process, WIP*). Given that our focus is not only on production processes, inventory could take the form of the number of insurance claims or the number of tax returns at the IRS. There are various reasons why we find inventory in processes, which we discuss in greater detail below. While many of us might initially feel uncomfortable with the wording, the inventory in the case of the interventional radiology unit is a group of patients.

• The time it takes a flow unit to get through the process is called the *flow time*. The flow time takes into account that the item (flow unit) may have to wait to be processed because there are other flow units (inventory) in the process potentially competing for the same resources. Flow time is an especially important performance metric in service environments or in other business situations that are sensitive to delays, such as make-to-order production, where the production of the process only begins upon the arrival of the customer order. In a radiology unit, flow time is something that patients are likely to care about: it measures the time from their arrival at the interventional radiology unit to the time patients can go home or return to their hospital unit.

• Finally, the rate at which the process is delivering output (measured in [flow units/unit of time], e.g., units per day) is called the *flow rate* or the *throughput rate*. The maximum rate with which the process can generate supply is called the *capacity* of the process. For December 2, the throughput of the interventional radiology unit was 11 patients per day.

Table 1.2 provides several examples of processes and their corresponding flow rates, inventory levels, and flow times.

You might be somewhat irritated that we have moved away from the idea of supply and demand mismatch for a moment. Moreover, we have not talked about profits so far.

FIGURE 1.6
The Process View of an Organization

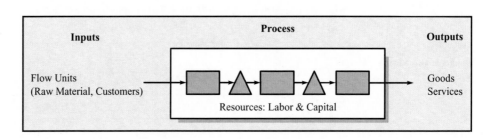

TABLE 1.2
Examples of Flow Rates, Inventories, and Flow Times

	U.S. Immigration	Champagne Industry	MBA Program	Large PC Manufacturer
Flow unit	Application for immigration benefit	Bottle of champagne	MBA student	Computer
Flow rate/ throughput	Approved or rejected visa cases: 6.3 million per year	260 million bottles per year	600 students per year	5,000 units per day
Flow time	Average processing time: 7.6 months	Average time in cellar: 3.46 years	2 years	10 days
Inventory	Pending cases: 4.0 million cases	900 million bottles	1,200 students	50,000 computers

However, note that increasing the maximum flow rate (capacity) avoids situations where we have insufficient supply to match demand. From a profit perspective, a higher flow rate translates directly into more revenues (you can produce a unit faster and thus can produce more units), assuming your process is currently *capacity constrained,* that is, there is sufficient demand that you could sell any additional output you make.

Shorter flow times reduce the time delay between the occurrence of demand and its fulfillment in the form of supply. Shorter flow times therefore also typically help to reduce demand–supply mismatches. In many industries, shorter flow times also result in additional unit sales and/or higher prices, which makes them interesting also from a broader management perspective.

Lower inventory results in lower working capital requirements as well as many quality advantages that we explore later in this book. A higher inventory also is directly related to longer flow times (explained below). Thus, a reduction in inventory also yields a reduction in flow time. As inventory is the most visible indication of a mismatch between supply and demand, we will now discuss it in greater detail.

1.3 Little's Law

At the end of October 2001, there was approximately $1.16 trillion of inventory in the United States and the inventory-to-sales ratio was 1.39. About one-third of that inventory was held by retailers, one-fifth by wholesalers, and the remainder by manufacturers. Over one-fourth of retail inventory is in the motor vehicle industry. The good news is that the inventory-to-sales ratio has been dropping over the last decade, from about 1.53 in 1992. The bad news is that there is still an enormous amount of capital tied up in inventory.

Accountants view inventory as an asset, but from an operations perspective, inventory often should be viewed as a liability. This is not a snub on accountants; inventory *should* be an asset on a balance sheet, given how accountants define an asset. But in common speech, the word *asset* means "desirable thing to have" and the dictionary defines *liability* as "something that works to one's disadvantage." In this sense, inventory can clearly be a liability. This is most visible in a service process such as a hospital unit, where patients in the waiting room obviously cannot be counted toward the assets of the health care system.

Let's take another visit to the interventional radiology unit. Even without much medical expertise, we can quickly find out which of the patients are currently undergoing care from some resource and which are waiting for a resource to take care of them. Similarly, if we took a quick walk through a factory, we could identify which parts of the inventory serve as raw materials, which ones are work-in-process, and which ones have completed the production process and now take the form of finished goods inventory.

However, taking a single walk through the process—dishwasher factory or interventional radiology unit—will not leave us with a good understanding of the underlying operations. All it will give us is a snapshot of what the process looked like at one single moment in time. Unfortunately, it is this same snapshot approach that underlies most management (accounting) reports: balance sheets itemize inventory into three categories (raw materials, WIP, finished goods); hospital administrators typically distinguish between pre- and postoperative patients. But such snapshots do not tell us *why* these inventories exist in the first place! Thus, a static, snapshot approach neither helps us to analyze business processes (why is there inventory?) nor helps us to improve them (is this the right amount of inventory?).

Now, imagine that instead of our single visit to the hospital unit, we would be willing to stay for some longer period of time. We arrive early in the morning and make ourselves comfortable at the entrance of the unit. Knowing that there are no patients in the interventional radiology unit overnight, we then start recording any arrival or departure of patients. In other words, we collect data concerning the patient inflow and outflow.

At the end of our stay, we can plot a graph similar to Figure 1.7. The upper of the two curves illustrates the cumulative number of patients who have entered the unit. The curve begins at time zero (7:00) and with zero patients. If we had done the same exercise in a unit with overnight patients, we would have recorded our initial patient count there. The lower of the two curves indicates the cumulative number of patients who have left the unit. Figure 1.7 shows us that by noon, seven patients have arrived, of which five have left the unit again.

At any given moment in time, the *vertical distance* between the upper curve and the lower curve corresponds to the number of patients in the interventional radiology unit, or—abstractly speaking—the inventory level. Thus, although we have not been inside the interventional radiology unit this day, we are able to keep track of the inventory level by comparing the cumulative inflow and outflow. For example, the inventory at noon consisted of two patients.

We also can look at the *horizontal distance* between the two lines. If the patients leave the unit in the same order they entered it, the horizontal gap would measure the exact amount of time each patient spent in the interventional radiology unit. More generally, given that the length of stay might vary across patients and patients do not necessarily leave the unit in the exact same sequence in which they entered it, the average gap between the two lines provides the average length of stay.

FIGURE 1.7
Cumulative Inflow and Outflow

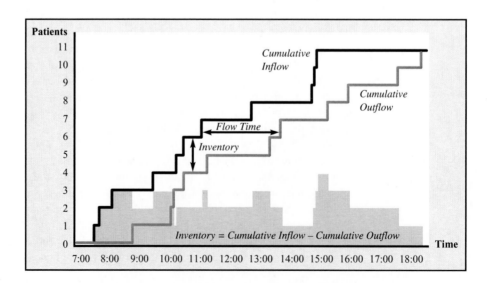

Thus, Figure 1.7 includes all three of the basic process performance measures we discussed on the previous page: flow rate (the slope of the two graphs), inventory (the vertical distance between the two graphs), and flow time (the horizontal distance between the two graphs).

Based on either the graph or the patient log, we can now compute these performance measures for December 2. We already know that the flow rate was 11 patients/day.

Next, consider inventory. Inventory changes throughout the day, reflecting the differences between inflow and outflow of patients. A "brute force" approach to compute average inventory is to count the inventory at every moment in time throughout the day, say every five minutes, and then take the average. For December 2, this computation yields an average inventory of 2.076 patients.

Next, consider the flow time, the time a patient spends in the unit. To compute that information, we need to add to the patient log, Table 1.1, the time each patient left the interventional radiology unit. The difference between arrival time and departure time would be the flow time for a given patient, which in turn would allow us to compute the average flow time across patients. This is shown in Table 1.3 and is in many ways similar to the two graphs in Figure 1.7. We can easily compute that on December 2, the average flow time was 2 hours, 4 minutes, and 33 seconds, or 2.076 hours.

At this point, you might ask: "Does the average inventory always come out the same as the average flow time?" The answer to this question is a profound *no*. However, the fact that the average inventory was 2.076 patients and the average flow time was 2.076 hours is no coincidence either.

To see how inventory and flow time relate to each other, let us review the three performance measures, flow rate, flow time, and inventory:

- Flow rate = 11 patients per day, which is equal to one patient per hour.
- Flow time = 2.076 hours.
- Inventory = 2.076 patients.

Thus, while inventory and flow time do not have to—and, in fact, rarely are—equal, they are linked in another form. We will now introduce this relationship as Little's Law (named after John D. C. Little).

$$\text{Average inventory } = \text{ Average flow rate } \times \text{ Average flow time} \qquad \text{(Little's Law)}$$

Many people think of this relationship as trivial. However, it is not. Its proof is rather complex for the general case (which includes—among other nasty things—variability) and by mathematical standards is very recent.

TABLE 1.3
Calculation of
Average Flow Time

Number	Patient Name	Arrival Time	Departure Time	Flow Time
1		7:35	8:50	1:15
2		7:45	10:05	2:20
3		8:10	10:10	2:00
4		9:30	11:15	1:45
5		10:15	10:30	0:15
6		10:30	13:35	3:05
7		11:05	13:15	2:10
8		12:35	15:05	2:30
9		14:30	18:10	3:40
10		14:35	15:45	1:10
11		14:40	17:20	2:40
			Average	2:04:33

Little's Law is useful in finding the third performance measure when the other two are known. For example, if you want to find out how long patients in a radiology unit spend waiting for their chest X-ray, you could do the following:

1. Observe the inventory of patients at a couple of random points during the day, giving you an average inventory. Let's say this number is seven patients: four in the waiting room, two already changed and waiting in front of the procedure room, and one in the procedure room.

2. Count the procedure slips or any other records showing how many patients were treated that day. This is the day's output. Let's say there were 60 patients over a period of 8 hours; we could say that we have a flow rate of $60/8 = 7.5$ patients/hour.

3. Use Little's Law to compute Flow time $=$ Inventory/Flow rate $= 7/7.5 = 0.933$ hour $= 56$ minutes. This tells us that, on average, it takes 56 minutes from the time a patient enters the radiology unit to the time his or her chest X-ray is completed. Note that this information would otherwise have to be computed by collecting additional data (e.g., see Table 1.3).

When does Little's Law hold? The short answer is *always*. For example, Little's Law does not depend on the sequence in which the flow units (e.g., patients) are served (remember FIFO and LIFO from your accounting class?). (However, the sequence could influence the flow time of a particular flow unit, e.g., the patient arriving first in the morning, but not the average flow time across all flow units.) Furthermore, Little's Law does not depend on randomness: it does not matter if there is variability in the number of patients or in how long treatment takes for each patient; all that matters is the average flow rate of patients and the average flow time.

In addition to the direct application of Little's Law, for example, in the computation of flow time, Little's Law is also underlying the computation of inventory costs as well as a concept known as inventory turns. This is discussed in the following section.

1.4   Inventory Turns and Inventory Costs

Using physical units as flow units (and, hence, as the inventory measure) is probably the most intuitive way to measure inventory. This could be vehicles at an auto retailer, patients in the hospital, or tons of oil in a refinery.

However, working with physical units is not necessarily the best method for obtaining an aggregate measure of inventory across different products: there is little value to saying you have 2,000 units of inventory if 1,000 of them are paper clips and the remaining 1,000 are computers. In such applications, inventory is often measured in some monetary unit, for example, $5 million worth of inventory.

Measuring inventory in a common monetary unit facilitates the aggregation of inventory across different products. This is why total U.S. inventory is reported in dollars. To illustrate the notion of monetary flow units, consider Kmart, a large U.S. retailer. Instead of thinking of Kmart's stores as sodas, toys, clothes, and bathroom tissues (physical units), we can think of its stores as processes transforming goods valued in monetary units into sales, which also can be evaluated in the form of monetary units.

As can easily be seen from Kmart's balance sheet, on January 29, 2002, the company held an inventory valued at $4.825 billion (see Table 1.4). Given that our flow unit now is the "individual dollar bill," we want to measure the flow rate through Kmart's operation.

The direct approach would be to take "sales" as the resulting flow. Yet, this measure is inflated by Kmart's gross profit margin; that is, a dollar of sales is measured in sales dollars, while a dollar of inventory is measured, given the present accounting practice, in a cost dollar. Thus, the appropriate measure for flow rate is the cost of goods sold, or COGS for short.

TABLE 1.4 **Excerpts from Financial Statements of Kmart and Wal-Mart (All Numbers in Millions)**

Source: Taken from 10-K filings.

	January 28, 1998	January 27, 1999	January 26, 2000	January 31, 2001	January 29, 2002
Kmart Corp.					
Inventory	$ 6,367	$ 6,536	$ 6,350	$ 5,796	$ 4,825
Income					
Total operating					
revenue	$ 33,674	$ 35,925	$ 37,028	$ 36,151	$ 30,762
Cost of goods sold	$ 26,319	$ 28,161	$ 29,732	$ 29,853	$ 26,258
Net income	$ 518	$ 364	($268)	($2,446)	($3,219)
Wal-Mart Stores Inc.					
Inventory	$ 16,497	$ 17,076	$ 19,793	$ 21,644	$ 22,749
Income					
Total operating					
revenue	$119,299	$139,208	$166,809	$193,295	$219,812
Cost of goods sold	$ 93,438	$108,725	$129,664	$150,255	$171,562
Net income	$ 3,526	$ 4,430	$ 5,377	$ 6,295	$ 6,671

With these two measures—flow rate and inventory—we can apply Little's Law to compute what initially might seem a rather artificial measure: how long does the average flow unit (dollar bill) spend within the Kmart system before being turned into sales, at which point the flow units will trigger a profit intake. This corresponds to the definition of flow time.

$$\text{Flow rate } = \text{ Cost of goods sold } = \$26,258 \text{ million/year}$$
$$\text{Inventory } = \$4,825 \text{ million}$$

Hence, we can compute flow time via Little's Law as

$$\text{Flow time } = \frac{\text{Inventory}}{\text{Flow rate}}$$
$$= \$4,825 \text{ million}/\$26,258 \text{ million/year } = 0.18 \text{ year } = 67 \text{ days}$$

Thus, we find that it takes Kmart—on average—67 days to translate a dollar investment into a dollar of—hopefully profitable—revenues. Note that if we conducted a similar analysis for the previous years, we would find that Kmart has improved this metric considerably from 1998 to 2002 (e.g., it took 88 days in 1998).

This calculation underlies the definition of another way of measuring inventory, namely in terms of *days of supply*. We could say that Kmart has 67 days of inventory in their process. In other words, the average item we find at Kmart spends 67 days in Kmart's supply chain.

Alternatively, we could say that Kmart turns over its inventory 365 days/year/67 days = 5.44 times per year. This measure is called *inventory turns*. Inventory turns is a common benchmark in the retailing environment and other supply chain operations:

$$\text{Inventory turns } = \frac{1}{\text{Flow time}}$$

TABLE 1.5
Inventory Turns and Margins for Selected Retail Segments

Source: Based on Gaur, Fisher, and Raman 2002.

Retail Segment	Examples	Annual Inventory Turns	Gross Margin
Apparel and accessory	Ann Taylor, GAP	4.57	37%
Catalog, mail-order	Spiegel, Lands End	8.60	39%
Department stores	Sears, JCPenney	3.87	34%
Drug and proprietary stores	Rite Aid, CVS	5.26	28%
Food stores	Albertson's, Safeway	10.78	26%
Hobby, toy/game stores	Toys R Us	2.99	35%
Home furniture/equipment	Bed Bath & Beyond, Linens N' Things	5.44	40%
Jewelry	Tiffany	1.68	42%
Radio, TV, consumer electronics	Best Buy, Circuit City, CompUSA	4.10	31%
Variety stores	Kmart, Wal-Mart, Target	4.45	29%

To illustrate this application of Little's Law further, consider Wal-Mart, Kmart's strongest competitor. Repeating the same calculations as outlined on the previous page, we find the following data about Wal-Mart:

$$
\begin{aligned}
\text{Cost of goods sold} &= \$171,562 \text{ million/year} \\
\text{Inventory} &= \$22,749 \text{ million} \\
\text{Flow time} &= \$22,749 \text{ million}/\$171,562 \text{ million/year} \\
&= 0.13 \text{ year} = 48.4 \text{ days} \\
\text{Inventory turns} &= 1/48.4 \text{ turns/day} \\
&= 365 \text{ days/year} \times 1/48.4 \text{ turns/day} = 7.54 \text{ turns per year}
\end{aligned}
$$

Thus, we find that Wal-Mart is able to achieve substantially higher inventory turns than Kmart. Table 1.5 summarizes inventory turn data for various segments of the retailing industry. Table 1.5 also provides information about gross margins in various retail settings (keep them in mind the next time you haggle for a new sofa or watch!).

Inventory requires substantial financial investments: the debt service on $1.16 trillion in the U.S. economy is obviously rather substantial even if the inventory is financed at an attractive rate of 10 percent. Yet, most companies would not be happy with a return on assets of 10 percent. Moreover, the inventory holding cost is substantially higher than the mere financial holding cost for a number of reasons:

- Inventory might become obsolete (think of the annual holding cost of a microprocessor).
- Inventory might physically perish (you don't want to think of the cost of holding fresh roses for a year).
- Inventory might disappear (also known as theft or shrink).
- Inventory requires storage space and other overhead cost (insurance, security, real estate, etc.).
- There are other less tangible costs of inventory that result from increased wait times (because of Little's Law, to be discussed in Chapter 3) and lower quality.

Given an annual cost of inventory (e.g., 20 percent per year) and the inventory turn information as computed above, we can compute the per-unit inventory cost that a process (or a supply chain) incurs. To do this, we take the annual holding cost and divide it by the number of times the inventory turns in a year:

$$
\text{Per-unit inventory costs} = \frac{\text{Annual inventory costs}}{\text{Annual inventory turns}}
$$

Exhibit 1.1

CALCULATING INVENTORY TURNS AND PER-UNIT INVENTORY COSTS

1. Look up the value of inventory from the balance sheet.
2. Look up the cost of goods sold (COGS) from the earnings statement; do *not* use sales!
3. Compute inventory turns as

$$\text{Inventory turns} = \frac{\text{COGS}}{\text{Inventory}}$$

4. Compute per-unit inventory costs as

$$\text{Per-unit inventory costs} = \frac{\text{Annual inventory costs}}{\text{Inventory turns}}$$

Note: The annual inventory cost needs to account for the cost of financing the inventory, the cost of depreciation, and other inventory-related costs the firm considers relevant (e.g., storage, theft).

For example, a company that works based on a 20 percent annual inventory cost and that turns its inventory six times per year incurs per-unit inventory costs of

$$\frac{20\% \text{ per year}}{6 \text{ turns per year}} = 3.33\%$$

In the case of Kmart (we earlier computed that the inventory turns 5.44 times per year), and assuming annual holding costs of 20 percent per year, this translates to inventory costs of more than 3.68 percent of the cost of goods sold (20%/5.44 = 3.68). The calculations to obtain per unit inventory costs are summarized in Exhibit 1.1.

To stay in the retailing context a little longer, consider a retailer of consumer electronics who has annual inventory costs of 30 percent (driven by financial costs and obsolescence). Assuming the retailer turns its inventory about four times per year (see Table 1.5.), we obtain a per-unit inventory cost of 30%/4 = 7.5%. Consider a TV in the retailer's assortment that is on the shelf with a price tag of $300 and is procured by the retailer for $200. Based on our calculation, we know that the retailer incurs a $200 × 7.5% = $15 inventory cost for each such TV that is sold. To put this number into perspective, consider Figure 1.8.

Figure 1.8 plots the relationship between gross margin and inventory turns for consumer electronics retailers (based on Gaur, Fisher, and Raman 2002). Note that this graph does not imply causality in this relationship. That is, the model does not imply that if a firm increases its gross margin, its inventory turns will decline commensurately. Instead, the way to look at Figure 1.8 is to think of gross margin for a given set of products as being fixed by the competitive environment. We can then make two interesting observations:

- A retailer can decide to specialize in products that turn very slowly to increase its margins. For example, Radio Shack is known for its high margins, as they carry many products in their assortment that turn only once or twice a year. In contrast, Best Buy is carrying largely very popular items, which exposes the company to stiffer competition and lower gross margins.
- For a given gross margin, we observe dramatic differences concerning inventory turns. For example, inventory turns vary between four and nine times for a 15 percent gross margin. Consider retailer A and assume that all retailers work with a 30 percent annual holding cost. Based on the annual inventory turns of 4.5, retailer A faces a 6.66 percent per-unit inventory cost. Now, compare this to competing retailer B, who turns its inventory eight times per year. Thus, retailer B operates with 3.75 percent per-unit inventory

13

FIGURE 1.8
Relationship between Inventory Turns and Gross Margin

Source: Based on Gaur, Fisher, and Raman 2002.

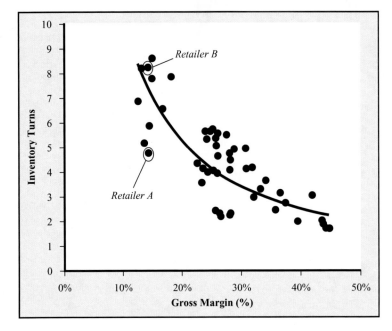

costs, almost a 3 percent cost advantage over retailer A. Given that net profits in this industry segment are around 2 percent of sales, such a cost advantage can make the difference between profits and bankruptcy.

1.5   Five Reasons to Hold Inventory

While Little's Law allows us to compute the average inventory in the process (as long as we know flow time and flow rate), it offers no help in answering the question we raised previously: Why is there inventory in the process in the first place? To understand the need for inventory, we can no longer afford to take the black-box perspective and look at processes from the outside. Instead, we have to look at the process in much more detail.

As we saw from Figure 1.7, inventory reflected a deviation between the inflow into a process and its outflow. Ideally, from an operations perspective, we would like Figure 1.7 to take the shape of two identical, straight lines, representing process inflow and outflow. Unfortunately, such straight lines with zero distance between them rarely exist in the real world. De Groote (1994) discusses five reasons for holding inventory, that is, for having the inflow line differ from the outflow line: (1) the time a flow unit spends in the process, (2) seasonal demand, (3) economies of scale, (4) separation of steps in a process, and (5) stochastic demand. Depending on the reason for holding inventory, inventories are given different names: pipeline inventory, seasonal inventory, cycle inventory, decoupling inventory/ buffers, and safety inventory. It should be noted that these five reasons are not necessarily mutually exclusive and that, in practice, there typically exist more than one reason for holding inventory.

Pipeline Inventory

This first reason for inventory reflects the time a flow unit has to spend in the process in order to be transformed from input to output. Even with unlimited resources, patients still need to spend time in the interventional radiology unit; their flow time would be the length of the critical path. We refer to this basic inventory on which the process operates as *pipeline inventory*.

For the sake of simplicity, let's assume that every patient would have to spend exactly 1.5 hours in the interventional radiology unit, as opposed to waiting for a resource to become available, and that we have one patient arrive every hour. How do we find the pipeline inventory in this case?

The answer is obtained through an application of Little's Law. Since we know two of the three performance measures, flow time and flow rate, we can figure out the third, in this case inventory: with a flow rate of one patient per hour and a flow time of 1.5 hours, the average inventory is

$$\text{Inventory} = 1[\text{patient/hour}] \times 1.5[\text{hours}] = 1.5 \text{ patients}$$

which is the number of patients undergoing some value-adding activity. This is illustrated by Figure 1.9.

In certain environments, you might hear managers make statements of the type "we need to achieve zero inventory in our process." If we substitute Inventory = 0 into Little's Law, the immediate result is that a process with zero inventory is also a process with zero flow rate (unless we have zero flow time, which means that the process does not do anything to the flow unit). Thus, as long as it takes an operation even a minimum amount of time to work on a flow unit, the process will always exhibit pipeline inventory. There can be no hospital without patients and no factory can operate without some work in process!

Little's Law also points us toward the best way to reduce pipeline inventory. As reducing flow rate (and with it demand and profit) is typically not a desirable option, the *only* other way to reduce pipeline inventory is by reducing flow time.

Seasonal Inventory

Seasonal inventory occurs when capacity is rigid and demand is variable. Two examples illustrate this second reason for inventory. Campbell's Soup sells more chicken noodle soup in January than in any other month of the year—not primarily because of cold weather, but because Campbell's discounts chicken noodle soup in January. June is the next biggest sales month, because Campbell's increases its price in July.

So much soup is sold in January that Campbell's starts production several months in advance and builds inventory in anticipation of January sales. Campbell's could wait longer to start production and thereby not build as much inventory, but it would be too costly to assemble the needed capacity (equipment and labor) in the winter only to dismantle that capacity at the end of January when it is no longer needed.

In other words, as long as it is costly to add and subtract capacity, firms will desire to smooth production relative to sales, thereby creating the need for seasonal inventory.

FIGURE 1.9
Pipeline Inventory

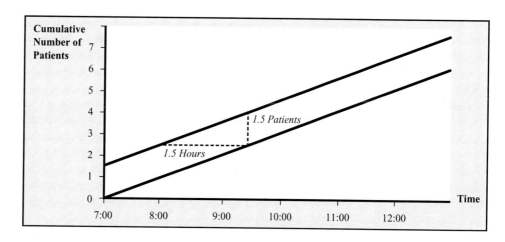

FIGURE 1.10
Seasonal Inventory—
Sugar

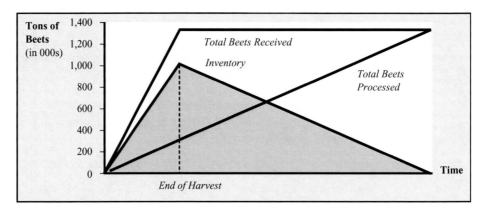

An extreme case of seasonal inventory can be found in the agricultural and food processing sector. Due to the nature of the harvesting season, Monitor Sugar, a large sugar cooperative in the U.S. Midwest, collects all raw material for their sugar production over a period of six weeks. At the end of the harvesting season, they have accumulated—in the very meaning of the word—a pile of sugar beets, about 1 million tons, taking the form of a 67-acre sugar beet pile.

Given that food processing is a very capital-intense operation, the process is sized such that the 1.325 million tons of beets received and the almost 1 million tons of inventory that is built allow for a nonstop operation of the production plant until the beginning of the next harvesting season. Thus, as illustrated by Figure 1.10, the production, and hence the product outflow, is close to constant, while the product inflow is zero except for the harvesting season.

Cycle Inventory

Throughout this book, we will encounter many situations in which it is economical to process several flow units collectively at a given moment in time to take advantage of scale economies in operations.

The scale economics in transportation processes provide a good example for the third reason for inventory. Whether a truck is dispatched empty or full, the driver is paid a fixed amount and a sizeable portion of the wear and tear on the truck depends on the mileage driven, not on the load carried. In other words, each truck shipment incurs a fixed cost that is independent of the amount shipped. To mitigate the sting of that fixed cost, it is tempting to load the truck completely, thereby dividing the fixed cost across the largest number of units.

In many cases, this indeed may be a wise decision. But a truck often carries more product than can be immediately sold. Hence, it takes some time to sell off the entire truck delivery. During that interval of time, there will be inventory. This inventory is labeled *cycle inventory* as it reflects that the transportation process follows a certain shipment cycle (e.g., a shipment every week).

Figure 1.11 plots the inventory level of a simple tray that is required during the operation in the interventional radiology unit. As we can see, there exists a "lumpy" inflow of units, while the outflow is relatively smooth. The reason for this is that—due to the administrative efforts related to placing orders for the trays—the hospital only places one order per week.

The major difference between cycle inventory and seasonal inventory is that seasonal inventory is due to temporary imbalances in supply and demand due to variable demand (soup) or variable supply (beets) while cycle inventory is created due to a cost motivation.

FIGURE 1.11
Cycle Inventory

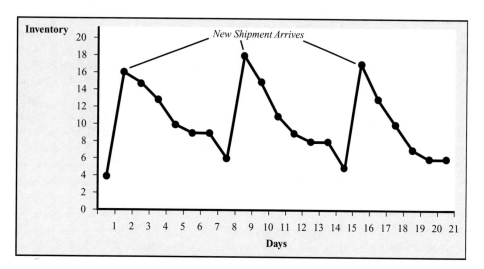

Decoupling Inventory/Buffers

Inventory between process steps can serve as buffers. An inventory buffer allows management to operate steps independently from each other. For example, consider two workers
in a garment factory. Suppose the first worker sews the collar onto a shirt and the second
sews the buttons. A buffer between them is a pile of shirts with collars but no buttons.
Because of that buffer, the first worker can stop working (e.g., to take a break, repair the
sewing machine, or change thread color) while the second worker keeps working. In other
words, buffers can absorb variations in flow rates by acting as a source of supply for a
downstream process step, even if the previous operation itself might not be able to create
this supply at the given moment in time.

An automotive assembly line is another example of a production process that uses buffers to decouple the various stations involved with producing the vehicle. In the absence
of such buffers, a disruption at any one station would lead to a disruption of all the other
stations, upstream and downstream. Think of a bucket brigade to fight a fire: There are no
buffers between firefighters in a bucket brigade, so nobody can take a break without stop-
ping the entire process.

Safety Inventory

The final reason for inventory is probably the most obvious, but also the most challenging: stochastic demand. Stochastic demand refers to the fact that we need to distinguish
between the predicted demand and the actually realized demand. In other words, we typically face variation in demand relative to our demand prediction. Note that this is different
from variations in predictable demand, which is called *seasonality,* like a sales spike of
Campbell's chicken noodle soup in January. Furthermore, stochastic demand can be present along with seasonal demand: January sales can be known to be higher than those for
other months (seasonal demand) and there can be variation around that known forecast
(stochastic demand).

Stochastic demand is an especially significant problem in retailing environments or at
the finished goods level of manufacturers. Take a book retailer that must decide how many
books to order of a given title. The book retailer has a forecast for demand, but forecasts
are (at best) correct on average. Order too many books and the retailer is faced with leftover inventory. Order too few and valuable sales are lost. This trade-off can be managed,
but not eliminated (unless there are zero forecast errors).

FIGURE 1.12
Safety Inventory at a Blood Bank

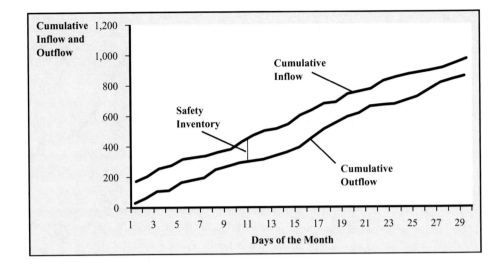

The resulting inventory thereby can be seen as a way to hedge against the underlying demand uncertainty. It might reflect a one-shot decision, for example, in the case of a book retailer selling short-life-cycle products such as newspapers or magazines. If we consider a title with a longer product life cycle (e.g., children's books), the book retailer will be able to replenish books more or less continuously over time.

Figure 1.12 shows the example of the blood bank in the Presbyterian Hospital in Philadelphia. While the detailed inflow and consumption of blood units vary over the course of the month, the hospital always has a couple of days of blood in inventory. Given that blood perishes quickly, the hospital wants to keep only a small inventory at its facility, which it replenishes from the regional blood bank operated by the Red Cross.

1.6 The Product–Process Matrix

Processes leading to the supply of goods or services can take many different forms. Some processes are highly automated, while others are largely manual. Some processes resemble the legendary Ford assembly line, while others resemble more the workshop in your local bike store. Empirical research in operations management, which has looked at thousands of processes, has identified five "clusters" or types of processes. Within each of the five clusters, processes are very similar concerning variables such as the number of different product variants they offer or the production volume they provide. Table 1.6 describes these different types of processes.

By looking at the evolution of a number of industries, Hayes and Wheelwright (1979) observed an interesting pattern, which they referred to as the product–process matrix (see Figure 1.13). The product–process matrix stipulates that over its life cycle, a product typically is initially produced in a job shop process. As the production volume of the product increases, the production process for the product moves from the upper left of the matrix to the lower right.

For example, the first automobiles were produced using job shops, typically creating one product at a time. Most automobiles were unique; not only did they have different colors or add-ons, but they differed in size, geometry of the body, and many other aspects. Henry Ford's introduction of the assembly line corresponded to a major shift along the diagonal of the product–process matrix. Rather than producing a couple of products in a job shop, Ford produced thousands of vehicles on an assembly line.

TABLE 1.6
Process Types and Their Characteristics

	Examples	Number of Different Product Variants	Product Volume (Units/Year)
Job shop	• Design company • Commercial printer • Formula 1 race car	High (100+)	Low (1–100)
Batch process	• Apparel sewing • Bakery • Semiconductor wafers	Medium (10–100)	Medium (100–100k)
Worker-paced line flow	• Auto assembly • Computer assembly	Medium (1–50)	High (10k–1M)
Machine-paced line flow	• Large auto assembly	Low (1–10)	High (10k–1M)
Continuous process	• Paper mill • Oil refinery • Food processing	Low (1–10)	Very high

Note that the "off-diagonals" in the product–process matrix (the lower left and the upper right) are empty. This reflects that it is neither economical to produce very high volumes in a job shop (imagine if all of the millions of new vehicles sold in the United States every year were handcrafted in the same manner as Gottlieb Daimler created the first automobile) nor does it make sense to use an assembly line in order to produce only a handful of products a year.

We have to admit that few companies—if any—would be foolish enough to produce a high-volume product in a job shop. However, identifying a process type and looking at the product–process matrix is more than an academic exercise in industrial history. The usefulness of the product–process matrix lies in two different points:

1. Similar process types tend to have similar problems. For example, assembly lines tend to have the problem of line balancing (some workers working harder than others). Batch-flow processes tend to be slow in responding to customer demand. Thus, once you

FIGURE 1.13
Product–Process Matrix

Source: Hayes and Wheelwright (1979).

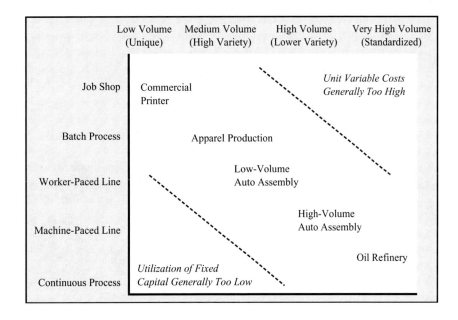

know a process type, you can quickly determine what type of problems the process is likely to face and what solution methods are most appropriate.

2. The "natural drift" of industries toward the lower right of Figure 1.13 enables you to predict how processes are likely to evolve in a particular industry. Consider, for example, the case of eye surgery. Up until the 1980s, corrective eye surgery was done in large hospitals. There, doctors would perform a large variety of very different eye-related cases. Fifteen years later, this situation had changed dramatically. Many highly specialized eye clinics have opened, most of them focusing on a limited set of procedures. These clinics achieve high volume and, because of the high volume and the lower variety of cases, can operate at much higher levels of efficiency. Similarly, semiconductor production equipment used to be assembled on a one-by-one basis, while now companies such as Applied Materials and Kulicke & Soffa operate worker-paced lines.

1.7 Summary

In this chapter, we emphasized the importance of looking at the operations of a firm not just in terms of the products that the firm supplies, but also at the processes that generate the supply. Looking at processes is especially important with respect to demand–supply mismatches. From the perspective of the product, such mismatches take the form of waiting times; from the perspective of the process, they take the form of inventory.

For any process, we can define three fundamental performance measures: inventory, flow time, and flow rate. The three measures are related by Little's Law, which states that the average inventory is equal to the average flow time multiplied by the average flow rate.

Little's Law can be used to find any of the three performance measures, as long as the other two measures are known. This is specifically important with respect to flow time, which is in practice frequently difficult to observe directly.

A measure related to flow time is inventory turns. Inventory turns, measured by 1/(flow time), captures how fast the flow units are transformed from input to output. It is an important benchmark in many industries, especially retailing. Inventory turns are also the basis of computing the inventory costs associated with one unit of supply.

1.8 Further Readings

De Groote (1994) is a very elegant note describing the basic roles of inventory. This note, as well as many other notes and articles by de Groote, takes a very "lean" perspective to operations management, resembling much more the tradition of economics as opposed to engineering.

Gaur, Fisher, and Raman (2002) provide an extensive study of retailing performance. They present various operational measures, including inventory turns, and show how they relate to financial performance measures.

The Hayes and Wheelwright (1979) reference is widely recognized as a pioneering article linking operations aspects to business strategy. Subsequent work by Hayes, Wheelwright, and Clark (1988) established operations as a key source for a firm's competitive advantage.

1.9 Practice Problems

Q 1.1* **(Dell)** What percentage of cost of a Dell computer reflects inventory costs? Assume Dell's yearly inventory cost is 40 percent to account for the cost of capital for financing the inventory, the warehouse space, and the cost of obsolescence. In other words, Dell incurs a cost of $40 for a $100 component that is in the company's inventory for one entire year. In 2001, Dell's 10-k reports showed that the company had $400 million in inventory and COGS of $26,442 million.

Q 1.2 **(Airline)** Consider the baggage check-in of a small airline. Check-in data indicate that from 9 a.m. to 10 a.m., 255 passengers checked in. Moreover, based on counting the number of

(* indicates that the solution is at the end of the book)

passengers waiting in line, airport management found that the average number of passengers waiting for check-in was 35. How long did the average passenger have to wait in line?

Q 1.3 **(Inventory Cost)** A manufacturing company producing medical devices reported $60,000,000 in sales over the last year. At the end of the same year, the company had $20,000,000 worth of inventory of ready-to-ship devices.

    a. Assuming that units in inventory are valued (based on COGS) at $1,000 per unit and are sold for $2,000 per unit, how fast does the company turn its inventory? The company uses a 25 percent per year cost of inventory. That is, for the hypothetical case that one unit of $1,000 would sit exactly one year in inventory, the company charges its operations division a $250 inventory cost.

    b. What—in absolute terms—is the per unit inventory cost for a product that costs $1,000?

Q 1.4 **(Apparel Retailing)** A large catalog retailer of fashion apparel reported $100,000,000 in revenues over the last year. On average, over the same year, the company had $5,000,000 worth of inventory in their warehouses. Assume that units in inventory are valued based on cost of goods sold (COGS) and that the retailer has a 100 percent markup on all products.

    a. How many times each year does the retailer turn its inventory? The company uses a 40 percent per year cost of inventory. That is, for the hypothetical case that one item of $100 COGS would sit exactly one year in inventory, the company charges itself a $40 inventory cost.

    b. What is the inventory cost for a $30 (COGS) item? You may assume that inventory turns are independent of the price.

Q 1.5 **(LaVilla)** LaVilla is a village in the Italian Alps. Given its enormous popularity among Swiss, German, Austrian, and Italian skiers, all of its beds are always booked in the winter season and there are, on average, 1,200 skiers in the village. On average, skiers stay in LaVilla for 10 days.

    a. How many new skiers are arriving—on average—in LaVilla every day?

    b. A study done by the largest hotel in the village has shown that skiers spend on average $50 per person on the first day and $30 per person on each additional day in local restaurants. The study also forecasts that—due to increased hotel prices—the average length of stay for the 2003/2004 season will be reduced to five days. What will be the percentage change in revenues of local restaurants compared to last year (when skiers still stayed for 10 days)? Assume that hotels continue to be fully booked!

Q 1.6 **(Highway)** While driving home for the holidays, you can't seem to get Little's Law out of your mind. You note that your average speed of travel is about 60 miles per hour. Moreover, the traffic report from the WXPN traffic chopper states that there is an average of 24 cars going in your direction on a one-quarter mile part of the highway. What is the flow rate of the highway (going in your direction) in cars per hour?

Q 1.7 **(Industrial Baking Process)** Strohrmann, a large-scale bakery in Pennsylvania, is laying out a new production process for their packaged bread, which they sell to several grocery chains. It takes 12 minutes to bake the bread. How large an oven is required so that the company is able to produce 4,000 units of bread per hour (measured in the number of units that can be baked simultaneously)?

Q 1.8 **(Mt. Kinley Consulting)** Mt. Kinley is a strategy consulting firm that divides its consultants into three classes: associates, managers, and partners. The firm has been stable in size for the last 20 years, ignoring growth opportunities in the 90s, but also not suffering from a need to downsize in the recession at the beginning of the 21st century. Specifically, there have been—and are expected to be—200 associates, 60 managers, and 20 partners.

The work environment at Mt. Kinley is rather competitive. After four years of working as an associate, a consultant goes "either up or out"; that is, becomes a manager or is dismissed from the company. Similarly, after six years, a manager either becomes a partner or is dismissed. The company recruits MBAs as associate consultants; no hires are made at the manager or partner level. A partner stays with the company for another 10 years (a total of 20 years with the company).

a. How many new MBA graduates does Mt. Kinley have to hire every year?

b. What are the odds that a new hire at Mt. Kinley will become partner (as opposed to being dismissed after 4 years or 10 years)?

Q 1.9   **(Major U.S. Retailers)** The following table shows financial data (year 2004) for Costco Wholesale and Wal-Mart, two major U.S. retailers.

	Costco	Wal-Mart
	Wholesale ($ Millions)	Stores ($ Millions)
Inventories	$ 3,643	$ 29,447
Sales (net)	$48,106	$286,103
COGS	$41,651	$215,493

Source: Compustat, WRDS.

Assume that both companies have an average annual holding cost rate of 30 percent (i.e., it costs both retailers $3 to hold an item that they procured for $10 for one entire year).

a. How many days, on average, does a product stay in Costco's inventory before it is sold? Assume that stores are operated 365 days a year.

b. How much lower is, on average, the inventory cost for Costco compared to Wal-Mart of a household cleaner valued at $5 COGS? Assume that the unit cost of the household cleaner is the same for both companies and that the price and the inventory turns of an item are independent.

Q 1.10   **(McDonald's)** The following figures are taken from the 2003 financial statements of McDonald's and Wendy's.[1] Figures are in million dollars.

	McDonald's	Wendy's
Inventory	$ 129.4	$ 54.4
Revenue	17,140.5	3,148.9
Cost of goods sold	11,943.7	1,634.6
Gross profit	5,196.8	1,514.4

a. In 2003, what were McDonald's inventory turns? What were Wendy's inventory turns?

b. Suppose it costs both McDonald's and Wendy's $3 (COGS) per their value meal offerings, each sold at the same price of $4. Assume that the cost of inventory for both companies is 30 percent a year. Approximately how much does McDonald's save in inventory cost *per value meal* compared to that of Wendy's? You may assume the inventory turns are independent of the price.

[1] Example adopted from an About.com article (http://beginnersinvest.about.com/cs/investinglessons/1/blles3mcwen.htm). Financial figures taken from Morningstar.com.

2

Understanding the Supply Process: Evaluating Process Capacity

In the attempt to match supply with demand, an important measure is the maximum amount that a process can produce in a given unit of time, a measure referred to as the *process capacity.* To determine the process capacity of an operation, we need to analyze the operation in much greater detail compared to the previous chapter. Specifically, we need to understand the various activities involved in the operation and how these activities contribute toward fulfilling the overall demand.

In this chapter, you will learn how to perform a process analysis. Unlike Chapter 1, where we felt it was sufficient to treat the details of the operation as a black box and merely focus on the performance measures inventory, flow time, and flow rate, we now will focus on the underlying process in great detail.

Despite this increase in detail, this chapter (and this book) is not taking the perspective of an engineer at operations. In fact, in this chapter, you will learn how to take a fairly technical and complex operation and simplify it to a level suitable for managerial analysis. This includes preparing a process flow diagram, finding the capacity and the bottleneck of the process, computing the utilization of various process steps, and computing a couple of other performance measures.

We will illustrate this new material with the Circored plant, a joint venture between the German engineering company Lurgi AG and the U.S. iron ore producer Cleveland Cliffs. The Circored plant converts iron ore (in the form of iron ore fines) into direct reduced iron (DRI) briquettes. Iron ore fines are shipped to the plant from mines in South America; the briquettes the process produces are shipped to various steel mills in the United States.

The example of the Circored process is particularly useful for our purposes in this chapter. The underlying process is complex and in many ways a masterpiece of process engineering (see Terwiesch and Loch [2002] for further details). At first sight, the process is so complex that it seems impossible to understand the underlying process behavior without a detailed background in engineering and metallurgy. This challenging setting allows us to demonstrate how process analysis can be used to "tame the beast" and create a managerially useful view of the process, avoiding any unnecessary technical details.

2.1 How to Draw a Process Flow Diagram

The best way to begin any analysis of an operation is by drawing a *process flow diagram.* A process flow diagram is a graphical way to describe the process and it will help us to structure the information that we collect during the case analysis or process improvement project. Before we turn to the question of how to draw a process flow diagram, first consider alternative approaches to how we could capture the relevant information about a process.

Looking at the plant from above (literally), we get a picture as is depicted in Figure 2.1. At the aggregate level, the plant consists of a large inventory of iron ore (input), the plant itself (the resource), and a large inventory of finished briquettes (output). In many ways, this corresponds to the black box approach to operations taken by economists and many other managerial disciplines.

In an attempt to understand the details of the underlying process, we could turn to the engineering specifications of the plant. Engineers are interested in a detailed description of the various steps involved in the overall process and how these steps are functioning. Such descriptions, typically referred to as specifications, were used in the actual construction of the plant. Figure 2.2 provides one of the numerous specification drawings for the Circored process.

Unfortunately, this attempt to increase our understanding of the Circored process is also only marginally successful. Like the photograph, this view of the process is also a rather static one: It emphasizes the equipment, yet provides us with little understanding of how the iron ore moves through the process. In many ways, this view of a process is similar to taking the architectural drawings of a hospital and hoping that this would lead to insights about what happens to the patients in this hospital.

In a third—and final—attempt to get our hands around this complex process, we change our perspective from the one of the visitor to the plant (photo in Figure 2.1) or the engineers who built the plant (drawing in Figure 2.2) to the perspective of the iron ore itself

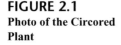

FIGURE 2.1
Photo of the Circored Plant

Source: Terwiesch and Loch 2002.

FIGURE 2.2   **Engineering Drawing**

Source: Terwiesch and Loch 2002.

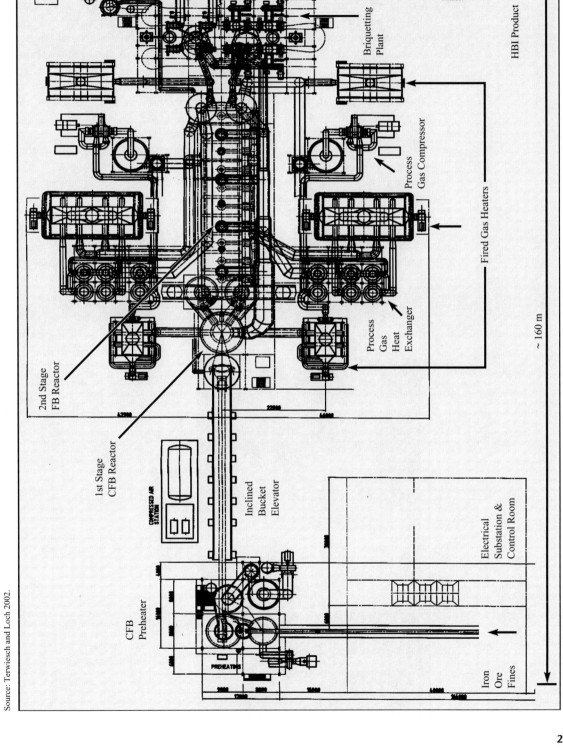

~110 m

~ 160 m

HBI Product

Briquetting
Plant

Process
Gas Compressor

Fired Gas Heaters

Process
Gas
Heat
Exchanger

2nd Stage
FB Reactor

1st Stage
CFB Reactor

COMPRESSED AIR
STATION

Inclined
Bucket
Elevator

Electrical
Substation &
Control Room

CFB
Preheater

PREHEATING

Iron
Ore
Fines

and how it flows through the process. Thus, we define a unit of iron ore—a ton, a pound, or a molecule—as our flow unit and "attach" ourselves to this flow unit as it makes its journey through the process. This is similar to taking the perspective of the patient in a hospital, as opposed to taking the perspective of the hospital resources.

To draw a process flow diagram, we first need to focus on a part of the process that we want to analyze in greater detail; that is, we need to define the *process boundaries* and an appropriate level of detail. The placement of the process boundaries will depend on the project we are working on. For example, in the operation of a hospital, one project concerned with patient waiting time might look at what happens to the patient waiting for a lab test (e.g., check-in, waiting time, encounter with the nurse). In this project, the encounter with the doctor who requested the lab test would be outside the boundaries of the analysis. Another project related to the quality of surgery, however, might look at the encounter with the doctor in great detail, while either ignoring the lab or treating it with less detail.

A process operates on flow units, which are the entities flowing through the process (e.g., patients in a hospital, cars in an auto plant, insurance claims at an insurance company). A process flow diagram is a collection of boxes, triangles, and arrows (see Figure 2.3). Boxes stand for process activities, where the operation adds value to the flow unit. Depending on the level of detail we choose, a process step (a box) can itself be a process.

Triangles represent waiting areas or *buffers* holding inventory. In contrast to a process step, inventories do not add value; thus, a flow unit does not have to spend time in them. However, as discussed in the previous chapter, there are numerous reasons why the flow unit might spend time in inventory even if it will not be augmented to a higher value there.

FIGURE 2.3
Elements of a Process

Source: Terwiesch and Loch 2002.

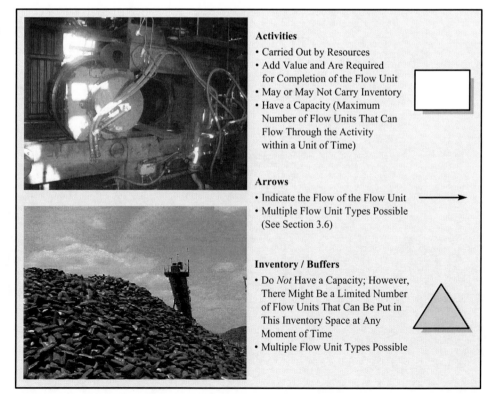

Activities
• Carried Out by Resources
• Add Value and Are Required for Completion of the Flow Unit
• May or May Not Carry Inventory
• Have a Capacity (Maximum Number of Flow Units That Can Flow Through the Activity within a Unit of Time)

Arrows
• Indicate the Flow of the Flow Unit
• Multiple Flow Unit Types Possible (See Section 3.6)

Inventory / Buffers
• Do *Not* Have a Capacity; However, There Might Be a Limited Number of Flow Units That Can Be Put in This Inventory Space at Any Moment of Time
• Multiple Flow Unit Types Possible

FIGURE 2.4
Process Flow
Diagram, First Step

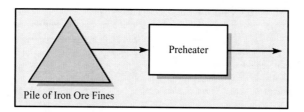

The arrows between boxes and triangles represent the route the flow unit takes through the process. If there are different flow units that take different routes through the process, it can be helpful to use different colors for the different routes. An example of this is given at the end of this chapter.

In the Circored plant, the first step the flow unit encounters in the process is the *pre-heater*, where the iron ore fines (which have a texture like large-grained sand) are dried and heated. The heating is achieved through an inflow of high-pressured air, which is blown into the preheater from the bottom. The high-speed air flow "fluidizes" the ore, meaning that the mixed air–ore mass (a "sandstorm") circulates through the system as if it was a fluid, while being heated to a temperature of approximately 850–900°C.

However, from a managerial perspective, we are not really concerned with the temperature in the preheater or the chemical reactions happening therein. For us, the preheater is a resource that receives iron ore from the initial inventory and processes it. In an attempt to take record of what the flow unit has experienced up to this point, we create a diagram similar to Figure 2.4.

From the preheater, a large bucket elevator transports the ore to the second process step, the *lock hoppers.* The lock hoppers consist of three large containers, separated by sets of double isolation valves. Their role is to allow the ore to transition from an oxygen-rich environment to a hydrogen atmosphere.

Following the lock hoppers, the ore enters the *circulating fluid bed reactor* (CFB, 1st reactor), where the actual reduction process begins. The reduction process requires the ore to be in the reactor for 15 minutes.

After this first reduction, the material flows into the *stationary fluid bed reactor* (FB, 2nd reactor). This second reaction takes about four hours. The reactor is the size of a medium two-family home and contains 400 tons of the hot iron ore at any given moment in time. In the meantime, our diagram from Figure 2.4. has extended to something similar to Figure 2.5.

A couple of things are worth noting at this point:

• When creating Figure 2.5, we decided to omit the bucket elevator. There is no clear rule on when it is appropriate to omit a small step and when a step would have to be included in the process flow diagram. A reasonably good rule of thumb is to only include those process steps that are likely to affect the process flow or the economics of the process. The bucket

FIGURE 2.5   Process Flow Diagram (to Be Continued)

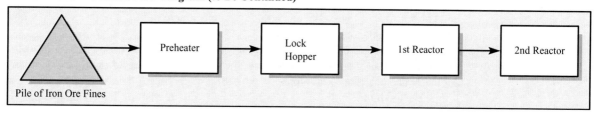

FIGURE 2.6 Completed Process Flow Diagram for the Circored Process

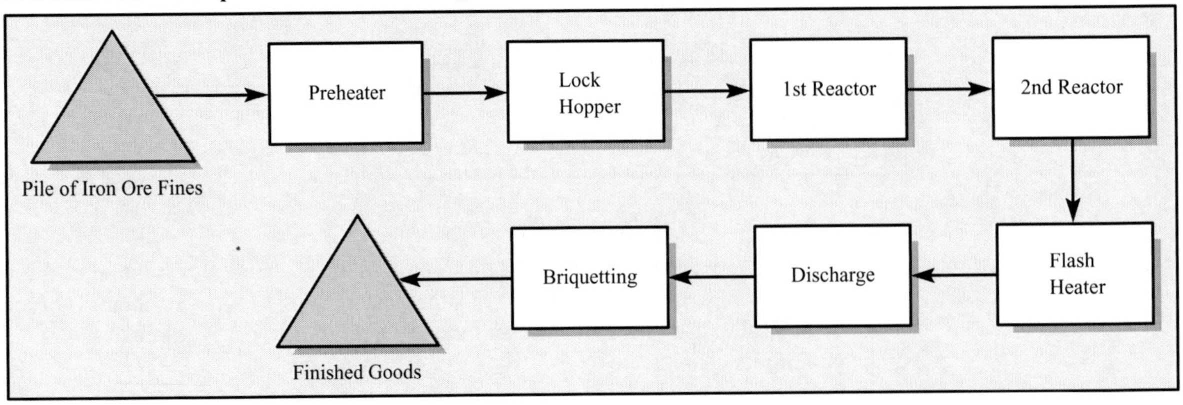

elevator is cheap, the flow units spend little time on it, and this transportation step never becomes a constraint for the process. So it is not included in our process flow diagram.

• The reaction steps are boxes, not triangles, although there is a substantial amount of ore in them, that is, they do hold inventory. The reduction steps are necessary, value-adding steps. No flow unit could ever leave the system without spending time in the reactors. This is why we have chosen boxes over triangles here.

Following the fluid bed reactor, the reduced iron enters the *flash heater*, in which a stream of high-velocity hydrogen carries the DRI to the top of the plant while simultaneously reheating it to a temperature of 685°C.

After the flash heater, the DRI enters the *pressure let-down system (discharger)*. As the material passes through the discharger, the hydrogen atmosphere is gradually replaced by inert nitrogen gas. Pressure and hydrogen are removed in a reversal of the lock hoppers at the beginning. Hydrogen gas sensors assure that material leaving this step is free of hydrogen gas and, hence, safe for briquetting.

Each of the three *briquetting* machines contains two wheels that turn against each other, each wheel having the negative of one-half of a briquette on its face. The DRI is poured onto the wheels from the top and is pressed into briquettes, or iron bars, which are then moved to a large pile of finished goods inventory.

This completes our journey of the flow unit through the plant. The resulting process flow diagram that captures what the flow unit has experienced in the process is summarized in Figure 2.6.

When drawing a process flow diagram, the sizes and the exact locations of the arrows, boxes, and triangles do not carry any special meaning. For example, in the context of Figure 2.6, we chose a "U-shaped" layout of the process flow diagram, as otherwise we would have had to publish this book in a larger format.

In the absence of any space constraints, the simplest way to draw a process flow diagram for a process such as Circored's is just as one long line. However, we should keep in mind that there are more complex processes; for example, a process with multiple flow units or a flow unit that visits one and the same resource multiple times. This will be discussed further at the end of the chapter.

Another alternative in drawing the process flow diagram is to stay much closer to the physical layout of the process. This way, the process flow diagram will look familiar for engineers and operators who typically work off the specification drawings (Figure 2.2) and it might help you to find your way around when you are visiting the "real" process. Such an approach is illustrated by Figure 2.7.

FIGURE 2.7 **Completed Process Flow Diagram for the Circored Process**

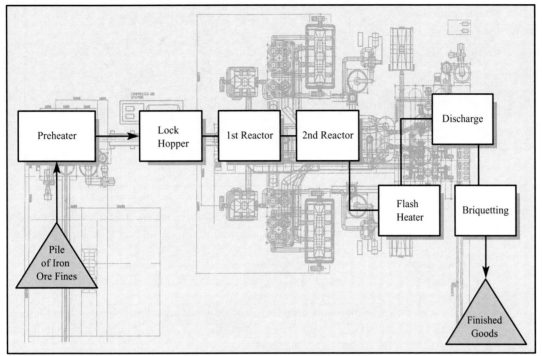

2.2 Bottleneck, Process Capacity, and Flow Rate (Throughput)

From a supply perspective, the most important question that arises is how much direct reduced iron a process can supply in a given unit of time, say one day. This measure is called the *process capacity*.

Note that the process capacity measures how much the process *can* produce, opposed to how much the process actually *does* produce. For example, consider a day where—due to a breakdown or another external event—the process does not operate at all. Its capacity would be unaffected by this, yet the flow rate would reduce to zero. This is similar to your car, which might be able to drive at 130 miles per hour (capacity), but typically—or better, hopefully—only drives at 65 miles per hour (flow rate).

Not only can capacity be measured at the level of the overall process, it also can be measured at the level of the individual resources that constitute the process. Similar to how we defined process capacity, we define the capacity of a resource as the maximum amount the resource can produce in a given time unit.

As the completion of a flow unit requires the flow unit to visit every one of the resources in the process, the overall process capacity is determined by the resource with the smallest capacity. We refer to that resource as the *bottleneck*. It provides the weakest link in the overall process chain, and, as we know, a chain is only as strong as its weakest link. More formally, we can write the process capacity as

Process capacity = Minimum{Capacity of Resource 1, . . . , Capacity of Resource n}

where there are a total of n resources. How much the process actually does produce will depend not only on its capability to create supply (process capacity), but also on the demand for its output as well as the availability of its input.

Thus, the flow rate or throughput of the process is determined as

Flow rate = Minimum{Available Input, Demand, Process Capacity}

FIGURE 2.8 **Supply-Constrained (left) and Demand-Constrained (right) Processes**

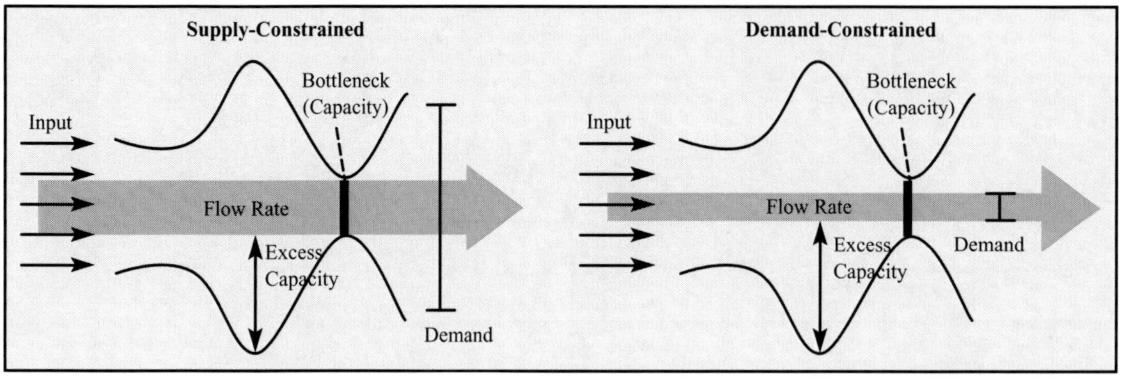

If demand is lower than supply (i.e., there is sufficient input available and the process has enough capacity), the process would produce at the rate of demand, independent of the process capacity. We refer to this case as *demand-constrained*. Note that in this definition demand also includes any potential requests for the accumulation of inventory. For example, while the demand for Campbell's chicken noodle soup might be lower than process capacity for the month of November, the process would not be demand-constrained if management decided to accumulate finished goods inventory in preparation for the high sales in the month of January. Thus, demand in our analysis refers to everything that is demanded from the process at a given time.

If demand exceeds supply, the process is *supply-constrained*. Depending on what limits product supply, the process is either input-constrained or capacity-constrained.

Figure 2.8 summarizes the concepts of process capacity and flow rate, together with the notion of demand- versus supply-constrained processes. In the case of the supply-constrained operation, there is sufficient input; thus, the supply constraint reflects a capacity constraint.

To understand how to find the bottleneck in a process and thereby determine the process capacity, consider each of the Circored resources. Note that all numbers are referring to tons of process output. The actual, physical weight of the flow unit might change over the course of the process.

Finding the bottleneck in many ways resembles the job of a detective in a crime story; each activity is a "suspect," in the sense that it could potentially constrain the overall supply of the process:

- The preheater can process 120 tons per hour.
- The lock hoppers can process 110 tons per hour.
- The analysis of the reaction steps is somewhat more complicated. We first observe that at any given moment of time, there can be, at maximum, 28 tons in the CFB reactor. Given that the iron ore needs to spend 15 minutes in the reactor, we can use Little's Law (see Chapter 1) to see that the maximum amount of ore that can flow through the reactor—and spend 15 minutes in the reactor—is

$$28 \text{ tons} = \text{Flow rate} \times 0.25 \text{ hour} \implies \text{Flow rate} = 112 \text{ tons/hour}$$

Thus, the capacity of the first reactor is 112 tons per hour. Note that a shorter reaction time in this case would translate to a higher capacity.

- We can apply a similar logic for the stationary reactor, which can hold up to 400 tons:

$$400 \text{ tons} = \text{Flow rate} \times 4 \text{ hours} \implies \text{Flow rate} = 100 \text{ tons/hour}$$

Thus, the capacity (the maximum possible flow rate through the resource) of the second reactor is 100 tons per hour.

TABLE 2.1
Capacity Calculation

Process Step	Calculations	Capacity
Preheater		120 tons per hour
Lock hoppers		110 tons per hour
CFB	Little's Law: Flow rate = 28 tons/0.25 hour	112 tons per hour
Stationary reactor	Little's Law: Flow rate = 400 tons/4 hours	100 tons per hour
Flash heater		135 tons per hour
Pressure let-down system		118 tons per hour
Briquetting machine	Consists of three machines: 3 × 55 tons per hour	165 tons per hour
Total process	Based on bottleneck, which is the stationary reactor	**100 tons per hour**

- The flash heater can process 135 tons per hour.
- The pressure let-down system has a capacity of 118 tons per hour.
- Each of the three briquetting machines has a capacity of 55 tons per hour. As the briquetting machines collectively form one resource, the capacity at the briquetting machines is simply 3 × 55 tons per hour = 165 tons per hour.

The capacity of each process step is summarized in Table 2.1.

Following the logic outlined above, we can now identify the stationary reactor as the bottleneck of the Circored process. The overall process capacity is computed as the minimum of the capacities of each resource (all units are in tons per hour):

$$\text{Process capacity} = \text{Minimum } \{120, 110, 112, 100, 135, 118, 165\} = 100$$

2.3 How Long Does It Take to Produce a Certain Amount of Supply?

There are many situations where we need to compute the amount of time required to create a certain amount of supply. For example, in the Circored case, we might ask, "How long does it take for the plant to produce 10,000 tons?" Once we have determined the flow rate of the process, this calculation is fairly straightforward. Let X be the amount of supply we want to fulfill. Then,

$$\text{Time to fullfill } X \text{ units } = \frac{X}{\text{Flow rate}}$$

To answer our question,

$$\text{Time to produce } 10,000 \text{ tons } = \frac{10,000 \text{ tons}}{100 \text{ tons/hour}} = 100 \text{ hours}$$

Note that this calculation assumes the process is already producing output, that is, the first unit in our 10,000 tons flows out of the process immediately. If the process started empty, it would take the first flow unit time to flow through the process.

Note that in the previous equation we use flow rate, which in our case is capacity because the system is supply-constrained. However, if our system were demand-constrained, then the flow rate would equal the demand rate.

2.4   Process Utilization and Capacity Utilization

Given the first-of-its-kind nature of the Circored process, the first year of its operation proved to be extremely difficult. In addition to various technical difficulties, demand for the product (reduced iron) was not as high as it could be, as the plant's customers (steel mills) had to be convinced that the output created by the Circored process would be of the high quality required by the steel mills.

While abstracting from details such as scheduled maintenance and inspection times, the plant was designed to achieve a process capacity of 876,000 tons per year (100 tons per hour × 24 hours/day × 365 days/year, see above), the demand for iron ore briquettes was only 657,000 tons. Thus, there existed a mismatch between demand and potential supply (process capacity).

A common measure of performance that quantifies this mismatch is process utilization. We define the utilization of a process as

$$\text{Process utilization} = \frac{\text{Flow rate}}{\text{Process capacity}}$$

Thus, to measure process utilization, we look at how much the process actually *does produce* relative to how much it *can produce* if it were running at full speed. This is in line with the example of a car driving at 65 miles per hour (flow rate), despite being able to drive at 130 miles per hour (capacity): the car utilizes 65/130 = 50 percent of its potential.

For the Circored case, the resulting utilization is

$$\text{Process utilization} = \frac{657,000 \text{ tons per year}}{876,000 \text{ tons per year}} = 0.75 = 75\%$$

In general, there are several reasons why a process might not produce at 100 percent utilization:

- If demand is less than supply, the process typically will not run at full capacity, but only produce at the rate of demand.
- If there is insufficient supply of the input of a process, the process will not be able to operate at capacity.
- If one or several process steps only have a limited availability (e.g., maintenance and breakdowns), the process might operate at full capacity while it is running, but then go into periods of not producing any output while it is not running.

As we did with process capacity and the capacity of individual resources, we can define utilization not only at the level of the entire process, but also at the level of the individual resources. The utilization of a resource is defined as follows:

$$\text{Utilization of resource} = \frac{\text{Flow rate}}{\text{Capacity of resource}}$$

Given that the bottleneck is the resource with the lowest capacity and that the flow rate through all resources is identical, the bottleneck is the resource with the highest utilization.

In the case of the Circored plant, the corresponding utilizations are provided by Table 2.2. Note that all resources in a process with only one flow unit have the same flow rate, which is equal to the overall process flow rate. In this case, this is a flow rate of 657,000 tons per year.

Measuring the utilization of equipment is particularly common in capital-intensive industries. Given limited demand and availability problems, the bottleneck in the Circored

TABLE 2.2
Utilization of the Circored Process Steps Including Downtime

Process Step	Calculations	Utilization
Preheater	657,000 tons/year/[120 tons/hour × 8,760 hours/year]	62.5%
Lock hoppers	657,000 tons/year/[110 tons/hour × 8,760 hours/year]	68.2%
CFB	657,000 tons/year/[112 tons/hour × 8,760 hours/year]	66.9%
Stationary reactor	657,000 tons/year/[100 tons/hour × 8,760 hours/year]	75%
Flash heater	657,000 tons/year/[135 tons/hour × 8,760 hours/year]	55.6%
Discharger	657,000 tons/year/[118 tons/hour × 8,760 hours/year]	63.6%
Briquetting	657,000 tons/year/[165 tons/hour × 8,760 hours/year]	45.5%
Total process	657,000 tons/year/[100 tons/hour × 8,760 hours/year]	**75%**

process did not operate at 100 percent utilization. We can summarize our computations graphically, by drawing a utilization profile. This is illustrated by Figure 2.9.

The utilization profile of the Circored process points at a small imbalance between various resources. We will look at a process environment, which is labor-intensive, where we will track the utilization of labor. All of the definitions we have seen up to this point are independent of whether the resource is a worker or a piece of equipment.

Utilization is a performance measure that should be handled with a great deal of care. Specifically, it should be emphasized that the objective of most businesses is to maximize profit, not to maximize utilization. As can be seen in Figure 2.9, there are two reasons in the Circored case for why an individual resource might not achieve 100 percent utilization, thus exhibiting excess capacity.

• First, given that no resource can achieve a higher utilization than the bottleneck, every process step other than the bottleneck will have a utilization gap relative to the bottleneck.

FIGURE 2.9 **Utilization Profile**

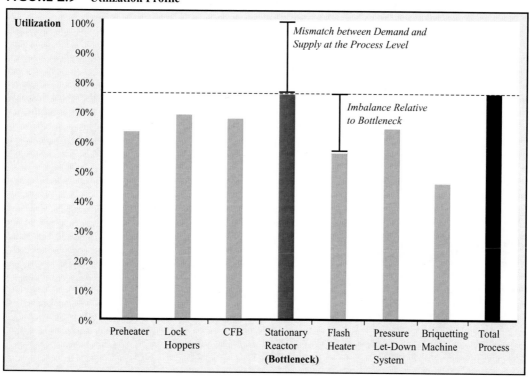

TABLE 2.3
Utilization of the
Circored Process
Steps Assuming
Unlimited Demand
and No Downtime

Process Step	Calculations	Utilization
Preheater	100/120	83.3%
Lock hoppers	100/110	90.9%
CFB	100/112	89.3%
Stationary reactor	100/100	100%
Flash heater	100/135	74.1%
Pressure let-down system	100/118	84.7%
Briquetting machine	100/165	60.6%
Total process	**100/100**	**100%**

- Second, given that the process might not always be capacity-constrained, but rather be input- or demand-constrained, even the bottleneck might not be 100 percent utilized. In this case, every resource in the process has a "base level" of excess capacity, corresponding to the difference between the flow rate and the bottleneck capacity.

Note that the second reason disappears if there is sufficient market demand and full resource availability. In this case, only the bottleneck achieves a 100 percent utilization level. If the bottleneck in the Circored plant were utilized 100 percent, we would obtain an overall flow rate of 876,000 tons per year, or, equivalently 100 tons per hour. The resulting utilization levels in that case are summarized in Table 2.3.

2.5 Workload and Implied Utilization

Given the way we defined utilization (the ratio between flow rate and capacity), utilization can never exceed 100 percent. Thus, utilization only carries information about excess capacity, in which case utilization is strictly less than 100 percent. In contrast, we cannot infer from utilization by how much demand exceeds the capacity of the process. This is why we need to introduce an additional measure.

We define the *implied utilization* of a resource as

$$\text{Implied utilization} = \frac{\text{Capacity requested by demand}}{\text{Available capacity}}$$

The implied utilization captures the mismatch between the capacity requested from a resource by demand (also called the *workload*) and the capacity currently available at the resource.

Assume that demand for the Circored ore would increase to 1,095,000 tons per year (125 tons per hour). Table 2.4 calculates the resulting levels of implied utilization for the Circored resources.

TABLE 2.4
Implied Utilization of
the Circored Process
Steps Assuming a
Demand of 125 Tons
per Hour and No
Downtime

Process Step	Calculations	Implied Utilization	Utilization
Preheater	125/120	104.2%	83.3%
Lock hoppers	125/110	113.6%	90.9%
CFB	125/112	111.6%	89.3%
Stationary reactor	125/100	125%	100%
Flash heater	125/135	92.6%	74.1%
Pressure let-down system	125/118	105.9%	84.7%
Briquetting machine	125/165	75.8%	60.6%
Total process	**125/100**	**125%**	**100%**

Several points in the table deserve further discussion:

- Unlike utilization, implied utilization can exceed 100 percent. Any excess over 100 percent reflects that a resource does not have the capacity available to meet demand.

- The fact that a resource has an implied utilization above 100 percent does not make it the bottleneck. As we see in Table 2.4, it is possible to have several resources with an implied utilization above 100 percent. However, there is only one bottleneck in the process! This is the resource where the implied utilization is the highest. In the Circored case, this is—not surprisingly—the stationary reactor. Would it make sense to say that the process has several bottlenecks? No! Given that we can only operate the Circored process at a rate of 100 tons per hour (the capacity of the stationary reactor), we have ore flow through every resource of the process at a rate of 100 tons per hour. Thus, while several resources have an implied utilization above 100 percent, all resources other than the stationary reactor have excess capacity (their utilizations in Table 2.4 are below 100 percent). That is why we should not refer to them as bottlenecks.

- Having said this, it is important to keep in mind that in the case of a capacity expansion of the process, it might be worthwhile to add capacity to these other resources as well, not just to the bottleneck. In fact, depending on the margins we make and the cost of installing capacity, we could make a case to install additional capacity for all resources with an implied utilization above 100 percent. In other words, once we add capacity to the current bottleneck, our new process (with a new bottleneck) could still be capacity-constrained, justifying additional capacity to other resources.

2.6 Multiple Types of Flow Units

Choosing an appropriate flow unit is an essential step when preparing a process flow diagram. While, for the examples we have discussed so far, this looked relatively straightforward, there are many situations that you will encounter where this choice requires more care. The two most common complications are

- The flow of the unit moving through the process breaks up into multiple flows. For example, in an assembly environment, following an inspection step, good units continue to the next processing step, while bad units require rework.
- There are multiple types of flow units, representing, for example, different customer types. In an emergency room, life-threatening cases follow a different flow than less complicated cases.

Consider the following example involving multiple product or customer types. An employment verification agency receives resumés from consulting firms and law firms with the request to validate information provided by their job candidates.

Consider the process flow diagram shown in Figure 2.10, which describes the process of handling the applicant's resumés. Note that while the three customer types share the first step and the last step in the process (filing and sending confirmation letter), they differ with respect to other steps:

- For internship positions, the agency provides information about the law school/ business school the candidate is currently enrolled in as well as previous institutions of higher education and, to the extent possible, provides information about the applicant's course choices and honors.
- For staff positions, the agency contacts previous employers and analyzes the letters of recommendation from those employers.

FIGURE 2.10   Process Flow Diagram with Multiple Product Types

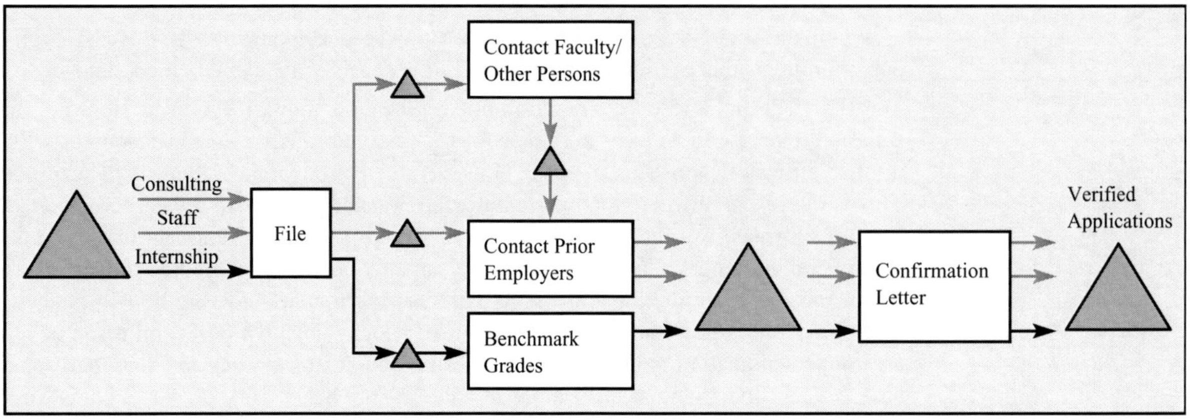

- For consulting/lawyer positions, the agency attempts to call former supervisors and/or colleagues in addition to contacting the previous employers and analyzes the letters of recommendation from those employers.

This *product mix* (different types of customers flowing through one process) complicates the process analysis. It is important to understand that the capacity of the process crucially depends on the product mix. For example, the process step "contact persons who have worked with the candidate" might have a very long activity time, resulting in a low capacity for this activity. However, if only 1 out of 100 applicants applies for a consulting position, this low capacity would not be a problem. Thus, the product mix can determine which resource is the bottleneck.

Thus, to find the bottleneck and to determine capacity in a multiproduct situation, we need to compare the available capacity with the requested capacity. The analysis is given in Table 2.5. Numbers that are raw data (i.e., that you would find in the case or by observing the real process) are printed in **bold.** Numbers that are derived by analysis are printed in *italics*.

TABLE 2.5   Finding the Bottleneck in the Multiproduct Case

	Activity Time	Number of Workers	Available Capacity	Requested Capacity [Applications/Hour] Workload				Implied Utilization
				Consulting	Staff	Interns	Total	
File	**3** [min./appl.]	**1**	*1/3* [appl./min.] = *20* [appl./hour]	3	11	4	18	*18/20 = 90%*
Contact persons	**20** [min./appl.]	**2**	*2/20* [appl./min.] = *6* [appl./hour]	3	0	0	3	*3/6 = 50%*
Contact employers	**15** [min./appl.]	**3**	*3/15* [appl./min.] = *12* [appl./hour]	3	11	0	14	*14/12 = 117%*
Grade/school analysis	**8** [min./appl.]	**2**	*2/8* [appl./min.] = *15* [appl./hour]	0	0	4	4	*4/15 = 27%*
Confirmation letter	**2** [min./appl.]	**1**	*1/2* [appl./min.] = *30* [appl./hour]	3	11	4	18	*18/30 = 60%*

We assume the demand is **180** applications a day, of which there are

- **30** for consulting positions,
- **110** for staff, and
- **40** for internship positions.

Assuming that the working day is 10 hours, demand is *3* consulting applications per hour, *11* staff applications per hour, and *4* applications for internships per hour.

When computing the workload of a given resource (requested capacity of a resource) as shown in Table 2.5, it is important to remember that some activities (e.g., filing the applications) are requested by all product types, whereas others (e.g., contacting faculty and former colleagues) are requested by one product type. This is (hopefully) clear by looking at the process flow diagram.

By dividing the requested capacity by the available capacity, we compute the implied utilization of the resource (see previous section). This allows us to find the "busiest" resource. In this case, this is "contact prior employers." As this ratio is above 100 percent, the process is capacity-constrained and, unless we can work overtime (i.e., add extra hours at the end of the day, in which case our available capacity would go up), we will not be able to process all the incoming applications.

As discussed previously, defining the flow unit in the presence of a product mix is somewhat more complicated. One approach to defining a flow unit is as follows:

- The flow is a "random" application.
- The application is a consulting application with probability 3/18, a staff position with 11/18 probability, and an internship application with 4/18 probability.

Alternatively, we could define the flow unit as "one minute of work." Then, we can compute the available capacity as (number of workers) $\times$ 60 [minutes/hour]. When we look at the requested capacity, we look at how many applications of a different type have to be processed within an hour and how many minutes of work each application requires at a given process step. For example, when we look at the process step File and staff applications, we know that

- There are 11 staff applications to be processed every hour.
- Each of them corresponds to three minutes of work.

Thus, there is a requested capacity (workload) of 33 minutes/hour for staff applications at process step File. In contrast, there is no requested capacity of staff applications for the process step Contact persons.

Table 2.6 summarizes the calculations for this alternative approach. Note that the two procedures to find the bottleneck in the case of a product mix are equivalent; that is, they yield the same bottleneck and the same levels of implied utilization.

There are two guiding principles to keep in mind when defining the flow unit:

- The capacity for each resource can be expressed in terms of that flow unit.
- Each type of demand can be expressed in terms of the number of flow units it requests.

For example, if the flow unit is "one application," then we can evaluate the capacity for each resource in terms of the number of applications processed per unit time. Furthermore, each demand type is exactly one application, so we can express the total number of applications requested for each resource. If the flow unit is "one minute of work," then we express the capacity of each resource in terms of the number of "minutes of work" per unit time, and, similarly, each demand type can be expressed in terms of number of "minutes of work" it requests from the resource.

TABLE 2.6   **Using "One Minute of Work" as the Flow Unit to Find the Bottleneck in the Multiproduct Case**

	Activity Time	Number of Workers	Available Capacity	Requested Capacity [Minutes/Hour] Workload				Implied Utilization
				Consulting	Staff	Interns	Total	
File	**3** [min./appl.]	**1**	60 [min./hour]	3 × 3	11 × 3	4 × 3	54	54/60 = 90%
Contact persons	**20** [min./appl.]	**2**	120 [min./hour]	3 × 20	0	0	60	60/120 = 50%
Contact employers	**15** [min./appl.]	**3**	180 [min./hour]	3 × 15	11 × 15	0	210	210/180 = 117%
Grade/school analysis	**8** [min./appl.]	**2**	120 [min./hour]	0	0	4 × 8	32	32/120 = 27%
Confirmation letter	**2** [min./appl.]	**1**	60 [min./hour]	3 × 2	11 × 2	4 × 2	36	36/60 = 60%

Neither of these two approaches is superior. As we have just seen, they lead to the same results. Thus, you can simply choose the approach that you find more intuitive or that seems easier to apply in a given setting.

The analysis shown above is a good first step in a process analysis with multiple flow units. It computes the implied utilization of each resource and hence can quickly determine if there exists enough capacity in the process or not. Yet, the analysis does not compute the actual flow rates through the process, as this analysis is somewhat more complex. It also does not show where a potential capacity expansion of a resource would be most beneficial.

To see the complications of doing a complete analysis of bottlenecks and flow rates in a process with multiple flow units, consider the following example. At the international arrival area of a major U.S. airport, 15 passengers arrive per minute, 10 of whom are U.S. citizens or permanent residents and 5 are visitors.

The immigration process is organized as follows. Passengers disembark their aircraft and use escalators to arrive in the main immigration hall. The escalators can transport up to 100 passengers per minute.

Following the escalators, passengers have to go through immigration. There exist separate immigration resources for U.S. citizens and permanent residents (they can handle 10 passengers per minute) and visitors (which can handle 3 visitors per minute). After immigration, all passengers pick up their luggage. Luggage handling (starting with getting the luggage off the plane and ending with moving the luggage onto the conveyor belts) has a capacity of 10 passengers per minute. Finally, all passengers go through customs, which has a capacity of 20 passengers per minute.

We calculate the implied utilization levels in Table 2.7. Based on the analysis we did before, we would call the immigration resource dedicated to visitors the bottleneck. However, the analysis of passenger flows and the accumulation of waiting lines are somewhat more complex. Consider the following information:

- There are three visitors per minute leaving immigration and moving on to receive their luggage.
- Together with the 10 passengers per minute who are U.S. citizens or permanent residents, this creates a flow of 13 passengers per minute at the luggage handling step.
- The luggage handling step, however, only has capacity for 10 passengers per minute. This suggests that lines will also exist at luggage handling, though it is not clear whether this line consists primarily of visitors or of U.S. citizens and permanent residents.

TABLE 2.7
Calculating Implied Utilization in Airport Example

Resource	Demand for U.S. Citizens and Permanent Residents [Pass./Min.]	Demand for Visitors [Pass./Min.]	Capacity [Pass./Min.]	Implied Utilization
Escalator	10	5	100	15/100 = 15%
Immigration— U.S. residents	10	0	10	10/10 = 100%
Immigration— visitors	0	5	3	5/3 = 167%
Luggage handling	10	5	10	15/10 = 150%
Customs	10	5	20	15/20 = 75%

The problem that this points to is that we have to decide how many passengers of the two types we want to serve at each resource. Assume our objective is to maximize the total number of passengers flowing through the system. Let US be the number of U.S. passengers and permanent residents served per minute and V be the number of visiting passengers served per minute. We can write:

$$Max\{US + V\}$$

Subject to $US \leq 10$, $V \leq 5$　(demand constraints)

$US \leq 10$, $V \leq 3$　(immigration)

$US + V \leq 10$　(luggage handling)

So the optimal solution is any combination of US and V such that $US + V = 10$. It could be $US = 7$ and $V = 3$ or $US = 10$ and $V = 0$.

Now, we can imagine two objectives for the airport, independent of the capacity of the resources and independent of the passenger demand.

- The airport might want to give priority to U.S. passengers, in which case it would operate at $V = 0$ and $US = 10$.

- The airport might want to achieve a fair flow, that is, the mix of passengers served should be the same as the mix of passengers arriving. If this is the case, we would operate at $V = 3.33$ and $US = 6.67$. Since $V = 3.33$ is not feasible, we might then add some U.S. passengers and permanent residents ($US = 7$) and reduce the visitor flow to $V = 3$.

So we observe that the flow rates through the process are not dictated by demand and capacity alone, but also depend on the objectives of the system. For this reason, the optimal flows are typically computed based on a network flow problem, a special form of a linear program that computes the flows to maximize profits while honoring the demand and resource constraints. This is somewhat more complicated than what we wanted to do in an introductory book, which is why we described it as we did.

2.7 Summary

Figure 2.11 is a summary of the major steps graphically. Exhibits 2.1 and 2.2 summarize the steps required to do the corresponding calculations for a single flow unit and multiple flow units respectively.

STEPS FOR BASIC PROCESS ANALYSIS WITH ONE TYPE OF FLOW UNIT

1. Find the capacity of every resource; if there are multiple resources performing the same activity, add their capacities together.
2. The resource with the lowest capacity is called the *bottleneck*. Its capacity determines the capacity of the entire process (*process capacity*).
3. The flow rate is found based on

$$\text{Flow Rate} = \text{Minimum \{Available input, Demand, Process capacity\}}$$

4. We find the utilization of the process as

$$\text{Process utilization} = \frac{\text{Flow rate}}{\text{Process capacity}}$$

Similarly, we find the utilization of each resource as

$$\text{Utilization of resource} = \frac{\text{Flow rate}}{\text{Capacity of resource}}$$

Any process analysis should begin with the creation of a process flow diagram. This is especially important for the case of multiple flow units, as their flows are typically more complex.

Next, we need to identify the bottleneck of the process. As long as there exists only one type of flow unit, this is simply the resource with the lowest capacity. However, for more general cases, we need to perform some extra analysis. Specifically, if there is a product mix, we have to compute the requested capacity (workload) at each resource and then compare it to the available capacity. This corresponds to computing the implied utilization, and we identify the bottleneck as the resource with the highest implied utilization.

Finally, once we have found the bottleneck, we can compute a variety of performance measures. As in the previous chapter, we are interested in finding the flow rate. The flow rate also allows us to compute the process utilization as well as the utilization profile across resources. Utilizations, while not necessarily a business goal by themselves, are important measures in many industries, especially capital-intensive industries.

FIGURE 2.11   Summary of Process Analysis

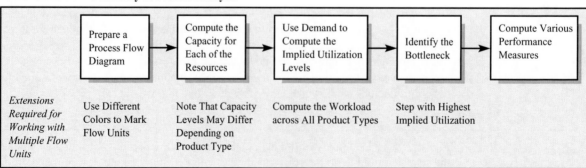

STEPS FOR BASIC PROCESS ANALYSIS WITH MULTIPLE TYPES OF FLOW UNITS

1. For each resource, compute the number of minutes that the resource can produce; this is 60 [min./hour] × Number of resources within the resource pool.
2. Create a process flow diagram, indicating how the flow units go through the process; use multiple colors to indicate the flow of the different flow units.
3. Create a table indicating how much workload each flow unit is consuming at each resource:

   - The rows of the table correspond to the resources in the process.
   - The columns of the table correspond to the different types of flow units.
   - Each cell of the table should contain one of the following:

   If flow unit does not visit the corresponding resource, Ø;
   Otherwise, demand per hour of the corresponding flow unit × activity time.
4. Add up the workload of each resource across all flow units.
5. Compute the implied utilization of each resource as

$$\text{Implied utilization} = \frac{\text{Result of step 3}}{\text{Result of step 1}}$$

The resource with the highest implied utilization is the bottleneck.

The above approach is based on Table 2.6; that is, the flow unit is "one minute of work."

2.8
Practice
Problems

Q 2.1* **(Process Analysis with One Flow Unit)** Consider a process consisting of three resources:

Resource	Activity Time [Min./Unit]	Number of Workers
1	10	2
2	6	1
3	16	3

What is the bottleneck? What is the process capacity? What is the flow rate if demand is eight units per hour? What is the utilization of each resource if demand is eight units per hour?

Q 2.2* **(Process Analysis with Multiple Flow Units)** Consider a process consisting of five resources that are operated eight hours per day. The process works on three different products, A, B, and C:

Resource	Number of Workers	Activity Time for A [Min./Unit]	Activity Time for B [Min./Unit]	Activity Time for C [Min./Unit]
1	2	5	5	5
2	2	3	4	5
3	1	15	0	0
4	1	0	3	3
5	2	6	6	6

Demand for the three different products is as follows: product A, 40 units per day; product B, 50 units per day; and product C, 60 units per day.

What is the bottleneck? What is the flow rate for each flow unit assuming that demand must be served in the mix described above (i.e., for every four units of A, there are five units of B and six units of C)?

(* indicates that the solution is at the end of the book)

Q 2.3   **(Cranberries)** International Cranberry Uncooperative (ICU) is a competitor to the National Cranberry Cooperative (NCC). At ICU, barrels of cranberries arrive on trucks at a rate of 150 barrels per hour and are processed continuously at a rate of 100 barrels per hour. Trucks arrive at a uniform rate over eight hours, from 6:00 a.m. until 2:00 p.m. Assume the trucks are sufficiently small so that the delivery of cranberries can be treated as a continuous inflow. The first truck arrives at 6:00 a.m. and unloads immediately, so processing begins at 6:00 a.m. The bins at ICU can hold up to 200 barrels of cranberries before overflowing. If a truck arrives and the bins are full, the truck must wait until there is room in the bins.

   a. What is the maximum number of barrels of cranberries that are waiting on the trucks at any given time?

   b. At what time do the trucks stop waiting?

   c. At what time do the bins become empty?

   d. ICU is considering using seasonal workers in addition to their regular workforce to help with the processing of cranberries. When the seasonal workers are working, the processing rate increases to 125 barrels per hour. The seasonal workers would start working at 10:00 a.m. and finish working when the trucks stop waiting. At what time would ICU finish processing the cranberries using these seasonal workers?

Q 2.4   **(Western Pennsylvania Milk Company)** The Western Pennsylvania Milk Company is producing milk at a fixed rate of 5,000 gallons/hour. The company's clients request 100,000 gallons of milk over the course of one day. This demand is spread out uniformly from 8 a.m. to 6 p.m. If there is no milk available, clients will wait until enough is produced to satisfy their requests.

   The company starts producing at 8 a.m. with 25,000 gallons in finished goods inventory. At the end of the day, after all demand has been fulfilled, the plant keeps on producing until the finished goods inventory has been restored to 25,000 gallons.

   When answering the following questions, treat trucks/milk as a continuous flow process. Begin by drawing a graph indicating how much milk is in inventory and how much milk is "back-ordered" over the course of the day.

   a. At what time during the day will the clients have to start waiting for their requests to be filled?

   b. At what time will clients stop waiting?

   c. Assume that the milk is picked up in trucks that hold 1,250 gallons each. What is the maximum number of trucks that are waiting?

   d. Assume the plant is charged $50 per hour per waiting truck. What are the total waiting time charges on a day?

Q 2.5   **(Bagel Store)** Consider a bagel store selling three types of bagels that are produced according to the process flow diagram outlined below. We assume the demand is **180** bagels a day, of which there are **30** grilled veggie, **110** veggie only, and **40** cream cheese. Assume that the workday is 10 hours long and each resource is staffed with one worker.

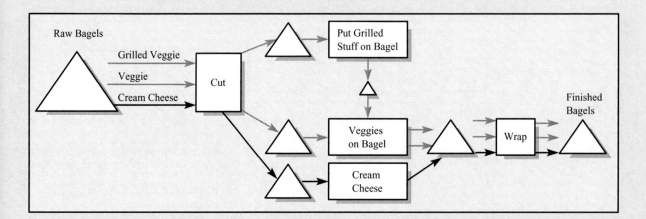

Moreover, we assume the following activity times:

	Cut	Grilled Stuff	Veggies	Cream Cheese	Wrap
Activity time	**3** [min./bagel]	**10** [min./bagel]	**5** [min./bagel]	**4** [min./bagel]	**2** [min./bagel]

Activity times are independent of which bagel type is processed at a resource (for example, cutting a bagel takes the same time for a cream cheese bagel as for a veggie bagel).

a. Where in the process is the bottleneck?

b. How many units can the process produce within one hour, assuming the product mix has to remain constant?

Q 2.6   **(Valley Forge Income Tax Advice)** VF is a small accounting firm supporting wealthy individuals in their preparation of annual income tax statements. Every December, VF sends out a short survey to their customers, asking for the information required for preparing the tax statements. Based on 24 years of experience, VF categorizes their cases into the following groups:

• Group 1 (new customers, easy): 15 percent of cases

• Group 2 (new customers, complex): 5 percent of cases

• Group 3 (repeat customers, easy): 50 percent of cases

• Group 4 (repeat customers, complex): 30 percent of cases

Here, "easy" versus "complex" refers to the complexity of the customer's earning situation.

In order to prepare the income tax statement, VF needs to complete the following set of activities. Activity times (and even which activities need to be carried out) depend on which group a tax statement falls into. All of the following activity times are expressed in minutes per income tax statement.

Group	Filing	Initial Meeting	Preparation	Review by Senior Accountant	Writing
1	20	30	120	20	50
2	40	90	300	60	80
3	20	No meeting	80	5	30
4	40	No meeting	200	30	60

The activities are carried out by the following three persons:

• Administrative support person: filing and writing.

• Senior accountant (who is also the owner): initial meeting, review by senior accountant.

• Junior accountant: preparation.

Assume that all three persons work eight hours per day and 20 days a month. For the following questions, assume the product mix as described above. Assume that there are 50 income tax statements arriving each month.

a. Which of the three persons is the bottleneck?

b. What is the (implied) utilization of the senior accountant? The junior accountant? The administrative support person?

c. You have been asked to analyze which of the four product groups is the most profitable. Which factors would influence the answer to this?

d. How would the process capacity of VF change if a new word processing system would reduce the time to write the income tax statements by 50 percent?

Q 2.7   **(Car Wash Supply Process)** CC Car Wash specializes in car cleaning services. The services offered by the company, the exact service time, and the resources needed for each of them are described in the table below:

Service	Description	Time	Resource Used
A. Wash	Exterior car washing and drying	10 min.	1 automated washing machine
B. Wax	Exterior car waxing	10 min.	1 automated waxing machine
C. Wheel cleaning	Detailed cleaning of all wheels	7 min.	1 employee
D. Interior cleaning	Detailed cleaning inside the car	20 min.	1 employee

The company offers the following packages to their customers:

- Package 1: Includes only car wash (service A).
- Package 2: Includes car wash and waxing (services A and B).
- Package 3: Car wash, waxing, and wheel cleaning (services A, B, and C).
- Package 4: All four services (A, B, C, and D).

Customers of CC Car Wash visit the station at a constant rate (you can ignore any effects of variability) of 40 customers per day. Of these customers, 40 percent buy Package 1, 15 percent buy Package 2, 15 percent buy Package 3, and 30 percent buy Package 4. The mix does not change over the course of the day. The store operates 12 hours a day.

a. What is the implied utilization of the employee doing the wheel cleaning service?

b. Which resource has the highest implied utilization?

For the next summer, CC Car Wash anticipates an increase in the demand to 80 customers per day. Together with this demand increase, there is expected to be a change in the mix of packages demanded: 30 percent of the customers ask for Package 1, 10 percent for Package 2, 10 percent for Package 3, and 50 percent for Package 4. The company will install an additional washing machine to do service A.

c. What will be the new bottleneck in the process?

d. How many customers a day will not be served? Which customers are going to wait? Explain your reasoning!

Q 2.8   (**Starbucks**) After an "all night" study session the day before their last final exam, four first-year MBA students decide to stop for some much-needed coffee at the campus Starbucks. They arrive at 8:30 a.m. and are dismayed to find a rather long line.

Fortunately for the students, a Starbucks executive happens to be in line directly in front of them. From her, they learn the following facts about this Starbucks location:

I. There are three employee types:

- There is a single **cashier** who takes all orders, prepares nonbeverage food items, grinds coffee, and pours drip coffee.
- There is a single **frozen drink maker** who prepares blended and iced drinks.
- There is a single **espresso drink maker** who prepares espressos, lattes, and steamed drinks.

II. There are typically four types of customers:

- **Drip coffee** customers order only drip coffee. This requires 20 seconds of the cashier's time to pour the coffee.
- **Blended and iced drink** customers order a drink that requires the use of the blender. These drinks take on average 2 minutes of work of the frozen drink maker.
- **Espresso drink** customers order a beverage that uses espresso and/or steamed milk. On average, these drinks require 1 minute of work of the espresso drink maker.
- **Ground coffee** customers buy one of Starbucks' many varieties of whole bean coffee and have it ground to their specification at the store. This requires a total of 1 minute of the cashier's time (20 seconds to pour the coffee and 40 seconds to grind the whole bean coffee).

III. The customers arrive uniformly at the following rates from 7 a.m. (when the store opens) until 10 a.m. (when the morning rush is over), with no customers arriving after 10 a.m.:

- **Drip coffee** customers: 25 per hour.
- **Blended and iced drink** customers: 20 per hour.
- **Espresso drink** customers: 70 per hour.
- **Ground coffee** customers: 5 per hour.

IV. Each customer spends, on average, 20 seconds with the cashier to order and pay.

V. Approximately 25 percent of all customers order food, which requires an additional 20 seconds of the cashier's time per transaction.

While waiting in line, the students reflect on these facts and with OPIM 631 fresh in mind they answer the following questions:

a. What is the implied utilization of the frozen drink maker?

b. Which resource has the highest implied utilization?

From their conversation with the executive, the students learn that Starbucks is considering a promotion on all scones (half price!), which marketing surveys predict will increase the percentage of customers ordering food to 30 percent (the overall arrival rates of customers will *not* change). However, the executive is worried about how this will affect the waiting times for customers.

c. How do the levels of implied utilization change as a response to this promotion?

Q 2.9   **(Paris Airport)** Kim Opim, an enthusiastic first-year MBA student, is on her flight over from Philadelphia (PHL) to Paris (CDG), where she will spend some time at INSEAD in Fontainebleau, France. Kim reflects upon how her educational experiences from her operations courses could help explain the long wait time that she experienced before she could enter the departure area of Terminal A at PHL. As an airline representative explained to Kim, there are four types of travelers in Terminal A:

- Experienced short-distance (short-distance international travel destinations are Mexico and various islands in the Atlantic) travelers: These passengers check in online and do not speak with any agent nor do they take any time at the kiosks.
- Experienced long-distance travelers: These passengers spend 3 minutes with an agent.
- Inexperienced short-distance travelers: These passengers spend 2 minutes at a kiosk; however, they do not require the attention of an agent.
- Inexperienced long-distance travelers: These passengers need to talk 5 minutes with an agent.

All passengers must pass through security, where they need 0.5 minutes independent of their type. From historical data, the airport is able to estimate the arrival rates of the different customer types at Terminal A of Philadelphia International:

- Experienced short-distance travelers: 100 per hour
- Experienced long-distance travelers: 80 per hour
- Inexperienced short-distance travelers: 80 per hour
- Inexperienced long-distance travelers: 40 per hour

At this terminal, there are four security check stations, six agents, and three electronic kiosks. Passengers arrive uniformly from 4 p.m. to 8 p.m., with the entire system empty prior to 4 p.m. (the "midafternoon lull") and no customers arriving after 8 p.m. All workers must stay on duty until the last passenger is entirely through the system (e.g., has passed through security).

a. What are the levels of implied utilization at each resource?

b. At what time has the last passenger gone through the system? Note: If passengers of one type have to wait for a resource, passengers that do not require service at the resource can pass by the waiting passengers!

c. Kim, an experienced long-distance traveler, arrived at 6 p.m. at the airport and attempted to move through the check-in process as quickly as she could. How long did she have to wait before she was checked at security?

d. The airline considers showing an educational program that would provide information about the airport's check-in procedures. Passenger surveys indicate that 80 percent of the inexperienced passengers (short or long distance) would subsequently act as experienced passengers (i.e., the new arrival rates would be 164 experienced short-distance, 112 experienced long-distance, 16 inexperienced short-distance, and 8 inexperienced long-distance [passengers/hour]). At what time has the last passenger gone through the system?

Chapter

3

Variability and Its Impact on Process Performance: Waiting Time Problems

For consumers, one of the most visible—and probably annoying—forms of supply–demand mismatches is waiting time. As consumers, we seem to spend a significant portion of our life waiting in line, be it in physical lines (supermarkets, check-in at airports) or in "virtual" lines (listening to music in a call center, waiting for a response e-mail).

It is important to distinguish between different types of waiting time:

• Waiting time predictably occurs when the expected demand rate exceeds the expected supply rate for some limited period of time. This happens especially in cases of constant capacity levels and demand that exhibits seasonality. This leads to implied utilization levels of over 100 percent for some time period. Queues forming at the gate of an airport after the flight is announced are an example of such queues.

• As we will see in the next section, in the presence of variability, queues also can arise if the implied utilization is below 100 percent. Such queues can thereby be fully attributed to the presence of variability, as there exists, on average, enough capacity to meet demand.

While the difference between these two types of waiting time probably does not matter much to the customer, it is of great importance from the perspective of operations management. The root cause for the first type of waiting time is a capacity problem; variability is only a secondary effect. Thus, when analyzing this type of a problem, we first should use the tools outlined in Chapter 2, instead of focusing on variability.

The root cause of the second type of waiting time is variability. This makes waiting time unpredictable, both from the perspective of the customer as well as from the perspective of the operation. Sometimes, it is the customer (demand) waiting for service (supply) and, sometimes, it is the other way around. Demand just never seems to match supply in these settings.

Analyzing waiting times and linking these waiting times to variability require the introduction of new analytical tools, which we present in this chapter. We will discuss the tools for analyzing waiting times based on the example of An-ser Services, a call-center operation in

Wisconsin that specializes in providing answering services for financial services, insurance companies, and medical practices. Specifically, the objective of this chapter is to

- Predict waiting times and derive some performance metrics capturing the service quality provided to the customer.
- Recommend ways of reducing waiting time by choosing appropriate capacity levels, redesigning the service system, and outlining opportunities to reduce variability.

3.1   Motivating Example: A Somewhat Unrealistic Call Center

For illustrative purposes, consider a call center with just one employee from 7 a.m. to 8 a.m. Based on prior observations, the call-center management estimates that, on average, a call takes 4 minutes to complete (e.g., giving someone driving directions) and there are, on average, 12 calls arriving in a 60-minute period, that is, on average, one call every 5 minutes.

What will be the average waiting time for a customer before talking to a customer service representative? From a somewhat naïve perspective, there should be no waiting time at all. Since the call center has a capacity of serving 60/4 = 15 calls per hour and calls arrive at a rate of 12 calls per hour, supply of capacity clearly exceeds demand. If anything, there seems to be excess service capacity in the call center since its utilization, which we defined previously as the ratio between flow rate and capacity, can be computed as

$$\text{Utilization} = \frac{\text{Flow rate}}{\text{Capacity}} = \frac{12 \text{ calls per hour}}{15 \text{ calls per hour}} = 80\%$$

First, consider the arrivals and service times as depicted in Figure 3.1. A call arrives exactly every 5 minutes and then takes exactly 4 minutes to be served. This is probably the weirdest call center that you have ever seen! No need to worry, we will return to "real operations" momentarily, but the following thought experiment will help you grasp how variability can lead to waiting time.

Despite its almost robotlike service times and the apparently very disciplined customer service representative ("sorry, 4 minutes are over; thanks for your call"), this call center has one major advantage: no incoming call ever has to wait.

FIGURE 3.1
A Somewhat Odd Service Process

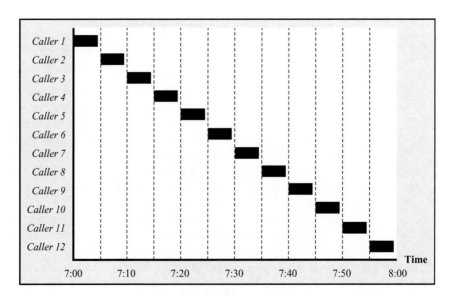

FIGURE 3.2
Data Gathered at a Call Center

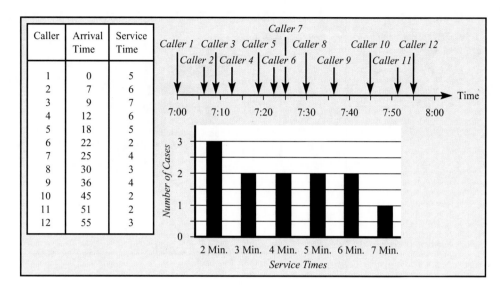

Assuming that calls arrive like kick scooters at an assembly line and are then treated by customer service representatives that act like robots reflects a common mistake managers make when calculating process performance. These calculations look at the process at an aggregate level and consider how much capacity is available over the entire hour (day, month, quarter), yet ignore how the requests for service are spaced out within the hour.

If we look at the call center on a minute-by-minute basis, a different picture emerges. Specifically, we observe that calls do not arrive like kick scooters appear at the end of the assembly line, but instead follow a much less systematic pattern, which is illustrated by Figure 3.2.

Moreover, a minute-by-minute analysis also reveals that the actual service durations also vary across calls. As Figure 3.2 shows, while the average service time is 4 minutes, there exist large variations across calls, and the actual activity times range from 2 minutes to 7 minutes.

Now, consider how the hour from 7:00 a.m. to 8:00 a.m. unfolds. As can be seen in Figure 3.2, the first call comes in at 7:00 a.m. This call will be served without waiting time, and it takes the customer service representative 5 minutes to complete the call. The following 2 minutes are idle time from the perspective of the call center (7:05–7:07). At 7:07, the second call comes in, requiring a 6-minute service time. Again, the second caller does not have to wait and will leave the system at 7:13. However, while the second caller is being served, at 7:09 the third caller arrives and now needs to wait until 7:13 before beginning the service.

Figure 3.3 shows the waiting time and service time for each of the 12 customers calling between 7:00 a.m. and 8:00 a.m. Specifically, we observe that

- Most customers do have to wait a considerable amount of time (up to 10 minutes) before being served. This waiting occurs, although, on average, there is plenty of capacity in the call center.

- The call center is not able to provide a consistent service quality, as some customers are waiting, while others are not.

- Despite long waiting times and—because of Little's Law—long queues (see lower part of Figure 3.3), the customer service representative incurs idle time repeatedly over the time period from 7 a.m. to 8 a.m.

Why does variability not average out over time? The reason for this is as follows. In the call center example, the customer service representative can only serve a customer if there is capacity *and* demand at the same moment in time. Therefore, capacity can never

FIGURE 3.3
Detailed Analysis of
Call Center

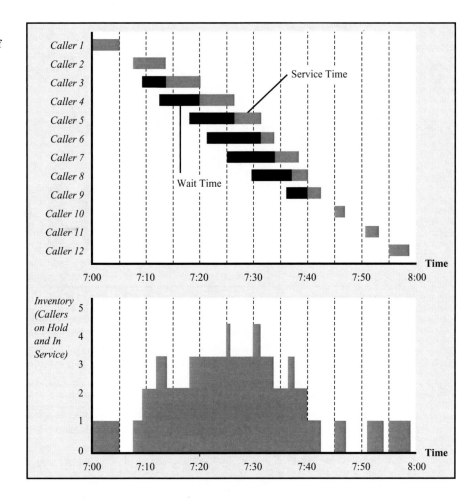

"run ahead" of demand. However, demand can "run ahead" of capacity, in which case the queue builds up. The idea that inventory can be used to decouple the supply process from demand, thereby restoring the flow rate to the level achievable in the absence of variability, is another version of the "buffer or suffer" principle that we already encountered. Thus, if a service organization attempts to achieve the flow-rate levels feasible based on averages, long waiting times will result (unfortunately, in those cases, it is the customer who gets "buffered" and "suffers").

Taking the perspective of a manager attempting to match supply and demand, our objectives have not changed. We are still interested in calculating the three fundamental performance measures of an operation: inventory, flow rate, and flow time. Yet, as the above example illustrated, we realize that the process analysis tools we have discussed up to this point in the book need to be extended to appropriately deal with variability.

3.2 Variability: Where It Comes From and How It Can Be Measured

As a first step toward restoring our ability to understand a process's basic performance measures in the presence of variability, we take a more detailed look at the concept of variability itself. Specifically, we are interested in the sources of variability and how to measure variability.

FIGURE 3.4
Variability and Where It Comes From

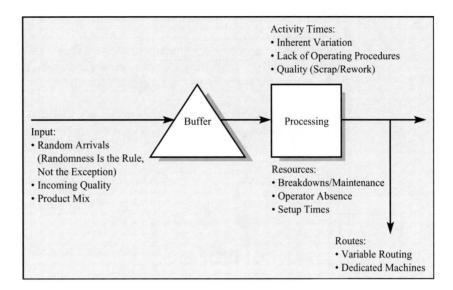

Why is there variability in a process to begin with? Drawing a simple (the most simple) process flow diagram suggests the following four sources of variability (these four sources are summarized in Figure 3.4):

• Variability from the inflow of flow units. The biggest source of variability in service organizations comes from the market itself. While some patterns of the customer-arrival process are predictable (e.g., in a hotel there are more guests checking out between 8 and 9 a.m. than between 2 and 3 p.m.), there always remains uncertainty about when the next customer will arrive.

• Variability in activity times. Whenever we are dealing with human operators at a resource, it is likely that there will be some variability in their behavior. Thus, if we would ask a worker at an assembly line to repeat a certain activity 100 times, we would probably find that some of these activities were carried out faster than others. Another source of variability in activity times that is specific to a service environment is that in most service operations, the customer him/herself is involved in many of the tasks constituting the activity time. At a hotel front desk, some guests might require extra time (e.g., the guest requires an explanation for items appearing on his or her bill), while others check out faster (e.g., simply use the credit card that they used for the reservation and only return their room key).

• Random availability of resources. If resources are subject to random breakdowns, for example, machine failures in manufacturing environments or operator absenteeism in service operations, variability is created.

• Random routing in case of multiple flow units in the process. If the path a flow unit takes through the process is itself random, the arrival process at each individual resource is subject to variability. Consider, for example, an emergency room in a hospital. Following the initial screening at the admissions step, incoming patients are routed to different resources. A nurse might handle easy cases, more complex cases might be handled by a general doctor, and severe cases are brought to specific units in the hospital (e.g., trauma center). Even if arrival times and service times are deterministic, this random routing alone is sufficient to introduce variability.

In general, any form of variability is measured based on the standard deviation. In our case of the call center, we could measure the variability of call durations based on collecting some data and then computing the corresponding standard deviation. The problem with this approach is that the standard deviation provides an *absolute* measure of variability. Does a standard deviation of 5 minutes indicate a high variability? A 5-minute standard deviation for call durations (activity times) in the context of a call center seems like a large number. In the context of a 2-hour surgery in a trauma center, a 5-minute standard deviation seems small.

For this reason, it is more appropriate to measure variability in *relative* terms. Specifically, we define the *coefficient of variation* of a random variable as

$$\text{Coefficient of variation} = \text{CV} = \frac{\text{Standard deviation}}{\text{Mean}}$$

As both the standard deviation and the mean have the same measurement units, the coefficient of variation is a unitless measure.

3.3 Analyzing an Arrival Process

Any process analysis we perform is only as good as the information we feed into our analysis. For this reason, Sections 3.3 and 3.4 focus on data collection and data analysis for the upcoming mathematical models. As a manager intending to apply some of the following tools, this data analysis is essential. However, as a student with only a couple of hours left to the final exam, you might be better off jumping straight to Section 3.5.

Of particular importance when dealing with variability problems is an accurate representation of the demand, which determines the timing of customer arrivals.

Assume we got up early and visited the call center of An-ser; say we arrived at their offices at 6:00 a.m. and we took detailed notes of what takes place over the coming hour. We would hardly have had the time to settle down when the first call comes in. One of the An-ser staff takes the call immediately. Twenty-three seconds later, the second call comes in; another 1:24 minutes later, the third call; and so on.

We define the time at which An-ser receives a call as the *arrival time*. Let AT_i denote the arrival time of the ith call. Moreover, we define the time between two consecutive arrivals as the *interarrival time*, IA. Thus, $IA_i = AT_{i+1} - AT_i$. Figure 3.5 illustrates these two definitions.

If we continue this data collection, we accumulate a fair number of arrival times. Such data are automatically recorded in call centers, so we could simply download a file that looks like Table 3.1.

Before we can move forward and introduce a mathematical model that predicts the effects of variability, we have to invest in some simple, yet important, data analysis. A major risk

FIGURE 3.5   **The Concept of Interarrival Times**

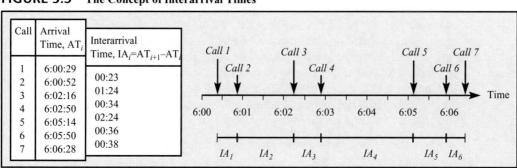

Call	Arrival Time, AT_i	Interarrival Time, $IA_i = AT_{i+1} - AT_i$
1	6:00:29	00:23
2	6:00:52	01:24
3	6:02:16	00:34
4	6:02:50	02:24
5	6:05:14	00:36
6	6:05:50	00:38
7	6:06:28	

TABLE 3.1 Call Arrivals at An-ser on April 2, 2002, from 6:00 a.m. to 10:00 a.m.

6:00:29	6:52:39	7:17:57	7:33:51	7:56:16	8:17:33	8:28:11	8:39:25	8:55:56	9:21:58
6:00:52	6:53:06	7:18:10	7:34:05	7:56:24	8:17:42	8:28:12	8:39:47	8:56:17	9:22:02
6:02:16	6:53:07	7:18:17	7:34:19	7:56:24	8:17:50	8:28:13	8:39:51	8:57:42	9:22:02
6:02:50	6:53:24	7:18:38	7:34:51	7:57:39	8:17:52	8:28:17	8:40:02	8:58:45	9:22:30
6:05:14	6:53:25	7:18:54	7:35:10	7:57:51	8:17:54	8:28:43	8:40:09	8:58:49	9:23:13
6:05:50	6:54:18	7:19:04	7:35:13	7:57:55	8:18:03	8:28:59	8:40:23	8:58:49	9:23:29
6:06:28	6:54:24	7:19:40	7:35:21	7:58:26	8:18:12	8:29:06	8:40:34	8:59:32	9:23:45
6:07:37	6:54:36	7:19:41	7:35:44	7:58:41	8:18:21	8:29:34	8:40:35	8:59:38	9:24:10
6:08:05	6:55:06	7:20:10	7:35:59	7:59:12	8:18:23	8:29:38	8:40:46	8:59:45	9:24:30
6:10:16	6:55:19	7:20:11	7:36:37	7:59:20	8:18:34	8:29:40	8:40:51	9:00:14	9:24:42
6:12:13	6:55:31	7:20:26	7:36:45	7:59:22	8:18:46	8:29:45	8:40:58	9:00:52	9:25:07
6:12:48	6:57:25	7:20:27	7:37:07	7:59:22	8:18:53	8:29:46	8:41:12	9:00:53	9:25:15
6:14:04	6:57:38	7:20:38	7:37:14	7:59:36	8:18:54	8:29:47	8:41:26	9:01:09	9:26:03
6:14:16	6:57:44	7:20:52	7:38:01	7:59:50	8:18:58	8:29:47	8:41:32	9:01:31	9:26:04
6:14:28	6:58:16	7:20:59	7:38:03	7:59:54	8:19:20	8:29:54	8:41:49	9:01:55	9:26:23
6:17:51	6:58:34	7:21:11	7:38:05	8:01:22	8:19:25	8:30:00	8:42:23	9:02:25	9:26:34
6:18:19	6:59:41	7:21:14	7:38:18	8:01:42	8:19:28	8:30:01	8:42:51	9:02:30	9:27:02
6:19:11	7:00:50	7:21:46	7:39:00	8:01:56	8:20:09	8:30:08	8:42:53	9:02:38	9:27:04
6:20:48	7:00:54	7:21:56	7:39:17	8:02:08	8:20:23	8:30:23	8:43:24	9:02:51	9:27:27
6:23:33	7:01:08	7:21:58	7:39:35	8:02:26	8:20:27	8:30:23	8:43:28	9:03:29	9:28:25
6:24:25	7:01:31	7:23:03	7:40:06	8:02:29	8:20:44	8:30:31	8:43:47	9:03:33	9:28:37
6:25:08	7:01:39	7:23:16	7:40:23	8:02:39	8:20:54	8:31:02	8:44:23	9:03:38	9:29:09
6:25:19	7:01:56	7:23:19	7:41:34	8:02:47	8:21:12	8:31:11	8:44:49	9:03:51	9:29:15
6:25:27	7:04:52	7:23:48	7:42:20	8:02:52	8:21:12	8:31:19	8:45:05	9:04:11	9:29:52
6:25:38	7:04:54	7:24:01	7:42:33	8:03:06	8:21:25	8:31:20	8:45:10	9:04:33	9:30:47
6:25:48	7:05:37	7:24:09	7:42:51	8:03:58	8:21:28	8:31:22	8:45:28	9:04:42	9:30:58
6:26:05	7:05:39	7:24:45	7:42:57	8:04:07	8:21:43	8:31:23	8:45:31	9:04:44	9:30:59
6:26:59	7:05:42	7:24:56	7:43:23	8:04:27	8:21:44	8:31:27	8:45:32	9:04:44	9:31:03
6:27:37	7:06:37	7:25:01	7:43:34	8:05:53	8:21:53	8:31:45	8:45:39	9:05:22	9:31:55
6:27:46	7:06:46	7:25:03	7:43:43	8:05:54	8:22:19	8:32:05	8:46:24	9:06:01	9:33:08
6:29:32	7:07:11	7:25:18	7:43:44	8:06:43	8:22:44	8:32:13	8:46:27	9:06:12	9:33:45
6:29:52	7:07:24	7:25:39	7:43:57	8:06:47	8:23:00	8:32:19	8:46:40	9:06:14	9:34:07
6:30:26	7:07:46	7:25:40	7:43:57	8:07:07	8:23:02	8:32:59	8:46:41	9:06:41	9:35:15
6:30:32	7:09:17	7:25:46	7:45:07	8:07:43	8:23:12	8:33:02	8:47:00	9:06:44	9:35:40
6:30:41	7:09:34	7:25:48	7:45:32	8:08:28	8:23:30	8:33:27	8:47:04	9:06:48	9:36:17
6:30:53	7:09:38	7:26:30	7:46:22	8:08:31	8:24:04	8:33:30	8:47:06	9:06:55	9:36:37
6:30:56	7:09:53	7:26:38	7:46:38	8:09:05	8:24:17	8:33:40	8:47:15	9:06:59	9:37:23
6:31:04	7:09:59	7:26:49	7:46:48	8:09:15	8:24:19	8:33:47	8:47:27	9:08:03	9:37:37
6:31:45	7:10:29	7:27:30	7:47:00	8:09:48	8:24:26	8:34:19	8:47:40	9:08:33	9:37:38
6:33:49	7:10:37	7:27:36	7:47:15	8:09:57	8:24:39	8:34:20	8:47:46	9:09:32	9:37:42
6:34:03	7:10:54	7:27:50	7:47:53	8:10:39	8:24:48	8:35:01	8:47:53	9:10:32	9:39:03
6:34:15	7:11:07	7:27:50	7:48:01	8:11:16	8:25:03	8:35:07	8:48:27	9:10:46	9:39:10
6:36:07	7:11:30	7:27:56	7:48:14	8:11:30	8:25:04	8:35:25	8:48:48	9:10:53	9:41:37
6:36:12	7:12:02	7:28:01	7:48:14	8:11:38	8:25:07	8:35:29	8:49:14	9:11:32	9:42:58
6:37:21	7:12:08	7:28:17	7:48:50	8:11:49	8:25:16	8:36:13	8:49:19	9:11:37	9:43:27
6:37:23	7:12:18	7:28:25	7:49:00	8:12:00	8:25:22	8:36:14	8:49:20	9:11:50	9:43:37
6:37:57	7:12:18	7:28:26	7:49:04	8:12:07	8:25:31	8:36:23	8:49:40	9:12:02	9:44:09
6:38:20	7:12:26	7:28:47	7:49:48	8:12:17	8:25:32	8:36:23	8:50:19	9:13:19	9:44:21
6:40:06	7:13:16	7:28:54	7:49:50	8:12:40	8:25:32	8:36:29	8:50:38	9:14:00	9:44:32
6:40:11	7:13:21	7:29:09	7:49:59	8:12:41	8:25:45	8:36:35	8:52:11	9:14:04	9:44:37
6:40:59	7:13:22	7:29:27	7:50:13	8:12:42	8:25:48	8:36:37	8:52:29	9:14:07	9:44:44
6:42:17	7:14:04	7:30:02	7:50:27	8:12:47	8:25:49	8:37:05	8:52:40	9:15:15	9:45:10
6:43:01	7:14:07	7:30:07	7:51:07	8:13:40	8:26:01	8:37:11	8:52:41	9:15:26	9:46:15
6:43:05	7:14:49	7:30:13	7:51:31	8:13:41	8:26:04	8:37:12	8:52:43	9:15:27	9:46:44
6:43:57	7:15:19	7:30:50	7:51:40	8:13:52	8:26:11	8:37:35	8:53:03	9:15:36	9:49:48
6:44:02	7:15:38	7:30:55	7:52:05	8:14:04	8:26:15	8:37:44	8:53:08	9:15:40	9:50:19
6:45:04	7:15:41	7:31:24	7:52:25	8:14:41	8:26:28	8:38:01	8:53:19	9:15:40	9:52:53
6:46:13	7:15:57	7:31:35	7:52:32	8:15:15	8:26:28	8:38:02	8:53:30	9:15:40	9:53:13
6:47:01	7:16:28	7:31:41	7:53:10	8:15:25	8:26:37	8:38:10	8:53:32	9:15:41	9:53:15
6:47:10	7:16:36	7:31:45	7:53:18	8:15:39	8:26:58	8:38:15	8:53:44	9:15:46	9:53:50
6:47:35	7:16:40	7:31:46	7:53:19	8:15:48	8:27:07	8:38:39	8:54:25	9:16:12	9:54:24
6:49:23	7:16:45	7:32:13	7:53:51	8:16:09	8:27:09	8:38:40	8:54:28	9:16:34	9:54:48
6:50:54	7:16:50	7:32:16	7:53:52	8:16:10	8:27:17	8:38:44	8:54:49	9:18:02	9:54:51
6:51:04	7:17:08	7:32:16	7:54:04	8:16:18	8:27:26	8:38:49	8:55:05	9:18:06	9:56:40
6:51:17	7:17:09	7:32:34	7:54:16	8:16:26	8:27:29	8:38:57	8:55:05	9:20:19	9:58:25
6:51:48	7:17:09	7:32:34	7:54:26	8:16:39	8:27:35	8:39:07	8:55:14	9:20:42	9:59:19
6:52:17	7:17:19	7:32:57	7:54:51	8:17:16	8:27:54	8:39:20	8:55:22	9:20:44	
6:52:17	7:17:22	7:33:13	7:55:13	8:17:24	8:27:57	8:39:20	8:55:25	9:20:54	
6:52:31	7:17:22	7:33:36	7:55:35	8:17:28	8:27:59	8:39:21	8:55:50	9:21:55	

related to any mathematical model or computer simulation is that these tools always provide us with a number (or a set of numbers), independent of the accuracy with which the inputs we enter into the equation reflect the real world.

Answering the following two questions before proceeding to any other computations improves the predictions of our models substantially.

- Is the arrival process *stationary;* that is, is the expected number of customers arriving in a certain time interval constant over the period we are interested in?
- Are the interarrival times *exponentially distributed,* and therefore form a so-called *Poisson* arrival process?

We now define the concepts of stationary arrivals and exponentially distributed interarrival times. We also describe how these two questions can be answered, both in general as well as in the specific setting of the call center described previously. We also discuss the importance of these two questions and their impact on the calculations in this chapter.

Stationary Arrivals

Consider the call arrival pattern displayed in Table 3.1. How tempting it is to put these data into a spreadsheet, compute the mean and the standard deviation of the interarrival times over that time period, and end the analysis of the arrival pattern at this point, assuming that the mean and the standard deviation capture the entire behavior of the arrival process. Five minutes with Excel, and we could be done!

However, a simple graphical analysis (Figure 3.6) of the data reveals that there is more going on in the arrival process than two numbers can capture. As we can see graphically in Figure 3.6, the average number of customers calling within a certain time interval (e.g., 15 minutes) is not constant over the day.

To capture such changes in arrival processes, we introduce the following definitions:

- An arrival process is said to be *stationary* if, for any time interval (e.g., an hour), the expected number of arrivals in this time interval only depends on the length of the time interval, not on the starting time of the interval (i.e., we can move a time interval of a fixed length forth and back on a time line without changing the expected number of arrivals). In the context of Figure 3.6, we see that the arrival process is not stationary. For example, if we take a 3-hour interval, we see that there are many more customers arriving from 6 to 9 a.m. than there are from 1 to 4 a.m.
- An arrival process exhibits *seasonality* if it is not stationary.

FIGURE 3.6
Seasonality over the Course of a Day

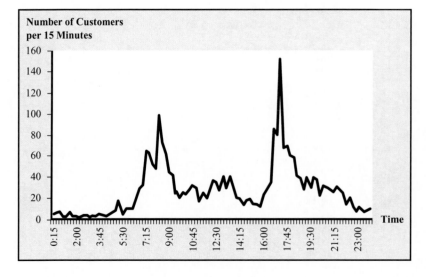

FIGURE 3.7 Test for Stationary Arrivals

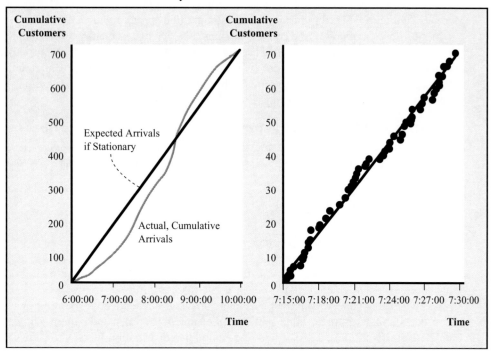

When analyzing an arrival process, it is important that we distinguish between changes in demand (e.g., the number of calls in 15 minutes) that are a result of variability and changes in demand that are a result of seasonality. Both variability and seasonality are unpleasant from an operations perspective. However, the effect of seasonality alone can be perfectly predicted ex ante, while this is not possible for the case of variability (we might know the expected number of callers for a day, but the actual number is a realization of a random variable).

Based on the data at hand, we observe that the arrival process is not stationary over a period of several hours. In general, a simple analysis determines whether a process is stationary.

1. Sort all arrival times so that they are increasing in time (label them as $AT_1 \ldots AT_n$).
2. Plot a graph with $(x\ AT_i; y = i)$ as illustrated by Figure 3.7.
3. Add a straight line from the lower left (first arrival) to the upper right (last arrival).

If the underlying arrival process is stationary, there will be no significant deviation between the graph you plotted and the straight line. In this case, however, in Figure 3.7 (left) we observe several deviations between the straight line and the arrival data. Specifically, we observe that for the first hour, fewer calls come in compared to the average arrival rate from 6 a.m. to 10 a.m. In contrast, around 8:30 a.m., the arrival rate becomes much higher than the average. Thus, our analysis indicates that the arrival process we face is not stationary.

When facing nonstationary arrival processes, the best way to proceed is to divide up the day (the week, the month) into smaller time intervals and have a separate arrival rate for each interval. If we then look at the arrival process within the smaller intervals—in our case, we use 15-minute intervals—we find that the seasonality within the interval is relatively low. In other words, within the interval, we come relatively close to a stationary arrival stream. The stationary behavior of the interarrivals within a 15-minute interval is illustrated by Figure 3.7 (right).

Figure 3.7 (left) is interesting to compare with Figure 3.7 (right): the arrival process behaves as stationary "at the micro-level" of a 15-minute interval, yet exhibits strong seasonality over the course of the entire day, as we observed in Figure 3.6. Note that the peaks in Figure 3.6 correspond to those time slots where the line of "actual, cumulative arrivals" in Figure 3.7 grows faster than the straight line "predicted arrivals."

In most cases in practice, the context explains this type of seasonality. For example, in the case of An-ser, the spike in arrivals corresponds to people beginning their day, expecting that the company they want to call (e.g., a doctor's office) is already "up and running." However, since many of these firms are not handling calls before 9 a.m., the resulting call stream is channeled to the answering service.

Exponential Interarrival Times

Interarrival times commonly are distributed following an *exponential distribution.* If IA is a random interarrival time and the interarrival process follows an exponential distribution, we have

$$\text{Probability } \{IA \leq t\} = 1 - e^{-\frac{t}{a}}$$

where a is the average interarrival time as defined above. Exponential functions are frequently used to model interarrival time in theory as well as practice, both because of their good fit with empirical data as well as their analytical convenience. If an arrival process has indeed exponential interarrival times, we refer to it as a *Poisson arrival process.*

It can be shown analytically that customers arriving independently from each other at the process (e.g., customers calling into a call center) form a demand pattern with exponential interarrival times. The shape of the cumulative distribution function for the exponential distribution is given in Figure 3.8. The average interarrival time is in minutes. An important property of the exponential distribution is that the standard deviation is also equal to the average, a.

Another important property of the exponential distribution is known as the *memoryless property.* The memoryless property simply states that the number of arrivals in the next time slot (e.g., 1 minute) is independent of when the last arrival has occurred.

To illustrate this property, consider the situation of an emergency room. Assume that, on average, a patient arrives every 10 minutes and no patients have arrived for the last

FIGURE 3.8   **Distribution Function of the Exponential Distribution (left) and an Example of a Histogram (right)**

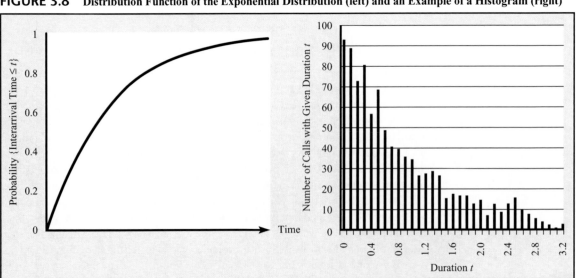

20 minutes. Does the fact that no patients have arrived in the last 20 minutes increase or decrease the probability that a patient arrives in the next 10 minutes? For an arrival process with exponential interarrival times, the answer is *no*.

Intuitively, we feel that this is a reasonable assumption in many settings. Consider, again, an emergency room. Given that the population of potential patients for the ER is extremely large (including all healthy people outside the hospital), we can treat new patients as arriving independently from each other (the fact that Joan Wiley fell off her mountain bike has nothing to do with the fact that Joe Hoop broke his ankle when playing basketball).

Because it is very important to determine if our interarrival times are exponentially distributed, we now introduce the following four-step diagnostic procedure:

1. Compute the interarrival times $IA_1 \ldots IA_n$.
2. Sort the interarrival times in increasing order; let a_i denote the *i*th smallest interarrival time (a_1 is the smallest interarrival time; a_n is the largest).
3. Plot pairs ($x = a_i$, $y = i/n$). The resulting graph is called an empirical distribution function.
4. Compare the graph with an exponential distribution with "appropriately chosen parameter." To find the best value for the parameter, we set the parameter of the exponential distribution equal to the average interarrival time we obtain from our data. If a few observations from the sample are substantially remote from the resulting curve, we might adjust the parameter for the exponential distribution "manually" to improve fit.

Figure 3.9 illustrates the outcome of this process. If the underlying distribution is indeed exponential, the resulting graph will resemble the analytical distribution as in the case of Figure 3.9. Note that this procedure of assessing the goodness of fit works also for any other distribution function.

Nonexponential Interarrival Times

In some cases, we might find that the interarrival times are not exponentially distributed. For example, we might encounter a situation where arrivals are scheduled (e.g., every hour), which typically leads to a lower amount of variability in the arrival process.

FIGURE 3.9
Empirical versus Exponential Distribution for Interarrival Times

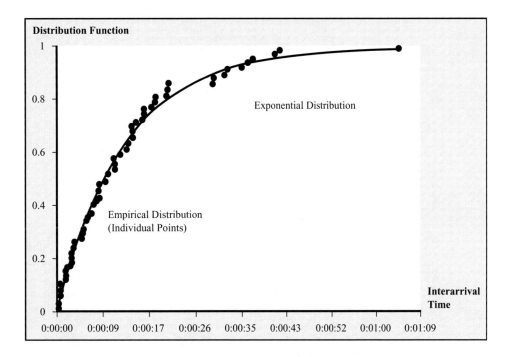

FIGURE 3.10
How to Analyze a
Demand/Arrival
Process

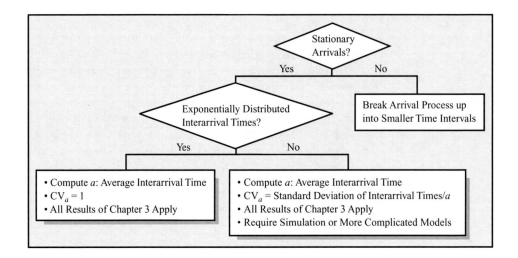

While in the case of the exponential distribution the mean interarrival time is equal to the standard deviation of interarrival times and, thus, one parameter is sufficient to characterize the entire arrival process, we need more parameters to describe the arrival process if interarrival times are not exponentially distributed.

Following our earlier definition of the coefficient of variation, we can measure the variability of an arrival (demand) process as

$$CV_a = \frac{\text{Standard deviation of interarrival time}}{\text{Average interarrival time}}$$

Given that for the exponential distribution the mean is equal to the standard deviation, its coefficient of variation is equal to 1.

Summary: Analyzing an Arrival Process

Figure 3.10 provides a summary of the steps required to analyze an arrival process. It also shows what to do if any of the assumptions required for the following models (Chapter 3) are violated.

3.4   Service Time Variability

Just as exact arrival time of an individual call is difficult to predict, so is the actual duration of the call. Thus, service processes also have a considerable amount of variability from the supply side. Figure 3.11 provides a summary of call durations (service times from the perspective of the customer service representative) for the case of the An-ser call center.

We observe that the variability in service times is substantial. While some calls were completed in less than a minute, others took more than 10 minutes! Thus, in addition to the variability of demand, variability also is created within the process.

There have been reports of numerous different shapes of activity time distributions. For the purposes of this book, we focus entirely on their mean and standard deviation. In other words, when we collect data, we do not explicitly model the distribution of the service times, but assume that the mean and standard deviation capture all the relevant information. This information is sufficient for all computations in Chapter 3.

FIGURE 3.11
Service Times in Call
Center

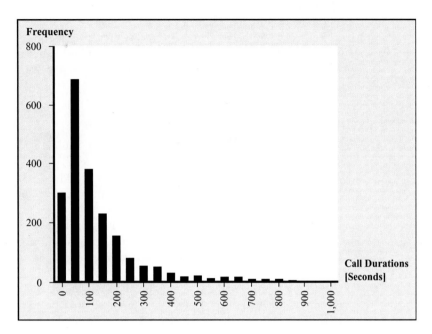

Based on the data summarized in Figure 3.11, we compute the mean call time as 120 seconds and the corresponding standard deviation as 150 seconds. As we have done with the interarrival times, we can now define the coefficient of variation, which we obtain by

$$CV_p = \frac{\text{Standard deviation of activity time}}{\text{Average activity time}}$$

As with the arrival process, we need to be careful not to confuse variability with seasonality. Seasonality in service times refers to known patterns of call durations as a function of the day of the week or the time of the day (as Figure 3.12 shows, calls take significantly longer on weekends than during the week). Call durations also differ depending on the time of the day.

FIGURE 3.12
**Average Call
Durations: Weekday
versus Weekend**

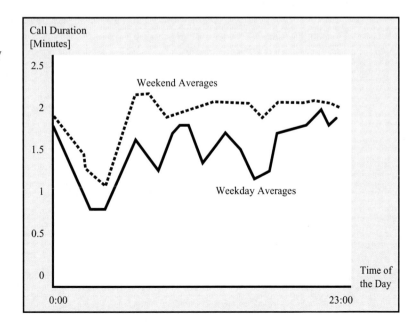

The models we introduce in Chapter 3 require a stationary service process (in the case of seasonality in the service process, just divide up the time line into smaller intervals, similar to what we did with the arrival process) but do not require any other properties (e.g., exponential distribution of service time). Thus, the standard deviation and mean of the service time are all we need to know.

3.5 Predicting the Average Waiting Time for the Case of One Resource

Based on our measures of variability, we now introduce a simple formula that restores our ability to predict the basic process performance measures: inventory, flow rate, and flow time.

In this chapter, we restrict ourselves to the most basic process diagram, consisting of one buffer with unlimited space and one single resource. This process layout corresponds to the call center example discussed above. Figure 3.13 shows the process flow diagram for this simple system.

Flow units arrive to the system following a demand pattern that exhibits variability. On average, a flow unit arrives every a time units. We labeled a as the average interarrival time. This average reflects the mean of interarrival times IA_1 to IA_n. After computing the standard deviation of the IA_1 to IA_n interarrival times, we can compute the coefficient of variation CV_a of the arrival process as discussed previously.

Assume that it takes on average p units of time to serve a flow unit. Similar to the arrival process, we can define p_1 to p_n as the empirically observed activity times and compute the coefficient of variation for the processing times, CV_p, accordingly. Given that there is only one single resource serving the arriving flow units, the capacity of the server can be written as $1/p$.

As discussed in the introduction to this chapter, we are considering cases in which the capacity exceeds the demand rate; thus, the resulting utilization is strictly less than 100 percent. If the utilization were above 100 percent, inventory would predictably build up and we would not need any sophisticated tools accounting for variability to predict that flow units will incur waiting times. However, the most important insight of this chapter is that flow units incur waiting time even if the server utilization is below 100 percent.

Given that capacity exceeds demand and assuming we never lose a customer (i.e., once a customer calls, he or she never hangs up), we are demand-constrained and, thus, the flow rate R is the demand rate. Specifically, since a customer arrives, on average, every a units of time, the flow rate $R = 1/a$. Recall that we can compute utilization as

$$\text{Utilization} = \frac{\text{Flow rate}}{\text{Capacity}} = \frac{1/a}{1/p} = p/a < 100\%$$

Note that, so far, we have not applied any concept that went beyond the deterministic process analysis we discussed in Chapter 2.

FIGURE 3.13
A Simple Process with One Queue and One Server

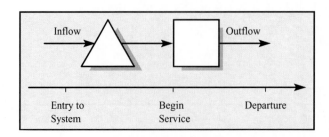

FIGURE 3.14
**A Simple Process
with One Queue and
One Server**

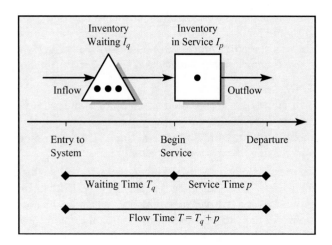

Now, take the perspective of a flow unit moving through the system (see Figure 3.14). A flow unit can spend time waiting in the queue (in a call center, this is the time when you listen to Music of the '70s). Let T_q denote the time the flow unit has to spend in the queue waiting for the service to begin. The subscript q denotes that this is only the time the flow unit waits in the queue. Thus, T_q does *not* include the actual service time, which we defined as p. Based on the waiting time in the queue T_q and the average service time p, we can compute the flow time (the time the flow unit will spend in the system) as

$$\text{Flow time} = \text{Time in queue} + \text{Activity time}$$
$$T = T_q + p$$

Instead of taking the perspective of the flow unit, we also can look at the system as a whole, wondering how many flow units will be in the queue and how many will be in service. Let I_q be defined as the inventory (number of flow units) that are in the queue and I_p be the number of flow units in process. Since the inventory in the queue I_q and the inventory in process I_p are the only places we can find inventory, we can compute the overall inventory in the system as $I = I_q + I_p$.

As long as there exists only one resource, I_p is a number between zero and one: sometimes there is a flow unit in service ($I_p = 1$); sometimes there is not ($I_p = 0$). The probability that at a random moment in time the server is actually busy, working on a flow unit, corresponds to the utilization. For example, if the utilization of the process is 30 percent, there exists a .3 probability that at a random moment in time the server is busy. Alternatively, we can say that over the 60 minutes in an hour, the server is busy for

$$.3 \times 60 \; [\text{minutes/hour}] = 18 \text{ minutes}$$

While the inventory in service I_p and the activity time p are relatively easy to compute, this is unfortunately not the case for the inventory in the queue I_q or the waiting time in the queue T_q.

Based on the activity time p, the utilization, and the variability as measured by the coefficients of variation for the interarrival time CV_a and the processing time CV_p, we can compute the average waiting time in the queue using the following formula:

$$\text{Time in queue} = \text{Activity time} \times \left(\frac{\text{Utilization}}{1 - \text{Utilization}} \right) \times \left(\frac{CV_a^2 + CV_p^2}{2} \right)$$

The formula does not require that the service times or the interarrival times follow a specific distribution. Yet, for the case of nonexponential interarrival times, the formula only approximates the expected time in the queue, as opposed to being 100 percent exact. The formula should be used only for the case of a stationary process (see Section 3.3 for the definition of a stationary process as well as for what to do if the process is not stationary).

The above equation states that the waiting time in the queue is the product of three factors:

- The waiting time is expressed as multiples of the activity time. However, it is important to keep in mind that the activity time also directly influences the utilization (as Utilization = Activity time/Interarrival time). Thus, one should not think of the waiting time as increasing linearly with the activity time.

- The second factor captures the utilization effect. Note that the utilization has to be less than 100 percent. If the utilization is equal to or greater than 100 percent, the queue continues to grow. This is not driven by variability, but simply by not having the requested capacity. We observe that the utilization factor is nonlinear and becomes larger and larger as the utilization level is increased closer to 100 percent. For example, for Utilization = 0.8, the utilization factor is $0.8/(1 - 0.8) = 4$; for Utilization = 0.9, it is $0.9/(1 - 0.9) = 9$; and for Utilization = 0.95, it grows to $0.95/(1 - 0.95) = 19$.

- The third factor captures the amount of variability in the system, measured by the average of the squared coefficient of variation of interarrival times CV_a and activity times CV_p. Since CV_a and CV_p affect neither the average activity time p nor the utilization u, we observe that the waiting time grows with the variability in the system.

The best way to familiarize ourselves with this newly introduced formula is to apply it and "see it in action." Toward that end, consider the case of the An-ser call center at 2:00 a.m. in the morning. An-ser is a relatively small call center and they receive very few calls at this time of the day (see Section 3.3 for detailed arrival information), so at 2:00 a.m., there is only one person handling incoming calls.

From the data we collected in the call center, we can quickly compute that the average activity time at An-ser at this time of the day is around 90 seconds. Given that we found in the previous section that the activity time does depend on the time of the day, it is important that we use the service time data representative for these early morning hours: Activity time p = 90 seconds.

Based on the empirical service times we collected in Section 3.4, we now compute the standard deviation of the service time to be 120 seconds. Hence, the coefficient of variation for the activity time is

$$CV_p = 120 \text{ seconds}/90 \text{ seconds} = 1.3333$$

From the arrival data we collected (see Figure 3.6), we know that at 2:00 a.m. there are 3 calls arriving in a 15-minute interval. Thus, the interarrival time is a = 5 minutes = 300 seconds. Given the activity time and the interarrival time, we can now compute the utilization as

$$\text{Utilization} = \text{Activity time/Interarrival time } (= p/a)$$
$$= 90 \text{ seconds}/300 \text{ seconds} = 0.3$$

Concerning the coefficient of variation of the interarrival time, we can take one of two approaches. First, we could take the observed interarrival times and compute the standard deviation empirically. Alternatively, we could view the arrival process during the time period as random. Given the good fit between the data we collected and the exponential distribution (see Figure 3.9), we assume that arrivals follow a Poisson process (interarrival times are exponentially distributed). This implies a coefficient of variation of

$$CV_a = 1$$

Substituting these values into the waiting time formula yields

$$\text{Time in queue} = \text{Activity time} \times \left(\frac{\text{Utilization}}{1 - \text{Utilization}} \right) \times \left(\frac{CV_a^2 + CV_p^2}{2} \right)$$

$$= 90 \times \frac{0.3}{1 - 0.3} \times \frac{1^2 + 1.3333^2}{2}$$

$$= 53.57 \text{ seconds}$$

Note that this result captures the average waiting time of a customer before getting served. To obtain the customer's total time spent for the call, including waiting time and service time, we need to add the activity time p for the actual service. Thus, the flow time can be computed as

$$T = T_q + p = 53.57 \text{ seconds} + 90 \text{ seconds} = 143.57 \text{ seconds}$$

It is important to point out that the value 53.57 seconds provides the average waiting time. The actual waiting times experienced by individual customers vary. Some customers get lucky and receive service immediately; others have to wait much longer than 53.57 seconds. This is discussed further below.

Waiting times computed based on the methodology outlined above need to be seen as long-run averages. This has the following two practical implications:

• If the system would start empty (e.g., in a hospital lab, where there are no patients before the opening of the waiting room), the first couple of patients are less likely to experience significant waiting time. This effect is transient: Once a sufficient number of patients have arrived, the system reaches a "steady-state." Note that given the 24-hour operation of An-ser, this is not an issue in this specific case.

• If we observe the system for a given time interval, it is unlikely that the average waiting time we observe within this interval is exactly the average we computed. However, the longer we observe the system, the more likely the expected waiting time T_q will indeed coincide with the empirical average. This resembles a casino, which cannot predict how much money a specific guest will win (or typically lose) in an evening, yet can well predict the economics of the entire guest population over the course of a year.

Now that we have accounted for the waiting time T_q (or the flow time T), we are able to compute the resulting inventory. With $1/a$ being our flow rate, we can use Little's Law to compute the average inventory I as

$$I = R \times T = \frac{1}{a} \times (T_q + p)$$

$$= 1/300 \times (53.57 + 90) = 0.479$$

Thus, there is, on average, about half a customer in the system (it is 2:00 a.m. after all . . .). This inventory includes the two subsets we defined as inventory in the queue (I_q) and inventory in process (I_p):

• I_q can be obtained by applying Little's Law, but this time, rather than applying Little's Law to the entire system (the waiting line and the server), we apply it only to the waiting line in isolation. If we think of the waiting line as a mini process in itself (the corresponding process flow diagram consists only of one triangle), we obtain a flow time of T_q. Hence,

$$I_q = 1/a \times T_q = 1/300 \times 53.57 = 0.179$$

- At any given moment in time, we also can look at the number of customers that are currently talking to the customer service representative. Since we assumed there would only be one representative at this time of the day, there will never be more than one caller at this stage. However, there are moments in time when no caller is served, as the utilization of the employee is well below 100 percent. The average number of callers in service can thus be computed as

$$I_p = \text{Probability\{0 callers talking to representative\}} \times 0$$
$$+ \text{Probability\{1 caller talking to representative\}} \times 1$$
$$I_p = (1 - u) \times 0 + u \times 1 = u$$

In this case, we obtain $I_p = 0.3$.

3.6   Predicting the Average Waiting Time for the Case of Multiple Resources

After analyzing waiting time in the presence of variability for an extremely simple process, consisting of just one buffer and one resource, we now turn to more complicated operations. Specifically, we analyze a waiting time model of a process consisting of one waiting area (queue) and a process step performed by multiple, identical resources.

We continue our example of the call center. However, now we consider time slots at more busy times over the course of the day, when there are many more customer representatives on duty in the An-ser call center. The basic process layout is illustrated in Figure 3.15.

Let m be the number of parallel servers we have available. Given that we have m servers working in parallel, we now face a situation where the average service time is likely to be much longer than the average interarrival time. Taken together, the m resources have a capacity of m/p, while the demand rate continues to be given by $1/a$. We can compute the utilization u of the service process as

$$\text{Utilization} = \frac{\text{Flow rate}}{\text{Capacity}} = \frac{1/\text{Interarrival time}}{(\text{Number of resources}/\text{Activity time})}$$
$$= \frac{1/a}{m/p} = \frac{p}{a \times m}$$

Similar to the case with one single resource, we are only interested in the cases of utilization levels below 100 percent.

FIGURE 3.15
A Process with One Queue and Multiple, Parallel Servers ($m = 5$)

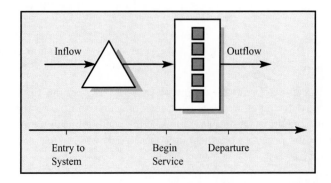

The flow unit will initially spend T_q units of time waiting for service. It then moves to the next available resource, where it spends p units of time for service. As before, the total flow time is the sum of waiting time and service time:

$$\text{Flow time} = \text{Waiting time in queue} + \text{Activity time}$$
$$T = T_q + p$$

Based on the activity time p, the utilization u, the coefficients of variation for both service (CV_p) and arrival process (CV_a) as well as the number of resources in the system (m), we can compute the average waiting time T_q using the following formula:[1]

$$\text{Time in queue} = \left(\frac{\text{Activity time}}{m} \right) \times \left(\frac{\text{Utilization}^{\sqrt{2(m+1)}-1}}{1 - \text{Utilization}} \right) \times \left(\frac{CV_a^2 + CV_p^2}{2} \right)$$

As in the case of one single resource, the waiting time is expressed as the product of the activity time, a utilization factor, and a variability factor. We also observe that for the special case of $m = 1$, the above formula is exactly the same as the waiting time formula for a single resource. Note that all other performance measures, including the flow time (T), the inventory in the system (I), and the inventory in the queue (I_q), can be computed as discussed before.

While the above expression does not necessarily seem an inviting equation to use, it can be programmed without much effort into a spreadsheet. Furthermore, it provides the average waiting time for a system that otherwise could only be analyzed with much more sophisticated software packages.

Unlike the waiting time formula for the single resource case, which provides an exact quantification of waiting times as long as the interarrival times follow an exponential distribution, the waiting time formula for multiple resources is an approximation. The formula works well for most settings we encounter, specifically if the ratio of utilization u to the number of servers m is large (u/m is high).

Now that we have computed waiting time, we can again use Little's Law to compute the average number of flow units in the waiting area I_q, the average number of flow units in service I_p, and the average number of flow units in the entire system $I = I_p + I_q$. Figure 3.16 summarizes the key performance measures.

[1] Hopp and Spearman (1996); the formula initially had been proposed by Sakasegawa (1977) and used successfully by Whitt (1983). For $m = 1$, the formula is exactly the same as in the previous section. The formula is an approximation for $m > 1$. An exact expression for this case does not exist.

FIGURE 3.16
Summary of Key Performance Measures

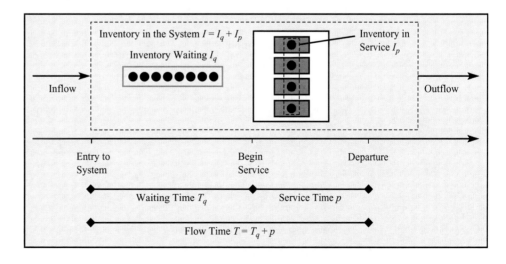

SUMMARY OF WAITING TIME CALCULATIONS

1. Collect the following data:

    - Number of servers, m
    - Activity time, p
    - Interarrival time, a
    - Coefficient of variation for interarrival (CV_a) and processing time (CV_p)

2. Compute utilization: $u = \dfrac{p}{a \times m}$

3. Compute expected waiting time:

$$T_q = \left(\frac{\text{Activity time}}{m}\right) \times \left(\frac{\text{Utilization}^{\sqrt{2(m+1)}-1}}{1 - \text{Utilization}}\right) \times \left(\frac{CV_a^2 + CV_a^2}{2}\right)$$

4. Based on T_q, we can compute the remaining performance measures as

$$\text{Flow time } T = T_q + p$$
$$\text{Inventory in service } I_p = m \times u$$
$$\text{Inventory in the queue } I_q = T_q/a$$
$$\text{Inventory in the system } I = I_p + I_q$$

Note that in the presence of multiple resources serving flow units, there can be more than one flow unit in service simultaneously. If u is the utilization of the process, it is also the utilization of each of the m resources, as they process demand at the same rate. We can compute the expected number of flow units at any of the m resources *in isolation* as

$$u \times 1 + (1 - u) \times 0 = u$$

Adding up across the m resources then yields

$$\text{Inventory in process } = \text{Number of resources} \times \text{Utilization}$$
$$I_p = m \times u$$

We illustrate the methodology using the case of An-ser services. Assuming we would work with a staff of 10 customer service representatives (CSRs) for the 8:00 a.m. to 8:15 a.m. time slot, we can compute the utilization as follows:

$$\text{Utilization } u = \frac{p}{a \times m} = \frac{90 \text{ [seconds/call]}}{11.39 \times 10 \text{ [seconds/call]}} = 0.79$$

where we obtained the interarrival time of 11.39 seconds between calls by dividing the length of the time interval (15 minutes = 900 seconds) by the number of calls received over the interval (79 calls). This now allows us to compute the average waiting time as

$$T_q = \left(\frac{p}{m}\right) \times \left(\frac{u^{\sqrt{2(m+1)}-1}}{1 - u}\right) \times \left(\frac{CV_a^2 + CV_p^2}{2}\right)$$
$$= \left(\frac{90}{10}\right) \times \left(\frac{0.79^{\sqrt{2(10+1)}-1}}{1 - 0.79}\right) \times \left(\frac{1 + 1.3333^2}{2}\right) = 24.98 \text{ seconds}$$

The most important calculations related to waiting times caused by variability are summarized in Exhibit 3.1.

3.7 Service Levels in Waiting Time Problems

So far, we have focused our attention on the average waiting time in the process. However, a customer requesting service from our process is not interested in the average time he or she waits in queue or the average total time to complete his or her request (waiting time T_q and flow time T respectively), but in the wait times that he or she experiences personally.

Consider, for example, a caller who has just waited for 15 minutes listening to music while on hold. This caller is likely to be unsatisfied about the long wait time. Moreover, the response from the customer service representative of the type "we are sorry for your delay, but our average waiting time is only 4 minutes" is unlikely to reduce this dissatisfaction.

Thus, from a managerial perspective, we not only need to analyze the average wait time, but also the likelihood that the wait time exceeds a certain *target wait time* (*TWT*). More formally, we can define the *service level* for a given target wait time as the percentage of customers that will begin service in TWT or less units of waiting time:

$$\text{Service level} = \text{Probability}\{\text{Waiting time} \leq \text{TWT}\}$$

This service level provides us with a way to measure to what extent the service is able to respond to demand within a consistent waiting time. A service level of 95 percent for a target waiting time of TWT = 2 minutes means that 95 percent of the customers are served in less than 2 minutes of waiting time.

Figure 3.17 shows the empirical distribution function (see Section 3.3 on how to create this graph) for waiting times at the An-ser call center for a selected time slot. Based on the graph, we can distinguish between two groups of customers. About 65 percent of the customers did not have to wait at all and received immediate service. The remaining 35 percent of the customers experienced a waiting time that strongly resembles an exponential distribution.

We observe that the average waiting time for the entire calling population (not just the ones who had to wait) was, for this specific sample, about 10 seconds. For a target wait time TWT = 30 seconds, we find a service level of 90 percent; that is, 90 percent of the callers had to wait 30 seconds or less.

FIGURE 3.17
Empirical Distribution of Waiting Times at An-ser

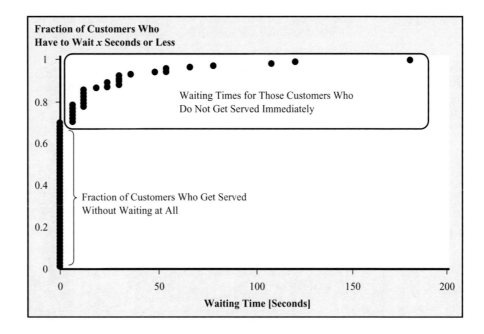

Service levels as defined above are a common performance measure for service operations in practice. They are used internally by the firm in charge of delivering a certain service. They also are used frequently by firms that want to outsource a service, such as a call center, as a way to contract (and track) the responsiveness of their service provider.

There is no universal rule of what service level is right for a given service operation. For example, responding to large public pressure, the German railway system (Deutsche Bundesbahn) has recently introduced a policy that 80 percent of the calls to their customer complaint number should be handled within 20 seconds. Previously, only 30 percent of the calls were handled within 20 seconds. How fast you respond to calls depends on your market position and the importance of the incoming calls for your business. A service level that worked for the German railway system in 2003 (30 percent within 20 seconds) is likely to be unacceptable in other, more competitive environments.

3.8   Economic Implications: Generating a Staffing Plan

So far, we have focused purely on analyzing the call center for a given number of customer service representatives (CSRs) on duty and predicted the resulting waiting times. This raises the managerial question of how many CSRs An-ser should have at work at any given moment in time over the day. The more CSRs we schedule, the shorter the waiting time, but the more we need to pay in terms of wages.

When making this trade-off, we need to balance the following two costs:

- Cost of waiting, reflecting increased line charges for 1-800 numbers and customer dissatisfaction (line charges are incurred for the actual talk time as well as for the time the customer is on hold).
- Cost of service, resulting from the number of CSRs available.

Additional costs that could be factored into the analysis are

- Costs related to customers calling into the call center but who are not able to gain access even to the waiting line, that is, they receive a busy signal (blocked customers).
- Costs related to customers who hang up while waiting for service.

In the case of An-ser, the average salary of a CSR is $10 per hour. Note that CSRs are paid independent of being idle or busy. Variable costs for a 1-800 number are about $0.05 per minute. A summary of various costs involved in managing a call center—or service operations in general—is given by Figure 3.18.

FIGURE 3.18
Economic Consequences of Waiting

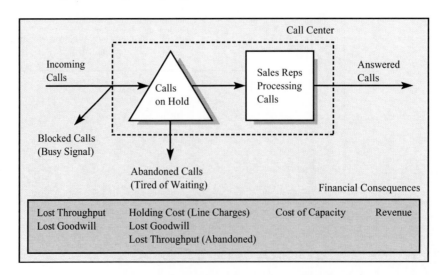

TABLE 3.2
Determining the Number of CSRs to Support Target Wait Time

Number of CSRs, m	Utilization $u = p/(a \times m)$	Expected Wait Time T_q [seconds] Based on Waiting Time Formula
8	0.99	1221.23
9	0.88	72.43
10	0.79	24.98
11	0.72	11.11
12	0.66	5.50
13	0.61	2.89
14	0.56	1.58

When deciding how many CSRs to schedule for a given time slot, we first need to decide on how responsive we want to be to our customers. For the purpose of our analysis, we assume that the management of An-ser wants to achieve an average wait time of 10 seconds. Alternatively, we also could set a service level and then staff according to a TWT constraint, for example, 95 percent of customers to be served in 20 seconds or less.

Now, for a given arrival rate, we need to determine the number of CSRs that will correspond to an average wait time of 10 seconds. Again, consider the time interval from 8:00 to 8:15 a.m. Table 3.2 shows the utilization level as well as the expected wait time for different numbers of customer service representatives. Note that using fewer than 8 servers would lead to a utilization above one, which would mean that queues would build up independent of variability, which is surely not acceptable.

Table 3.2 indicates that adding CSRs leads to a reduction in waiting time. For example, while a staff of 8 CSRs would correspond to an average waiting time of about 20 minutes, the average waiting time falls below 10 seconds once a twelfth CSR has been added. Thus, working with 12 CSRs allows An-ser to meet its target of an average wait time of 10 seconds. In this case, the actual service would be even better and we expect the average wait time for this specific time slot to be 5.50 seconds.

Providing a good service level does come at the cost of increased labor. The more CSRs are scheduled to serve, the lower is their utilization. We defined the cost of direct labor as

$$\text{Cost of direct labor} = \frac{\text{Total wages per unit of time}}{\text{Flow rate per unit of time}}$$

where the total wages per unit of time are determined by the number of CSRs m times their wage rate (in our case, $10 per hour or 16.66 cents per minute) and the flow rate is determined by the arrival rate. Therefore,

$$\text{Cost of direct labor} = \frac{m \times 16.66 \text{ cents/minute}}{1/a} = a \times m \times 16.66 \text{ cents/minute}$$

An alternative way of writing the cost of labor uses the definition of utilization ($u = p/(a \times m)$). Thus, in the above equation, we can substitute p/u for $a \times m$ and obtain

$$\text{Cost of direct labor} = \frac{p \times 16.66 \text{ cents/minute}}{u}$$

This way of writing the cost of direct labor has a very intuitive interpretation: The actual activity time p is inflated by a factor of 1/Utilization to appropriately account for idle time. For example,

TABLE 3.3
Economic
Implications of
Various Staffing
Levels

Number of Servers	Utilization	Cost of Labor per Call	Cost of Line Charges per Call	Total Cost per Call
8	0.988	0.2531	1.0927	1.3458
9	0.878	0.2848	0.1354	0.4201
10	0.790	0.3164	0.0958	0.4122
11	0.718	0.3480	0.0843	0.4323
12	0.658	0.3797	0.0796	0.4593
13	0.608	0.4113	0.0774	0.4887
14	0.564	0.4429	0.0763	0.5193
15	0.527	0.4746	0.0757	0.5503

if utilization were 50 percent, we are charged a $1 of idle time penalty for every $1 we spend on labor productively. In our case, the utilization is 66 percent; thus, the cost of direct labor is

$$\text{Cost of direct labor} = \frac{1.5 \text{ minutes/call} \times 16.66 \text{ cents/minute}}{0.66} = 38 \text{ cents/call}$$

This computation allows us to extend Table 3.2 to include the cost implications of the various staffing scenarios (our calculations do not consider any cost of lost goodwill). Specifically, we are interested in the impact of staffing on the cost of direct labor per call as well as in the cost of line charges.

Not surprisingly, we can see in Table 3.3 that moving from a very high level of utilization of close to 99 percent (using 8 CSRs) to a more responsive service level, for example, as provided by 12 CSRs, leads to a significant increase in labor cost.

At the same time, though, line charges drop from over $1 per call to almost $0.075 per call. Note that $0.075 per call is the minimum charge that can be achieved based on staffing changes, as it corresponds to the pure talk time.

Adding line charges and the cost of direct labor allows us to obtain total costs. In Table 3.3, we observe that total costs are minimized when we have 10 CSRs in service.

However, we need to be careful in labeling this point as the optimal staffing level, as the total cost number is a purely internal measure and does not take into account any information about the customer's cost of waiting. For this reason, when deciding on an appropriate staffing level, it is important to set acceptable service levels for waiting times as done in Table 3.2 and then staffing up to meet these service levels (opposed to minimizing internal costs).

If we repeat the analysis that we have conducted for the 8:00 to 8:15 a.m. time slot over the 24 hours of the day, we obtain a staffing plan. The staffing plan accounts for both the seasonality observed throughout the day as well as the variability and the resulting need for extra capacity. This is illustrated by Figure 3.19.

When we face a nonstationary arrival process as in this case, a common problem is to decide into how many intervals one should break up the time line to have close to a stationary arrival process within a time interval (in this case, 15 minutes). While we cannot go into the theory behind this topic, the basic intuition is this: It is important that the time intervals are large enough so that

- We have enough data to come up with reliable estimates for the arrival rate of the interval (e.g., if we had worked with 30-second intervals, our estimates for the number of calls arriving within a 30-second time interval would have been less reliable).
- Over the course of an interval, the queue needs sufficient time to reach a "steady state"; this is achieved if we have a relatively large number of arrivals and service completions within the duration of a time interval (more than 10).

FIGURE 3.19
Staffing and
Incoming Calls over
the Course of a Day

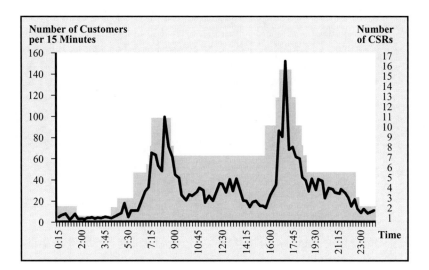

In practice, finding a staffing plan can be somewhat more complicated, as it needs to account for

* Breaks for the operators.
* Length of work period. It is typically not possible to request an operator to show up for work for only a one-hour time slot. Either one has to provide longer periods of time or one would have to temporarily route calls to other members of the organization (supervisor, back-office employees).

Despite these additional complications, the analysis outlined above captures the most important elements typical for making supply-related decisions in service environments.

3.9 Impact of Pooling: Economies of Scale

Consider a process that currently corresponds to two (m) demand arrival processes that are processed by two (m) identical servers. If demand cannot be processed immediately, the flow unit waits in front of the server where it initially arrived. An example of such a system is provided in Figure 3.20 (left).

Here is an interesting question: Does combining the two systems into a single system with one waiting area and two (m) identical servers lead to lower average waiting times? We refer to such a combination of multiple resources into one "mega-resource" as *pooling*.

FIGURE 3.20
The Concept of
Pooling

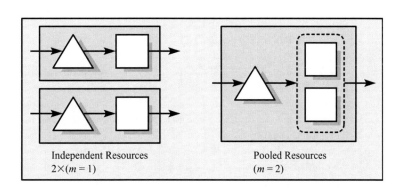

Consider, for example, two small food services at an airport. For simplicity, assume that both of them have a customer arrival stream with an average interarrival time a of 4 minutes and a coefficient of variation equal to one. The activity time p is three minutes per customer and the coefficient of variation for the service process also is equal to one. Consequently, both food services face a utilization of $p/a = 0.75$.

Using our waiting time formula, we compute the average waiting time as

$$T_q = \text{Activity time} \times \left(\frac{\text{Utilization}}{1 - \text{Utilization}}\right) \times \left(\frac{CV_a^2 + CV_p^2}{2}\right)$$

$$= 3 \times \left(\frac{0.75}{1 - 0.75}\right) \times \left(\frac{1 + 1}{2}\right)$$

$$= 3 \times (0.75/0.25) = 9 \text{ minutes}$$

Now compare this with the case in which we combine the capacity of both food services to serve the demand of both services. The capacity of the pooled process has increased by a factor of two and now is $\frac{2}{3}$ unit per minute. However, the demand rate also has doubled: If there was one customer every four minutes arriving for service 1 and one customer every four minutes arriving for service 2, the pooled service experiences an arrival rate of one customer every $a = 2$ minutes (i.e., two customers every four minutes is the same as one customer every two minutes).

We can compute the utilization of the pooled process as

$$u = \frac{p}{a \times m}$$

$$= 3/(2 \times 2) = 0.75$$

Observe that the utilization has not changed compared to having two independent services. Combining two processes with a utilization of 75 percent leads to a pooled system with a 75 percent utilization. However, a different picture emerges when we look at the waiting time of the pooled system. Using the waiting time formula for multiple resources, we can write

$$T_q = \left(\frac{\text{Activity time}}{m}\right) \times \left(\frac{\text{Utilization}^{\sqrt{2(m+1)}-1}}{1 - \text{Utilization}}\right) \times \left(\frac{CV_a^2 + CV_p^2}{2}\right)$$

$$= \left(\frac{3}{2}\right) \times \left(\frac{0.75^{\sqrt{2(2+1)}-1}}{1 - 0.75}\right) = 3.95 \text{ minutes}$$

In other words, the pooled process on the right of Figure 3.20 can serve the same number of customers using the same service time (and thereby having the same utilization), but in only *half* the waiting time!

While short of being a formal proof, the intuition for this result is as follows. The pooled process uses the available capacity more effectively, as it prevents the case that one resource is idle while the other faces a backlog of work (waiting flow units). Thus, pooling identical resources balances the load for the servers, leading to shorter waiting times. This behavior is illustrated in Figure 3.21.

Figure 3.21 illustrates that for a given level of utilization, the waiting time decreases with the number of servers in the resource pool. This is especially important for higher levels of utilization. While for a system with one single server waiting times tend to "go through the

FIGURE 3.21
How Pooling Can
Reduce Waiting Time

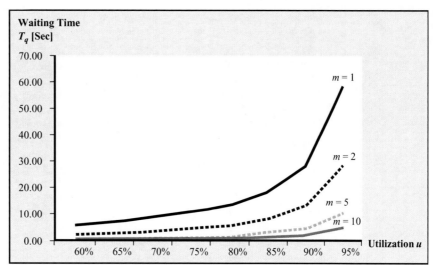

roof " once the utilization exceeds 85 percent, a process consisting of 10 identical servers can still provide reasonable service even at utilizations approaching 95 percent.

Given that a pooled system provides better service than individual processes, a service organization can benefit from pooling identical branches or work groups in one of two forms:

- The operation can use pooling to reduce customer waiting time without having to staff extra workers.
- The operation can reduce the number of workers while maintaining the same responsiveness.

These economic benefits of pooling can be illustrated nicely within the context of the An-ser case discussed above. In our analysis leading to Table 3.2, we assumed that there would be 79 calls arriving per 15-minute time interval and found that we would need 12 CSRs to serve customers with an average wait time of 10 seconds or less.

Assume we could pool An-ser's call center with a call center of comparable size; that is, we would move all CSRs to one location and merge both call centers' customer populations. Note that this would not necessarily require the two call centers to "move in" with each other; they could be physically separate as long as the calls are routed through one joint network.

Without any consolidation, merging the two call centers would lead to double the number of CSRs and double the demand, meaning 158 calls per 15-minute interval. What would be the average waiting time in the pooled call center? Or, alternatively, if we maintained an average waiting time of 10 seconds or less, how much could we reduce our staffing level? Table 3.4 provides the answers to these questions.

First, consider the row of 24 CSRs, corresponding to pooling the entire staff of the two call centers. Note specifically that the utilization of the pooled call center is not any different from what it was in Table 3.2. We have doubled the number of CSRs, but we also have doubled the number of calls (and thus cut the interarrival time by half). With 24 CSRs, we expect an average waiting time of 1.2 seconds (compared to almost 6 seconds before).

Alternatively, we could take the increased efficiency benefits resulting from pooling by reducing our labor cost. We also observe from Table 3.4 that a staff of 20 CSRs would be able to answer calls with an average wait time of 10 seconds. Thus, we could increase

TABLE 3.4
Pooling Two Call Centers

Number of CSRs	Utilization	Expected Wait Time [seconds]	Labor Cost per Call	Line Cost per Call	Total Cost
16	0.988	588.15	0.2532	0.5651	0.8183
17	0.929	72.24	0.2690	0.1352	0.4042
18	0.878	28.98	0.2848	0.0992	0.3840
19	0.832	14.63	0.3006	0.0872	0.3878
20	0.790	8.18	0.3165	0.0818	0.3983
21	0.752	4.84	0.3323	0.0790	0.4113
22	0.718	2.97	0.3481	0.0775	0.4256
23	0.687	1.87	0.3639	0.0766	0.4405
24	0.658	1.20	0.3797	0.0760	0.4558
25	0.632	0.79	0.3956	0.0757	0.4712
26	0.608	0.52	0.4114	0.0754	0.4868
27	0.585	0.35	0.4272	0.0753	0.5025
28	0.564	0.23	0.4430	0.0752	0.5182
29	0.545	0.16	0.4589	0.0751	0.5340
30	0.527	0.11	0.4747	0.0751	0.5498

utilization to almost 80 percent, which would lower our cost of direct labor from $0.3797 to $0.3165. Given an annual call volume of about 700,000 calls, such a saving would be of significant impact for the bottom line.

Despite the nice property of pooled systems outlined above, pooling should not be seen as a silver bullet. Specifically, pooling benefits are much lower than expected (and potentially negative) in the following situations:

• Pooling benefits are significantly lower when the systems that are pooled are not truly independent. Consider, for example, the idea of pooling waiting lines before cash registers in supermarkets, similar to what is done at airport check-ins. In this case, the individual queues are unlikely to be independent, as customers in the current, nonpooled layout will intelligently route themselves to the queue with the shortest waiting line. Pooling in this case will have little, if any, effect on waiting times.

• Similar to the concept of line balancing we introduced earlier in this book, pooling typically requires the service workforce to have a broader range of skills (potentially leading to higher wage rates). For example, an operator sufficiently skilled that she can take orders for hiking and running shoes, as well as provide answering services for a local hospital, will likely demand a higher wage rate than someone who is just trained to do one of these tasks.

• In many service environments, customers value being treated consistently by the same person. Pooling several lawyers in a law firm might be desirable from a waiting-time perspective but ignores the customer desire to deal with one point of contact in the law firm.

• Similarly, pooling can introduce additional setups. In the law-firm example, a lawyer unfamiliar with the situation of a certain client might need a longer time to provide some quick advice on the case and this extra setup time mitigates the operational benefits from pooling.

• Pooling can backfire if pooling combines different customer classes because this might actually increase the variability of the service process. Consider two clerks working in a retail bank, one of them currently in charge of simple transactions (e.g., activity time of 2 minutes per customer), while the other one is in charge of more complex cases (e.g., activity time of 10 minutes). Pooling these two clerks makes the service process more variable and might actually increase waiting time.

3.10   Priority Rules in Waiting Lines

Choosing an appropriate level of capacity helps to prevent waiting lines from building up in a process. However, in a process with variability, it is impossible to eliminate waiting lines entirely. Given, therefore, that at some point in time some customers will have to wait before receiving service, we need to decide on the order in which we permit them access to the server. This order is determined by a *priority rule,* sometimes also referred to as a queuing discipline.

Customers are assigned priorities by adding a (small) step at the point in the process where customers arrive. This process step is called the *triage step.* At triage, we collect information about some of the characteristics of the arriving customer, which we use as input for the priority rule. Below we discuss priority rules based on the following characteristics:

- The service time or the expected service time of the customer (service-time-dependent priority rules).
- Service-time-independent priority rules, including priority rules based on customer arrival time and priority rules based on customer importance or urgency.

Service-Time-Dependent Priority Rules

If it is possible to observe the customer's service time or his or her expected service time prior to initiating the service process, this information should be incorporated when assigning a priority to the customer. The most commonly used service-time-dependent priority rule is the shortest processing time (SPT) rule.

Under the SPT rule, the next available server is allocated to the customer with the shortest (expected) processing time of all customers currently in the waiting line. The SPT rule is extremely effective and performs well, with respect to the expected waiting time as well as to the variance of the waiting time. If the service times are not dependent on the sequence with which customers are processed, the SPT rule can be shown to lead to the shortest average flow time. Its basic intuition is summarized by Figure 3.22.

Service-Time-Independent Priority Rules

In many cases, it is difficult or impossible to assess the service time or even the expected service time prior to initiating the service process. Moreover, if customers are able to misrepresent their service time, then they have an incentive to suggest that their service time is less than it really is when the SPT rule is applied (e.g., "Can I just ask a quick question? . . ."). In contrast, the customer arrival time is easy to observe and difficult for the customer to manipulate.

For example, a call center receiving calls for airline reservations knows the sequence with which callers arrive but does not know which customer has already gathered all relevant information and is ready to order and which customer still requires explanation and discussion.

FIGURE 3.22   **The Shortest Processing Time (SPT) Rule (used in the right case)**

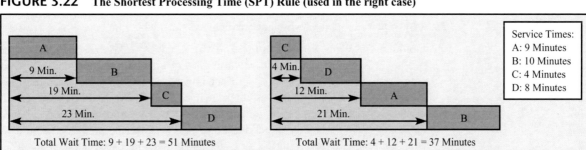

The most commonly used priority rule based on arrival times is the first-come, first-served (FCFS) rule. With the FCFS rule, the next available server is allocated to the customer in the waiting line with the earliest arrival time.

In addition to using arrival time information, many situations in practice require that characteristics such as the urgency or the importance of the case are considered in the priority rule. Consider the following two examples:

- In an emergency room, a triage nurse assesses the urgency of each case and then assigns a priority to the patient. Severely injured patients are given priority, independent of their arrival times.

- Customers calling in for investor services are likely to experience different priorities, depending on the value of their invested assets. Customers with an investment of greater than $5 million are unlikely to wait, while customers investing only several thousand dollars might wait for 20 minutes or more.

Such urgency-based priority rules are also independent of the service time. In general, when choosing a service-time-independent priority rule, the following property should be kept in mind: Whether we serve customers in the order of their arrival, in the reverse order of their arrival (last-come, first-served), or even in alphabetical order, the expected waiting time does not change. Thus, higher priority service (shorter waiting time) for one customer always requires lower priority (longer waiting time) for other customers.

From an implementation perspective, one last point is worth noting. Using priority rules other than FCFS might be perceived as unfair by the customers who arrived early and are already waiting the longest. Thus, while the average waiting time does not change, serving latecomers first increases the variance of the waiting time. Since variability in waiting time is not desirable from a service-quality perspective, the following property of the FCFS rule is worth remembering: Among service-time-independent priority rules, the FCFS rule minimizes the variance of waiting time and flow time.

3.11   Reducing Variability

In this chapter, we have provided some new methods to evaluate the key performance measures of flow rate, flow time, and inventory in the presence of variability. We also have seen that variability is the enemy of all operations (none of the performance measures improves as variability increases). Thus, in addition to just taking variability as given and adjusting our models to deal with variability, we should always think about ways to reduce variability.

Ways to Reduce Arrival Variability

One—somewhat obvious—way of achieving a match between supply and demand is by "massaging" demand such that it corresponds exactly to the supply process. This is basically the idea of *appointment systems* (also referred to as reservation systems in some industries).

Appointment systems have the potential to reduce the variability in the arrival process as they encourage customers to arrive at the rate of service. However, one should not overlook the problems associated with appointment systems, which include

- Appointment systems do not eliminate arrival variability. Customers do not perfectly arrive at the scheduled time (and some might not arrive at all, "no-shows"). Consequently, any good appointment system needs ways to handle these cases (e.g., extra charge or extra waiting time for customers arriving late). However, such actions are typically very difficult to implement, due to what is perceived to be "fair" and/or "acceptable," or because variability in service times prevents service providers from always keeping on schedule (and if the doctor has the right to be late, why not the patient?).

- What portion of the available capacity should be reserved in advance. Unfortunately, the customers arriving at the last minute are frequently the most important ones: emergency operations in a hospital do not come through an appointment system and business travelers paying 5 to 10 times the fare of low-price tickets are not willing to book in advance.

The most important limitation, however, is that appointment systems might reduce the variability of the arrival process as seen by the operation, but they do not reduce the variability of the true underlying demand. Consider, for example, the appointment system of a dental office. While the system (hopefully) reduces the time the patient has to wait before seeing the dentist on the day of the appointment, this wait time is not the only performance measure that counts, as the patient might already have waited for three months between requesting to see the dentist and the day of the appointment. Thus, appointment systems potentially hide a much larger supply–demand mismatch and, consequently, any good implementation of an appointment system includes a continuous measurement of both of the following:

- The inventory of customers who have an appointment and are now waiting for the day they are scheduled to go to the dentist.
- The inventory of customers who wait for an appointment in the waiting room of the dentist.

In addition to the concept of appointment systems, we can attempt to influence the customer arrival process (though, for reasons similar to the ones discussed, not the true underlying demand pattern) by providing incentives for customers to avoid peak hours. Frequently observed methods to achieve this include

- Early-bird specials at restaurants or bars.
- Price discounts for hotels during off-peak days (or seasons).
- Price discounts in transportation (air travel, highway tolls) depending on the time of service.
- Pricing of air travel depending on the capacity that is already reserved.

It is important to point out that, strictly speaking, the first three items do not reduce variability; they level expected demand and thereby reduce seasonality (remember that the difference between the two is that seasonality is a pattern known already ex ante). The fourth item refers to the concept of revenue management.

Ways to Reduce Service Time Variability

In addition to reducing variability by changing the behavior of our customers, we also should consider how to reduce internal variability. However, when attempting to standardize activities (reducing the coefficient of variation of the service times) or shorten activity times, we need to find a balance between operational efficiency (call durations) and the quality of service experienced by the customer (perceived courtesy).

Figure 3.23 compares five of An-ser's operators for a specific call service along these two dimensions. We observe that operators NN, BK, and BJ are achieving relatively short call durations while being perceived as friendly by the customers (based on recorded calls). Operator KB has shorter call durations, yet also scores lower on courtesy. Finally, operator NJ has the longest call durations and is rated medium concerning courtesy.

Based on Figure 3.23, we can make several interesting observations. First, observe that there seems to exist a frontier capturing the inherent trade-off between call duration and courtesy. Once call durations for this service go below 2.5 minutes, courtesy seems hard to maintain. Second, observe that operator NJ is away from this frontier, as he is neither

FIGURE 3.23
Operator
Performance
Concerning Call
Duration and
Courtesy

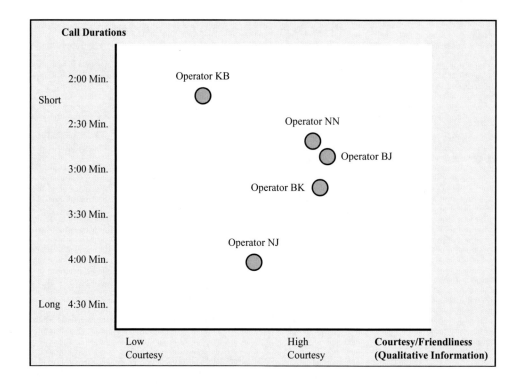

overly friendly nor fast. Remarkably, this operator also has the highest variability in call durations, which suggests that he is not properly following the operating procedures in place (this is not visible in the graph).

To reduce the inefficiencies of operators away from the frontier (such as NJ), call centers invest heavily in training and technology. For example, technology allows operators to receive real-time instruction of certain text blocks that they can use in their interaction with the customer (scripting). Similarly, some call centers have instituted training programs in which operators listen to tapes of other operators or have operators call other operators with specific service requests. Such steps reduce both the variability of service times as well as their means and, therefore, represent substantial improvements in operational performance.

There are other improvement opportunities geared primarily toward reducing the variability of the service times:

• Although in a service environment (or in a make-to-order production setting) the operator needs to acknowledge the idiosyncrasy of each customer, the operator still can follow a consistent process. For example, a travel agent in a call center might use predefined text blocks (scripts) for his or her interaction with the customer (welcome statement, first question, potential up-sell at the end of the conversation). This approach allowed operators NN, BK, and BJ in Figure 3.23 to be fast and friendly. Thus, being knowledgeable about the process (when to say what) is equally important as being knowledgeable about the product (what to say).

• Activity times in a service environment—unlike activity times in a manufacturing context—are not under the complete control of the resource. The customer him/herself plays a crucial part in the activity at the resource, which automatically introduces a certain amount of variability (e.g., having the customer provide his or her credit card number, having the customer bag the groceries, etc.) What is the consequence of this? At least from a variability perspective, the answer is clear: Reduce the involvement of the customer during the service at a scarce resource wherever possible (note that if the customer involvement does not occur at a scarce resource, having the customer be involved and thereby do part of the work might be very desirable, e.g., in a self-service setting).

• Variability in service times frequently reflects quality problems. In manufacturing environments, this could include reworking a unit that initially did not meet specifications. However, rework also occurs in service organizations (e.g., a patient who is released from the intensive care unit but later on readmitted to intensive care can be thought of as rework).

3.12 Summary

In this chapter, we have analyzed the impact of variability on waiting times. As we expected from our more qualitative discussion of variability in the beginning of this chapter, variability causes waiting times, even if the underlying process operates at a utilization level of less than 100 percent. In this chapter, we have outlined a set of tools that allows us to quantify this waiting time, with respect to both the average waiting time (and flow time) as well as the service level experienced by the customer.

There exists an inherent tension between resource utilization (and thereby cost of labor) and responsiveness: Adding service capacity leads to shorter waiting times but higher costs of labor (see Figure 3.24). Waiting times grow steeply with utilization levels. Thus, any responsive process requires excess capacity. Given that capacity is costly, it is important that only as much capacity is installed as is needed to meet the service objective in place for the process. In this chapter, we have outlined a method that allows a service operation to find the point on the frontier that best supports their business objectives (service levels).

However, our results should be seen not only as a way to predict/quantify the waiting time problem. They also outline opportunities for improving the process. Improvement opportunities can be broken up into capacity-related opportunities and system-design-related opportunities, as summarized below.

FIGURE 3.24
Balancing Efficiency with Responsiveness

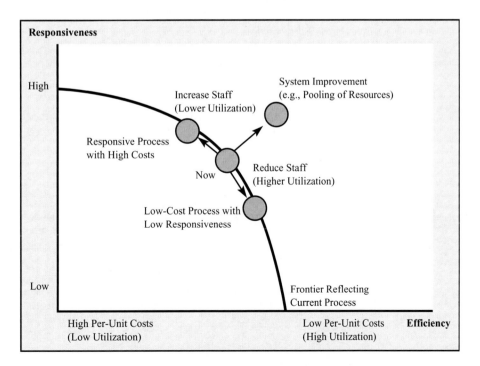

Capacity-Related Improvements

Operations benefit from flexibility in capacity, as this allows management to adjust staffing levels to predicted demand. For example, the extent to which a hospital is able to have more doctors on duty at peak flu season is crucial in conducting the staffing calculations outlined in this chapter. A different form of flexibility is given by the operation's ability to increase capacity in the case of unpredicted demand. For example, the extent to which a bank can use supervisors and front-desk personnel to help with unexpected spikes in inbound calls can make a big difference in call center waiting times. This leads to the following two improvement opportunities:

- Demand (and sometimes supply) can exhibit seasonality over the course of the day. In such cases, the waiting time analysis should be done for individual time intervals over which the process behaves relatively stationary. System performance can be increased to the extent the organization is able to provide time-varying capacity levels that mirror the seasonality of demand (e.g., Figure 3.19).

- In the presence of variability, a responsive process cannot avoid excess capacity, and thereby will automatically face a significant amount of idle time. In many operations, this idle time can be used productively for tasks that are not (or at least are less) time critical. Such work is referred to as background work. For example, operators in a call center can engage in outbound calls during times of underutilization.

System-Design-Related Improvements

Whenever we face a trade-off between two conflicting performance measures, in this case between responsiveness and efficiency, finding the right balance between the measures is important. However, at least equally important is the attempt to improve the underlying process, shifting the frontier and allowing for higher responsiveness and lower cost (see Figure 3.24). In the context of services suffering from variability-induced waiting times, the following improvement opportunities should be considered:

- By combining similar resources into one joint resource pool (pooling resources), we are able to either reduce wait times for the same amount of capacity or reduce capacity for the same service level. Processes that face variability thereby exhibit very strong scale economies.

- Variability is not exogenous and we should remember to reduce variability wherever possible.

- By introducing a triage step before the actual service process that sequences incoming flow units according to a priority rule (service-time-dependent or service-time-independent), we can reduce the average wait time, assign priority to the most important flow units, or create a waiting system that is perceived as fair by customers waiting in line.

3.13 Further Reading

Gans, Koole, and Mandelbaum (2003) is a recent overview on call-center management from a queuing theory perspective. Further quantitative tools on queueing can be found in Hillier and Lieberman (2002).

Hall (1997) is a very comprehensive and real-world-focused book that provides numerous tools related to variability and its consequences in services and manufacturing.

3.14 Practice Problems

Q 3.1* **(Online Retailer)** Customers send e-mails to a help desk of an online retailer every 2 minutes, on average, and the standard deviation of the interarrival time is also 2 minutes. The online retailer has three employees answering e-mails. It takes on average 4 minutes to write a response e-mail. The standard deviation of the service times is 2 minutes.

(* indicates that the solution is at the end of the book)

a. Estimate the average customer wait before being served.

b. How many e-mails would there be, on average, that have been submitted to the online retailer but not yet answered?

Q 3.2   **(My-law.com)** My-law.com is a recent start-up trying to cater to customers in search of legal services who are intimidated by the idea of talking to a lawyer or simply too lazy to enter a law office. Unlike traditional law firms, My-law.com allows for extensive interaction between lawyers and their customers via telephone and the Internet. This process is used in the upfront part of the customer interaction, largely consisting of answering some basic customer questions prior to entering a formal relationship.

In order to allow customers to interact with the firm's lawyers, customers are encouraged to send e-mails to my-lawyer@My-law.com. From there, the incoming e-mails are distributed to the lawyer who is currently "on call." Given the broad skills of the lawyers, each lawyer can respond to each incoming request.

E-mails arrive from 8 a.m. to 6 p.m. at a rate of 10 e-mails per hour (coefficient of variation for the arrivals is 1). At each moment in time, there is exactly one lawyer "on call," that is, sitting at his or her desk waiting for incoming e-mails. It takes the lawyer, on average, 5 minutes to write the response e-mail. The standard deviation of this is 4 minutes.

a. What is the average time a customer has to wait for the response to his/her e-mail, ignoring any transmission times? *Note:* This includes the time it takes the lawyer to start writing the e-mail *and* the actual writing time.

b. How many e-mails will a lawyer have received at the end of a 10-hour day?

c. When not responding to e-mails, the lawyer on call is encouraged to actively pursue cases that potentially could lead to large settlements. How much time on a 10-hour day can a My-law.com lawyer dedicate to this activity (assume the lawyer can instantly switch between e-mails and work on a settlement)?

To increase the responsiveness of the firm, the board of My-law.com proposes a new operating policy. Under the new policy, the response would be highly standardized, reducing the standard deviation for writing the response e-mail to 0.5 minute. The average writing time would remain unchanged.

d. How would the amount of time a lawyer can dedicate to the search for large settlement cases change with this new operating policy?

e. How would the average time a customer has to wait for the response to his/her e-mail change? *Note:* This includes the time until the lawyer starts writing the e-mail *and* the actual writing time.

Q 3.3   **(Car Rental Company)** The airport branch of a car rental company maintains a fleet of 50 SUVs. The interarrival time between requests for an SUV is 2.4 hours, on average, with a standard deviation of 2.4 hours. There is no indication of a systematic arrival pattern over the course of a day. Assume that, if all SUVs are rented, customers are willing to wait until there is an SUV available. An SUV is rented, on average, for 3 days, with a standard deviation of 1 day.

a. What is the average number of SUVs parked in the company's lot?

b. Through a marketing survey, the company has discovered that if it reduces its daily rental price of $80 by $25, the average demand would increase to 12 rental requests per day and the average rental duration will become 4 days. Is this price decrease warranted? Provide an analysis!

c. What is the average time a customer has to wait to rent an SUV? Please use the initial parameters rather than the information in (b).

d. How would the waiting time change if the company decides to limit all SUV rentals to *exactly* 4 days? Assume that if such a restriction is imposed, the average interarrival time will increase to 3 hours, with the standard deviation changing to 3 hours.

Q 3.4   **(Tom Opim)** The following situation refers to Tom Opim, a first-year MBA student. In order to pay the rent, Tom decides to take a job in the computer department of a local department store. His only responsibility is to answer telephone calls to the department, most of which are inquiries about store hours and product availability. As Tom is the only person answering calls, the manager of the store is concerned about queuing problems.

Currently, the computer department receives an average of one call every 3 minutes, with a standard deviation in this interarrival time of 3 minutes.

Tom requires an average of 2 minutes to handle a call. The standard deviation in this activity time is 1 minute.

The telephone company charges $5.00 per hour for the telephone lines whenever they are in use (either while a customer is in conversation with Tom or while waiting to be helped).

Assume that there are no limits on the number of customers that can be on hold and that customers do not hang up even if forced to wait a long time.

a. For one of his courses, Tom has to read a book (*The Pole,* by E. Silvermouse). He can read 1 page per minute. Tom's boss has agreed that Tom could use his idle time for studying, as long as he drops the book as soon as a call comes in. How many pages can Tom read during an 8-hour shift?

b. How long does a customer have to wait, on average, before talking to Tom?

c. What is the average total cost of telephone lines over an 8-hour shift? Note that the department store is billed whenever a line is in use, including when a line is used to put customers on hold.

Q 3.5 **(Atlantic Video)** Atlantic Video, a small video rental store in Philadelphia, is open 24 hours a day, and—due to its proximity to a major business school—experiences customers arriving around the clock. A recent analysis done by the store manager indicates that there are 30 customers arriving every hour, with a standard deviation of interarrival times of 2 minutes. This arrival pattern is consistent and is independent of the time of day. The checkout is currently operated by one employee, who needs on average 1.7 minutes to check out a customer. The standard deviation of this check-out time is 3 minutes, primarily as a result of customers taking home different numbers of videos.

a. If you assume that every customer rents at least one video (i.e., has to go to the checkout), what is the average time a customer has to wait in line before getting served by the checkout employee, not including the actual checkout time (within 1 minute)?

b. If there are no customers requiring checkout, the employee is sorting returned videos, of which there are always plenty waiting to be sorted. How many videos can the employee sort over an 8-hour shift (assume no breaks) if it takes exactly 1.5 minutes to sort a single video?

c. What is the average number of customers who are at the checkout desk, either waiting or currently being served (within 1 customer)?

d. Now assume *for this question only* that 10 percent of the customers do not rent a video at all and therefore do not have to go through checkout. What is the average time a customer has to wait in line before getting served by the checkout employee, not including the actual checkout time (within 1 minute)? Assume that the coefficient of variation for the arrival process remains the same as before.

e. As a special service, the store offers free popcorn and sodas for customers waiting in line at the checkout desk. (*Note:* The person who is currently being served is too busy with paying to eat or drink.) The store owner estimates that every minute of customer waiting time costs the store 75 cents because of the consumed food. What is the optimal number of employees at checkout? Assume an hourly wage rate of $10 per hour.

Q 3.6 **(RentAPhone)** RentAPhone is a new service company that provides European mobile phones to American visitors to Europe. The company currently has 80 phones available at Charles de Gaulle Airport in Paris. There are, on average, 25 customers per day requesting a phone. These requests arrive uniformly throughout the 24 hours the store is open. (*Note:* This means customers arrive at a faster rate than 1 customer per hour.) The corresponding coefficient of variation is 1.

Customers keep their phones on average 72 hours. The standard deviation of this time is 100 hours.

Given that RentAPhone currently does not have a competitor in France providing equally good service, customers are willing to wait for the telephones. Yet, during the waiting period, customers are provided a free calling card. Based on prior experience, RentA-Phone found that the company incurred a cost of $1 per hour per waiting customer, independent of day or night.

a. What is the average number of telephones the company has in its store?

b. How long does a customer, on average, have to wait for the phone?

c. What are the total monthly (30 days) expenses for telephone cards?

d. Assume RentAPhone could buy additional phones at $1,000 per unit. Is it worth it to buy one additional phone? Why?

e. How would waiting time change if the company decides to limit all rentals to *exactly* 72 hours? Assume that if such a restriction is imposed, the number of customers requesting a phone would be reduced to 20 customers per day.

Q 3.7   **(Webflux, Inc.)** Webflux is an Internet-based DVD rental business specializing in hard-to-find, obscure films. Its operating model is as follows. When a customer finds a film on the Webflux Web site and decides to watch it, she puts it in the virtual shopping cart. If a DVD is available, it is shipped immediately (assume it can be shipped during weekends and holidays, too). If not available, the film remains in the customer's shopping cart until a rented DVD is returned to Webflux, at which point it is shipped to the customer if she is next in line to receive it. Webflux maintains an internal queue for each film and a returned DVD is shipped to the first customer in the queue (first-in, first-out).

Webflux has one copy of the 1990 film *Sundown, the Vampire in Retreat,* starring David Carradine and Bruce Campbell. The average time between requests for the DVD is 10 days, with a coefficient of variation of 1. On average, a customer keeps the DVD for 5 days before returning it. It also takes 1 day to ship the DVD to the customer and 1 day to ship it from the customer back to Webflux. The standard deviation of the time between shipping the DVD out from Webflux and receiving it back is 7 days (i.e., it takes on average 7 days to (a) ship it, (b) have it with the customer, and (c) ship it back); hence, the coefficient of variation of this time is 1.

a. What is the average time that a customer has to wait to receive *Sundown, the Vampire in Retreat* DVD after the request? Recall it takes 1 day for a shipped DVD to arrive at a customer address (i.e., in your answer, you have to include the 1-day shipping time).

b. On average, how many customers are in Webflux's internal queue for *Sundown?* Assume customers do not cancel their items in their shopping carts.

Thanks to David Carradine's renewed fame after the recent success of *Kill Bill Vol. I* and *II* which he starred in, the demand for *Sundown* has spiked. Now the average interarrival time for the DVD requests at Webflux is 3 days. Other numbers (coefficient of variation, time in a customer's possession, shipping time) remain unchanged. *For the following question only,* assume sales are lost for customers who encounter stockouts; that is those who cannot find a DVD on the Webflux Web site simply navigate away without putting it in the shopping cart.

c. To satisfy the increased demand, Webflux is considering acquiring a second copy of the *Sundown* DVD. If Webflux owns a total of two copies of *Sundown* DVDs (whether in Webflux's internal stock, in customer's possession, or in transit), what percentage of the customers are turned away because of a stockout?

Q 3.8   **(Security Walking Escorts)** A university offers a walking escort service to increase security around campus. The system consists of specially trained uniformed professional security officers that accompany students from one campus location to another. The service is operated 24 hours a day, seven days a week. Students request a walking escort by phone. Requests for escorts are received, on average, every 5 minutes with a coefficient of variation of 1. After receiving a request, the dispatcher contacts an available escort (via a mobile phone), who immediately proceeds to pick up the student and walk her/him to her/

his destination. If there are no escorts available (that is, they are all either walking a student to her/his destination or walking to pick up a student), the dispatcher puts the request in a queue until an escort becomes available. An escort takes, on average, 25 minutes for picking up a student and taking her/him to her/his desired location (the coefficient of variation of this time is also 1). Currently, the university has 8 security officers who work as walking escorts.

a. How many security officers are, on average, available to satisfy a new request?

b. How much time does it take—on average—from the moment a student calls for an escort to the moment the student arrives at her/his destination?

For the next two questions, consider the following scenario. During the period of final exams, the number of requests for escort services increases to 19.2 per hour (one request every 3.125 minutes). The coefficient of variation of the time between successive requests equals 1. However, if a student requesting an escort finds out from the dispatcher that her/his request would have to be put in the queue (i.e., all security officers are busy walking other students), the student cancels the request and proceeds to walk on her/his own.

c. How many students per hour who called to request an escort end up canceling their request and go walking on their own?

d. University security regulations require that at least 80 percent of the students' calls to request walking escorts have to be satisfied. What is the minimum number of security officers that are needed in order to comply with this regulation?

Q 3.9 **(Mango Electronics Inc.)** Mango Electronics Inc. is a *Fortune* 500 company that develops and markets innovative consumer electronics products. The development process proceeds as follows.

Mango researches new technologies to address unmet market needs. Patents are filed for products that have the requisite market potential. Patents are granted for a period of 20 years starting from the date of issue. After receiving a patent, the patented technologies are then developed into marketable products at five independent development centers. Each product is only developed at one center. Each center has all the requisite skills to bring any of the products to market (a center works on one product at a time). On average, Mango files a patent every 7 months (with standard deviation of 7 months). The average development process lasts 28 months (with standard deviation of 56 months).

a. What is the utilization of Mango's development facilities?

b. How long does it take an average technology to go from filing a patent to being launched in the market as a commercial product?

c. How many years of patent life are left for an average product launched by Mango Electronics?

Q 3.10 **(UPS Shipping)** A UPS employee, Davis, packs and labels three types of packages: basic packages, business packages, and oversized packages. Business packages take priority over basic packages and oversized packages because those customers paid a premium to have guaranteed two-day delivery. During his nine-hour shift, he has, on average, one container of packages containing a variety of basic, business, and oversized packages to process every 3 hours. As soon as Davis processes a package, he passes it to the next employee, who loads it onto a truck. The times it takes him to process the three different types of packages and the average number of packages per container are shown in the table below.

	Basic	Business	Oversized
Average number of minutes to label and package each unit	5 minutes	4 minutes	6 minutes
Average number of units per container	10	10	5

Davis currently processes packages from each container as follows. First, he processes all business packages in the container. Then he randomly selects either basic packages or oversized packages for processing until the container is empty. However, his manager suggested to Davis that, for each container, he should process all the business packages first, second the basic packages, and last the oversized packages.

a. If Davis follows his supervisor's advice, what will happen to Davis's utilization?

b. What will happen to the average time that a package spends in the container?

Chapter 4

Simulation

After reading this chapter you will:

1. Recognize key concepts related to discrete event simulation.
2. Understand how simulation models are constructed.
3. See examples of simulations developed using spreadsheets.
4. Compare the advantages and disadvantages of simulation.

Service

Simulation has become a standard tool in business. In manufacturing, simulation is used to determine production schedules, inventory levels, and maintenance procedures; to plan capacity, resource requirements, and processes; and more. In services, simulation is widely used to analyze waiting lines and schedule operations. Often, when a mathematical technique fails, we turn to simulation.

4.1 Definition of Simulation

Although the term *simulation* can have various meanings depending on its application, in business, it generally refers to using a computer to perform experiments on a model of a real system. Examples of other types of simulation are airplane flight simulators, video games, and virtual reality animation. Simulation experiments may be undertaken before a real system is operational, to aid in its design, to see how the system might react to changes in its operating rules, or to evaluate the system's response to changes in its structure. Simulation is particularly appropriate to situations in which the size or complexity of the problem makes the use of optimizing techniques difficult or impossible. Thus, job shops, which are characterized by complex queuing problems, have been studied extensively via simulation, as have certain types of inventory, layout, and maintenance problems (to name but a few). Simulation also can be used in conjunction with traditional statistical and management science techniques.

In addition, simulation is useful in training managers and workers in how the real system operates, in demonstrating the effects of changes in system variables, in real-time control, and in developing new ideas about how to run the business.

4.2 Simulation Methodology

Exhibit 4.1 is a flowchart of the major phases in a simulation study. In this section, we develop each phase with particular reference to the key factors noted at the right of the chart.

Exhibit 4.1

MAJOR PHASES IN A SIMULATION STUDY

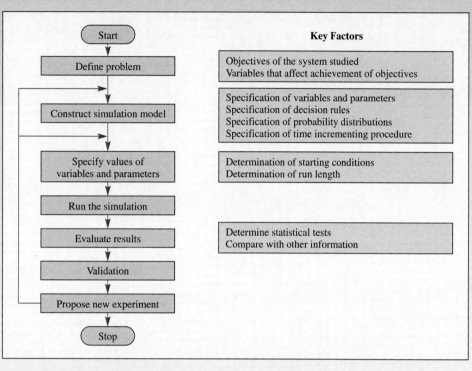

Problem Definition

Problem definition for purposes of simulation differs little from problem definition for any other tool of analysis. Essentially, it entails specifying the objectives and identifying the relevant controllable and uncontrollable variables of the system to be studied. Consider the example of a fish market. The objective of the market's owner is maximizing the profit on sales of fish. The relevant controllable variable (that is, under the control of the decision maker) is the ordering rule; the relevant uncontrollable variables are the daily demand levels for fish and the amount of fish sold. Other possible objectives also could be specified, such as to maximize profit from the sale of lobsters or to maximize sales revenue.

Constructing a Simulation Model

A feature that distinguishes simulation from techniques such as linear programming or queuing theory is the fact that a simulation model must be custom built for each problem situation. (A linear programming model, in contrast, can be used in a variety of situations with only a restatement of the values for the objective function and constraint equations.) There are simulation languages that make the model building easier, however. We discuss this subject later in this chapter. The unique nature of each simulation model means that the procedures discussed later for building and executing a model represent a synthesis of various approaches to simulation and are guidelines rather than rigid rules.

Parameters
Variables

Specification of Variables and Parameters   The first step in constructing a simulation model is determining which properties of the real system should be fixed (called **parameters**) and which should be allowed to vary throughout the simulation run (called **variables**). In a fish market, the variables are the amount of fish ordered, the amount

Exhibit 4.2

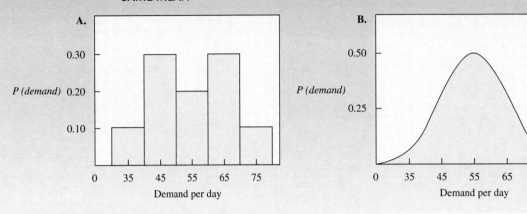

ACTUAL DISTRIBUTION OF DEMAND AND NORMAL DISTRIBUTION WITH THE SAME MEAN

demanded, and the amount sold; the parameters are the cost of the fish and the selling price of the fish. In most simulations, the focus is on the status of the variables at different points in time, such as the number of pounds of fish demanded and sold each day.

Decision rules

Specification of Decision Rules   Decision rules (or operating rules) are sets of conditions under which the behavior of the simulation model is observed. These rules are either directly or indirectly the focus of most simulation studies. In many simulations, decision rules are priority rules (for example, which customer to serve first, which job to process first). In certain situations, these can be quite involved, taking into account a large number of variables in the system. For example, an inventory ordering rule could be stated in such a way that the amount to order would depend on the amount in inventory, the amount previously ordered but not received, the amount backordered, and the desired safety stock.

Distributions

Specification of Probability Distributions   Two categories of distributions can be used for simulation: empirical frequency distributions and standard mathematical distributions. An empirical distribution is derived from observing the relative frequencies of some event, such as arrivals in a line or demand for a product. In other words, it is a custom-built demand distribution that is relevant only to a particular situation. It might appear like the one shown on the left side of Exhibit 4.2. Such distributions have to be determined by direct observation or detailed analysis of records. (We show how to use these later in the waiting line simulation example.) But often demand, for example, can reasonably be assumed to closely approximate a standard mathematical distribution such as the normal or Poisson. This greatly simplifies data collection and computerization.

Time incrementing

Specification of Time-Incrementing Procedure   In a simulation model, time can be advanced by one of two methods: (1) fixed-time increments or (2) variable-time increments. Under both methods of time incrementing, the concept of a simulated clock is important. In the fixed-time increment method, uniform clock-time increments (such as minutes, hours, or days) are specified and the simulation proceeds by fixed intervals from one time period to the next. At each point in clock time, the system is scanned to determine if any events are to occur. If they are, the events are simulated and time is advanced; if they are not, time is still advanced by one unit.

In the variable-time increment method, clock time is advanced by the amount required to initiate the next event.

RANDOMLY DISTRIBUTED NORMAL NUMBERS

1.23481	−1.66161	1.49673	−.26990	−.23812	.34506
1.54221	.02629	1.22318	.52304	.18124	.20790
.19126	1.18250	1.00826	.24826	−1.35882	.70691
−.54929	−.87214	−2.75470	−1.19941	−1.45402	.16760
1.14463	−.23153	1.11241	1.08497	−.28185	−.17022
−.63248	−.04776	−.55806	.04496	1.16515	2.24938
−.29988	.31052	−.49094	−.00926	−.28278	−.95339
−.32855	−.93166	−.04187	−.94171	1.64410	−.96893
.35331	.56176	−.98726	.82752	.32468	.36915
.72576					
.04406					

4.1 Example

Relating Random Numbers to a Standard Distribution

Step by Step

To illustrate how to relate random numbers to a standard distribution, suppose that daily demand for newspapers from a vending machine is normally distributed with a mean of 55 and standard deviation of 10. (This distribution is shown on the right side of Exhibit 4.2.) Under this assumption, the generation of daily demand would employ a table of randomly distributed normal numbers (or deviates) in conjunction with the statistical formula $D_n = \bar{x} + Z_n\sigma$ (terms defined later).[1]

Solution

1. Draw a five- or six-digit number from Exhibit 4.3. The entries in this table are randomly developed deviate values that pertain to a normal distribution having a mean of 0 and a standard deviation of 1. The term deviate refers to the number of standard deviations some value is from the mean and, in this case, represents the number of standard deviations that any day's demand is from the mean demand. In the preceding formula for Dn, it would be the value for Z on day n. If we are simulating Day 1 and using the first entry in Exhibit 4.3, then Z1 5 1.23481. A negative deviate value means simply that the particular level of demand will be less than the mean, not that demand will be a negative value.

2. Substitute the value of Z_1, along with the predetermined values for x and σ, into the formula

$$D_n = \bar{x} + Z_n\sigma$$

where

D_n = Demand on day n
$\bar{x}$ = Mean demand (55 in this example)
σ = Estimated standard deviation (10 in this example)
z_n = Number of standard deviations from the mean on day n

Thus $D_n = 55 + (1.23481)(10)$.

3. Solve for D_n:

$$D_n = 55 + 12.3481$$
$$D_n = 67.3481$$

4. Repeat Steps 1 to 3, using different normal deviates from the table until the desired number of days have been simulated. ●

89

Which method is most appropriate? Experience suggests that the fixed-time increment is desirable when events of interest occur with regularity or when the number of events is large, with several commonly occurring in the same time period. The variable-time increment method is generally desirable, taking less computer run time, when there are relatively few events occurring within a considerable amount of time. It ignores time intervals where nothing happens and immediately advances to the next point when some event does take place.

Specifying Values of Variables and Parameters

A variable, by definition, changes in value as the simulation progresses, but it must be given an initial starting value. The value of a parameter, remember, stays constant; however, it may be changed as different alternatives are studied in other simulations.

Determining Starting Conditions   Determining starting conditions for variables is a major tactical decision in simulation. This is because the model is biased by the set of initial starting values until the model has settled down to a steady state. To cope with this problem, analysts have followed various approaches such as (1) discarding data generated during the early parts of the run, (2) selecting starting conditions that reduce the duration of the warm-up period, or (3) selecting starting conditions that eliminate bias. To employ any of these alternatives, however, the analyst must have some idea of the range of output data expected. Therefore, in one sense, the analyst biases results. On the other hand, one of the unique features of simulation is that it allows judgment to enter into the design and analysis of the simulation; so if the analyst has some information that bears on the problem, it should be included.

Run length
(run time)

Determining Run Length   The length of the simulation run (**run length** or **run time**) depends on the purpose of the simulation. Perhaps the most common approach is to continue the simulation until it has achieved equilibrium. In the fish market example, this would mean that simulated fish sales correspond to their historical relative frequencies. Another approach is to run the simulation for a set period such as a month, a year, or a decade and see if the conditions at the end of the period appear reasonable. A third approach is to set run length so that a sufficiently large sample is gathered for purposes of statistical hypothesis testing. This alternative is considered further in the next section.

Evaluating Results

The types of conclusions that can be drawn from a simulation depend, of course, on the degree to which the model reflects the real system, but they also depend on the design of the simulation in a statistical sense. Indeed, many analysts view simulation as a form of hypothesis testing, with each simulation run providing one or more pieces of sample data that are amenable to formal analysis through inferential statistical methods. Statistical procedures commonly used in evaluating simulation results include analysis of variance, regression analysis, and t tests.

In most situations, the analyst has other information available with which to compare the simulation results: past operating data from the real system, operating data from the performance of similar systems, and the analyst's own intuitive understanding of the real system's operation. However, information obtained from these sources is probably not sufficient to validate the conclusions derived from the simulation. Thus, the only true test of a simulation is how well the real system performs after the results of the study have been implemented.

Validation

In this context, *validation* refers to testing the computer program to ensure that the simulation is correct. Specifically, it is a check to see whether the computer code is a valid translation of the flowchart model and whether the simulation adequately represents the real system. Errors may arise in the program from mistakes in the coding or from mistakes in logic. Mistakes in coding are usually easily found because the program is most likely not executed by the computer. Mistakes in logic, however, present more of a challenge. In these cases, the program runs but fails to yield correct results.

To deal with this problem, the analyst has three alternatives: (1) have the program print out all calculations and verify these calculations by separate computation, (2) simulate present conditions and compare the results with the existing system, or (3) pick some point in the simulation run and compare its output to the answer obtained from solving a relevant mathematical model of the situation at that point. Even though the first two approaches have obvious drawbacks, they are more likely to be employed than the third, because if we had a relevant mathematical model in mind, we would probably be able to solve the problem without the aid of simulation.

Proposing a New Experiment

Based on the simulation results, a new simulation experiment may be in order. We might like to change many of the factors: parameters, variables, decision rules, starting conditions, and run length. As for parameters, we might be interested in replicating the simulation with several different costs or prices of a product to see what changes would occur. Trying different decision rules would obviously be in order if the initial rules led to poor results or if these runs yielded new insights into the problem. (The procedure of using the same stream of random numbers is a good general approach in that it sharpens the differences among alternatives and permits shorter runs.) Also, the values from the previous experiment may be useful starting conditions for subsequent simulations.

Finally, whether trying different run lengths constitutes a new experiment rather than a replication of a previous experiment depends on the types of events that occur in the system operation over time. It might happen, for example, that the system has more than one stable level of operation and that reaching the second level is time dependent. Thus, while the first series of runs of, say, 100 periods shows stable conditions, doubling the length of the series may provide new and distinctly different but equally stable conditions. In this case, running the simulation over 200 time periods could be thought of as a new experiment.

Computerization

When using a computer model, we reduce the system to be studied to a symbolic representation to be run on a computer. Although it is beyond this book's scope to detail the technical aspects of computer modeling, some that bear directly on simulation are

1. Computer language selection.
2. Flowcharting.
3. Coding.
4. Data generation.
5. Output reports.
6. Validation.

We say more about simulation programs and languages at the end of this chapter.

Output Reports   General-purpose languages permit the analyst to specify any type of output report (or data) desired, providing one is willing to pay the price in programming effort. Special-purpose languages have standard routines that can be activated by one or two program statements to print out such data as means, variances, and standard deviations. Regardless of language, however, our experience has been that too much data from a simulation can be as dysfunctional to problem solving as too little data; both situations tend to obscure important, truly meaningful information about the system under study.

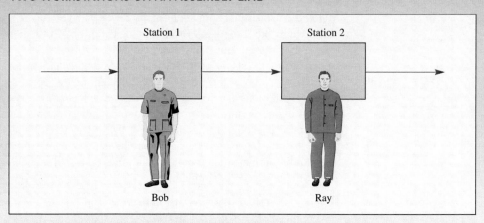

4.3   Simulating Waiting Lines

Waiting lines that occur in series and parallel (such as in assembly lines and work centers) usually cannot be solved mathematically. However, because waiting lines are often easily simulated on a computer, we have chosen a two-stage assembly line as our second simulation example.

Example: A Two-Stage Assembly Line

Consider an assembly line that makes a product of significant physical size such as a refrigerator, stove, car, boat, TV, or furniture. Exhibit 4.4 shows two workstations on such a line.

The size of the product is an important consideration in assembly-line analysis and design because the number of products that can exist at each workstation affects worker performance. If the product is large, then the workstations are dependent on each other. Exhibit 4.4, for example, shows Bob and Ray working on a two-stage line where Bob's output in Station 1 is fed to Ray in Station 2. If the workstations are adjacent, leaving no room for items between them, then Bob, by working slowly, would cause Ray to wait. Conversely, if Bob completes a product quickly (or if Ray takes longer to finish the task), then Bob must wait for Ray.

In this simulation, assume that Bob, the first worker on the line, can pull over a new item to work on whenever needed. We concentrate our analysis on the interaction between Bob and Ray.

Objective of the Study   We would like to answer a number of questions about the assembly line from this study. A partial list would be

- What is the average performance time of each worker?
- What is the output rate of product through this line?
- How much time does Bob wait for Ray?
- How much time does Ray wait for Bob?
- If the space between the two stations were increased so that items could be stored there and give workers some independence, how would this affect output rates, wait times, and so on?

Exhibit 4.5

DATA COLLECTION FORM FOR WORKER OBSERVATION

Seconds to Complete Task	Bob		Ray	
		Totals		Totals
5–14.99	IIII	4	IIII	4
15–24.99	JHI I	6	JHI	5
25–34.99	JHI JHI	10	JHI I	6
35–44.99	JHI JHI JHI JHI	20	JHI II	7
45–54.99	JHI JHI JHI JHI JHI JHI JHI JHI	40	JHI JHI	10
55–64.99	JHI JHI I	11	JHI III	8
65–74.99	JHI	5	JHI I	6
75–84.99	IIII	4	IIII	4
		100		50

Data Collection To simulate this system, we need the performance times of Bob and Ray. One way to collect these data is to divide the range of performance times into segments and then observe each worker. A simple check or tally mark in each of these segments results in a useful histogram of data.

Exhibit 4.5 shows the data collection form used to observe the performances of Bob and Ray. To simplify the procedure, performance time was divided into 10-second intervals. Bob was observed for 100 repetitions of the work task and Ray was observed just 50 times. The number of observations does not have to be the same, but the more there are and the smaller the size of the time segments, the more accurate the study will be. The trade-off is that more observations and smaller segments take more time and more people (as well as more time to program and run a simulation).

Exhibit 4.6 contains the random number intervals assigned that correspond to the same ratio as the actual observed data. For example, Bob had 4 out of 100 times at 10 seconds. Therefore, if we used 100 numbers, we would assign 4 of those numbers as corresponding to 10 seconds. We could have assigned any four numbers, for example, 42, 18, 12, and 93. However, these would be a nuisance to search for, so we assign consecutive numbers, such as 00, 01, 02, and 03.

There were 50 observations of Ray. There are two ways we could assign random numbers. First, we could use just 50 numbers (say, 00–49) and ignore any numbers over that. However, this is wasteful because we would discard 50 percent of all the numbers from the list. Another choice would be to double the frequency number. For example, rather than assign, say, numbers 0–03 to account for the 4 observations out of 50 that took 10 seconds, we could assign numbers 00–07 to represent 8 observations out of 100, which is double the observed number but the same frequency. Actually, for this example and the speed of computers, the savings of time by doubling is insignificant.

Exhibit 4.7 shows a hand simulation of 10 items processed by Bob and Ray. The random numbers used were from Appendix H, starting at the first column of two numbers and working downward.

Assume that we start out at time 00 and run it in continuous seconds (not bothering to convert this to hours and minutes). The first random number is 56 and corresponds to Bob's performance at 50 seconds on the first item. The item is passed to Ray, who starts at 50 seconds. Relating the next random number, 83, to Exhibit 4.6, we find that Ray takes 70 seconds to complete the item. In the meantime, Bob starts on the next item at time

Exhibit 4.6

Seconds	Time Frequencies for Bob (Operation 1)	RN Intervals	Time Frequencies for Ray (Operation 2)	RN Intervals
10	4	00–03	4	00–07
20	6	04–09	5	08–17
30	10	10–19	6	18–29
40	20	20–39	7	30–43
50	40	40–79	10	44–63
60	11	80–90	8	64–79
70	5	91–95	6	80–91
80	4	96–99	4	92–99
	100		50	

50 and takes 50 seconds (random number 55), finishing at time 100. However, Bob cannot start on the third item until Ray gets through with the first item at time 120. Bob, therefore, has a wait time of 20 seconds. (If there was storage space between Bob and Ray, this item could have been moved out of Bob's workstation, and Bob could have started the next item at time 100.) The remainder of the exhibit was calculated following the same pattern: obtaining a random number, finding the corresponding processing time, noting the wait time (if any), and computing the finish time. Note that with no storage space between Bob and Ray, there was considerable waiting time for both workers.

We can now answer some questions and make some statements about the system. For example,

The output time averages 60 seconds per unit (the complete time 600 for Ray divided by 10 units).

Utilization of Bob is $\frac{470}{530} = 88.7$ percent.

Utilization of Ray is $\frac{430}{550} = 78.2$ percent (disregarding the initial startup wait for the first item of 50 seconds).

The average performance time for Bob is $\frac{470}{10} = 47$ seconds.

The average performance time for Ray is $\frac{430}{10} = 43$ seconds.

We have demonstrated how this problem would be solved in a simple manual simulation. A sample of 10 is really too small to place much confidence in, so this problem should be run on a computer for several thousand iterations. (We extend this same problem further in the next section of this chapter.)

It is also vital to study the effect of item storage space between workers. The problem would be run to see what the throughput time and worker utilization times are with no storage space between workers. A second run should increase this storage space to one unit, with the corresponding changes noted. Repeating the runs for two, three, four, and so on, offers management a chance to compute the additional cost of space compared with the increased use. Such increased space between workers may require a larger building, more materials and parts in the system, material handling equipment, and a transfer machine, plus added heat, light, building maintenance, and so on.

These also would be useful data for management to see what changes in the system would occur if one worker position was automated. The assembly line could be simulated using data from the automated process to see if such a change would be cost justified.

Exhibit 4.7

SIMULATION OF BOB AND RAY—TWO-STAGE ASSEMBLY LINE

Item Number	Bob						Ray				
	Random Number	Start Time	Performance Time	Finish Time	Wait Time	Storage Space	Random Number	Start Time	Performance Time	Finish Time	Wait Time
1	56	00	50	50		0	83	50	70	120	50
2	55	50	50	100	20	0	47	120	50	170	
3	84	120	60	180		0	08	180	20	200	10
4	36	180	40	220		0	05	220	10	230	20
5	26	220	40	260		0	42	260	40	300	30
6	95	260	70	330		0	95	330	80	410	30
7	66	330	50	380	30	0	17	410	20	430	
8	03	410	10	420	10	0	21	430	30	460	
9	57	430	50	480		0	31	480	40	520	20
10	69	480	50	530		0	90	530	70	600	10
			470		60				430		170

4.4 Spreadsheet Simulation

As we have stated throughout this book, spreadsheets such as Microsoft® Excel are very useful for a variety of problems. Exhibit 4.8 shows Bob and Ray's two-stage assembly line on an Excel® spreadsheet. The procedure follows the same pattern as our manual display in Exhibit 4.7.

The total simulation on Excel® passed through 1,200 iterations (shown in Exhibit 4.9); that is, 1,200 parts were finished by Ray. Simulation, as an analytic tool, has an advantage over quantitative methods in that it is dynamic, whereas analytic methods show long-run average performance. As you can see in Exhibit 4.9A, there is an unmistakable startup (or transient) phase. We could even raise some questions about the long-term operation of the line because it does not seem to have settled to a constant (steady state) value, even after the 1,200 items. Exhibit 4.9A shows 100 items that pass through the Bob and Ray two-stage system. Notice the wide variation in time for the first units completed. These figures are the average time that units take. It is a cumulative number; that is, the first unit takes the time generated by the random numbers. The average time for two units is the average time of the sum of the first and second units. The average time for three units is the average time for the sum of the first three units, and so on. This display could have almost any starting shape, not necessarily what we have shown. It all depends on the stream of random numbers. What we can be sure of is that the times do oscillate for a while until they settle down as units are finished and smooth the average.

Exhibit 4.9B shows the average time that parts spend in the system. At the start, the display shows an increasing amount of time in the system. This can be expected because the system started empty and there are no interruptions for parts passing from Bob to Ray. Often parts enter the system and may have to wait between stages as work-in-process; this causes delays for subsequent parts and adds to the waiting time. As time goes on, however, stability should occur unless the capacity of the second stage is less than the first stage's. In our present case, we did not allow space between them. Therefore, if Bob finished first, he had to wait for Ray. If Ray finished first, he had to wait for Bob.

Exhibit 4.8

Excel: Two-Stage Assembly

BOB AND RAY TWO-STAGE ASSEMBLY LINE ON MICROSOFT EXCEL®

		Bob					Ray						Average
Item	RN	Start Time	Perf. Time	Finish Time	Wait Time	RN	Start Time	Perf. time	Finish Time	Wait Time	Average Time/Unit	Total Time	Time in System
1	93	0	70	70	0	0	70	10	80	70	80.0	80	80.0
2	52	70	50	120	0	44	120	50	170	40	85.0	100	90.0
3	15	120	30	150	20	72	170	60	230	0	76.7	110	96.7
4	64	170	50	220	10	35	230	40	270	0	67.5	100	97.5
5	86	230	60	290	0	2	290	10	300	20	60.0	70	92.0
6	20	290	40	330	0	82	330	70	400	30	66.7	110	95.0
7	83	330	60	390	10	31	400	40	440	0	62.9	110	97.1
8	89	400	60	460	0	13	460	20	480	20	60.0	80	95.0
9	69	460	50	510	0	53	510	50	560	30	62.2	100	95.6
10	41	510	50	560	0	48	560	50	610	0	61.0	100	96.0
11	32	560	40	600	10	13	610	20	630	0	57.3	70	93.6
12	1	610	10	620	10	67	630	60	690	0	57.5	80	92.5
13	11	630	30	660	30	91	690	70	760	0	58.5	130	95.4
14	2	690	10	700	60	76	760	60	820	0	58.6	130	97.9
15	11	760	30	790	30	41	820	40	860	0	57.3	100	98.0
16	55	820	50	870	0	34	870	40	910	10	56.9	90	97.5
17	18	870	30	900	10	28	910	30	940	0	55.3	70	95.9
18	39	910	40	950	0	53	950	50	1000	10	55.6	90	95.6
19	13	950	30	980	20	41	1000	40	1040	0	54.7	90	95.3
20	7	1000	20	1020	20	21	1040	30	1070	0	53.5	70	94.0
21	29	1040	40	1080	0	54	1080	50	1130	10	53.8	90	93.8
22	58	1080	50	1130	0	39	1130	40	1170	0	53.2	90	93.6
23	95	1130	70	1200	0	70	1200	60	1260	30	54.8	130	95.2
24	27	1200	40	1240	20	60	1260	50	1310	0	54.6	110	95.8
25	59	1260	50	1310	0	93	1310	80	1390	0	55.6	130	97.2
26	85	1310	60	1370	20	51	1390	50	1440	0	55.4	130	98.5
27	12	1390	30	1420	20	35	1440	40	1480	0	54.8	90	98.1
28	34	1440	40	1480	0	51	1480	50	1530	0	54.6	90	97.9
29	60	1480	50	1530	0	87	1530	70	1600	0	55.2	120	98.6
30	97	1530	80	1610	0	29	1610	30	1640	10	54.7	110	99.0

Exhibit 4.9C shows the results of simulating Bob and Ray completing 1,200 units of product. Compare these figures to those that we obtained simulating 10 items by hand. Not too bad, is it? The average performance time for Bob is shown as 46.48 seconds. This is close to the weighted average of what you would expect in the long run. For Bob it is (10 × 4 + 20 × 6 + 30 × 10 etc.) 100 = 45.9 seconds. Ray's expected time is (10 × 4 + 20 × 5 + 30 × 6 etc.) 50 = 46.4 seconds.

The two-stage assembly line simulation is a good example of a specially designed spreadsheet for analyzing this problem. More general simulation programs built within Excel® are available. John McClain, professor of operations management at Cornell University, has developed two simulation spreadsheets that can be used to demonstrate a variety of common systems. These spreadsheets have been included on this book's Web site.

Excel: LineSim

A. Average Time per Unit of Output (Finish Time/ Number of Units)

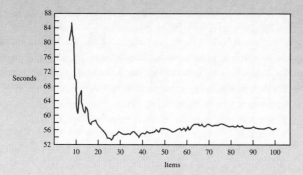

B. Average Time the Product Spends in the System

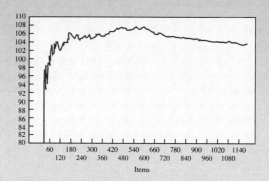

C. Results of Simulating 1,200 Units Processed by Bob and Ray

	Bob	Ray	Unit
Utilization	0.81	0.85	
Average wait time	10.02	9.63	
Average performance time	46.48	46.88	
Average time per unit			57.65
Average time in system			103.38

Excel: CellSim

The first spreadsheet, titled "LineSim," is designed to analyze a simple serial production line. This is a system with a series of machines; the output of one machine goes to a storage area, which is the input to the next machine. The spreadsheet can be easily configured for different numbers of machines, different buffer sizes, and numerous processing time distributions. In addition, machine breakdowns and repairs can be modeled. The second spreadsheet, "CellSim," is similar but allows machines to be arranged more generally. We thank Professor McClain for making these spreadsheets available.

4.5   Simulation Programs and Languages

Simulation models can be classified as *continuous* or *discrete*. Continuous models are based on mathematical equations and therefore are continuous, with values for all points in time. In contrast, discrete simulation occurs only at specific points. For example, customers arriving at a bank teller's window would be discrete simulation. The simulation jumps from point to point: the arrival of a customer, the start of a service, the ending of service, the arrival of the next customer, and so on. Discrete simulation also can be triggered to run by units of time (daily, hourly, minute by minute). This is called *event simulation;* points in between either have no value to our simulation or cannot be computed because of the lack of some sort of mathematical relationship to link the succeeding events. Operations and supply management applications almost exclusively use discrete (event) simulation.

Simulation programs also can be categorized as general-purpose and special-purpose. General-purpose softwares allow programmers to build their own models. Examples are SLAM II, SIMSCRIPT II.5, SIMAN, GPSS/H, GPSS/PC, PC-MODEL, and RESQ. Special-purpose software simulation programs are specially built to simulate specific applications, for example, Extend and SIMFACTORY. In a specialized simulation for manufacturing, for example, provisions in the model allow for specifying the number of work centers, their description, arrival rates, processing time, batch sizes, quantities of work in process, available resources including labor, sequences, and so on. Additionally, the program may allow the observer to watch the animated operation and see the quantities and flows throughout the system as the simulation is running. Data are collected, analyzed, and presented in a form most suitable for that type of application. The software package called Extend is featured in the Breakthrough box titled "Animation and Simulation Software."

4.6 Break-through

Animation and Simulation Software

Call centers are a good application for simulation. They are easy to model, and information is available about the service time, arrival rates, renege times, and the paths that the calls take through the center. In this call center, there are four types of calls arriving at random intervals and four types of agents who are able to answer the calls. Each agent type is specialized in a particular call type. However, some agents are able to answer calls of different types.

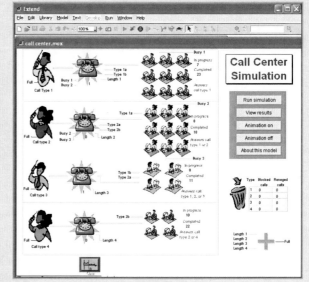

This was quickly modeled using Extend, a product of Imagine That! company. The product makes extensive use of animation so that the user can actually watch the call center operate. You can learn more about this product at http://www.imaginethatinc.com.

Hospital Overcrowding Solutions are Found with Simulation

Thanks to increased life expectancy through improved health care coupled with shifting population demographics, hospitals everywhere are becoming increasingly overcrowded. Limited health care budgets are forcing hospitals to explore creative solutions. But creative solutions can be risky, so they need to be carefully evaluated. From the standpoint of cost, the earlier a solution can be evaluated and either accepted or rejected, the better.

Along these lines, the outpatient laboratory at Bay Medical Center was experiencing serious capacity constraints. Adding to its difficulties, a renovation designed to improve efficiency actually added to the overcrowding problem. Dave Nall, a management engineer for Bay Medical Center, ran a study to evaluate several alternatives and make recommendations designed to reduce bottlenecks and improve patient flow through the outpatient laboratory. The objective of this study was to develop and evaluate alternative ways of reducing overcrowding at the outpatient laboratory.

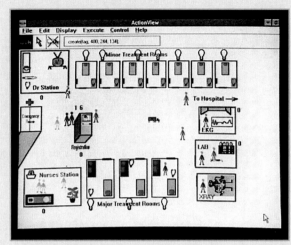

Solution

The key technology employed by Dave in conducting this analysis was computer simulation. Dave had used computer simulation numerous times in the past and had found that it was an efficient way to both gain insight into the problem and evaluate the solutions.

Through discussions with managers responsible for the outpatient laboratory, Dave built a network describing the patient's flow through the laboratory as it was currently configured. Then data were collected on the times required for patients to receive the various services they might need as well as the travel time between rooms where the services were provided. From this information, Dave constructed a computer simulation of the baseline laboratory configuration.

Dave then modified the computer simulation and used it to study issues relating to three categories of solutions to outpatient laboratory overcrowding: (1) changing staff, including both medical and administrative staff; (2) utilizing another clinic as an overflow laboratory; and (3) possibly redesigning the laboratory facility itself.

With respect to staffing, the computer simulation verified that the medical staff currently employed was indeed the optimal number. However, Dave found that the administrative functions, if anything, were overstaffed and that a staff reduction could take place with no appreciable reduction in patient service. Staffing was not the key problem. With respect to the option of utilizing another laboratory for overflow, there were significant opportunities for improving throughput if other patients could be enticed to use another laboratory. Although the simulation did not tell him how to get the patients to use an alternative laboratory, it did allow Dave to quantify the benefits of implementing policies that would increase alternative laboratory usage by 5 percent, 10 percent, and so on. With respect to redesign of the existing outpatient laboratory, Dave determined that, with a relatively minor redesign of the facility and a procedural change, the laboratory would become significantly more productive. Increased productivity would, of course, lead to better patient service.

Benefits

Individually, no one could have accurately guessed the impact of the different ways of addressing overcrowding at the outpatient laboratory at Bay Medical Center. Through the results of the simulation analysis and the insights gained, Dave was able to assess the relative merits of each alternative as well as predict their impact. With a small investment in Dave's time, Bay Medical Center was able to make informed decisions with an understanding of both costs and benefits. As a result, the right decisions were made, money was saved, and patients were better served.

Source: Micro Analysis and Design Micro Saint Simulation Software. © 2004 Micro Analyses & Design. Used with Permission.

Service

Service

Many software simulation programs are available. How, then, do you choose a program from a long list? The first step is to understand the different types of simulation. Then it becomes a matter of reviewing programs on the market to find one that fits your specific needs. (See the Breakthrough box titled "Hospital Overcrowding Solutions Are Found with Simulation" for a successful application of a commercial program.)

As a last comment on simulation programs, do not rule out spreadsheets for simulation. As you noticed, we simulated Bob and Ray on a spreadsheet in the preceding section. Spreadsheets are becoming quite user-friendly and are adding many features such as allowing random number generation and asking what-if questions. The simplicity in using a spreadsheet for simulation may well compensate for any needed reduction in the complexity of the problem in order to use the spreadsheet.

@RISK is an add-in program that works with Microsoft Excel®. The program adds many useful simulation-related functions to the spreadsheet. Using @RISK automates the process of taking random values from a specified distribution function, automates the recalculation of the spreadsheet with the new random values, and captures output values and statistics. @RISK simplifies the process of building and running spreadsheet simulations.[2]

Desirable Features of Simulation Software

Simulation software takes a while to learn to use. Once specific software is learned, the tendency is to stay with it for a long time, so the choice must be made carefully. Simulation software should

1. Be capable of being used interactively as well as allowing complete runs.
2. Be user-friendly and easy to understand.
3. Allow modules to be built and then connected. In this way, models can be worked on separately without affecting the rest of the system.
4. Allow users to write and incorporate their own routines; no simulation program can provide for all needs.
5. Have building blocks that contain built-in commands (such as statistical analysis or decision rules for where to go next).
6. Have macro capability, such as the ability to develop machining cells.
7. Have material flow capability. Operations involve the movement of material and people; the program should be able to model trucks, cranes, conveyers, and so on.
8. Output standard statistics such as cycle times, utilizations, and wait times.
9. Allow a variety of data analysis alternatives for both input and output data.
10. Have animation capabilities to display graphically the product flow through the system.
11. Permit interactive debugging of the model so the user can trace flows through the model and more easily find errors.[3]

4.7 Advantages and Disadvantages of Simulation

The following is not intended as a comprehensive list of reasons why one should elect to use or not use simulation as a technique. Rather, we state some of the generally accepted advantages and disadvantages.

Advantages

1. Developing the model of a system often leads to a better understanding of the real system.
2. Time can be compressed in simulation; years of experience in the real system can be compressed into seconds or minutes.
3. Simulation does not disrupt ongoing activities of the real system.
4. Simulation is far more general than mathematical models and can be used where conditions are not suitable for standard mathematical analysis.
5. Simulation can be used as a game for training experience.
6. Simulation provides a more realistic replication of a system than mathematical analysis.
7. Simulation can be used to analyze transient conditions, whereas mathematical techniques usually cannot.
8. Many standard packaged models, covering a wide range of topics, are available commercially.
9. Simulation answers what-if questions.

Disadvantages

1. Although a great deal of time and effort may be spent to develop a model for simulation, there is no guarantee that the model will, in fact, provide good answers.
2. There is no way to prove that a simulation model's performance is completely reliable. Simulation involves numerous repetitions of sequences that are based on randomly generated occurrences. An apparently stable system can, with the right combination of events—however unlikely—explode.
3. Depending on the system to be simulated, building a simulation model can take anywhere from an hour to 100 worker years. Complicated systems can be very costly and take a long time.
4. Simulation may be less accurate than mathematical analysis because it is randomly based. If a given system can be represented by a mathematical model, it may be better to use than simulation.
5. A significant amount of computer time may be needed to run complex models.
6. The technique of simulation, while making progress, still lacks a standardized approach. Therefore, models of the same system built by different individuals may differ widely.

4.8 Summary

We could make the statement that anything that can be done mathematically can be done with simulation. However, simulation is not always the best choice. Mathematical analysis, when appropriate to a specific problem, is usually faster and less expensive. Also, it is usually provable as far as the technique is concerned, and the only real question is whether the system is adequately represented by the mathematical model.

Simulation, however, has nothing fixed; there are no boundaries to building a model or making assumptions about the system. Expanding computer power and memory have pushed out the limits of what can be simulated. Further, the continued development of simulation languages and programs—both general-purpose programs (SIMAN, SLAM) and special-purpose programs (Extend, Process Model, SIMFACTORY, Optima!)—have made the entire process of creating simulation models much easier.

4.9
Key Terms

Parameters Properties of a simulation model that are fixed.

Variables Properties of a simulation model that are allowed to vary throughout the simulation run. The results of the simulation are analyzed through these variables.

Decision rules Logic that controls the behavior of a simulation.

Distributions The probability distributions that are used to model the random events in a simulation.

Time incrementing The process of moving through time in a simulation.

Run length (or run time) The duration of a simulation in simulated time or number of events.

4.10
Solved
Problems

Solved Problem 1

To use an old statistical example for simulation, if an urn contains 100 balls, of which 10 percent are green, 40 percent are red, and 50 percent are spotted, develop a simulation model of the process of drawing balls at random from the urn. Each time a ball is drawn and its color noted, it is replaced. Use the following random numbers as you desire.

Simulate drawing 10 balls from the urn. Show which numbers you have used.

26768	66954	83125	08021
42613	17457	55503	36458
95457	03704	47019	05752
95276	56970	84828	05752

Solution

Assign random numbers to the balls to correspond to the percentage present in the urn.

	Random Number
10 green balls	00–09
40 red balls	10–49
50 spotted balls	50–99

Many possible answers exist, depending on how the random numbers were assigned and which numbers were used from the list provided in the problem.

For the random number sequence above and using the first two numbers of those given, we obtain

RN	Color	RN	Color
26	Red	17	Red
42	Red	3	Green
95	Spotted	56	Spotted
95	Spotted	83	Spotted
66	Spotted	55	Spotted

For the 10 there were 1 green, 3 red, and 6 spotted balls—a good estimate based on a sample of only 10!

Solved Problem 2

A rural clinic receives a delivery of fresh plasma once each week from a central blood bank. The supply varies according to demand from other clinics and hospitals in the region but ranges between four and nine pints of the most widely used blood type, type O. The number of patients per week requiring this blood varies from zero to four, and each patient may need from one to four pints. Given the following delivery quantities, patient distribution, and demand per patient, what would be the number of pints in excess or short for a six-week period? Use simulation to derive your answer. Consider that plasma is storable and there is currently none on hand.

Patient Distribution					
Delivery Quantities		**Patients per week**		**Demand Per Patient**	
Pints per week	**Probability**	**Reauiring Blood**	**Probability**	**Pints**	**Probability**
4	0.15	0	0.25	1	0.40
5	0.20	1	0.25	2	0.30
6	0.25	2	0.30	3	0.20
7	0.15	3	0.15	4	0.10
8	0.15	4	0.05		
9	0.10				

Solution

First, develop a random number sequence; then simulate.

Delivery			Number of Patients			Patient Demand		
Pints	**Probability**	**Random Number**	**Blood**	**Probability**	**Random Number**	**Pints**	**Probability**	**Random Number**
4	.15	00–14	0	.25	00–24	1	.40	00–39
5	.20	15–34	1	.25	25–49	2	.30	40–69
6	.25	35–59	2	.30	50–79	3	.20	70–89
7	.15	60–74	3	.15	80–94	4	.10	90–99
8	.15	75–89	4	.05	95–99			
9	.10	90–99						

Week No	Beginning Inventory	Quantity Delivered		Total Blood on Hand	Patients Needing Blood		Patient	Quantity Needed		Number of Pints Remaining
		RN	**Pints**		**Rn**	**Patient**		**RN**	**Pints**	
1	0	74	7	7	85	3	First	21	1	6
							Second	06	1	5
							Third	71	3	2
2	2	31	5	7	28	1		96	4	3
3	3	02	4	7	72	2	First	12	1	6
							Second	67	2	4
4	4	53	6	10	44	1		23	1	9
5	9	16	5	14	16	0				14
6	14	40	6	20	83	3	First	65	2	18
							Second	34	1	17
							Third	82	3	14
7	14									

At the end of six weeks, there were 14 pints on hand

4.11
Review and Discussion Questions

1. Why is simulation often called a technique of last resort?

2. What roles does statistical hypothesis testing play in simulation?

3. What determines whether a simulation model is valid?

4. Must you use a computer to get good information from a simulation? Explain.

5. What methods are used to increment time in a simulation model? How do they work?

6. What are the pros and cons of starting a simulation with the system empty? With the system in equilibrium?

7. Distinguish between known mathematical distributions and empirical distributions. What information is needed to simulate using a known mathematical distribution?

8. What is the importance of run length in simulation? Is a run of 100 observations twice as valid as a run of 50? Explain.

4.12
Problems

1. Classroom Simulation: Fish Forwarders

   This is a competitive exercise designed to test players' skills at setting inventory ordering rules over a 10-week planning horizon. Maximum profit at the end determines the winner.

   Fish Forwarders supplies fresh shrimp to a variety of customers in the New Orleans area. It orders cases of shrimp from fleet representatives at the beginning of each week to meet a demand from its customers at the middle of the week. Shrimp are subsequently delivered to Fish Forwarders and then, at the end of the week, to its customers.

   Both the supply of shrimp and the demand for shrimp are uncertain. The supply may vary as much as 610 percent from the amount ordered, and, by contract, Fish Forwarders must purchase this supply. The probability associated with this variation is 210 percent, 30 percent of the time; 0 percent, 50 percent of the time; and 110 percent, 20 percent of the time. Weekly demand for shrimp is normally distributed with a mean of 800 cases and standard deviation of 100 cases.

   A case of shrimp costs Fish Forwarders $30 and sells for $50. Any shrimp not sold at the end of the week are sold to a cat-food company at $4 per case. Fish Forwarders may, if it chooses, order the shrimp flash-frozen by the supplier at dockside, but this raises the cost of a case by $4 and, hence, costs Fish Forwarders $34 per case.

   Procedure for play. The game requires that each week a decision be made as to how many cases to order of regular shrimp and of flash-frozen shrimp. The number ordered may be any amount. The instructor plays the role of referee and supplies the random numbers. The steps in playing the game are as follows:

   a. Decide on the order amount of regular shrimp or flash-frozen shrimp and enter the figures in column 3 of the worksheet. (See Exhibit 4.10.) Assume that there is no opening inventory of flash-frozen shrimp.

   b. Determine the amount that arrives and enter it under "Orders received." To accomplish this, the referee draws a random number from a uniform random number table (such as that in Appendix H) and finds its associated level of variation from the following random number intervals: 00 to 29 5 210 percent, 30 to 79 5 0 percent, and 80 to 99 5 110 percent. If the random number is, say, 13, the amount of variation will be 210 percent. Thus, if you decide to order 1,000 regular cases of shrimp and 100 flash-frozen cases, the amount you would actually receive would be 1,000 2 0.10(1,000), or 900 regular cases, and 100 2 0.10(100), or 90 flash-frozen cases. (Note that the variation is the same for both regular and flash-frozen shrimp.) These amounts are then entered in column 4.

   c. Add the amount of flash-frozen shrimp in inventory (if any) to the quantity of regular and flash-frozen shrimp just received and enter this amount in column 5. This would be 990, using the figures provided earlier.

   d. Determine the demand for shrimp. To accomplish this, the referee draws a random normal deviate value from Exhibit 4.3 or Appendix H and enters it into the equation at the top of

(1) Week	(2) Flash-frozen inventory	(3) Orders placed		(4) Orders received		(5) Available (regular and flash-frozen)	(6) Demand (800 + 100Z)	(7) Sales (minimum of demand or available)	(8) Excess		(9) Shortages
		Regular	Flash-frozen	Regular	Flash-frozen				Regular	Flash	
1											
2											
3											
4											
5											
6											
7		MARDI GRAS					*				
8											
9											
10											
Total											

*Flash-frozen only.

column 6. Thus, if the deviate value is 21.76, demand for the week is 800 1 100(21.76), or 624.

e. IDetermine the amount sold. This will be the lesser of the amount demanded (column 6) and the amount available (column 5). Thus, if a player has received 990 and demand is 624, the quantity entered will be 624 (with 990 2 624, or 366, left over).

f. Determine the excess. The amount of excess is simply that quantity remaining after demand for a given week is filled. Always assume that regular shrimp are sold before the flash-frozen. Thus, if we use the 366 figure obtained in e, the excess would include all the original 90 cases of flash-frozen shrimp.

g. Determine shortages. This is simply the amount of unsatisfied demand each period, and it occurs only when demand is greater than sales. (Because all customers use the shrimp within the week in which they are delivered, backorders are not relevant.) The amount of shortage (in cases of shrimp) is entered in column 9.

Profit determination. Exhibit 4.11 is provided for determining the profit achieved at the end of play. The values to be entered in the table are obtained by summing the relevant columns of Exhibit 4.10 and making the calculations.

Assignment. Simulate operations for a total of 10 weeks. It is suggested that a 10-minute break be taken at the end of Week 5, allowing the players to evaluate how they may improve their performance. They might also wish to plan an ordering strategy for the week of Mardi Gras, when no shrimp will be supplied.

2. The manager of a small post office is concerned that the growing township is overloading the one-window service being offered. Sample data are collected on 100 individuals who arrive for service:

Using the following random number sequence, simulate six arrivals; estimate the average customer waiting time and the average idle time for clerks.

RN: 08, 74, 24, 34, 45, 86, 31, 32, 45, 21, 10, 67, 60, 17, 60, 87, 74, 96

Revenue from sales ($50 × Col. 7)	$_____	
Revenue from salvage ($4 × Col. 8 reg.)	$_____	
Total revenue		$_____
Cost of regular purchases ($30 × Col. 4 reg.)	$_____	
Cost of flash-frozen purchases ($34 × Col. 4 flash)	$_____	
Cost of holding flash-frozen shrimp ($2 × Col. 8 flash)	$_____	
Cost of shortages ($20 × Col. 9)	$_____	
Total cost		$_____
Profit		$_____

Time between Arrivals (Minutes)	Frequency	Service Time (Minutes)	Frequency
1	8	1.0	12
2	35	1.5	21
3	34	2.0	36
4	17	2.5	19
5	6	3.0	7
	100	3.5	5
			100

3. Thomas Magnus, a private investigator, has been contacted by a potential client in Kamalo, Molokai. The call came just in time because Magnus is down to his last $10. Employment, however, is conditional on Magnus's meeting the client at Kamalo within eight hours. Magnus, presently at the Masters' residence in Kipahulu, Maui, has three alternative ways to get to Kamalo. Magnus may

a. Drive to the native village of Honokahua and take an outrigger to Kamalo.

b. Drive to Honokahua and swim the 10 miles across Pailolo Channel to Kamalo.

c. Drive to Hana and ask his friend T. C. to fly him by helicopter to Kamalo.

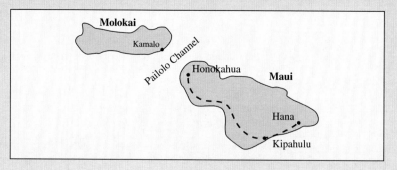

If option *a* is chosen, driving times to Honokahua are given in Distribution 1. Once at Honokahua, Magnus must negotiate with the friendly Tai natives. Negotiations always include a few Mai Tais, so if Magnus begins to negotiate, swimming becomes impossible. Negotiations center on how much each of the three outrigger crew members will be paid. Negotiation time, crew pay, and outrigger travel time are in Distributions 3, 4, and 5, respectively. You may assume each crew member is paid the same amount. If crew pay totals more than $10, Magnus is out of luck—trip time may then be taken to be infinity.

If option *b* is chosen, driving times to Honokahua and swimming times are given in Distributions 1 and 6.

If option *c* is chosen, driving times to Hana are given in Distribution 2. T. C., however, is at the airport only 10 percent of the time. If T. C. is not at the airport, Magnus will wait for him to arrive. Magnus's waiting time is given by Distribution 8. T. C. may refuse to fly for the $10 Magnus has available; Magnus puts the probability of T. C. refusing to fly for $10 at 30 percent. You may assume negotiation time is zero. If T. C. refuses, Magnus will drive to Honokahua via Kipahulu and swim to Kamalo. Helicopter flying times are given in Distribution 7.

Simulate each of the three alternative transportation plans *twice* and, based on your simulation results, calculate the average trip time for each plan. Use the following random numbers in the order they appear; do not skip any random numbers.

RN: 7, 3, 0, 4, 0, 5, 3, 5, 6, 1, 6, 6, 4, 8, 4, 9, 0, 7, 7, 1, 7, 0, 6, 8, 8, 7, 9, 0, 1, 2, 9, 7, 3, 2, 3, 8, 6, 0, 6, 0, 5, 9, 7, 9, 6, 4, 7, 2, 8, 7, 8, 1, 7, 0, 5

Distribution 1: Time to Drive from Kipahulu to Honokahua (Hours)

Time	Probability	RN
1	.2	0–1
1.5	.6	2–7
2	.2	8–9

Distribution 2: Time to Drive from Kipahulu to Hana and Vice Versa (Hours)

Time	Probability	RN
.5	.2	0–1
1	.7	2–8
1.5	.1	9

Distribution 3: Negotiation Time (Hours)

Time	Probability	RN
1	.2	0–1
1.5	.3	2–4
2	.3	5–7
2.5	.2	8–9

Distribution 4: Outrigger Pay per Crew Member

Pay	Probability	RN
$2	.3	0–2
3	.3	3–5
4	.4	6–9

Distribution 5: Outrigger Travel Time from Honokahua to Kamalo (Hours)

Time	Probability	RN
3	.1	0
4	.5	1–5
5	.4	6–9

Distribution 6: Time to Swim from Honokahua to Kamalo (Hours)

Time	Probability	RN
5	.2	0–1
6	.6	2–7
7	.2	8–9

Distribution 7: Time to Fly from Hana to Kamalo (Hours)

Time	Probability	RN
1	.1	0
1.5	.7	1–7
2	.2	8–9

Distribution 8: Magnus's Waiting Time at Airport (Hours)

Time	Probability	RN
1	.1	0
2	.2	1–2
3	.4	3–6
4	.3	7–9

4. A bank of machines in a manufacturing shop breaks down according to the following interarrival time distribution. The time it takes one repairperson to complete the repair of a machine is given in the service time distribution:

Interarrival Time (Hours)	P(X)	RN	Service Time (Hours)	P(X)	RN
.5	.30	0–29	.5	.25	0–24
1.0	.22	30–51	1.0	.20	25–44
1.5	.16	52–67	2.0	.25	45–69
2.0	.10	68–77	3.0	.15	70–84
3.0	.14	78–91	4.0	.10	85–94
4.0	.08	92–99	5.0	.05	95–99
	1.00			1.00	

Simulate the breakdown of five machines. Calculate the average machine downtime using two repairpersons and the following random number sequence. (Both repairpersons cannot work on the same machine.)

RN: 30, 81, 02, 91, 51, 08, 28, 44, 86, 84, 29, 08, 37, 34, 99

5. Jennifer Jones owns a small candy store she operates herself. A study was made observing the time between customers coming into the store and the time that Jones took to serve them. The following data were collected from 100 customers observed:

Interarrival Time (Minutes)	Number of Observations	Service Time (Minutes)	Number of Observations
1	5	1	10
2	10	2	15
3	10	3	15
4	15	4	20
5	15	5	15
6	20	6	10
7	10	7	8
8	8	8	4
9	5	9	2
10	2	10	1

Simulate the system (all of the arrivals and services) until 10 customers pass through the system and are serviced.

How long does the average customer spend in the system? Use Appendix H to obtain random numbers.

6. A professional football coach has six running backs on his squad. He wants to evaluate how injuries might affect his stock of running backs. A minor injury causes a player to be removed from the game and miss only the next game. A major injury puts the player out of action for the rest of the season. The probability of a major injury in a game is 0.05. There is at most one major injury per game. The probability distribution of minor injuries per game is

Number of Injuries	Probability
0	.2
1	.5
2	.22
3	.05
4	.0254
	.005
	1.000

Injuries seem to happen in a completely random manner, with no discernible pattern over the season. A season is 10 games.

Using the following random numbers, simulate the fluctuations in the coach's stock of running backs over the season. Assume that he hires no additional running backs during the season.

RN: 044, 392, 898, 615, 986, 959, 558, 353, 577, 866, 305, 813, 024, 189, 878, 023, 285, 442, 862, 848, 060, 131, 963, 874, 805, 105, 452

7. At Tucson Mills, minor breakdowns of machines occur frequently. The occurrence of breakdowns and the service time to fix the machines are randomly distributed. Management is concerned with minimizing the cost of breakdowns. The cost per hour for the machines to be down is $40. The cost of service repairpersons is $12 per hour. A preliminary study has produced the following data on times between successive breakdowns and their service times:

Relative Frequency of Breakdowns						
Time between breakdowns (in minutes)	4	5	6	7	8	9
Relative frequency	.10	.30	.25	.20	.10	.05

Relative Frequency of Service Times						
Service time (in minutes)	4	5	6	7	8	9
Relative frequency	.10	.40	.20	.15	.10	.05

Simulate 30 breakdowns under two conditions: with one service repairperson and with two service repairpersons.

Use the following random number sequence to determine time between breakdowns:
RN: 85, 16, 65, 76, 93, 99, 65, 70, 58, 44, 02, 85, 01, 97, 63, 52, 53, 11, 62, 28, 84, 82, 27, 20, 39, 70, 26, 21, 41, 81

Use the following random number sequence to determine service times:
RN: 68, 26, 85, 11, 16, 26, 95, 67, 97, 73, 75, 64, 26, 45, 01, 87, 20, 01, 19, 36, 69, 89, 81, 81, 02, 05, 10, 51, 24, 36

   a. Drive to the native ville simulations, calculate
      (1) The total idle time for the service repairpersons under each condition.
      (2) The total delay caused by waiting for a service repairperson to begin working on a breakdown.
   b. Determine the lowest-cost approach.

8. Jethro's service station has one gasoline pump. Because everyone in Kornfield County drives big cars, there is room at the station for only three cars, including the car at the pump. Cars arriving when three cars are already at the station drive on to another station. Use the following probability distributions to simulate the arrival of four cars to Jethro's station:

Use the following random number sequence:

Interarrival time (Minutes)	$P(X)$	RN	Service Time (Minutes)	$P(X)$	RN
10	.40	0–39	5	.45	0–44
20	.35	40–74	10	.30	45–74
30	.20	75–94	15	.20	75–94
40	.05	95–99	20	.05	95–99

RN: 99, 00, 73, 09, 38, 53, 72, 91

How many cars go to another station? What is the average time a car spends at the station?

9. You have been hired as a consultant by a supermarket chain to answer a basic question: How many items per customer should be permitted in the fast checkout line? This is no trivial question for the chain's management; your findings will be the basis for corporate policy for all 2,000 stores. The vice president of operations has given you one month to do the study and two assistants to help you gather the data.

In starting this study, you decide to avoid queuing theory as the tool for analysis (because of your concern about the reliability of its assumptions) and instead opt for simulation. Given the following data, explain in detail how you would go about your analysis, stating (1) the criteria you would use in making your recommendation, (2) what additional data you would need to set up your simulation, (3) how you would gather the preliminary data, (4) how you would set up the problem for simulation, and (5) which factors would affect the applicability of your findings to all of the stores.

Store locations	The United States and Canada
Hours of operation	16 per day
Average store size	9 checkout stands including fast checkout
Available checkers	7 to 10 (some engage in stocking activities when not at a checkout stand)

10. The saga of Joe from Chapter 19 (Problem 12, page 649) continues. Joe has the opportunity to do a big repair job for a local motorcycle club. (Their cycles were accidentally run over by a garbage truck.) The compensation for the job is good, but it is vital that the total repair time for the five cycles be less than 40 hours. (The leader of the club has stated that he would be very distressed if the cycles were not available for a planned rally.) Joe knows from experience that repairs of this type often entail several trips between processes for a given cycle, so estimates of time are difficult to provide. Still, Joe has the following historical data about the probability that a job will start in each process, processing time in each process, and transitional probabilities between each pair of processes:

Process	Probability of Job Starting in Process	Processing Time Probability (hours)			Probability of Going from Process to Other Processes or Completion (Out)			
		1	2	3	Frame	Engine Work	Painting	Out
Frame repair	0.5	0.2	0.4	0.4	—	0.4	0.4	0.2
Engine work	0.3	0.6	0.1	0.3	0.3	—	0.4	0.3
Painting	0.2	0.3	0.3	0.4	0.1	0.1	—	0.8

Given this information, use simulation to determine the repair times for each cycle. Display your results on a Gantt chart showing an FCFS schedule. (Assume that only one cycle can be worked on at a time in each process.) Based on your simulation, what do you recommend Joe do next?

11. "Eat at Helen's" has decided to add a drive-up window to the restaurant. Due to limited capital, there is enough space for only two cars in the drive-up window lane (one being served and one waiting). Helen would like to know how many customers are bypassing her restaurant due to the limited space in the drive-up window lane. Simulate 10 cars as they attempt to use the drive-up window using the following distributions and random numbers:Use the following two-digit random numbers for this problem:

Time between Arrivals (Minutes)	Probability	Service Time (Minutes)	Probability
1	0.40	1	0.20
2	0.30	2	0.40
3	0.15	3	0.40
4	0.15		

Arrivals: 37, 60, 79, 21, 85, 71, 48, 39, 31, 35
Service: 66, 74, 90, 95, 29, 72, 17, 55, 15, 36

12. Jane's Auto World has a policy of placing an order for 27 of the most popular model whenever inventory reaches 20. Lead time on delivery is two weeks, and 25 automobiles are currently on hand. Simulate 15 weeks' worth of sales using the following probabilities that were derived from historical information:

Sales per Week	Probability	Sales per Week	Probability
5	.05	10	.20
6	.05	11	.20
7	.10	12	.10
8	.10	13	.05
9	.10	14	.05

Use the following random numbers for sales: 23, 59, 82, 83, 61, 00, 48, 33, 06, 32, 82, 51, 54, 66, 55.

Does this policy appear to be appropriate? Explain.

13. A local newspaper vendor sells papers for $.50. The papers cost her $.40, giving her a $.10 profit on each one she sells. From past experience, she knows that

   20% of the time she sells 100 papers
   20% of the time she sells 150 papers
   30% of the time she sells 200 papers
   30% of the time she sells 250 papers

   Assuming that she believes that the cost of a lost sale is $.05 and any unsold papers cost her $.25, simulate her profit outlook over 5 days if she orders 200 papers for each of the 5 days. Use the following random numbers: 51, 07, 55, 87, 53.

14. The daily demand for a high-energy drink from a given vending machine is 20, 21, 22, or 23 with probabilities 0.4, 0.3, 0.2, or 0.1, respectively. Assume the following random numbers have been generated: 08, 54, 74, 66, 52, 58, 03, 22, 89, and 85. Using these numbers, generate the daily drink sales for 10 days.

4.13 Advanced Case: Understanding the Impact of Variability on the Capacity of a Production System

Excel: LineSim

This exercise, which uses LineSim, is an opportunity to study the impact that variability in processing time has on the capacity of a simple serial production system. Much more complex systems could be studied, but our hope is that by studying this simple system, you will gain insight that can be applied to more complex systems..

The system we are studying is similar to the two-stage assembly line discussed in this chapter; here we look at a three-stage assembly line. In practice, assembly lines have many more workstations, but completing an exercise with more workstations would take considerably longer. If you do not believe that your results can be generalized to a larger system, feel free to expand your study.

For this study, we use the Serial Line Simulator (LineSim) that is included on this book's Web site. This Microsoft Excel® spreadsheet simulates a simple serial production line. We are indebted to John McClain at the Johnson Graduate School of Management, Cornell University, for allowing us to use his innovative spreadsheet.

Goal of this Exercise
Our goal in this exercise is that you learn firsthand how variability can impact the performance of multistage production systems. A common approach used to reduce the impact of variability is through some type of buffering mechanism. To be more specific, in our system, variability exists in the amount of time that it takes to perform work at a workstation. In analyzing the system, we use the average time to complete each unit, so sometimes it takes longer and sometimes less time. It probably seldom takes exactly the average time

When there is variability, production engineers put buffer stations between each workstation. These buffers allow the variability to be smoothed so that the variability in one workstation has less impact on the other workstations. An interesting question to study with simulation is if these buffers are eliminated, or if there are 100 units between each workstation, how would this change the performance of the system?

Details of the Exercise
Start with the spreadsheet as Professor McClain configures it initially. Click the "Design" tab, and note that we have a three-station assembly line. The stations are named "Joe," "Next's," and "M2." There is a buffer area downstream from "Joe" with a capacity of one unit and another downstream from "Next's" with a capacity of one unit. The way this simulation is designed, "Joe" will always have something to work on and "M2" can always deposit finished work in a storage area.

Notice that the processing time distribution is Shifted Exponential with a mean of 5 and a standard deviation of 5. The shape of this distribution, described in the "Instructions" tab, shows that there is much process time variation. Answer the following question before going on to the next part of the exercise:

Question 1: How many units would you expect to be able to produce over 100 time periods?

Click the "Run" tab and, using the default values for "Run-In Time," "Run Length," and "Repetitions," run the simulation. Tabulate the average utilization at each machine based on the five repetitions, and tabulate the mean and standard deviation of the output of the system (these data are in the "Machine" worksheet).

Question 2: How many units did you actually produce per 100 time periods? Explain any difference between your simulation result and your estimate made in Question 1.

Next map the impact that increased buffer inventory has on the output of the system. You can change the buffer behind "Joe" and "Next's" by changing the inventory cell designated "Joe's Inventory" (this is on the "Design" worksheet) and then clicking "Make Storage Areas Like #1."

Question 3: Create a graph that shows the impact of changing the buffer stock on the output of the system. Consider buffer levels that vary from 0 to a maximum of 20 units. What can you conclude from your experiment?

Finally, experiment with the impact of a bottleneck in the system.

Question 4: What would be the impact on system performance if "M2" had a processing time that averaged 6 time units? (Assume that "Joe" and "Next's" still run at an average of 5.) What happens to the inventory after "Joe" and "Next's"? Does varying the size of these inventories have any impact?

Question 5: What happens if instead of "M2" being the bottleneck, "Joe" is the bottleneck? Do the buffers at "Joe" and "Next's" have any impact?

Keep your answers brief; your entire report, including graphs, should be no longer than two double-spaced pages.

4.14 Super Quiz

1. This is a powerful tool that allows one to perform experiments using a computer model of a real system.
2. To allow the computer model to consider variability in such items as demand and processing times, these are used.
3. This is the logic that controls the behavior of the simulation.
4. This is the duration of simulation in simulation time or events.
5. This is the term used to check to see whether the computer code adequately represents the real system.
6. True/False: Simulation is most useful when a problem can be solved mathematically.
7. A simulation that jumps from one point in time directly to a second, and then to a third, and so on, is classified as this.

1. Simulation 2. Random numbers 3. Decision rules 4. Run length (or run time) 5. Validation 6. False 7. Discrete

4.15 Selected Bibliography

Kelton, W. D. *Simulation with Arena.* 4th ed. New York: McGraw-Hill, 2006.

Ross, S. M. *Simulation.* 4th ed. Burlington, MA: Academic Press, Elsevier, 2006.

Winston, W. L. *Simulation Modeling Using @RISK.* Belmont, CA: Wadsworth, 2000.

4.16 Footnotes

1. The basic formula is $Z = \frac{x - \mu}{\sigma}$, which when restated in terms of x appears as $x = \mu - Z\sigma$. We then substituted Dn for x and $\bar{x}$ for μ to relate the method more directly to the sample problem.
2. See W. L. Winston, *Simulation Modeling Using @RISK* (Belmont, CA: Wadsworth, 2000). @RISK is a product of Palisade Corporation (http://www.palisade.com).
3. S. W. Haider and J. Banks, "Simulation Software Products for Analyzing Manufacturing Systems," *Industrial Engineering* 18, no. 7 (July 1986), pp. 982103.

Chapter 5

Linear Programming Using the Excel Solver

The key to profitable operations is making the best use of available resources of people, material, plant and equipment, and money. Today's manager has a powerful mathematical modeling tool available for this purpose with linear programming. In this chapter, we will show how the use of the Microsoft Excel Solver to solve LP problems opens a whole new world to the innovative manager and provides an invaluable addition to the technical skill set for those who seek careers in consulting. In this chapter, we use a product-planning problem to introduce this tool. Here we find the optimal mix of products that have different costs and resource requirements. This problem is certainly relevant to today's competitive market. Extremely successful companies provide a mix of products, from standard to high-end luxury models. All these products compete for the use of limited production and other capacity. Maintaining the proper mix of these products over time can significantly bolster earnings and the return on a firm's assets.

We begin with a quick introduction to linear programming and conditions under which the technique is applicable. Then we solve a simple product-mix problem. Other linear programming applications appear throughout the rest of the book.

5.1 Introduction

Linear programming (LP)

Linear programming (or simply **LP**) refers to several related mathematical techniques used to allocate limited resources among competing demands in an optimal way. LP is the most widely used of the approaches falling under the general heading of mathematical optimization techniques and has been applied to many operations management problems. The following are typical applications:

Aggregate sales and operations planning: Finding the minimum-cost production schedule. The problem is to develop a three- to six-month plan for meeting expected demand given constraints on expected production capacity and workforce size. Relevant costs considered in the problem include regular and overtime labor rates, hiring and firing, subcontracting, and inventory carrying cost.

Service/manufacturing productivity analysis: Comparing how efficiently different service and manufacturing outlets are using their resources compared to the best-performing unit. This is done using an approach called data envelopment analysis.

Product planning: Finding the optimal product mix where several products have different costs and resource requirements. Examples include finding the optimal blend of chemicals for gasoline, paints, human diets, and animal feeds. Examples of this problem are covered in this chapter.

Product routing: Finding the optimal way to produce a product that must be processed sequentially through several machine centers, with each machine in the center having its own cost and output characteristics.

Vehicle/crew scheduling: Finding the optimal way to use resources such as aircraft, buses, or trucks and their operating crews to provide transportation services to customers and materials to be moved between different locations.

Process control: Minimizing the amount of scrap material generated by cutting steel, leather, or fabric from a roll or sheet of stock material.

Inventory control: Finding the optimal combination of products to stock in a network of warehouses or storage locations.

Distribution scheduling: Finding the optimal shipping schedule for distributing products between factories and warehouses or between warehouses and retailers.

Plant location studies: Finding the optimal location of a new plant by evaluating shipping costs between alternative locations and supply and demand sources.

Material handling: Finding the minimum-cost routings of material-handling devices (such as forklift trucks) between departments in a plant, or hauling materials from a supply yard to work sites by trucks, for example. Each truck might have different capacity and performance capabilities.

Linear programming is gaining wide acceptance in many industries due to the availability of detailed operating information and the interest in optimizing processes to reduce cost. Many software vendors offer optimization options to be used with enterprise resource planning systems. Some firms refer to these as *advanced planning option, synchronized planning*, and *process optimization.*

For linear programming to pertain in a problem situation, five essential conditions must be met. First, there must be *limited resources* (such as a limited number of workers, equipment, finances, and material); otherwise there would be no problem. Second, there must be an *explicit objective* (such as maximize profit or minimize cost). Third, there must be *linearity* (two is twice as much as one; if three hours are needed to make a part, then two parts would take six hours and three parts would take nine hours). Fourth, there must be *homogeneity* (the products produced on a machine are identical, or all the hours available from a worker are equally productive). Fifth, there must be *divisibility*: Normal linear programming assumes products and resources can be subdivided into fractions. If this subdivision is not possible (such as flying half an airplane or hiring one-fourth of a person), a modification of linear programming, called *integer programming*, can be used.

When a single objective is to be maximized (like profit) or minimized (like costs), we can use linear programming. When multiple objectives exist, *goal programming* is used. If a problem is best solved in stages or time frames, *dynamic programming* is employed. Other restrictions on the nature of the problem may require that it be solved by other variations of the technique, such as *nonlinear programming* or *quadratic programming.*

5.2 The Linear Programming Model

Stated formally, the linear programming problem entails an optimizing process in which nonnegative values for a set of decision variables $x_1, x_2, \ldots, x_n$ are selected so as to maximize (or minimize) an objective function in the form

$$\text{Maximize (minimize) } Z = C_1X_1 + C_2X_2 + \ldots + C_nX_n$$

subject to resource constraints in the form

$$A_{11}X_1 + A_{12}X_2 + \ldots + A_{1n}X_n \leq B_1$$
$$A_{21}X_1 + A_{22}X_2 + \ldots + A_{2n}X_n \leq B_2$$
.
.
.
$$A_{m1}X_1 + A_{m2}X_2 + \ldots + A_{mn}X_n \leq B_m$$

where C_n, A_{mn}, and B_m are given constants.

Depending on the problem, the constraints also may be stated with equal signs ($=$) or greater-than-or-equal-to signs ($\geq$).

5.1 Example

Puck and Pawn Company

Step by Step

Tutorial: Intro to Solver

We describe the steps involved in solving a simple linear programming model in the context of a sample problem, that of Puck and Pawn Company, which manufactures hockey sticks and chess sets. Each hockey stick yields an incremental profit of $2, and each chess set, $4. A hockey stick requires 4 hours of processing at machine center A and 2 hours at machine center B. A chess set requires 6 hours at machine center A, 6 hours at machine center B, and 1 hour at machine center C. Machine center A has a maximum of 120 hours of available capacity per day, machine center B has 72 hours, and machine center C has 10 hours.

If the company wishes to maximize profit, how many hockey sticks and chess sets should be produced per day?

Solution

Formulate the problem in mathematical terms. If H is the number of hockey sticks and C is the number of chess sets, to maximize profit the objective function may be stated as

$$\text{Maximize } Z = \$2H + \$4C$$

The maximization will be subject to the following constraints:

$$4H + 6C \leq 120 \quad \text{(machine center A constraint)}$$
$$2H + 6C \leq 72 \quad \text{(machine center B constraint)}$$
$$1C \leq 10 \quad \text{(machine center C constraint)}$$
$$H, C \geq 0 \; \bullet$$

This formulation satisfies the five requirements for standard LP stated in the first section of this chapter:

1. There are limited resources (a finite number of hours available at each machine center).
2. There is an explicit objective function (we know what each variable is worth and what the goal is in solving the problem).
3. The equations are linear (no exponents or cross-products).
4. The resources are homogeneous (everything is in one unit of measure, machine hours).
5. The decision variables are divisible and nonnegative (we can make a fractional part of a hockey stick or chess set; however, if this were deemed undesirable, we would have to use integer programming).

5.3   Graphical Linear Programming

Graphical linear programming

Though limited in application to problems involving two decision variables (or three variables for three-dimensional graphing), **graphical linear programming** provides a quick insight into the nature of linear programming. We describe the steps involved in the graphical method in the context of Puck and Pawn Company. The following steps illustrate the graphical approach:

1. **Formulate the problem in mathematical terms.**   The equations for the problem are given above.
2. **Plot constraint equations.**   The constraint equations are easily plotted by letting one variable equal zero and solving for the axis intercept of the other. (The inequality portions of the restrictions are disregarded for this step.) For the machine center A constraint equation, when $H = 0$, $C = 20$, and when $C = 0$, $H = 30$. For the machine center B constraint equation, when $H = 0$, $C = 12$, and when $C = 0$, $H = 36$. For the machine center C constraint equation, $C = 10$ for all values of H. These lines are graphed in Exhibit 5.1.
3. **Determine the area of feasibility.**   The direction of inequality signs in each constraint determines the area where a feasible solution is found. In this case, all inequalities are of the less-than-or-equal-to variety, which means it would be impossible to produce any combination of products that would lie to the right of any constraint line on the graph. The region of feasible solutions is unshaded on the graph and forms a convex polygon. A convex polygon exists when a line drawn between any two points in the polygon stays within the boundaries of that polygon. If this condition of convexity does not exist, the problem is either incorrectly set up or is not amenable to linear programming.
4. **Plot the objective function.**   The objective function may be plotted by assuming some arbitrary total profit figure and then solving for the axis coordinates, as was done for the constraint equations. Other terms for the objective function when used in this context are the *iso-profit* or *equal contribution line*, because it shows all possible production combinations for any given profit figure. For example, from the dotted line closest to the origin on the graph, we can determine all possible combinations of hockey sticks and chess sets that yield $32 by picking a point on the line and reading the number of each product that can be made at that point. The combination yielding $32 at point *a* would be 10 hockey sticks and three chess sets. This can be verified by substituting $H = 10$ and $C = 3$ in the objective function:

$$\$2(10) + \$4(3) = \$20 + \$12 = \$32$$

GRAPH OF HOCKEY STICK AND CHESS SET PROBLEM

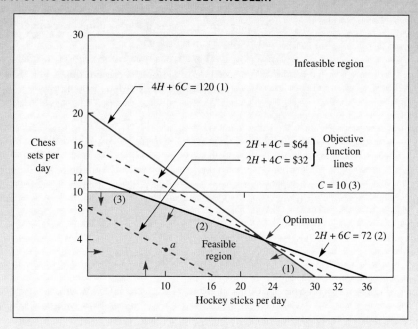

H	C	Explanation
0	120/6 = 20	Intersection of Constraint (1) and C axis
120/4 = 30	0	Intersection of Constraint (1) and H axis
0	72/6 = 12	Intersection of Constraint (2) and C axis
72/2 = 36	0	Intersection of Constraint (2) and H axis
0	10	Intersection of Constraint (3) and C axis
0	32/4 = 8	Intersection of $32 iso-profit line (objective function) and C axis
32/2 = 16	0	Intersection of $32 iso-profit line and H axis
0	64/4 = 16	Intersection of $64 iso-profit line and C axis
64/2 = 32	0	Intersection of $64 iso-profit line and H axis

5. **Find the optimum point.** It can be shown mathematically that the optimal combination of decision variables is always found at an extreme point (corner point) of the convex polygon. In Exhibit 5.1, there are four corner points (excluding the origin), and we can determine which one is the optimum by either of two approaches. The first approach is to find the values of the various corner solutions algebraically. This entails simultaneously solving the equations of various pairs of intersecting lines and substituting the quantities of the resultant variables in the objective function. For example, the calculations for the intersection of $2H + 6C = 72$ and $C = 10$ are as follows:

Substituting $C = 10$ in $2H + 6C = 72$ gives $2H + 6(10) = 72$, $2H = 12$, or $H = 6$. Substituting $H = 6$ and $C = 10$ in the objective function, we get

$$\text{Profit} = \$2H + \$4C = \$2(6) + \$4(10)$$
$$= \$12 + \$40 = \$52$$

117

A variation of this approach is to read the *H* and *C* quantities directly from the graph and substitute these quantities into the objective function, as shown in the previous calculation. The drawback in this approach is that in problems with a large number of constraint equations, there will be many possible points to evaluate, and the procedure of testing each one mathematically is inefficient.

The second and generally preferred approach entails using the objective function or iso-profit line directly to find the optimum point. The procedure involves simply drawing a straight line *parallel* to any arbitrarily selected initial iso-profit line so the iso-profit line is farthest from the origin of the graph. (In cost minimization problems, the objective would be to draw the line through the point closest to the origin.) In Exhibit 5.1, the dashed line labeled $2*H* + $4*C* = $64 intersects the most extreme point. Note that the initial arbitrarily selected iso-profit line is necessary to display the slope of the objective function for the particular problem.[1] This is important since a different objective function (try Profit = 3*H* + 3*C*) might indicate that some other point is farthest from the origin. Given that $2*H* + $4*C* = $64 is optimal, the amount of each variable to produce can be read from the graph: 24 hockey sticks and four chess sets. No other combination of the products yields a greater profit.

5.4 Linear Programming Using Microsoft Excel

Spreadsheets can be used to solve linear programming problems. Microsoft Excel has an optimization tool called *Solver* that we will demonstrate by solving the hockey stick and chess problem. We invoke the Solver from the Data tab. A dialogue box requests information required by the program. The following example describes how our sample problem can be solved using Excel.

If the Solver option does not appear in your Data tab, click on Excel Options → Add-Ins, select the Solver Add-In, and then click OK. Solver should then be available directly from the Data tab for future use.

In the following example, we work in a step-by-step manner, setting up a spreadsheet and then solving our Puck and Pawn Company problem. Our basic strategy is to first define the problem within the spreadsheet. Following this, we invoke the Solver and feed it required information. Finally, we execute the Solver and interpret results from the reports provided by the program.

Step 1: Define Changing Cells   A convenient starting point is to identify cells to be used for the decision variables in the problem. These are *H* and *C*, the number of hockey sticks and the number of chess sets to produce. Excel refers to these cells as changing cells in Solver. Referring to our Excel screen (Exhibit 5.2), we have designated B4 as the location for the number of hockey sticks to produce and C4 for the number of chess sets. Note that we have set these cells equal to 2 initially. We could set these cells to anything, but a value other than zero will help verify that our calculations are correct.

Step 2: Calculate Total Profit (or Cost)   This is our objective function and is calculated by multiplying profit associated with each product by the number of units produced. We have placed the profits in cells B5 and C5 ($2 and $4), so the profit is calculated by the following equation: B4*B5 + C4*C5, which is calculated in cell D5. Solver refers to this as the Target Cell, and it corresponds to the objective function for a problem.

Step 3: Set Up Resource Usage   Our resources are machine centers A, B, and C as defined in the original problem. We have set up three rows (9, 10, and 11) in our spreadsheet, one for each resource constraint. For machine center A, 4 hours of processing time are used

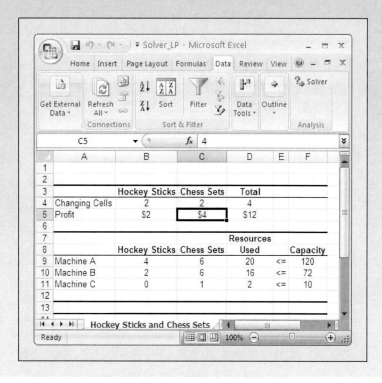

**Excel:
Solver LP**

for each hockey stick produced (cell B9) and 6 hours for each chess set (cell C9). For a particular solution, the total amount of the machine center A resource used is calculated in D9 (B9*B4 + C9*C4). We have indicated in cell E9 that we want this value to be less than the 120-hour capacity of machine center A, which is entered in F9. Resource usage for machine centers B and C is set up in the exact same manner in rows 10 and 11.

Step 4: Set Up Solver Go to the Data tab and select the Solver option.

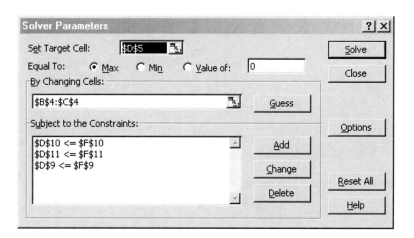

1. Set Target Cell: is set to the location where the value that we want to optimize is calculated. This is the profit calculated in D5 in our spreadsheet.
2. Equal To: is set to Max since the goal is to maximize profit.
3. By Changing Cells: are the cells that Solver can change to maximize profit. Cells B4 through C4 are the changing cells in our problem.
4. Subject to the Constraints: corresponds to our machine center capacity. Here we click on Add and indicate that the total used for a resource is less than or equal to the capacity available. A sample for machine center A follows. Click OK after each constraint is specified.

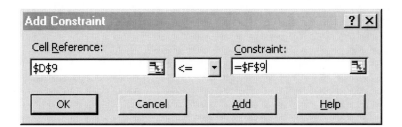

5. Clicking on Options allows us to tell Solver what type of problem we want it to solve and how we want it solved. Solver has numerous options, but we will need to use only a few. The screen is shown below.

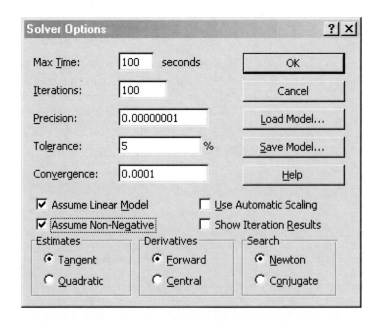

Most of the options relate to how Solver attempts to solve nonlinear problems. These can be very difficult to solve, and optimal solutions difficult to find. Luckily our problem is a linear problem. We know this since our constraints and our objective function are all calculated using linear equations. Click on Assume Linear Model to tell Solver that we want to use the linear programming option for solving the problem. In addition, we know our changing cells (decision variables) must be numbers that are greater than or equal to zero since it makes no sense to make a negative number of hockey sticks or chess sets. We indicate this by selecting Assume Non-Negative as an option. We are now ready to actually solve the problem. Click OK to return to the Solver Parameters box.

Step 5: Solve the Problem   Click Solve. We immediately get a Solver Results acknowledgment like that shown below.

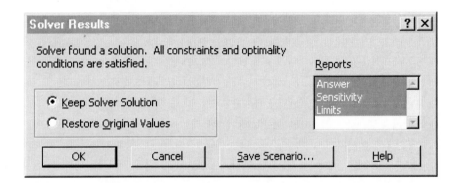

Solver acknowledges that a solution was found that appears to be optimal. On the right side of this box are options for three reports: an Answer Report, a Sensitivity Report, and a Limits Report. Click on each report to have Solver provide these. After highlighting the reports, click OK to exit back to the spreadsheet. Three new tabs have been created that correspond to these reports.

The most interesting reports for our problem are the Answer Report and the Sensitivity Report, both of which are shown in Exhibit 5.3. The Answer Report shows the final answers for the total profit ($64) and the amounts produced (24 hockey sticks and 4 chess sets). In the constraints section of the Answer Report, the status of each resource is given. All of machine A and machine B are used, and there are six units of slack for machine C.

The Sensitivity Report is divided into two parts. The first part, titled "Adjustable Cells," corresponds to objective function coefficients. The profit per unit for the hockey sticks can be either up or down $0.67 (between $2.67 and $1.33) without having an impact on the solution. Similarly, the profit of the chess sets could be between $6 and $3 without changing the solution. In the case of machine A, the right-hand side could increase to 144 (120 + 24) or decrease to 84 with a resulting $0.33 increase or decrease per unit in the objective function. The right-hand side of machine B can increase to 90 units or decrease to 60 units with the same $0.33 change for each unit in the objective function. For machine C, the right-hand side could increase to infinity (1E+30 is scientific notation for a very large number) or decrease to 4 units with no change in the objective function.

EXCEL SOLVER ANSWER AND SENSITIVITY REPORTS

Answer Report

Target Cell (Max)

Cell	Name	Original Value	Final Value
$D$5	Profit Total	$12	$64

Adjustable Cells

Cell	Name	Original Value	Final Value
$B$4	Changing Cells Hockey Sticks	2	24
$C$4	Changing Cells Chess Sets	2	4

Constraints

Cell	Name	Cell Value	Formula	Status	Slack
$D$11	Machine C Used	4	$D$11<=$F$11	Not Binding	6
$D$10	Machine B Used	72	$D$10<=$F$10	Binding	0
$D$9	Machine A Used	120	$D$9<=$F$9	Binding	0

Sensitivity Report

Adjustable Cells

Cell	Name	Final Value	Reduced Cost	Objective Coefficient	Allowable Increase	Allowable Decrease
$B$4	Changing Cells Hockey Sticks	24	0	2	0.666666667	0.666666667
$C$4	Changing Cells Chess Sets	4	0	4	2	1

Constraints

Cell	Name	Final Value	Shadow Price	Constraint R.H. Side	Allowable Increase	Allowable Decrease
$D$11	Machine C Used	4	0	10	1E+30	6
$D$10	Machine B Used	72	0.333333333	72	18	12
$D$9	Machine A Used	120	0.333333333	120	24	36

5.5 Key Terms

Linear programming (LP) Refers to several related mathematical techniques used to allocate limited resources among competing demands in an optimal way.

Graphical linear programming Provides a quick insight into the nature of linear programming.

5.6 Solved Problems

Solved Problem 1

A furniture company produces three products: end tables, sofas, and chairs. These products are processed in five departments: the saw lumber, fabric cutting, sanding, staining, and assembly departments. End tables and chairs are produced from raw lumber only, and the sofas require lumber and fabric. Glue and thread are plentiful and represent a relatively insignificant cost that is included in operating expense. The specific requirements for each product are as follows:

Resource or Activity (quantity available per month)	Required per End Table	Required per Sofa	Required per Chair
Lumber (4,350 board feet)	10 board feet @ $10/foot = $100/table	7.5 board feet @ $10/foot = $75	4 board feet @ $10/foot = $40
Fabric (2,500 yards)	None	10 yards @ $17.50/ yard = $175	None
Saw lumber (280 hours)	30 minutes	24 minutes	30 minutes
Cut fabric (140 hours)	None	24 minutes	None
Sand (280 hours)	30 minutes	6 minutes	30 minutes
Stain (140 hours)	24 minutes	12 minutes	24 minutes
Assemble (700 hours)	60 minutes	90 minutes	30 minutes

The company's direct labor expenses are $75,000 per month for the 1,540 hours of labor, at $48.70 per hour. Based on current demand, the firm can sell 300 end tables, 180 sofas, and 400 chairs per month. Sales prices are $400 for end tables, $750 for sofas, and $240 for chairs. Assume that labor cost is fixed and the firm does not plan to hire or fire any employees over the next month.

Required:

1. What is the most limiting resource to the furniture company?
2. Determine the product mix needed to maximize profit at the furniture company. What is the optimal number of end tables, sofas, and chairs to produce each month?

Solution

Define X_1 as the number of end tables, X_2 as the number of sofas, and X_3 as the number of chairs to produce each month. Profit is calculated as the revenue for each item minus the cost of materials (lumber and fabric), minus the cost of labor. Since labor is fixed, we subtract this out as a total sum. Mathematically we have $(400 - 100)X_1 + (750 - 75 - 175)X_2 + (240 - 40)X_3 - 75,000$. Profit is calculated as follows:

$$\text{Profit} = 300X_1 + 500X_2 + 200X_3 - 75,000$$

Constraints are the following:

Lumber: $10X_1 + 7.5X_2 + 4X_3 \leq 4,350$
Fabric: $10X_2 \leq 2,500$
Saw: $.5X_1 + .4X_2 + .5X_3 \leq 280$
Cut: $.4X_2 \leq 140$
Sand: $.5X_1 + .1X_2 + .5X_3 \leq 280$
Stain: $.4X_1 + .2X_2 + .4X_3 \leq 140$
Assemble: $1X_1 + 1.5X_2 + .5X_3 \leq 700$
Demand:

Table: $X_1 \leq 300$
Sofa: $X_2 \leq 180$
Chair: $X_3 \leq 400$

Step 1: Define Changing Cells These are B3, C3, and D3. Note that these cells have been set equal to zero.

	E4		f_x =B4*$B$3+C4*$C$3+D4*$D$3-75000				
	A	B	C	D	E	F	
1	Furniture Company						
2		End Tables	Sofas	Chairs	Total	Limit	
3	Changing cells	0	0	0			
4	Profit	$300	$500	$200	-$75,000		
5							
6	Lumber	10	7.5	4	0	4350	
7	Fabric	0	10	0	0	2500	
8	Saw	0.5	0.4	0.5	0	280	
9	Cut fabric	0	0.4	0	0	140	
10	Sand	0.5	0.1	0.5	0	280	
11	Stain	0.4	0.2	0.4	0	140	
12	Assemble	1	1.5	0.5	0	700	
13	Table Demand	1			0	300	
14	Sofa Demand		1		0	180	
15	Chair Demand			1	0	400	
16							

H ◀ ▶ H\ Solved Problem
Ready   NUM

Step 2: Calculate Total Profit This is E4 (this is equal to B3 times the $300 revenue associated with each end table, plus C3 times the $500 revenue for each sofa, plus D3 times the $200 revenue associated with each chair). Note the $75,000 fixed expense that has been subtracted from revenue to calculate profit.

Step 3: Set Up Resource Usage In cells E6 through E15, the usage of each resource is calculated by multiplying B3, C3, and D3 by the amount needed for each item and summing the product (for example, E6 = B3*B6 + C3*C6 + D3*D6). The limits on these constraints are entered in cells F6 to F15.

Step 4: Set Up Solver Go to Tools and select the Solver option.

Solver Parameters

Set Target Cell: $E$4

Equal To: ● Max ○ Min ○ Value of: 0

By Changing Cells:
$B$3:$D$3   Guess

Subject to the Constraints:
$E$6:$E$15 <= $F$6:$F$15   Add   Change   Delete

Solve   Close   Options   Reset All   Help

a. Set Target Cell: is set to the location where the value that we want to optimize is calculated. This is the profit calculated in E4 in this spreadsheet.

b. Equal To: is set to Max since the goal is to maximize profit.

c. By Changing Cells: are the cells that Solver can change to maximize profit (cells B3 through D3 in this problem).

d. Subject to the Constraints: is where a constraint set is added; we indicate that the range E6 to E15 must be less than or equal to F6 to F15.

Add Constraint ? | X

Cell Reference: | | Constraint:
$E$6:$E$15 | <= ▼ | =$F$6:$F$15

OK | Cancel | Add | Help

Step 5: Set Options   There are many options here, but for our purposes we just need to indicate Assume Linear Model and Assume Non-Negative. Assume Linear Model means all of our formulas are simple linear equations. Assume Non-Negative indicates that changing cells must be greater than or equal to zero. Click OK and we are ready to solve our problem.

Solver Options ? | X

Max Time: 100 seconds | OK
Iterations: 100 | Cancel
Precision: 0.000001 | Load Model...
Tolerance: 5 % | Save Model...
Convergence: 0.0001 | Help

☑ Assume Linear Model   ☐ Use Automatic Scaling
☑ Assume Non-Negative   ☐ Show Iteration Results

Estimates | Derivatives | Search
◉ Tangent | ◉ Forward | ◉ Newton
○ Quadratic | ○ Central | ○ Conjugate

Step 6: Solve the Problem   Click Solve. We can see the solution and two special reports by highlighting items on the Solver Results acknowledgment that is displayed after a solution is found. Note that in the following report, Solver indicates that it has found a solution and all constraints and optimality conditions are satisfied. In the Reports box on the right, the Answer, Sensitivity, and Limits options have been highlighted, indicating that we would like to see these items. After highlighting the reports, click OK to exit back to the spreadsheet.

Solver Results ? | X

Solver found a solution. All constraints and optimality conditions are satisfied.

Reports
Answer
Sensitivity
Limits

◉ Keep Solver Solution
○ Restore Original Values

OK | Cancel | Save Scenario... | Help

Note that three new tabs have been created: an Answer Report, a Sensitivity Report, and a Limits Report. The Answer Report indicates in the Target Cell section that the profit associated with this solution is $93,000 (we started at −$75,000). From the Target Cell section, we should make 260 end tables, 180 sofas, and no chairs. From the Constraints section, notice that the only constraints limiting profit are the staining capacity and the demand for sofas. We can see this from the column indicating whether a constraint is binding or nonbinding. Nonbinding constraints have slack, as indicated in the last column.

Target Cell (Max)

Cell	Name	Original Value	Final Value
$E$4	Profit Total	−$75,000	$93,000

Adjustable Cells

Cell	Name	Original Value	Final Value
$B$3	Changing cells End Tables	0	260
$C$3	Changing cells Sofas	0	180
$D$3	Changing cells Chairs	0	0

Constraints

Cell	Name	Cell Value	Formula	Status	Slack
$E$6	Lumber Total	3950	$E$6<=$F$6	Not Binding	400
$E$7	Fabric Total	1800	$E$7<=$F$7	Not Binding	700
$E$8	Saw Total	202	$E$8<=$F$8	Not Binding	78
$E$9	Cut fabric Total	72	$E$9<=$F$9	Not Binding	68
$E$10	Sand Total	148	$E$10<=$F$10	Not Binding	132
$E$11	Stain Total	140	$E$11<=$F$11	Binding	0
$E$12	Assemble Total	530	$E$12<=$F$12	Not Binding	170
$E$13	Table Demand Total	260	$E$13<=$F$13	Not Binding	40
$E$14	Sofa Demand Total	180	$E$14<=$F$14	Binding	0
$E$15	Chair Demand Total	0	$E$15<=$F$15	Not Binding	400

Of course, we may not be too happy with this solution since we are not meeting all the demand for tables, and it may not be wise to totally discontinue the manufacturing of chairs.

The Sensitivity Report (shown below) gives additional insight into the solution. The Adjustable Cells section of this report shows the final value for each cell and the reduced cost. The reduced cost indicates how much the target cell value would change if a cell that was currently set to zero were brought into the solution. Since the end tables (B3) and sofas (C3) are in the current solution, their reduced cost is zero. For each chair (D3) that we make, our target cell would be reduced $100 (just round these numbers for interpretation purposes). The final three columns in the adjustable cells section of the report are the Objective Coefficient from the original spreadsheet and columns titled Allowable Increase and Allowable Decrease. Allowable Increase and Decrease show by how much the value of the corresponding coefficient could change so there would not be a change in the changing cell values (of course, the target cell value would change). For example, revenue for each end table could be as high as $1,000 ($300 + $700) or as low as $200 ($300 − $100), and we would still want to produce 260 end tables. Keep in mind that these values assume nothing else is changing in the problem. For the allowable increase value for sofas, note the value 1E+30. This is a very large number, essentially infinity, represented in scientific notation.

For the Constraints section of the report, the actual final usage of each resource is given in Final Value. The Shadow Price is the value to our target cell for each unit increase in the resource. If we could increase staining capacity, it would be worth $750 per hour. The Constraint Right-Hand Side

Adjustable Cells

Cell	Name	Final Value	Reduced Cost	Objective Coefficient	Allowable Increase	Allowable Decrease
$B$3	Changing cells End Tables	260	0	299.9999997	700.0000012	100.0000004
$C$3	Changing cells Sofas	180	0	500.0000005	1E+30	350.0000006
$D$3	Changing cells Chairs	0	−100.0000004	199.9999993	100.0000004	1E+30

Constraints

Cell	Name	Final Value	Shadow Price	Constraint R.H. Side	Allowable Increase	Allowable Decrease
$E$6	Lumber Total	3950	0	4350	1E+30	400
$E$7	Fabric Total	1800	0	2500	1E+30	700
$E$8	Saw Total	202	0	280	1E+30	78
$E$9	Cut fabric Total	72	0	140	1E+30	68
$E$10	Sand Total	148	0	280	1E+30	132
$E$11	Stain Total	140	749.9999992	140	16	104
$E$12	Assemble Total	530	0	700	1E+30	170
$E$13	Table Demand Total	260	0	300	1E+30	40
$E$14	Sofa Demand Total	180	350.0000006	180	70	80
$E$15	Chair Demand Total	0	0	400	1E+30	400

is the current limit on the resource. Allowable Increase is the amount the resource could be increased while the shadow price is still valid. Another 16 hours' work of staining capacity could be added with a value of $750 per hour. Similarly, the Allowable Decrease column shows the amount the resource could be reduced without changing the shadow price. There is some valuable information available in this report.

The Limits Report provides additional information about our solution.

Cell	Target Name	Value				
$E$4	Profit Total	$93,000				
Cell	Adjustable Name	Value	Lower Limit	Target Result	Upper Limit	Target Result
$B$3	Changing cells End Tables	260	0	15000	260.0000002	93000
$C$3	Changing cells Sofas	180	0	3000	180	93000
$D$3	Changing cells Chairs	0	0	93000	0	93000

Total profit for the current solution is $93,000. Current value for B3 (end tables) is 260 units. If this were reduced to 0 units, profit would be reduced to $15,000. At an upper limit of 260, profit is $93,000 (the current solution). Similarly, for C3 (sofas), if this were reduced to 0, profit would be reduced to $3,000. At an upper limit of 180, profit is $93,000. For D3 (chairs), if this were reduced to 0, profit is $93,000 (current solution), and in this case the upper limit on chairs is also 0 units.

Acceptable answers to the questions are as follows:

1. *What is the most limiting resource to the furniture company?*
   In terms of our production resources, staining capacity is really hurting profit at this time. We could use another 16 hours of capacity.

2. *Determine the product mix needed to maximize profit at the furniture company.*
   The product mix would be to make 260 end tables, 180 sofas, and no chairs.

Of course, we have only scratched the surface with this solution. We could actually experiment with increasing staining capacity. This would give insight into the next most limiting resource. We also could run scenarios where we are required to produce a minimum number of each product, which is probably a more realistic scenario. This could help us determine how we could possibly reallocate the use of labor in our shop.

Solved Problem 2

It is 2:00 on Friday afternoon and Joe Bob, the head chef (grill cook) at Bruce's Diner, is trying to decide the best way to allocate the available raw material to the four Friday night specials. The decision has to be made in the early afternoon because three of the items must be started now (Sloppy Joes, Tacos, and Chili). The table below contains the information on the food in inventory and the amounts required for each item.

Food	Cheese Burger	Sloppy Joes	Taco	Chili	Available
Ground Beef (lbs.)	0.3	0.25	0.25	0.4	100 lbs.
Cheese (lbs.)	0.1	0	0.3	0.2	50 lbs.
Beans (lbs.)	0	0	0.2	0.3	50 lbs.
Lettuce (lbs.)	0.1	0	0.2	0	15 lbs.
Tomato (lbs.)	0.1	0.3	0.2	0.2	50 lbs.
Buns	1	1	0	0	80 buns
Taco Shells	0	0	1	0	80 shells

One other fact relevant to Joe Bob's decision is the estimated market demand and selling price.

	Cheese Burger	Sloppy Joes	Taco	Chili
Demand	75	60	100	55
Selling Price	$2.25	$2.00	$1.75	$2.50

Joe Bob wants to maximize revenue since he has already purchased all the materials that are sitting in the cooler.

Required:

1. What is the best mix of the Friday night specials to maximize Joe Bob's revenue?
2. If a supplier offered to provide a rush order of buns at $1.00 a bun, is it worth the money?

Solution

Define X_1 as the number of Cheese Burgers, X_2 as the number of Sloppy Joes, X_3 as the number of Tacos, and X_4 as the number of bowls of chili made for the Friday night specials.

$$\text{Revenue} = \$2.25\, X_1 + \$2.00\, X_2 + \$1.75\, X_3 + \$2.50\, X_4$$

Constraints are the following:

Ground Beef: $0.30\, X_1 + 0.25\, X_2 + 0.25\, X_3 + 0.40\, X_4 \le 100$

Cheese: $0.10\, X_1 + 0.30\, X_3 + 0.20\, X_4 \le 50$

Beans: $0.20\, X_3 + 0.30\, X_4 \le 50$

Lettuce: $0.10\, X_1 + 0.20\, X_3 \le 15$

Tomato: $0.10\, X_1 + 0.30\, X_2 + 0.20\, X_3 + 0.20\, X_4 \le 50$

Buns: $X_1 + X_2 \leq 80$

Taco Shells: $X_3 \leq 80$

Demand

Cheese Burger $X_1 \leq 75$

Sloppy Joes $X_2 \leq 60$

Taco $X_3 \leq 100$

Chili $X_4 \leq 55$

Step 1: Define the Changing Cells   These are B3, C3, D3, and E3. Note the values in the changing cell are set to 10 each so the formulas can be checked.

	F7		fx =SUMPRODUCT($B$3:$E$3,B7:E7)					
	A	B	C	D	E	F	G	H
1								
2		Cheese Burger	Sloppy Joes	Taco	Chili			
3	Changing Cells	10	10	10	10			
4		>=	>=	>=	>=			
5	Demand	75	60	100	55			
6						Total		
7	Revenue	$ 2.25	$ 2.00	$ 1.75	$ 2.50	$ 85.00		
8								
9								
10	Food	Cheese Burger	Sloppy Joes	Taco	Chili	Total		Available
11	Ground Beef (lbs.)	0.3	0.25	0.25	0.4	12.00 <=		100
12	Cheese (lbs.)	0.1	0	0.3	0.2	6.00 <=		50
13	Beans (lbs.)	0	0	0.2	0.3	5.00 <=		50
14	Lettuce (lbs.)	0.1	0	0.2	0	3.00 <=		15
15	Tomato (lbs.)	0.1	0.3	0.2	0.2	8.00 <=		50
16	Buns	1	1	0	0	20.00 <=		80
17	Taco Shells	0	0	1	0	10.00 <=		80
18								

Step 2: Calculate Total Revenue   This is in cell F7 (this is equal to B3 times the $2.25 for each cheese burger, plus C3 times the $2.00 for a Sloppy Joe, plus D3 times the $1.75 for each taco, plus E3 times the $2.50 for each bowl of chili; the SUMPRODUCT function in Excel was used to make this calculation faster). Note that the current value is $85, which is a result of selling 10 of each item.

Step 3: Set Up the Usage of the Food   In cells F11 to F17, the usage of each food is calculated by multiplying the changing cells row times the per item use in the table and then summing the result. The limits on each of these food types are given in H11 through H17.

Step 4: Set Up Solver and Select the Solver Option

a. Set Target Cell: is set to the location where the value that we want to optimize is calculated. The revenue is calculated in F7 in this spreadsheet.

b. Equal to: is set to Max since the goal is to maximize revenue.

c. By Changing Cells: are the cells that tell how many of each special to produce.

d. Subject to the Constraints: is where we add two separate constraints, one for demand and one for the usage of food.

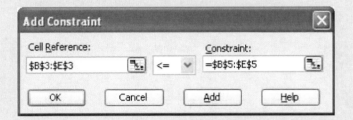

Step 5: Set Options Click on Options. We will leave all the settings as the default values and only need to make sure of two changes: (1) check the Assume Linear Model option and (2) check the Assume Non-Negative option. These two options make sure that Solver knows that this is a linear programming problem and that all changing cells should be nonnegative. Click OK to return to the Solver Parameters screen.

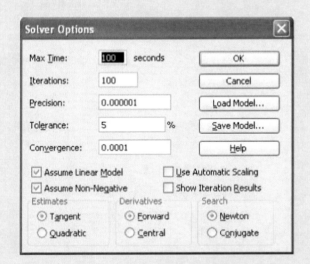

Step 6: Solve the Problem Click Solve. We will get a Solver Results box. Make sure it says that it has the following statement: "Solver found a solution. All constraints and optimality conditions are satisfied."

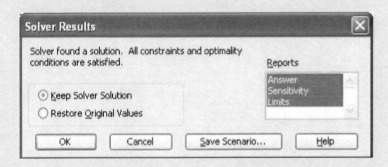

On the right-hand side of the box, there is an option for three reports: Answer, Sensitivity, and Limit. Click on all three reports and then click OK; this will exit you back to the spreadsheet, but you will have three new worksheets in your workbook.

The answer report indicates that the target cell has a final solution of $416.25 and started at $85. From the adjustable cells area we can see that we should make 20 cheese burgers, 60 Sloppy Joes, 65 tacos, and 55 bowls of chili. This answers the first requirement from the problem of what the mix of Friday night specials should be.

Target Cell (Max)

Cell	Name	Original Value	Fiinal Value
$F$7	Revenue Total	$85.00	$416.25

Adjustable Cells

Cell	Name	Original Value	Final Value
$B$3	Changing Cells Cheese Burger	10	20
$C$3	Changing Cells Sloppy Joes	10	60
$D$3	Changing Cells Taco	10	65
$E$3	Changing Cells Chili	10	55

Constraints

Cell	Name	Cell Value	Formula	Status	Slack
$F$11	Ground Beef (lbs.) Total	59.25	$F$11<=$H$11	Not Binding	40.75
$F$12	Cheese (lbs.) Total	32.50	$F$12<=$H$12	Not Binding	17.5
$F$13	Beans (lbs.) Total	29.50	$F$13<=$H$13	Not Binding	20.5
$F$14	Lettuce (lbs.) Total	15.00	$F$14<=$H$14	Binding	0
$F$15	Tomato (lbs.) Total	44.00	$F$15<=$H$15	Not Binding	6
$F$16	Buns Total	80.00	$F$16<=$H$16	Binding	0
$F$17	Taco Shells Total	65.00	$F$17<=$H$17	Not Binding	15
$B$3	Changing Cells Cheese Burger	20	$B$3<=$B$5	Not Binding	55
$C$3	Changing Cells Sloppy Joes	60	$C$3<=$C$5	Binding	0
$D$3	Changing Cells Taco	65	$D$3<=$D$5	Not Binding	35
$E$3	Changing Cells Chili	55	$E$3<=$E$5	Binding	0

The second required answer was whether it is worth it to pay a rush supplier $1 a bun for additional buns. The answer report shows us that the buns constraint was binding. This means that if we had more buns, we could make more money. However, the answer report does not tell us whether a rush order of buns at $1 a bun is worthwhile. In order to answer that question, we have to look at the sensitivity report.

Adjustable Cells

Cell	Name	Final Value	Reduced Cost	Objective Coefficient	Allowable Increase	Allowable Decrease
$B$3	Changing Cells Cheese Burger	20	0	2.25	0.625	1.375
$C$3	Changing Cells Sloppy Joes	60	0.625	2	1E+30	0.625
$D$3	Changing Cells Taco	65	0	1.75	2.75	1.25
$E$3	Changing Cells Chili	55	2.5	2.5	1E+30	2.5

We have highlighted the buns row to answer the question. We can see that buns have a shadow price of $1.38. This shadow price means that each additional bun will generate $1.38 of profit. We also can see that other foods such as ground beef have a shadow price of $0. The items with a shadow price of $0 add nothing to profit since we are currently not using all that we have now. The other important piece of information that we have on the buns is that they are only worth $1.38 up until the next 55 buns and that is why the allowable increase is 55. We also can see that a pound of lettuce is worth $8.75. It might be wise to also look for a rush supplier of lettuce so we can increase our profit on Friday nights.

Constraints

Cell	Name	Final Value	Shadow Price	Constraint R.H. Side	Allowable Increase	Allowable Decrease
$F$11	Ground Beef (lbs.) Total	59.25	0.00	100	1E+30	40.75
$F$12	Cheese (lbs.) Total	32.50	0.00	50	1E+30	17.5
$F$13	Beans (lbs.) Total	29.50	0.00	50	1E+30	20.5
$F$14	Lettuce (lbs.) Total	15.00	8.75	15	3	13
$F$15	Tomato (lbs.) Total	44.00	0.00	50	1E+30	6
$F$16	Buns Total	80.00	1.38	80	55	20
$F$17	Taco Shells Total	65.00	0.00	80	1E+30	15

Acceptable answers to the questions are as follows:

1. *What is the best mix of the Friday night specials to maximize Joe Bob's revenue?*
   20 cheese burgers, 60 Sloppy Joes, 65 tacos, and 55 bowls of chili.
2. *If a supplier offered to provide a rush order of buns at $1.00 a bun, is it worth the money?*
   Yes, each additional bun brings in $1.38, so if they cost us $1, then we will net $0.38 per bun.
   However, this is true only up to 55 additional buns.

5.7 Problems

1. Solve the following problem with Excel Solver:
$$\text{Maximize } Z = 3X + Y.$$
$$12X + 14Y \leq 85$$
$$3X + 2Y \leq 18$$
$$Y \leq 4$$

2. Solve the following problem with Excel Solver:
$$\text{Minimize } Z = 2A + 4B.$$
$$4A + 6B \geq 120$$
$$2A + 6B \geq 72$$
$$B \geq 10$$

3. A manufacturing firm has discontinued production of a certain unprofitable product line. Considerable excess production capacity was created as a result. Management is considering devoting this excess capacity to one or more of three products: X_1, X_2, and X_3.
   Machine hours required per unit are

	Product		
Machine Type	X_1	X_2	X_3
Milling machine	8	2	3
Lathe	4	3	0
Grinder	2	0	1

The available time in machine hours per week is

	Machine Hours per Week
Milling machines	800
Lathes	480
Grinders	320

The salespeople estimate they can sell all the units of X_1 and X_2 that can be made. But the sales potential of X_3 is 80 units per week maximum.

Unit profits for the three products are

	Unit Profits
X_1	$20
X_2	6
X_3	8

a. Set up the equations that can be solved to maximize the profit per week.

b. Solve these equations using the Excel Solver.

c. What is the optimal solution? How many of each product should be made, and what should the resultant profit be?

d. What is this situation with respect to the machine groups? Would they work at capacity, or would there be unused available time? Will X_3 be at maximum sales capacity?

e. Suppose that an additional 200 hours per week can be obtained from the milling machines by working overtime. The incremental cost would be $1.50 per hour. Would you recommend doing this? Explain how you arrived at your answer.

4. A diet is being prepared for the University of Arizona dorms. The objective is to feed the students at the least cost, but the diet must have between 1,800 and 3,600 calories. No more than 1,400 calories can be starch, and no fewer than 400 can be protein. The varied diet is to be made of two foods: A and B. Food A costs $0.75 per pound and contains 600 calories, 400 of which are protein and 200 starch. No more than two pounds of food A can be used per resident. Food B costs $0.15 per pound and contains 900 calories, of which 700 are starch, 100 are protein, and 100 are fat.

a. Write the equations representing this information.

b. Solve the problem graphically for the amounts of each food that should be used.

5. Repeat Problem 4 with the added constraint that not more than 150 calories shall be fat and that the price of food has escalated to $1.75 per pound for food A and $2.50 per pound for food B.

6. Logan Manufacturing wants to mix two fuels, A and B, for its trucks to minimize cost. It needs no fewer than 3,000 gallons to run its trucks during the next month. It has a maximum fuel storage capacity of 4,000 gallons. There are 2,000 gallons of fuel A and 4,000 gallons of fuel B available. The mixed fuel must have an octane rating of no less than 80.

When fuels are mixed, the amount of fuel obtained is just equal to the sum of the amounts put in. The octane rating is the weighted average of the individual octanes, weighted in proportion to the respective volumes.

The following is known: Fuel *A* has an octane of 90 and costs $1.20 per gallon. Fuel *B* has an octane of 75 and costs $0.90 per gallon.

    a. Write the equations expressing this information.

    b. Solve the problem using the Excel Solver, giving the amount of each fuel to be used. State any assumptions necessary to solve the problem.

7. You are trying to create a budget to optimize the use of a portion of your disposable income. You have a maximum of $1,500 per month to be allocated to food, shelter, and entertainment. The amount spent on food and shelter combined must not exceed $1,000. The amount spent on shelter alone must not exceed $700. Entertainment cannot exceed $300 per month. Each dollar spent on food has a satisfaction value of 2, each dollar spent on shelter has a satisfaction value of 3, and each dollar spent on entertainment has a satisfaction value of 5.

    Assuming a linear relationship, use the Excel Solver to determine the optimal allocation of your funds.

8. C-town brewery brews two beers: Expansion Draft and Burning River. Expansion Draft sells for $20 per barrel, while Burning River sells for $8 per barrel. Producing a barrel of Expansion Draft takes 8 pounds of corn and 4 pounds of hops. Producing a barrel of Burning River requires 2 pounds of corn, 6 pounds of rice, and 3 pounds of hops. The brewery has 500 pounds of corn, 300 pounds of rice, and 400 pounds of hops. Assuming a linear relationship, use Excel Solver to determine the optimal mix of Expansion Draft and Burning River that maximizes C-town's revenue.

9. BC Petrol manufactures three chemicals at their chemical plant in Kentucky: BCP1, BCP2, and BCP3. These chemicals are produced in two production processes known as zone and man. Running the zone process for an hour costs $48 and yields three units of BCP1, one unit of BCP2, and one unit of BCP3. Running the man process for one hour costs $24 and yields one unit of BCP1 and one unit of BCP2. To meet customer demands, at least 20 units of BCP1, 10 units of BCP2, and 6 units of BCP3 must be produced daily. Assuming a linear relationship, use Excel Solver to determine the optimal mix of processes zone and man to minimize costs and meet BC Petrol daily demands.

10. A farmer in Wood County has 900 acres of land. She is going to plant each acre with corn, soybeans, or wheat. Each acre planted with corn yields a $2,000 profit; each with soybeans yields $2,500 profit; and each with wheat yields $3,000 profit. She has 100 workers and 150 tons of fertilizer. The table below shows the requirement per acre of each of the crops. Assuming a linear relationship, use Excel Solver to determine the optimal planting mix of corn, soybeans, and wheat to maximize her profits.

	Corn	Soybeans	Wheat
Labor (workers)	0.1	0.3	0.2
Fertilizer (tons)	0.2	0.1	0.4

5.8 Selected Bibliography

Anderson, D. R.; D. J. Sweeney; and T. A. Williams. *An Introduction to Management Science.* 11th ed. Mason, OH. South-Western, 2005.

Kelly, Julia, and Curt Simmons. *The Unofficial Guide to Microsoft Excel 2007.* New York: John Wiley & Sons, 2007.

Winston, W. L., and S. C. Albright. *Practical Management Science.* 3rd ed. Mason, OH: South-Western, 2006.

5.9 Footnote

1. The slope of the objective function is -2. If P = profit, $P = \$2H + \$4C$; $\$2H = P + \$4C$; $H = P/2 - 2C$. Thus, the slope is -2.

Chapter  6

Demand Management and Forecasting

After reading this chapter you will:

1. Understand the role of forecasting as a basis for supply chain planning.
2. Compare the differences between independent and dependent demand.
3. Identify the basic components of independent demand: average, trend, seasonal, and random variation.
4. Describe the common qualitative forecasting techniques such as the Delphi method and Collaborative Forecasting.
5. Show how to make a time series forecast using regression, moving averages, and exponential smoothing.
6. Use decomposition to forecast when trend and seasonality is present.

6.1   Walmart's Data Warehouse

Walmart's size and power in the retail industry is having a huge influence in the database industry. Walmart manages one of the world's largest data warehouses with more than 35 terabytes of data. A terabyte is equal to 1,024 gigabytes or a trillion bytes. Your computer is probably 500–750 gigabytes. Walmart's formula for success—getting the right product on the appropriate shelf at the lowest price—owes much to the company's multimillion-dollar investment in data warehousing. Walmart has more detail than most of its competitors on what's going on by product, by store, and by day.

The systems track point of sale data at each store, inventory levels by store, products in transit, market statistics, customer demographics, finance, product returns, and supplier performance. The data are used for three broad areas of decision support: analyzing trends, managing inventory, and understanding customers. What emerges are "personality traits" for each of Walmart's 3,000 or so outlets, which Walmart managers use to determine product mix and presentation for each store.

Data mining is next. Walmart has developed a demand-forecasting application that looks at individual items for individual stores to decide the seasonal sales profile of each item. The system keeps a year's worth of data on the sales of 100,000 products and predicts which items will be needed in each store.

Walmart is now doing market-basket analysis. Data are collected on items that make up a shopper's total purchase so that the company can analyze relationships and patterns in customer purchases. The data warehouse is made available over the Web to its store managers and suppliers.

Forecasts are vital to every business organization and for every significant management decision. Forecasting is the basis of corporate long-run planning. In the functional areas of finance and accounting, forecasts provide the basis for budgetary planning and cost control. Marketing relies on sales forecasting to plan new products, compensate sales personnel, and make other key decisions. Production and operations personnel use forecasts to make periodic decisions involving supplier selection, process selection, capacity planning, and facility layout, as well as for continual decisions about purchasing, production planning, scheduling, and inventory.

In considering what forecasting approach to use it is important to consider the purpose of the forecast. Some forecasts are for very high-level demand analysis. What do we expect the demand to be for a group of products over the next year, for example? Some forecasts are used to help set the strategy of how, in an aggregate sense, we will meet demand. We will call these **strategic forecasts**. Relative to the material in the book, strategic forecasts are most appropriate when making decisions related to overall strategy, capacity, production process design, service process design, sourcing (Chapter 8), location and distribution design, and in sales and operations planning . These all involve relatively long-term decisions that relate to how demand will be met strategically.

Forecasts are also needed for how a firm operates processes on a day-to-day basis. For example, when should the inventory for an item be replenished, or how much production should we schedule for an item next week? These are **tactical forecasts** where the goal is to estimate demand in the relative short term, a few weeks or months. These forecasts are important to ensure that in the short term we are able to meet customer lead time expectations and other criteria related to the availability of our products and services.

These are points within the supply chain where inventory is positioned to allow processes or entities in the supply chain to operate independently. For example, if a product is stocked at a retailer, the customer pulls the item from the shelf and the manufacturer never sees a customer order. Inventory acts as a buffer to separate the customer from the manufacturing process. Selection of decoupling points is a strategic decision that

Strategic forecasts

Tactical forecasts

Supply Chain

Service

determines customer lead times and can greatly impact inventory investment. The closer this point is to the customer, the quicker the customer can be served. Typically, a trade-off is involved where quicker response to customer demand comes at the expense of greater inventory investment, because finished goods inventory is more expensive than raw material inventory.

Forecasting is needed at these decoupling points to set appropriate inventory levels for these buffers. The actual setting of these levels is the topic of Chapter 7, Inventory Control, but an essential input into those decisions is a forecast of expected demand and the expected error associated with that demand. If, for example, we are able to forecast demand very accurately, then inventory levels can be set precisely to expected customer demand. On the other hand, if predicting short-term demand is difficult, then extra inventory to cover this uncertainty will be needed.

The same is true relative to service settings where inventory is not used to buffer demand. Here capacity availability relative to expected demand is the issue. If we can predict demand in a service setting very accurately, then tactically all we need to do is ensure that we have the appropriate capacity in the short term. When demand is not predictable then excess capacity may be needed if servicing customers quickly is important.

Bear in mind that a perfect forecast is virtually impossible. Too many factors in the business environment cannot be predicted with certainty. Therefore, rather than search for the perfect forecast, it is far more important to establish the practice of continual review of forecasts and to learn to live with inaccurate forecasts. This is not to say that we should not try to improve the forecasting model or methodology or even to try to influence demand in a way that reduces demand uncertainty. When forecasting, a good strategy is to use two or three methods and look at them for the commonsense view. Will expected changes in the general economy affect the forecast? Are changes in our customers' behaviors that will impact demand not being captured by our current approaches? In this chapter we look at both *qualitative* techniques that use managerial judgment and also *quantitative* techniques that rely on mathematical models. In our view, combining these techniques is essential to a good forecasting process that is appropriate to the decisions being made.

6.2   Demand Management

The purpose of demand management is to coordinate and control all sources of demand so the supply chain can be run efficiently and the product delivered on time.

Where does demand for a firm's product or service come from, and what can a firm do to manage it? There are two basic sources of demand: dependent demand and independent demand. **Dependent demand** is the demand for a product or service caused by the demand for other products or services. For example, if a firm sells 1,000 tricycles, then 1,000 front wheels and 2,000 rear wheels are needed. This type of internal demand needs no forecast, just a tabulation. As to how many tricycles the firm might sell, this is called **independent demand** because its demand cannot be derived directly from that of other products.[1] We discuss dependence and independence more fully in Chapter 7.

Dependent demand

Independent demand

There is not much a firm can do about dependent demand. It must be met (although the product or service can be purchased rather than produced internally). But there is a lot a firm can do about independent demand—if it wants to. The firm can:

1. **Take an active role to influence demand.**   The firm can apply pressure on its sales force, it can offer incentives both to customers and to its own personnel, it can wage campaigns to sell products, and it can cut prices. These actions can increase demand. Conversely, demand can be decreased through price increases or reduced sales efforts.

2. **Take a passive role and simply respond to demand.**   There are several reasons a firm may not try to change demand but simply accept what happens. If a firm is running at full capacity, it may not want to do anything about demand. Other reasons are a firm may be powerless to change demand because of the expense to advertise; the market may be fixed in size and static; or demand is beyond its control (such as in the case of sole supplier). There are other competitive, legal, environmental, ethical, and moral reasons that market demand is passively accepted.

A great deal of coordination is required to manage these dependent, independent, active, and passive demands. These demands originate both internally and externally in the form of new product sales from marketing, repair parts for previously sold products from product service, restocking from the factory warehouses, and supply items for manufacturing. In this chapter, our primary interest is in forecasting for independent items.

6.3   Types of Forecasting

Forecasting can be classified into four basic types: *qualitative, time series analysis, causal relationships,* and *simulation.*

Time series analysis

Qualitative techniques are subjective or judgmental and are based on estimates and opinions. **Time series analysis**, the primary focus of this chapter, is based on the idea that data relating to past demand can be used to predict future demand. Past data may include several components, such as trend, seasonal, or cyclical influences, and are described in the following section. Causal forecasting, which we discuss using the linear regression technique, assumes that demand is related to some underlying factor or factors in the environment. Simulation models allow the forecaster to run through a range of assumptions about the condition of the forecast. In this chapter we focus on

Exhibit 6.1

HISTORICAL PRODUCT DEMAND CONSISTING OF A GROWTH TREND AND SEASONAL DEMAND

Excel:
Components
of Demand

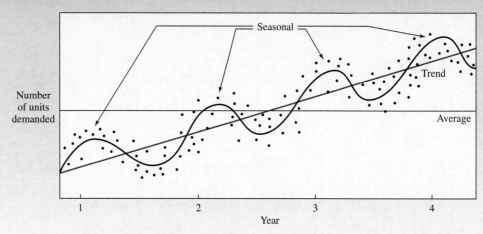

qualitative and time series techniques since these are most often used in supply chain planning and control.

6.4   Components of Demand

In most cases, demand for products or services can be broken down into six components: average demand for the period, a trend, seasonal element, cyclical elements, random variation, and autocorrelation. Exhibit 6.1 illustrates a demand over a four-year period, showing the average, trend, and seasonal components and randomness around the smoothed demand curve.

Cyclical factors are more difficult to determine because the time span may be unknown or the cause of the cycle may not be considered. Cyclical influence on demand may come from such occurrences as political elections, war, economic conditions, or sociological pressures.

Random variations are caused by chance events. Statistically, when all the known causes for demand (average, trend, seasonal, cyclical, and autocorrelative) are subtracted from total demand, what remains is the unexplained portion of demand. If we cannot identify the cause of this remainder, it is assumed to be purely random chance.

Autocorrelation denotes the persistence of occurrence. More specifically, the value expected at any point is highly correlated with its own past values. In waiting line theory, the length of a waiting line is highly autocorrelated. That is, if a line is relatively long at one time, then shortly after that time, we would expect the line still to be long.

When demand is random, it may vary widely from one week to another. Where high autocorrelation exists, demand is not expected to change very much from one week to the next.

Trend lines are the usual starting point in developing a forecast. These trend lines are then adjusted for seasonal effects, cyclical elements, and any other expected events that may influence the final forecast. Exhibit 6.2 shows four of the most common types of trends. A linear trend is obviously a straight continuous relationship. An S-curve is typical of a product growth and maturity cycle. The most important point in the S-curve is where the trend changes from slow growth to fast growth, or from fast to slow. An asymptotic trend starts with the highest demand growth at the beginning but then tapers off. Such a

Exhibit 6.2

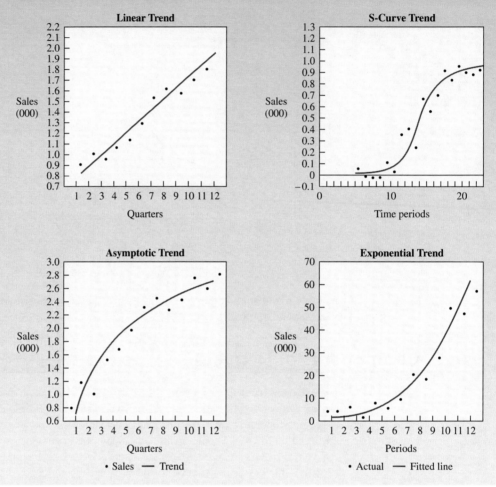

COMMON TYPES OF TRENDS

curve could happen when a firm enters an existing market with the objective of saturating and capturing a large share of the market. An exponential curve is common in products with explosive growth. The exponential trend suggests that sales will continue to increase—an assumption that may not be safe to make.

A widely used forecasting method plots data and then searches for the curve pattern (such as linear, S-curve, asymptotic, or exponential) that fits best. The attractiveness of this method is that because the mathematics for the curve are known, solving for values for future time periods is easy.

Sometimes our data do not seem to fit any standard curve. This may be due to several causes essentially beating the data from several directions at the same time. For these cases, a simplistic but often effective forecast can be obtained by simply plotting data.

6.5 Time Series Analysis

Time series forecasting models try to predict the future based on past data. For example, sales figures collected for the past six weeks can be used to forecast sales for the seventh week. Quarterly sales figures collected for the past several years can be used to

Exhibit 6.3

A GUIDE TO SELECTING AN APPROPRIATE FORECASTING METHOD

Forecasting Method	Amount of Historical Data	Data Pattern	Forecast Horizon
Linear regression	10 to 20 observations for seasonally at least 5 observations per season	Stationary, trend, and seasonality	Short to medium
Simple moving average	6 to 12 months, weekly data are often usedW	Data should be stationary (i.e., no trend or seasonality)	Short
Weighted moving average and simple exponential smoothing	5 to 10 observations needed to start	Data should be stationary	Short
Exponential smoothing with trend	5 to 10 observations needed to start	Stationary and trend	Short

forecast future quarters. Even though both examples contain sales, different forecasting time series models would likely be used.

Exhibit 6.3 shows the time series models discussed in the chapter and some of their characteristics. Terms such as *short, medium*, and *long* are relative to the context in which they are used. However, in business forecasting *short term* usually refers to under three months; *medium term*, three months to two years; and *long term*, greater than two years. We would generally use short-term forecasts for tactical decisions such as replenishing inventory or scheduling employees in the near term and medium-term forecasts for planning a strategy for meeting demand over the next six months to a year and a half. In general, the short-term models compensate for random variation and adjust for short-term changes (such as consumers' responses to a new product). They are especially good for measuring the current variability in demand, which is useful for setting safety stock levels or estimating peak loads in a service setting. Medium-term forecasts are useful for capturing seasonal effects, and long-term models detect general trends and are especially useful in indentifying major turning points.

Which forecasting model a firm should choose depends on:

1. Time horizon to forecast.
2. Data availability.
3. Accuracy required.
4. Size of forecasting budget.
5. Availability of qualified personnel.

In selecting a forecasting model, there are other issues such as the firm's degree of flexibility. (The greater the ability to react quickly to changes, the less accurate the forecast needs to be.) Another item is the consequence of a bad forecast. If a large capital investment decision is to be based on a forecast, it should be a good forecast.

Linear Regression Analysis

Regression can be defined as a functional relationship between two or more correlated variables. It is used to predict one variable given the other. The relationship is usually

Exhibit 6.4

Excel:
Forecasting

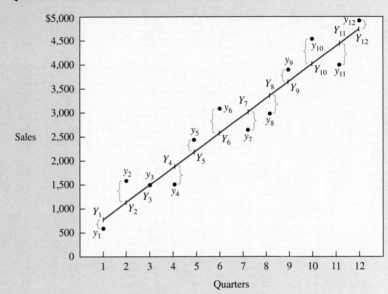

Linear regression
forecasting

developed from observed data. The data should be plotted first to see if they appear linear or if at least parts of the data are linear. *Linear regression* refers to the special class of regression where the relationship between variables forms a straight line.

The linear regression line is of the form $Y = a + bX$, where Y is the value of the dependent variable that we are solving for, a is the Y intercept, b is the slope, and X is the independent variable. (In time series analysis, X is units of time.)

Linear regression is useful for long-term forecasting of major occurrences and aggregate planning. For example, linear regression would be very useful to forecast demands for product families. Even though demand for individual products within a family may vary widely during a time period, demand for the total product family is surprisingly smooth.

The major restriction in using **linear regression forecasting** is, as the name implies, that past data and future projections are assumed to fall about a straight line. Although this does limit its application, sometimes, if we use a shorter period of time, linear regression analysis can still be used. For example, short segments of the longer period may be approximately linear.

Linear regression is used both for time series forecasting and for causal relationship forecasting. When the dependent variable (usually the vertical axis on a graph) changes as a result of time (plotted as the horizontal axis), it is time series analysis. If one variable changes because of the change in another variable, this is a causal relationship (such as the number of deaths from lung cancer increasing with the number of people who smoke).

We use the following example to demonstrate linear least squares regression analysis.

We discuss the possible existence of seasonal components in the next section on decomposition of a time series.

Step by Step

6.1 Example

Least Squares Method

A firm's sales for a product line during the 12 quarters of the past three years were as follows:

Quarter	Sales	Quarter	Sales
1	600	7	2,600
2	1,550	8	2,900
3	1,500	9	3,800
4	1,500	10	4,500
5	2,400	11	4,000
6	3,100	12	4,900

The firm wants to forecast each quarter of the fourth year—that is, quarters 13, 14, 15, and 16.

Solution

The least squares equation for linear regression is

$$Y = a + bx \qquad \text{[6.1]}$$

where

Y = Dependent variable computed by the equation
y = The actual dependent variable data point (used below)
a = Y intercept
b = Slope of the line
x = Time period

The least squares method tries to fit the line to the data *that minimizes the sum of the squares of the vertical distance* between each data point and its corresponding point on the line. If a straight line is drawn through the general area of the points, the difference between the point and the line is $y - Y$. Exhibit 6.4 shows these differences. The sum of the squares of the differences between the plotted data points and the line points is

$$(y_1 - Y_1)^2 + (y_2 - Y_2)^2 + \cdots + (y_{12} - Y_{12})^2$$

The best line to use is the one that minimizes this total.

As before, the straight line equation is

$$Y = a + bx$$

Previously we determined a and b from the graph. In the least squares method, the equations for a and b are

$$a = \bar{y} - b\bar{x} \qquad \text{[6.2]}$$

$$b = \frac{\sum xy - n\bar{x} \cdot \bar{y}}{\sum x^2 - n\bar{x}^2} \qquad \text{[6.3]}$$

where

a = Y intercept
b = Slope of the line
$\bar{y}$ = Average of all ys
$\bar{x}$ = Average of all xs
x = x value at each data point
y = y value at each data point

n = Number of data points
Y = Value of the dependent variable computed with the regression equation

Exhibit 6.5 shows these computations carried out for the 12 data points in the problem. Note that the final equation for Y shows an intercept of 441.6 and a slope of 359.6. The slope shows that for every unit change in X, Y changes by 359.6.

Strictly based on the equation, forecasts for periods 13 through 16 would be

$$Y_{13} = 441.6 + 359.6(13) = 5,116.4$$
$$Y_{14} = 441.6 + 359.6(14) = 5,476.0$$
$$Y_{15} = 441.6 + 359.6(15) = 5,835.6$$
$$Y_{16} = 441.6 + 359.6(16) = 6,195.2$$

The standard error of estimate, or how well the line fits the data, is[2]

$$S_{yx} = \sqrt{\frac{\sum_{i=1}^{n}(y_i - Y_i)^2}{n - 2}}$$

[6.4]

The standard error of estimate is computed from the second and last columns of Exhibit 6.5:

$$S_{yx} = \sqrt{\frac{(600 - 801.3)^2 + (1,550 - 1,160.9)^2 + (1,500 - 1,520.5)^2 + \cdots + (4,900 - 4,757.1)^2}{10}}$$

$$= 363.9$$

Microsoft Excel has a very powerful regression tool designed to perform these calculations. To use the tool, a table is needed that contains data relevant to the problem (see Exhibit 6.6). The tool is part of the Data Analysis ToolPak that is accessed from the Tools menu (or Data tab in Excel 2007) (you may need to add this to your Tools options by using the Add-In option under Tools).

To use the tool, first input the data in two columns in your spreadsheet, then access the Regression option from the Tools → Data Analysis menu. Next, specify the Y Range, which is B2:B13, and the X Range, which is A2:A13 in our example. Finally, an Output Range is specified. This is where you would like the results of the regression analysis placed in your spreadsheet. In the example, A16 is entered. Some of the information provided goes beyond what we have covered, but what you are looking for is the Intercept and X Variable coefficients that correspond to the intercept and slope values in the linear equation. These are in rows 32 and 33 in Exhibit 6.6. ●

Decomposition of a Time Series

A *time series* can be defined as chronologically ordered data that may contain one or more components of demand: trend, seasonal, cyclical, autocorrelation, and random. *Decomposition* of a time series means identifying and separating the time series data into these components. In practice, it is relatively easy to identify the trend (even without mathematical analysis, it is usually easy to plot and see the direction of movement) and the seasonal component (by comparing the same period year to year). It is considerably more difficult to identify the cycles (these may be many months or years long), autocorrelation, and random components. (The forecaster usually calls random anything left over that cannot be identified as another component.)

When demand contains both seasonal and trend effects at the same time, the question is how they relate to each other. In this description, we examine two types of seasonal variation: *additive* and *multiplicative*.

LEAST SQUARES REGRESSION ANALYSIS

**Excel:
Forecasting**

(1)	(2)	(3)	(4)	(5)	(6)
x	y	xy	x^2	y^2	Y
1	600	600	1	360,000	801.3
2	1,550	3,100	4	2,402,500	1,160.9
3	1,500	4,500	9	2,250,000	1,520.5
4	1,500	6,000	16	2,250,000	1,880.1
5	2,400	12,000	25	5,760,000	2,239.7
6	3,100	18,600	36	9,610,000	2,599.4
7	2,600	18,200	49	6,760,000	2,959.0
8	2,900	23,200	64	8,410,000	3,318.6
9	3,800	34,200	81	14,440,000	3,678.2
10	4,500	45,000	100	20,250,000	4,037.8
11	4,000	44,000	121	16,000,000	4,397.4
12	4,900	58,800	144	24,010,000	4,757.1
78	33,350	268,200	650	112,502,500	

$\bar{x} = 6.5 \quad b = 359.6153$
$\bar{y} = 2,779.17 \quad a = 441.6666$
Therefore, $Y = 441.66 + 359.6x$
$\qquad S_{yx} = 363.9$

Additive Seasonal Variation   Additive seasonal variation simply assumes that the seasonal amount is a constant no matter what the trend or average amount is.

$$\text{Forecast including trend and seasonal} = \text{Trend} + \text{Seasonal}$$

Exhibit 6.7A shows an example of increasing trend with constant seasonal amounts.

Multiplicative Seasonal Variation   In multiplicative seasonal variation, the trend is multiplied by the seasonal factors.

$$\text{Forecast including trend and seasonal} = \text{Trend} \times \text{Seasonal factor}$$

Exhibit 6.7B shows the seasonal variation increasing as the trend increases because its size depends on the trend.

The multiplicative seasonal variation is the usual experience. Essentially, this says that the larger the basic amount projected, the larger the variation around this that we can expect.

Seasonal Factor (or Index)   A seasonal factor is the amount of correction needed in a time series to adjust for the season of the year.

We usually associate *seasonal* with a period of the year characterized by some particular activity. We use the word *cyclical* to indicate other than annual recurrent periods of repetitive activity.

The following examples show how seasonal indexes are determined and used to forecast (1) a simple calculation based on past seasonal data and (2) the trend and seasonal index from a hand-fit regression line. We follow this with a more formal procedure for the decomposition of data and forecasting using least squares regression.

EXCEL REGRESSION TOOL

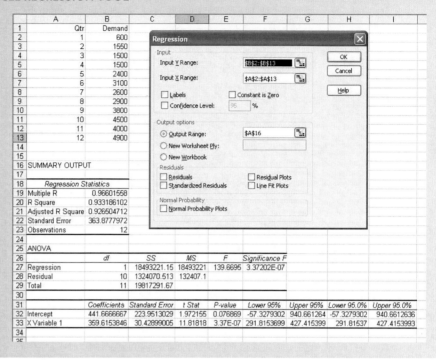

	A	B	C	D	E	F	G	H	I
1	Qtr	Demand							
2	1	600							
3	2	1550							
4	3	1500							
5	4	1500							
6	5	2400							
7	6	3100							
8	7	2600							
9	8	2900							
10	9	3800							
11	10	4500							
12	11	4000							
13	12	4900							
14									
15									
16	SUMMARY OUTPUT								
17									
18	*Regression Statistics*								
19	Multiple R	0.96601558							
20	R Square	0.933186102							
21	Adjusted R Square	0.926504712							
22	Standard Error	363.8777972							
23	Observations	12							
24									
25	ANOVA								
26		df	SS	MS	F	Significance F			
27	Regression	1	18493221.15	18493221	139.6695	3.37202E-07			
28	Residual	10	1324070.513	132407.1					
29	Total	11	19817291.67						
30									
31		Coefficients	Standard Error	t Stat	P-value	Lower 95%	Upper 95%	Lower 95.0%	Upper 95.0%
32	Intercept	441.6666667	223.9513029	1.972155	0.076869	-57.3279302	940.661264	-57.3279302	940.6612636
33	X Variable 1	359.6153846	30.42899005	11.81818	3.37E-07	291.8153699	427.415399	291.81537	427.4153993
34									

Companies such as Toro manufacture lawnmowers and snow blowers to match seasonal demand. Using the same equipment and assembly lines provides better capacity utilization, workforce stability, productivity, and revenue.

ADDITIVE AND MULTIPLICATIVE SEASONAL VARIATION SUPERIMPOSED ON CHANGING TREND

Excel: Forecasting

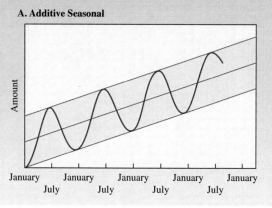

A. Additive Seasonal

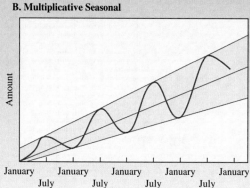

B. Multiplicative Seasonal

6.2 Example

Simple Proportion

Assume that in past years, a firm sold an average of 1,000 units of a particular product line each year. On the average, 200 units were sold in the spring, 350 in the summer, 300 in the fall, and 150 in the winter. The seasonal factor (or index) is the ratio of the amount sold during each season divided by the average for all seasons.

Solution

In this example, the yearly amount divided equally over all seasons is $1,000 \div 4 = 250$. The seasonal factors therefore are

	Past Sales	Average Sales for Each Season (1,000/4)	Seasonal Factor
Spring	200	250	200/250 = 0.8
Summer	350	250	350/250 = 1.4
Fall	300	250	300/250 = 1.2
Winter	150	250	150/250 = 0.6
Total	1,000		

Using these factors, if we expected demand for next year to be 1,100 units, we would forecast the demand to occur as

	Expected Demand for Next Year	Average Sales for Each Season (1,100/4)		Seasonal Factor		Next Year's Seasonal Forecast
Spring		275	×	0.8	=	220
Summer		275	×	1.4	=	385
Fall		275	×	1.2	=	330
Winter		275	×	0.6	=	165
Total	1,100					

The seasonal factor may be periodically updated as new data are available. The following example shows the seasonal factor and multiplicative seasonal variation.

6.3 Example

Computing Trend and Seasonal Factor from a Hand-Fit Straight Line

Step by Step

Here we must compute the trend as well as the seasonal factors.

Solution

We solve this problem by simply hand fitting a straight line through the data points and measuring the trend and intercept from the graph. Assume the history of data is

Quarter	Amount		Quarter	Amount
I–2008	300		I–2009	520
II–2008	200		II–2009	420
III–2008	220		III–2009	400
IV–2008	530		IV–2009	700

First, we plot as in Exhibit 4.8 and then visually fit a straight line through the data. (Naturally, this line and the resulting equation are subject to variation. We show how to do this using regression in the next section.) The equation for the line is

$$\text{Trend}_t = 170 + 55t$$

Our equation was derived from the intercept 170 plus a rise of $(610 - 170) \div 8$ periods. Next we can derive a seasonal index by comparing the actual data with the trend line as in Exhibit 6.8. The seasonal factor was developed by averaging the same quarters in each year.

We can compute the 2010 forecast including trend and seasonal factors (FITS) as follows:

$$\text{FITS}_t = \text{Trend} \times \text{Seasonal}$$
$$\text{I—2010 FITS}_9 = [170 + 55(9)]1.25 = 831$$
$$\text{II—2010 FITS}_{10} = [170 + 55(10)]0.78 = 562$$
$$\text{III—2010 FITS}_{11} = [170 + 55(11)]0.69 = 535$$
$$\text{IV—2010 FITS}_{12} = [170 + 55(12)]1.25 = 1,038 \;\bullet$$

Decomposition Using Least Squares Regression Decomposition of a time series means finding the series' basic components of trend, seasonal, and cyclical. Indexes are calculated for seasons and cycles. The forecasting procedure then reverses the process by projecting the trend and adjusting it by the seasonal and cyclical indexes, which were determined in the decomposition process. More formally, the process is:

1. Decompose the time series into its components.
   a. Find seasonal component.
   b. Deseasonalize the demand.
   c. Find trend component.

**Excel:
Forecasting**

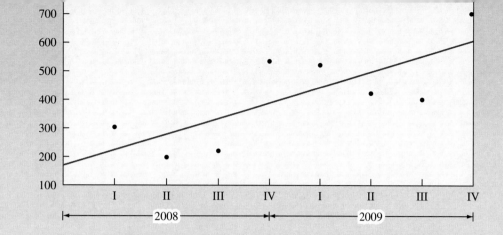

Quarter	Actual Amount	From Trend Equation $Tt = 170 + 55t$	Ratio of Actual ÷ Trend	Seasonal Factor (Average of Same Quarters in Both Years)
2008				
I	300	225	1.33	
II	200	280	.71	
III	220	335	.66	I—1.25
IV	530	390	1.36	II—0.78
2009				III—0.69
I	520	445	1.17	IV—1.25
II	420	500	.84	
III	400	555	.72	
IV	700	610	1.15	

2. Forecast future values of each component.

   a. Project trend component into the future.

   b. Multiply trend component by seasonal component.

Note that the random component is not included in this list. We implicitly remove the random component from the time series when we average as in step 1. It is pointless to attempt a projection of the random component in step 2 unless we have information about some unusual event, such as a major labor dispute, that could adversely affect product demand (and this would not really be random).

Exhibit 6.9 shows the decomposition of a time series using least squares regression and the same basic data we used in our first regression example. Each data point corresponds to using a single three-month quarter of the three-year (12-quarter) period. Our objective is to forecast demand for the four quarters of the fourth year.

Step 1. Determine the seasonal factor (or index). Exhibit 6.9 summarizes the calculations needed. Column 4 develops an average for the same quarters in the three-year

(1) Period (x)	(2) Quarter	(3) Actual Demand (y)	(4) Average of the Same Quarters of Each Year	(5) Seasonal Factor	(6) Deseasonalized Demand (yd) Col. (3) ÷ Col. (5)	(7) x^2 (Col. 1)^2	(8) $x \times yd$ Col. (1) × Col. (6)
1	I	600	(600 + 2,400 + 3,800)/3 = 2,266.7	0.82	735.7	1	735.7
2	II	1,550	(1,550 + 3,100 + 4,500)/3 = 3,050	1.10	1,412.4	4	2,824.7
3	III	1,500	(1,500 + 2,600 + 4,000)/3 = 2,700	0.97	1,544.0	9	4,631.9
4	IV	1,500	(1,500 + 2,900 + 4,900)/3 = 3,100	1.12	1,344.8	16	5,379.0
5	I	2,400		0.82	2,942.6	25	14,713.2
6	II	3,100		1.10	2,824.7	36	16,948.4
7	III	2,600		0.97	2,676.2	49	18,733.6
8	IV	2,900		1.12	2,599.9	64	20,798.9
9	I	3,800		0.82	4,659.2	81	41,932.7
10	II	4,500		1.10	4,100.4	100	41,004.1
11	III	4,000		0.97	4,117.3	121	45,290.1
12	IV	4,900		1.12	4,392.9	144	52,714.5
78		33,350		12.03	33,350.1*	650	265,706.9

$$\bar{x} = \frac{78}{12} = 6.5 \qquad b = \frac{\sum xy_d - n\bar{x}\bar{y}_d}{\sum x^2 - n\bar{x}^2} = \frac{265,706.9 - 12(6.5)2,779.2}{650 - 12(6.5)^2} = 342.2$$

$\bar{y}_d = 33,350/12 = 2,779.2 \qquad a = \bar{y}_d - b\bar{x} = 2,779.2 - 342.2(6.5) = 554.9$

Therefore, $Y = a + bx = 554.9 + 342.2x$

*Column 3 and column 6 totals should be equal at 33,350. Differences are due to rounding. Column 5 was rounded to two decimal places.

period. For example, the first quarters of the three years are added together and divided by 3. A seasonal factor is then derived by dividing that average by the general average for all 12 quarters $\left(\frac{33,350}{12}, \text{ or } 2,779\right)$. For example, this first quarter seasonal factor is $\frac{2,266.7}{2,779} = 0.82$. These are entered in column 5. Note that the seasonal factors are identical for similar quarters in each year.

Step 2. Deseasonalize the original data. To remove the seasonal effect on the data, we divide the original data by the seasonal factor. This step is called the deseasonalization of demand and is shown in column 6 of Exhibit 6.9.

Step 3. Develop a least squares regression line for the deseasonalized data. The purpose here is to develop an equation for the trend line Y, which we then modify with the seasonal factor. The procedure is the same as we used before:

$$Y = a + bx$$

Exhibit 6.10

STRAIGHT LINE GRAPH OF DESEASONALIZED EQUATION

Excel:
Forecasting

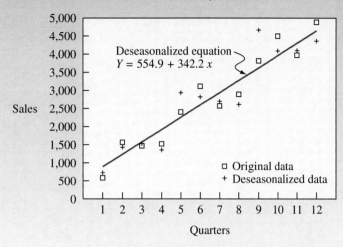

where

y_d = Deseasonalized demand (see Exhibit 6.9)
x = Quarter
Y = Demand computed using the regression equation $Y = a + bx$
a = Y intercept
b = Slope of the line

The least squares calculations using columns 1, 7, and 8 of Exhibit 6.9 are shown in the lower section of the exhibit. The final deseasonalized equation for our data is $Y = 554.9 + 342.2x$. This straight line is shown in Exhibit 6.10.

Step 4. Project the regression line through the period to be forecast. Our purpose is to forecast periods 13 through 16. We start by solving the equation for Y at each of these periods (shown in step 5, column 3).

Step 5. Create the final forecast by adjusting the regression line by the seasonal factor. Recall that the Y equation has been deseasonalized. We now reverse the procedure by multiplying the quarterly data we derived by the seasonal factor for that quarter:

Period	Quarter	Y from Regression Line	Seasonal Factor	Forecast (Y × Seasonal Factor)
13	1	5,003.5	0.82	4,102.87
14	2	5,345.7	1.10	5,880.27
15	3	5,687.9	0.97	5,517.26
16	4	6,030.1	1.12	6,753.71

Our forecast is now complete. The procedure is generally the same as what we did in the hand-fit previous example. In the present example, however, we followed a more formal procedure and computed the least squares regression line as well.

Exhibit 6.11

PREDICTION INTERVALS FOR LINEAR TREND

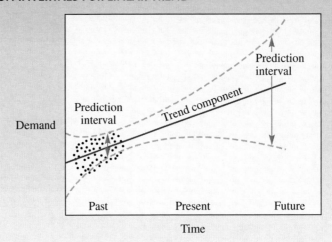

Error Range When a straight line is fitted through data points and then used for forecasting, errors can come from two sources. First, there are the usual errors similar to the standard deviation of any set of data. Second, there are errors that arise because the line is wrong. Exhibit 6.11 shows this error range. Instead of developing the statistics here, we will briefly show why the range broadens. First, visualize that one line is drawn that has some error such that it slants too steeply upward. Standard errors are then calculated for this line. Now visualize another line that slants too steeply downward. It also has a standard error. The total error range, for this analysis, consists of errors resulting from both lines as well as all other possible lines. We included this exhibit to show how the error range widens as we go further into the future.

Simple Moving Average

When demand for a product is neither growing nor declining rapidly, and if it does not have seasonal characteristics, a moving average can be useful in removing the random fluctuations for forecasting. Although *moving averages* are frequently centered, it is more convenient to use past data to predict the following period directly. To illustrate, a centered five-month average of January, February, March, April, and May gives an average centered on March. However, all five months of data must already exist. If our objective is to forecast for June, we must project our moving average—by some means—from March to June. If the average is not centered but is at the forward end, we can forecast more easily, though we may lose some accuracy. Thus, if we want to forecast June with a five-month moving average, we can take the average of January, February, March, April, and May. When June passes, the forecast for July would be the average of February, March, April, May, and June. This is how Exhibit 6.12 was computed.

Although it is important to select the best period for the moving average, there are several conflicting effects of different period lengths. The longer the moving average period, the more the random elements are smoothed (which may be desirable in many cases). But if there is a trend in the data—either increasing or decreasing—the moving average has the adverse characteristic of lagging the trend. Therefore, while a shorter time span produces

FORECAST DEMAND BASED ON A THREE- AND A NINE-WEEK SIMPLE MOVING AVERAGE

Excel: Forecasting

Week	Demand	3 Week	9 Week	Week	Demand	3 Week	9 Week
1	800			16	1,700	2,200	1,811
2	1,400			17	1,800	2,000	1,800
3	1,000			18	2,200	1,833	1,811
4	1,500	1,067		19	1,900	1,900	1,911
5	1,500	1,300		20	2,400	1,967	1,933
6	1,300	1,333		21	2,400	2,167	2,011
7	1,800	1,433		22	2,600	2,233	2,111
8	1,700	1,533		23	2,000	2,467	2,144
9	1,300	1,600		24	2,500	2,333	2,111
10	1,700	1,600	1,367	25	2,600	2,367	2,167
11	1,700	1,567	1,467	26	2,200	2,367	2,267
12	1,500	1,567	1,500	27	2,200	2,433	2,311
13	2,300	1,633	1,556	28	2,500	2,333	2,311
14	2,300	1,833	1,644	29	2,400	2,300	2,378
15	2,000	2,033	1,733	30	2,100	2,367	2,378

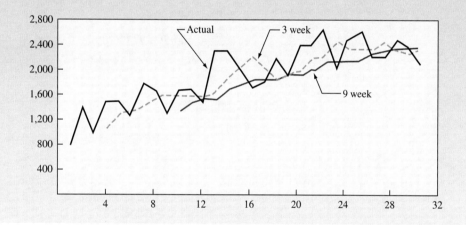

more oscillation, there is a closer following of the trend. Conversely, a longer time span gives a smoother response but lags the trend.

The formula for a simple moving average is

$$F_t = \frac{A_{t-1} + A_{t-2} + A_{t-3} + \cdots + A_{t-n}}{n}$$ [6.5]

where

$$F_t = \text{Forecast for the coming period}$$
$$n = \text{Number of periods to be averaged}$$
$$A_{t-1} = \text{Actual occurrence in the past period}$$
$$A_{t-2}, A_{t-3}, \text{ and } A_{t-n} = \text{Actual occurrences two periods ago, three periods ago, and so on up to } n \text{ periods ago}$$

153

A plot of the data in Exhibit 6.12, shows the effects of various lengths of the period of a moving average. We see that the growth trend levels off at about the 23rd week. The three-week moving average responds better in following this change than the nine-week average, although overall, the nine-week average is smoother.

The main disadvantage in calculating a moving average is that all individual elements must be carried as data because a new forecast period involves adding new data and dropping the earliest data. For a three- or six-period moving average, this is not too severe. But plotting a 60-day moving average for the usage of each of 20,000 items in inventory would involve a significant amount of data.

Weighted Moving Average

Whereas the simple moving average gives equal weight to each component of the moving average database, a weighted moving average allows any weights to be placed on each element, providing, of course, that the sum of all weights equals 1. For example, a department store may find that in a four-month period, the best forecast is derived by using 40 percent of the actual sales for the most recent month, 30 percent of two months ago, 20 percent of three months ago, and 10 percent of four months ago. If actual sales experience was

Month 1	Month 2	Month 3	Month 4	Month 5
100	90	105	95	?

the forecast for month 5 would be

$$F_5 = 0.40(95) + 0.30(105) + 0.20(90) + 0.10(100)$$
$$= 38 + 31.5 + 18 + 10$$
$$= 97.5$$

The formula for a weighted moving average is

$$F_t = w_1 A_{t-1} + w_2 A_{t-2} + \cdots + wn A_{t-n} \qquad \textbf{[6.6]}$$

where

w_1 = Weight to be given to the actual occurrence for the period $t-1$
w_2 = Weight to be given to the actual occurrence for the period $t-2$
w_n = Weight to be given to the actual occurrence for the period $t-n$
n = Total number of periods in the forecast

Although many periods may be ignored (that is, their weights are zero) and the weighting scheme may be in any order (for example, more distant data may have greater weights than more recent data), the sum of all the weights must equal 1.

$$\sum_{i=1}^{n} w_i = 1$$

Suppose sales for month 5 actually turned out to be 110. Then the forecast for month 6 would be

$$F_6 = 0.40(110) + 0.30(95) + 0.20(105) + 0.10(90)$$
$$= 44 + 28.5 + 21 + 9$$
$$= 102.5$$

Choosing Weights   Experience and trial and error are the simplest ways to choose weights. As a general rule, the most recent past is the most important indicator of what to expect in the future, and, therefore, it should get higher weighting. The past month's revenue or plant capacity, for example, would be a better estimate for the coming month than the revenue or plant capacity of several months ago.

However, if the data are seasonal, for example, weights should be established accordingly. Bathing suit sales in July of last year should be weighted more heavily than bathing suit sales in December (in the Northern Hemisphere).

The weighted moving average has a definite advantage over the simple moving average in being able to vary the effects of past data. However, it is more inconvenient and costly to use than the exponential smoothing method, which we examine next.

Exponential Smoothing

In the previous methods of forecasting (simple and weighted moving averages), the major drawback is the need to continually carry a large amount of historical data. (This is also true for regression analysis techniques, which we soon will cover.) As each new piece of data is added in these methods, the oldest observation is dropped, and the new forecast is calculated. In many applications (perhaps in most), the most recent occurrences are more indicative of the future than those in the more distant past. If this premise is valid—that the importance of data diminishes as the past becomes more distant—then **exponential smoothing** may be the most logical and easiest method to use.

Exponential smoothing

The reason this is called exponential smoothing is that each increment in the past is decreased by $(1 - \alpha)$. If α is 0.05, for example, weights for various periods would be as follows (α is defined below):

	Weighting at $\alpha = 0.05$
Most recent weighting $= \alpha(1 - \alpha)^0$	0.0500
Data one time period older $= \alpha(1 - \alpha)^1$	0.0475
Data two time periods older $= \alpha(1 - \alpha)^2$	0.0451
Data three time periods older $= \alpha(1 - \alpha)^3$	0.0429

Therefore, the exponents 0, 1, 2, 3, . . . , give it its name.

Exponential smoothing is the most used of all forecasting techniques. It is an integral part of virtually all computerized forecasting programs, and it is widely used in ordering inventory in retail firms, wholesale companies, and service agencies.

Exponential smoothing techniques have become well accepted for six major reasons:

1. Exponential models are surprisingly accurate.
2. Formulating an exponential model is relatively easy.
3. The user can understand how the model works.
4. Little computation is required to use the model.
5. Computer storage requirements are small because of the limited use of historical data.
6. Tests for accuracy as to how well the model is performing are easy to compute.

Smoothing constant alpha (α)

In the exponential smoothing method, only three pieces of data are needed to forecast the future: the most recent forecast, the actual demand that occurred for that forecast period, and a **smoothing constant alpha (α)**. This smoothing constant determines the level of smoothing and the speed of reaction to differences between forecasts and actual occurrences. The value for the constant is determined both by the nature of the product and by the manager's sense of what constitutes a good response rate. For example, if a firm produced a standard item with relatively stable demand, the reaction rate to differences between actual and forecast demand would tend to be small, perhaps just 5 or 10 percentage points. However, if the

Exhibit 6.13

EXPONENTIAL FORECASTS VERSUS ACTUAL DEMAND FOR UNITS OF A PRODUCT OVER TIME SHOWING THE FORECAST LAG

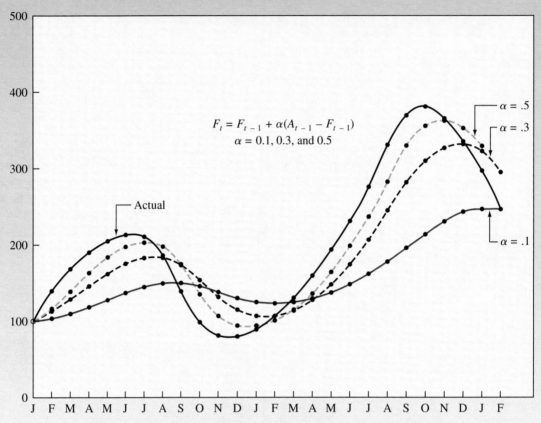

firm were experiencing growth, it would be desirable to have a higher reaction rate, perhaps 15 to 30 percentage points, to give greater importance to recent growth experience. The more rapid the growth, the higher the reaction rate should be. Sometimes users of the simple moving average switch to exponential smoothing but like to keep the forecasts about the same as the simple moving average. In this case, α is approximated by $2 \div (n + 1)$, where n is the number of time periods.

The equation for a single exponential smoothing forecast is simply

$$F_t = F_{t-1} + \alpha(A_{t-1} - F_{t-1}) \qquad \text{[6.7]}$$

where

$F_t =$ The exponentially smoothed forecast for period t

$F_{t-1} =$ The exponentially smoothed forecast made for the prior period

$A_{t-1} =$ The actual demand in the prior period

$\alpha =$ The desired response rate, or smoothing constant

This equation states that the new forecast is equal to the old forecast plus a portion of the error (the difference between the previous forecast and what actually occurred).[3]

To demonstrate the method, assume that the long-run demand for the product under study is relatively stable and a smoothing constant (α) of 0.05 is considered appropriate.

If the exponential method were used as a continuing policy, a forecast would have been made for last month.[4] Assume that last month's forecast (F_{t-1}) was 1,050 units. If 1,000 actually were demanded, rather than 1,050, the forecast for this month would be

$$F_t = F_{t-1} + \alpha(A_{t-1} - F_{t-1})$$
$$= 1,050 + 0.05(1,000 - 1,050)$$
$$= 1,050 + 0.05(-50)$$
$$= 1,047.5 \text{ units}$$

Because the smoothing coefficient is small, the reaction of the new forecast to an error of 50 units is to decrease the next month's forecast by only $2\frac{1}{2}$ units.

Single exponential smoothing has the shortcoming of lagging changes in demand. Exhibit 6.13 presents actual data plotted as a smooth curve to show the lagging effects of the exponential forecasts. The forecast lags during an increase or decrease but overshoots when a change in direction occurs. Note that the higher the value of alpha, the more closely the forecast follows the actual. To more closely track actual demand, a trend factor may be added. Adjusting the value of alpha also helps. This is termed *adaptive forecasting*. Both trend effects and adaptive forecasting are briefly explained in following sections.

Trend Effects in Exponential Smoothing   Remember that an upward or downward trend in data collected over a sequence of time periods causes the exponential forecast to always lag behind (be above or below) the actual occurrence. Exponentially smoothed forecasts can be corrected somewhat by adding in a trend adjustment. To correct the trend, we need two smoothing constants. Besides the smoothing constant α, the trend equation also uses a **smoothing constant delta (δ)**. The delta reduces the impact of the error that occurs between the actual and the forecast. If both alpha and delta are not included, the trend overreacts to errors.

To get the trend equation going, the first time it is used the trend value must be entered manually. This initial trend value can be an educated guess or a computation based on observed past data.

The equation to compute the forecast including trend (FIT) is

$$\text{FIT}_t = F_t + T_t \qquad\qquad \textbf{[6.8]}$$
$$F_t = \text{FIT}_{t-1} + \alpha(A_{t-1} - \text{FIT}_{t-1}) \qquad\qquad \textbf{[6.9]}$$
$$T_t = T_{t-1} + \delta(F_t - \text{FIT}_{t-1}) \qquad\qquad \textbf{[6.10]}$$

where

F_t = The exponentially smoothed forecast for period t
T_t = The exponentially smoothed trend for period t
FIT_t = The forecast including trend for period t
FIT_{t-1} = The forecast including trend made for the prior period
A_{t-1} = The actual demand for the prior period
α = Smoothing constant
δ = Smoothing constant

Choosing the Appropriate Value for Alpha   Exponential smoothing requires that the smoothing constant alpha (α) be given a value between 0 and 1. If the real demand is stable (such as demand for electricity or food), we would like a small alpha to lessen the effects of short-term or random changes. If the real demand is rapidly increasing or decreasing (such as in fashion items or new small appliances), we would like a large alpha to try to keep up with the change. It would be ideal if we could predict which alpha we should use. Unfortunately, two things work against us. First, it would take some passage of time to determine the alpha that would best fit our actual data. This would be tedious to follow

(margin note) Smoothing constant delta (δ)

6.4 Example

Forecast Including Trend

Assume an initial starting F_t of 100 units, a trend of 10 units, an alpha of 0.20, and a delta of 0.30. If actual demand turned out to be 115 rather than the forecast 100, calculate the forecast for the next period.

Step by Step

Solution

Adding the starting forecast and the trend, we have

$$\text{FIT}_{t-1} = F_{t-1} + T_{t-1} = 100 + 10 = 110$$

The actual A_{t-1} is given as 115. Therefore,

$$F_t = \text{FIT}_{t-1} + \alpha(A_{t-1} - \text{FIT}_{t-1})$$
$$= 110 + 0.2(115 - 110) = 111.0$$
$$T_t = T_{t-1} + \delta(F_t - \text{FIT}_{t-1})$$
$$= 10 + 0.3(111 - 110) = 10.3$$
$$\text{FIT}_t = F_t + T_t = 111.0 + 10.3 = 121.3$$

If, instead of 121.3, the actual turned out to be 120, the sequence would be repeated and the forecast for the next period would be

$$F_{t+1} = 121.3 + 0.2(120 - 121.3) = 121.04$$
$$T_{t+1} = 10.3 + 0.3(121.04 - 121.3) = 10.22$$
$$\text{FIT}_{t+1} = 121.04 + 10.22 = 131.26 \; \bullet$$

and revise. Second, because demands do change, the alpha we pick this week may need to be revised soon. Therefore, we need some automatic method to track and change our alpha values.

There are two approaches to controlling the value of alpha. One uses various values of alpha. The other uses a tracking signal.

1. **Two or more predetermined values of alpha.**   The amount of error between the forecast and the actual demand is measured. Depending on the degree of error, different values of alpha are used. If the error is large, alpha is 0.8; if the error is small, alpha is 0.2.
2. **Computed values for alpha.**   A tracking alpha computes whether the forecast is keeping pace with genuine upward or downward changes in demand (as opposed to random changes). In this application, the tracking alpha is defined as the exponentially smoothed actual error divided by the exponentially smoothed absolute error. Alpha changes from period to period within the possible range of 0 to 1.

Forecast Errors

In using the word *error,* we are referring to the difference between the forecast value and what actually occurred. In statistics, these errors are called *residuals.* As long as the forecast value is within the confidence limits, as we discuss later in "Measurement of Error," this is not really an error. But common usage refers to the difference as an error.

Demand for a product is generated through the interaction of a number of factors too complex to describe accurately in a model. Therefore, all forecasts certainly contain some error. In discussing forecast errors, it is convenient to distinguish between *sources of error* and the *measurement of error.*

Sources of Error

Errors can come from a variety of sources. One common source that many forecasters are unaware of is projecting past trends into the future. For example, when we talk about statistical errors in regression analysis, we are referring to the deviations of observations from our regression line. It is common to attach a confidence band (that is, statistical control limits) to the regression line to reduce the unexplained error. But when we then use this regression line as a forecasting device by projecting it into the future, the error may not be correctly defined by the projected confidence band. This is because the confidence interval is based on past data; it may not hold for projected data points and therefore cannot be used with the same confidence. In fact, experience has shown that the actual errors tend to be greater than those predicted from forecast models.

Errors can be classified as bias or random. *Bias errors* occur when a consistent mistake is made. Sources of bias include the failure to include the right variables; the use of the wrong relationships among variables; employing of the wrong trend line; a mistaken shift in the seasonal demand from where it normally occurs; and the existence of some undetected secular trend. *Random errors* can be defined as those that cannot be explained by the forecast model being used.

Measurement of Error

Several common terms used to describe the degree of error are *standard error, mean squared error* (or *variance*), and *mean absolute deviation.* In addition, tracking signals may be used to indicate any positive or negative bias in the forecast.

Standard error is discussed in the section on linear regression in this chapter. Because the standard error is the square root of a function, it is often more convenient to use the function itself. This is called the mean square error or variance.

Mean absolute deviation (MAD)

The **mean absolute deviation (MAD)** was in vogue in the past but subsequently was ignored in favor of standard deviation and standard error measures. In recent years, MAD has made a comeback because of its simplicity and usefulness in obtaining tracking signals. MAD is the average error in the forecasts, using absolute values. It is valuable because MAD, like the standard deviation, measures the dispersion of some observed value from some expected value.

MAD is computed using the differences between the actual demand and the forecast demand without regard to sign. It equals the sum of the absolute deviations divided by the number of data points, or, stated in equation form,

$$\text{MAD} = \frac{\sum_{i=1}^{n} |A_t - F_t|}{n}$$ **[6.11]**

where

t = Period number
A = Actual demand for the period
F = Forecast demand for the period
n = Total number of periods
$||$ = A symbol used to indicate the absolute value disregarding positive and negative signs

Exhibit 6.14

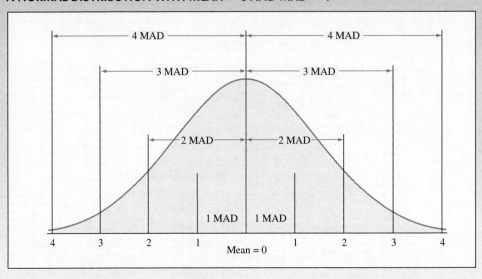

When the errors that occur in the forecast are normally distributed (the usual case), the mean absolute deviation relates to the standard deviation as

$$1 \text{ standard deviation} = \sqrt{\frac{\pi}{2}} \times \text{MAD, or approximately 1.25 MAD}$$

Conversely,

$$1 \text{ MAD} = 0.8 \text{ standard deviation}$$

The standard deviation is the larger measure. If the MAD of a set of points was found to be 60 units, then the standard deviation would be 75 units. In the usual statistical manner, if control limits were set at plus or minus 3 standard deviations (or ± 63.75 MADs), then 99.7 percent of the points would fall within these limits.

Mean absolute percent error (MAPE)

An additional measure of error that is often useful is the **mean absolute percent error (MAPE)**. This measure gauges the error relative to the average demand. For example, if the MAD is 10 units and average demand is 20 units, the error is large and significant, but relatively insignificant on an average demand of 1,000 units. MAPE is calculated by taking the MAD and dividing by the average demand,

$$\text{MAPE} = \frac{\text{MAD}}{\text{Average demand}} \qquad \textbf{[6.12]}$$

This is a useful measure because it is an estimate of how much error to expect with a forecast. So if the MAD were 10 and average demand 20, the MAPE would be 50 percent $\left(\frac{10}{20} = 50\right)$. In the case of an average demand of 1,000 units, the MAPE would be only 1 percent $\left(\frac{10}{1,000} = 1\right)$.

Tracking signal

A **tracking signal** is a measurement that indicates whether the forecast average is keeping pace with any genuine upward or downward changes in demand. As used in forecasting, the tracking signal is the *number* of mean absolute deviations that the forecast value is above or below the actual occurrence. Exhibit 6.14 shows a normal distribution with a mean of 0 and a MAD equal to 1. Thus, if we compute the tracking signal and find it equal to minus 2, we can see that the forecast model is providing forecasts that are quite a bit above the mean of the actual occurrences.

Exhibit 6.15

COMPUTING THE MEAN ABSOLUTE DEVIATION (MAD), THE RUNNING SUM OF FORECAST ERRORS (RSFE), AND THE TRACKING SIGNAL (TS) FROM FORECAST AND ACTUAL DATA

**Excel:
Forecasting**

Month	Demand Forecast	Actual	Deviation	RSFE	Abs. Dev.	Sum of Abs. Dev.	MAD*	$TS = \dfrac{RSFE^\dagger}{MAD}$
1	1,000	950	−50	−50	50	50	50	−1
2	1,000	1,070	+70	+20	70	120	60	.33
3	1,000	1,100	+100	+120	100	220	73.3	1.64
4	1,000	960	−40	+80	40	260	65	1.2
5	1,000	1,090	+90	+170	90	350	70	2.4
6	1,000	1,050	+50	+220	50	400	66.7	3.3

*For month 6, MAD = 400 ÷ 6 = 66.7.

$\dagger$For month 6, $TS = \dfrac{RSFE}{MAD} = \dfrac{220}{66.7} = 3.3$ MADs.

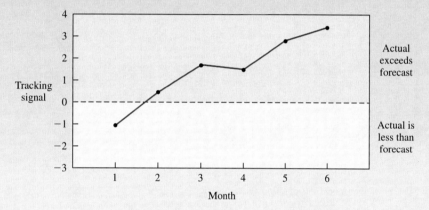

A tracking signal (TS) can be calculated using the arithmetic sum of forecast deviations divided by the mean absolute deviation:

$$TS = \frac{RSFE}{MAD} \qquad\qquad \textbf{[6.13]}$$

where

RSFE = The running sum of forecast errors, considering the nature of the error. (For example, negative errors cancel positive errors and vice versa.)

MAD = The average of all the forecast errors (disregarding whether the deviations are positive or negative). It is the average of the absolute deviations.

Exhibit 6.15 illustrates the procedure for computing MAD and the tracking signal for a six-month period where the forecast had been set at a constant 1,000 and the actual demands that occurred are as shown. In this example, the forecast, on the average, was off by 66.7 units and the tracking signal was equal to 3.3 mean absolute deviations.

We can get a better feel for what the MAD and tracking signal mean by plotting the points on a graph. Though this is not completely legitimate from a sample-size standpoint, we plotted each month in Exhibit 6.15 to show the drift of the tracking signal. Note that it drifted from minus 1 MAD to plus 3.3 MADs. This happened because actual demand was greater than the forecast in four of the six periods. If the actual demand does not fall below the forecast to offset the continual positive RSFE, the tracking signal would continue to rise and we would conclude that assuming a demand of 1,000 is a bad forecast.

6.5 Example

Forecasting Using a Causal Relationship

Step by Step

The Carpet City Store in Carpenteria has kept records of its sales (in square yards) each year, along with the number of permits for new houses in its area.

Number of Housing Starts		
Year	Permits	Sales (in Sq. Yds.)
1999	18	13,000
2000	15	12,000
2001	12	11,000
2002	10	10,000
2003	20	14,000
2004	28	16,000
2005	35	19,000
2006	30	17,000
2007	20	13,000

Carpet City's operations manager believes forecasting sales is possible if housing starts are known for that year. First, the data are plotted in Exhibit 6.16, with

x = Number of housing start permits

y = Sales of carpeting

Because the points appear to be in a straight line, the manager decides to use the linear relationship $Y = \alpha + bx$. We solve this problem by hand fitting a line. We also could solve for this equation using least squares regression as we did earlier.

Solution

Projecting the hand-fit line causes it to intercept the Y axis at about 7,000 yards. This could be interpreted as the demand when no new houses are built, that is, probably as replacement for old carpeting. To estimate the slope, two points are selected, such as

Year	x	y
2005	10	10,000
2009	30	17,000

From algebra the slope is calculated as

$$b = \frac{y(2009) - y(2005)}{x(2009) - x(2005)} = \frac{17,000 - 10,000}{30 - 10} = \frac{7,000}{20} = 350$$

The manager interprets the slope as the average number of square yards of carpet sold for each new house built in the area. The forecasting equation is therefore

$$Y = 7,000 + 350x$$

Now suppose that there are 25 permits for houses to be built in 2010. The 2010 sales forecast would therefore be

$$7,000 + 350(25) = 15,750 \text{ square yards}$$

In this problem, the lag between filing the permit with the appropriate agency and the new homeowner coming to Carpet City to buy carpet makes a causal relationship feasible for forecasting. ●

Exhibit 6.16

Excel:
Forecasting

CAUSAL RELATIONSHIP: SALES TO HOUSING STARTS

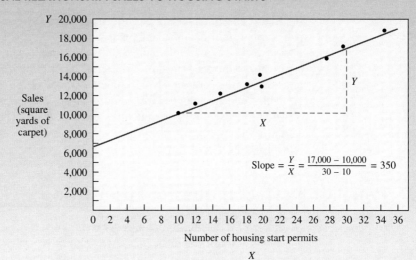

$$\text{Slope} = \frac{Y}{X} = \frac{17{,}000 - 10{,}000}{30 - 10} = 350$$

6.6 Causal Relationship Forecasting

Causal relationship

Causal relationship forecasting uses independent variables other than time to predict future demand. To be of value for the purpose of forecasting, any independent variable must be a leading indicator. For example, we can expect that an extended period of rain will increase sales of umbrellas and raincoats. The rain causes the sale of rain gear. This is a **causal relationship**, where one occurrence causes another. If the causing element is known far enough in advance, it can be used as a basis for forecasting.

The first step in causal relationship forecasting is to find those occurrences that are really the causes. Often leading indicators are not causal relationships, but in some indirect way, they may suggest that some other things might happen. Other noncausal relationships just seem to exist as a coincidence. The following shows one example of a forecast using a causal relationship.

Multiple Regression Analysis

Another forecasting method is multiple regression analysis, in which a number of variables are considered, together with the effects of each on the item of interest. For example, in the home furnishings field, the effects of the number of marriages, housing starts, disposable income, and the trend can be expressed in a multiple regression equation as

$$S = B + B_m(M) + B_h(H) + B_i(I) + B_t(T)$$

where
- S = Gross sales for year
- B = Base sales, a starting point from which other factors have influence
- M = Marriages during the year
- H = Housing starts during the year

163

I = Annual disposable personal income

T = Time trend (first year = 1, second = 2, third = 3, and so forth)

B_m, B_h, B_i, and B_t represent the influence on expected sales of the numbers of marriages and housing starts, income, and trend.

Forecasting by multiple regression is appropriate when a number of factors influence a variable of interest—in this case, sales. Its difficulty lies with the mathematical computation. Fortunately, standard computer programs for multiple regression analysis are available, relieving the need for tedious manual calculation.

Microsoft Excel supports the time series analysis techniques described in this section. These functions are available under the Data Analysis tools for exponential smoothing, moving averages, and regression.

6.7 Qualitative Techniques in Forecasting

Service

Qualitative forecasting techniques generally take advantage of the knowledge of experts and require much judgment. These techniques typically involve processes that are well defined to those participating in the forecasting exercise. For example, in the case of forecasting the demand for new fashions merchandise in a retail store, the firm can include a combination of typical customers to express preferences and store managers who understand product mix and store volumes, where they view the merchandise and run through a series of exercises designed to bring the group to a consensus estimate. The point is that these are not wild guesses as to the expected demand but rather involve a well-thought-out and structured decision-making approach.

These techniques are most useful when the product is new or there is little experience with selling into a new region. Here such information as knowledge of similar products, the habits of customers in the area, and how the product will be advertised and introduced may be important to estimate demand successfully. In some cases it may even be useful to consider industry data and the experience of competing firms in making estimates of expected demand.

The following are samples of qualitative forecasting techniques.

A number of firms, including the gilmore research group, now offer marketers software or databases to help them more accurately forecast sales for specific market areas, products, or segments.

Market Research

Firms often hire outside companies that specialize in *market research* to conduct this type of forecasting. You may have been involved in market surveys through a marketing class. Certainly you have not escaped e-mails asking you about product preferences, your income, habits, and so on.

Market research is used mostly for product research in the sense of looking for new product ideas, likes and dislikes about existing products, which competitive products within a particular class are preferred, and so on. Again, the data collection methods are primarily surveys and interviews.

Panel Consensus

In a *panel consensus,* the idea that two heads are better than one is extrapolated to the idea that a panel of people from a variety of positions can develop a more reliable forecast than a narrower group. Panel forecasts are developed through open meetings with free exchange of ideas from all levels of management and individuals. The difficulty with this open style is that lower employee levels are intimidated by higher levels of management. For example, a salesperson in a particular product line may have a good estimate of future product demand but may not speak up to refute a much different estimate given by the vice president of marketing. The Delphi technique (which we discuss shortly) was developed to try to correct this impairment to free exchange.

When decisions in forecasting are at a broader, higher level (as when introducing a new product line or concerning strategic product decisions such as new marketing areas), the term *executive judgment* is generally used. The term is self-explanatory: a higher level of management is involved.

Historical Analogy

In trying to forecast demand for a new product, an ideal situation would be where an existing product or generic product could be used as a model. There are many ways to classify such analogies—for example, complementary products, substitutable or competitive products, and products as a function of income. Again, you have surely gotten a deluge of mail advertising products in a category similar to a product purchased via catalog, the Internet, or mail order. If you buy a DVD through the mail, you will receive more mail about new DVDs and DVD players. A causal relationship would be that demand for compact discs is caused by demand for DVD players. An analogy would be forecasting the demand for digital videodisc players by analyzing the historical demand for VCRs. The products are in the same general category of electronics and may be bought by consumers at similar rates. A simpler example would be toasters and coffee pots. A firm that already produces toasters and wants to produce coffee pots could use the toaster history as a likely growth model.

Delphi Method

As we mentioned under panel consensus, a statement or opinion of a higher-level person will likely be weighted more than that of a lower-level person. The worst case is where lower-level people feel threatened and do not contribute their true beliefs. To prevent this problem, the *Delphi method* conceals the identity of the individuals participating in the study. Everyone has the same weight. Procedurally, a moderator creates a questionnaire and distributes it to participants. Their responses are summed and given back to the entire group along with a new set of questions.

The step-by-step procedure for the Delphi method is:

1. Choose the experts to participate. There should be a variety of knowledgeable people in different areas.
2. Through a questionnaire (or e-mail), obtain forecasts (and any premises or qualifications for the forecasts) from all participants.
3. Summarize the results and redistribute them to the participants along with appropriate new questions.
4. Summarize again, refining forecasts and conditions, and again develop new questions.
5. Repeat step 4 if necessary. Distribute the final results to all participants.

The Delphi technique can usually achieve satisfactory results in three rounds. The time required is a function of the number of participants, how much work is involved for them to develop their forecasts, and their speed in responding.

6.8 Web-Based Forecasting: Collaborative Planning, Forecasting, and Replenishment (CPFR)[5]

Collaborative
Planning,
Forecasting, and
Replenishment
(CPFR)

**Supply
Chain**

Collaborative Planning, Forecasting, and Replenishment (CPFR) is a Web-based tool used to coordinate demand forecasting, production and purchase planning, and inventory replenishment between supply chain trading partners. CPFR is being used as a means of integrating all members of an *n*-tier supply chain, including manufacturers, distributors, and retailers. As depicted in Exhibit 6.17, the ideal point of collaboration utilizing CPFR is the retail-level demand forecast, which is successively used to synchronize forecasts, production, and replenishment plans upstream through the supply chain.

Although the methodology is applicable to any industry, CPFR applications to date have largely focused on the food, apparel, and general merchandise industries. The potential benefits of sharing information for enhanced planning visibility in any supply chain are enormous. Various estimates for cost savings attributable to improved supply chain coordination have been proposed, including $30 billion annually in the food industry alone.[6]

CPFR's objective is to exchange selected internal information on a shared Web server in order to provide for reliable, longer-term future views of demand in the supply chain. CPFR uses a cyclic and iterative approach to derive consensus supply chain forecasts. It consists of the following five steps:

Step 1. Creation of a front-end partnership agreement. This agreement specifies (1) objectives (e.g., inventory reductions, lost sale elimination, lower product obsolescence) to be gained through collaboration, (2) resource requirements (e.g., hardware, software, performance metrics) necessary for the collaboration, and (3) expectations of confidentiality concerning the prerequisite trust necessary to share sensitive company information, which represents a major implementation obstacle.

Step 2. Joint business planning. Typically partners create partnership strategies, design a joint calendar identifying the sequence and frequency of planning activities to follow that affect product flows, and specify exception criteria for handling planning variances between the trading partners' demand forecasts.

Step 3. Development of demand forecasts. Forecast development may follow preexisting company procedures. Retailers should play a critical role as shared *point-of-sale* (POS) data permit the development of more accurate and timely expectations (compared with extrapolated warehouse withdrawals or aggregate store orders) for both retailers and vendors. Given the frequency of forecast generation and the potential for vast numbers of items requiring forecast preparation, a simple forecast procedure such as a moving average is commonly used within CPFR. Simple techniques are easily used in conjunction with expert knowledge of promotional or pricing events to modify forecast values accordingly.

Step 4. Sharing forecasts. Retailer (order forecasts) and vendor (sales forecasts) then electronically post their latest forecasts for a list of products on a shared, dedicated server. The server examines pairs of corresponding forecasts and issues an exception notice for any forecast pair where the difference exceeds a preestablished safety margin (e.g., 5 percent). If the safety margin is exceeded, planners from both firms may collaborate electronically to derive a consensus forecast.

Step 5. Inventory replenishment. Once the corresponding forecasts are in agreement, the order forecast becomes an actual order, which commences the replenishment

Exhibit 6.17

Supply Chain

n-TIER SUPPLY CHAIN WITH RETAIL ACTIVITIES

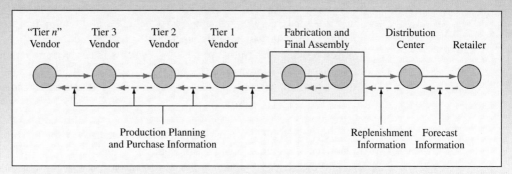

process. Each of these steps is then repeated iteratively in a continuous cycle, at varying times, by individual products and the calendar of events established between trading partners. For example, partners may review the front-end partnership agreement annually, evaluate the joint business plans quarterly, develop forecasts weekly to monthly, and replenish daily.

The early exchange of information between trading partners provides for reliable, longer-term future views of demand in the supply chain. The forward visibility based upon information sharing leads to a variety of benefits within supply chain partnerships.

As with most new corporate initiatives, there is skepticism and resistance to change. One of the largest hurdles hindering collaboration is the lack of trust over complete information sharing between supply chain partners. The conflicting objective between the profit-maximizing vendor and the cost-minimizing customer gives rise to adversarial supply chain relationships. Sharing sensitive operating data may enable one trading partner to take advantage of the other. Similarly, the potential loss of control is a barrier to implementation. Some companies are rightfully concerned about the idea of placing strategic data such as financial reports, manufacturing schedules, and inventory values online. Companies open themselves to security breaches. The front-end partnership agreements, nondisclosure agreements, and limited information access may help overcome these fears.

6.9 Summary

Developing a forecasting system is not easy. However, it must be done because forecasting is fundamental to any planning effort. In the short run, a forecast is needed to predict the requirements for materials, products, services, or other resources to respond to changes in demand. Forecasts permit adjusting schedules and varying labor and materials. In the long run, forecasting is required as a basis for strategic changes, such as developing new markets, developing new products or services, and expanding or creating new facilities.

For medium and long-term strategic forecasts that lead to heavy financial commitments, great care should be taken to derive the forecast. Several approaches should be used. Regression analysis or multiple regression analysis are best suited for these problems. These provide a basis for discussion. Economic factors, product trends, growth factors, and competition, as well as myriad other possible variables, need to be considered and the forecast adjusted to reflect the influence of each.

Short- and intermediate-term forecasting (such as required for inventory control as well as staffing and material scheduling) may be satisfied with simpler models, such as exponential smoothing with perhaps an adaptive feature or a seasonal index. In these applications, thousands of items are usually being forecast. The forecasting routine should therefore be simple and run quickly on a computer. The routines also should detect and respond rapidly to definite short-term changes in demand while at the same time ignoring the occasional spurious demands. Exponential smoothing, when monitored by management to control the value of alpha, is an effective technique.

Web-based collaborative forecasting systems that use combinations of the forecasting methods will be the wave of the future in many industries. Information sharing between trading partners with direct links into each firm's ERP system ensures rapid and error-free information, at very low cost.

In summary, forecasting is tough. A perfect forecast is like a hole in one in golf: great to get but we should be satisfied just to get close to the cup—or, to push the analogy, just to land on the green. The ideal philosophy is to create the best forecast that you reasonably can and then hedge by maintaining flexibility in the system to account for the inevitable forecast error.

6.10 Key Terms

Strategic forecasts Medium and long-term forecasts that are used to make decisions related to design and plans for meeting demand.

Tactical forecasts Short-term forecasts used as input for making day-to-day decisions related to meeting demand.

Dependent demand Requirements for a product or service caused by the demand for other products or services. This type of internal demand does not need a forecast, but can be calculated based on the demand for the other products or services.

Independent demand Demand that cannot be directly derived from the demand for other products.

Time series analysis A type of forecast in which data relating to past demand are used to predict future demand.

Linear regression forecasting A forecasting technique that assumes that past data and future projections fall around a straight line.

Exponential smoothing A time series forecasting technique in which each increment of past demand data is decreased by $(1 - \alpha)$.

Smoothing constant alpha (α) The parameter in the exponential smoothing equation that controls the speed of reaction to differences between forecasts and actual demand.

Smoothing constant delta (δ) An additional parameter used in an exponential smoothing equation that includes an adjustment for trend.

Mean absolute deviation (MAD) The average forecast error using absolute values of the error of each past forecast.

Mean absolute percent error (MAPE) The mean absolute deviation divided by the average demand. The average error expressed as a percentage of demand.

Tracking signal A measure that indicates whether the forecast average is keeping pace with any genuine upward or downward changes in demand.

Causal relationship A situation in which one event causes another. If the event is far enough in the future, it can be used as a basis for forecasting.

Collaborative Planning, Forecasting, and Replenishment (CPFR) An Internet tool to coordinate forecasting, production, and purchasing in a firm's supply chain.

6.11 Formula Review

Least squares regression

$$Y = a + bx \qquad [6.1]$$

$$a = \bar{y} - b\bar{x} \qquad [6.2]$$

$$b = \frac{\Sigma xy - n\bar{x}\cdot\bar{y}}{\Sigma x^2 - n\bar{x}^2} \qquad [6.3]$$

Standard error of estimate

$$S_{yx} = \sqrt{\frac{\sum_{i=1}^{n}(y_i - Y_i)^2}{n-2}} \qquad [6.4]$$

Simple moving average

$$F_t = \frac{A_{t-1} + A_{t-2} + A_{t-3} + \cdots + A_{t-n}}{n} \qquad [6.5]$$

Weighted moving average

$$F_t = w_1 A_{t-1} + w_2 A_{t-2} + \cdots + w_n A_{t-n} \qquad [6.6]$$

Single exponential smoothing

$$F_t = F_{t-1} + \alpha(A_{t-1} - F_{t-1}) \qquad [6.7]$$

Exponential smoothing with trend

$$\text{FIT}_t = F_t + T_t \qquad [6.8]$$

$$F_t = \text{FIT}_{t-1} + \alpha(A_{t-1} - \text{FIT}_{t-1}) \qquad [6.9]$$

$$T_t = T_{t-1} + \delta(F_t - \text{FIT}_{t-1}) \qquad [6.10]$$

Mean absolute deviation

$$\text{MAD} = \frac{\sum_{i=1}^{n}|A_t - F_t|}{n} \qquad [6.11]$$

Mean absolute percent error

$$\text{MAPE} = \frac{\text{MAD}}{\text{Average demand}} \qquad [6.12]$$

Tracking signal

$$\text{TS} = \frac{\text{RSFE}}{\text{MAD}} \qquad [6.13]$$

6.12 Solved Problems

Excel: Forecasting

Solved Problem 1

Here are quarterly data for the past two years. From these data, prepare a forecast for the upcoming year using decomposition.

Period	Actual	Period	Actual
1	300	5	416
2	540	6	760
3	885	7	1191
4	580	8	760

Solution

(Note that the values you obtain may be slightly different due to rounding. The values given here were obtained using an Excel spreadsheet.)

(1)	(2)	(3)	(4)	(5)
Period x	Actual y	Period Average	Seasonal Factor	Deseasonalized Demand
1	300	358	0.527	568.99
2	540	650	0.957	564.09
3	885	1,038	1.529	578.92
4	580	670	0.987	587.79
5	416		0.527	789.01
6	760		0.957	793.91
7	1,191		1.529	779.08
8	760		0.987	770.21
Total	5,432	2,716	8.0	
Average	679	679	1	

Column 3 is seasonal average. For example, the first-quarter average is

$$\frac{300 + 416}{2} = 358$$

Column 4 is the quarter average (column 3) divided by the overall average (679). Column 5 is the actual data divided by the seasonal index. To determine x^2 and xy, we can construct a table as follows:

	Period x	Deseasonalized Demand (y_d)	x^2	xy
	1	568.99	1	569.0
	2	564.09	4	1128.2
	3	578.92	9	1736.7
	4	587.79	16	2351.2
	5	789.01	25	3945.0
	6	793.91	36	4763.4
	7	779.08	49	5453.6
	8	770.21	64	6161.7
Sums	36	5,432	204	26,108.8
Average	4.5	679		

Now we calculate regression results for deseasonalized data.

$$b = \frac{(26108) - (8)(4.5)(679)}{(204) - (8)(4.5)^2} = 39.64$$

$$a = \overline{Y} - b\overline{x}$$

$$a = 679 - 39.64(4.5) = 500.6$$

Therefore, the deseasonalized regression results are

$$Y = 500.6 + 39.64x$$

Period	Trend Forecast		Seasonal Factor		Final Forecast
9	857.4	×	0.527	=	452.0
10	897.0	×	0.957	=	858.7
11	936.7	×	1.529	=	1431.9
12	976.3	×	0.987	=	963.4

**Excel:
Forecasting**

Solved Problem 2

Sunrise Baking Company markets doughnuts through a chain of food stores. It has been experiencing over- and underproduction because of forecasting errors. The following data are its demand in dozens of doughnuts for the past four weeks. Doughnuts are made for the following day; for example, Sunday's doughnut production is for Monday's sales, Monday's production is for Tuesday's sales, and so forth. The bakery is closed Saturday, so Friday's production must satisfy demand for both Saturday and Sunday.

	4 Weeks Ago	3 Weeks Ago	2 Weeks Ago	Last Week
Monday	2,200	2,400	2,300	2,400
Tuesday	2,000	2,100	2,200	2,200
Wednesday	2,300	2,400	2,300	2,500
Thursday	1,800	1,900	1,800	2,000
Friday	1,900	1,800	2,100	2,000
Saturday				
Sunday	2,800	2,700	3,000	2,900

Make a forecast for this week on the following basis:

a. Daily, using a simple four-week moving average.

b. Daily, using a weighted average of 0.40, 0.30, 0.20, and 0.10 for the past four weeks.

c. Sunrise is also planning its purchases of ingredients for bread production. If bread demand had been forecast for last week at 22,000 loaves and only 21,000 loaves were actually demanded, what would Sunrise's forecast be for this week using exponential smoothing with $\alpha = 0.10$?

d. Suppose, with the forecast made in c, this week's demand actually turns out to be 22,500. What would the new forecast be for the next week?

Solution

a. Simple moving average, four-week.

$$\text{Monday} \quad \frac{2{,}400 + 2{,}300 + 2{,}400 + 2{,}200}{4} = \frac{9{,}300}{4} = 2{,}325 \text{ doz.}$$

$$\text{Tuesday} \quad = \frac{8{,}500}{4} = 2{,}125 \text{ doz.}$$

$$\text{Wednesday} \quad = \frac{9{,}500}{4} = 2{,}375 \text{ doz.}$$

$$\text{Thursday} \quad = \frac{7{,}500}{4} = 1{,}875 \text{ doz.}$$

$$\text{Friday} \quad = \frac{7{,}800}{4} = 1{,}950 \text{ doz.}$$

$$\text{Saturday and Sunday} \quad = \frac{11{,}400}{4} = 2{,}850 \text{ doz.}$$

b. Weighted average with weights of .40, .30, .20, and .10.

	(.10)		(.20)		(.30)		(.40)		
Monday	220	+	480	+	690	+	960	=	2,350
Tuesday	200	+	420	+	660	+	880	=	2,160
Wednesday	230	+	480	+	690	+	1,000	=	2,400
Thursday	180	+	380	+	540	+	800	=	1,900
Friday	190	+	360	+	630	+	800	=	1,980
Saturday and Sunday	280	+	540	+	900	+	1,160	=	2,880
	1,300	+	2,660	+	4,110	+	5,600	=	13,670

c. Exponentially smoothed forecast for bread demand

$$F_t = F_{t-1} + \alpha(A_{t-1} - F_{t-1})$$
$$= 22{,}000 + 0.10(21{,}000 - 22{,}000)$$
$$= 22{,}000 - 100 = 21{,}900 \text{ loaves}$$

d. Exponentially smoothed forecast

$$F_{t+1} = 21{,}900 + .10(22{,}500 - 21{,}900)$$
$$= 21{,}900 + .10(600) = 21{,}960 \text{ loaves}$$

Solved Problem 3

Here are the actual demands for a product for the past six quarters. Using focus forecasting rules 1 through 5, find the best rule to use in predicting the third quarter of this year.

	Quarter			
	I	**II**	**III**	**IV**
Last year	1,200	700	900	1,100
This year	1,400	1,000		

Solution

Rule 1: Next three months' demand = Last three months' demand.

Testing this on the last three months, $F_{II} = A_I$; therefore, $F_{II} = 1{,}400$.
Actual demand was 1,000, so $\frac{1{,}000}{1{,}400} = 71.4\%$.

Rule 2: This quarter's demand equals demand in the same quarter last year.
The forecast for the second quarter this year will therefore be 700, the amount for that quarter last year.

Actual demand was 1,000, and $\frac{1{,}000}{700} = 142.9\%$.

Rule 3: 10 percent more than last quarter.

$$F_{II} = 1{,}400 \times 1.10 = 1{,}540$$
Actual was 1,000, and $\frac{1{,}000}{1{,}540} = 64.9\%$.

Rule 4: 50 percent more than same quarter last year.

$$F_{II} = 700 \times 1.50 = 1{,}050$$
Actual was 1,000, and $\frac{1{,}000}{1{,}050} = 95.2\%$.

Rule 5: Same rate of increase or decrease as last three months.

$$\frac{1{,}400}{1{,}200} = 1.167$$

$$F_{II} = 700 \times 1.167 = 816.7$$

Actual was 1,000, so $\frac{1{,}000}{816.7} = 122.4\%$.

Rule 4 was the closest in predicting the recent quarter—95.2 percent, or just 4.8 percent under. Using this rule (50 percent more than the same quarter last year), we would forecast the third quarter this year as 50 percent more than the third quarter last year, or

$$F_{III} = 1.50\,A_{III} \quad \text{(last year)}$$
$$F_{III} = 1.50(900) = 1{,}350 \text{ units}$$

This year

**Excel:
Forecasting**

Solved Problem 4

A specific forecasting model was used to forecast demand for a product. The forecasts and the corresponding demand that subsequently occurred are shown below. Use the MAD and tracking signal technique to evaluate the accuracy of the forecasting model.

	Actual	Forecast
October	700	660
November	760	840
December	780	750
January	790	835
February	850	910
March	950	890

Solution

Evaluate the forecasting model using MAD and tracking signal.

	Actual Demand	Forecast Demand	Actual Deviation	Cumulative Deviation (RSFE)	Absolute Deviation
October	700	660	40	40	40
November	760	840	−80	−40	80
December	780	750	30	−10	30
January	790	835	−45	−55	45
February	850	910	−60	−115	60
March	950	890	60	−55	60
				Total dev. =	315

$$\text{MAD} = \frac{315}{6} = 52.5$$
$$\text{Tracking signal} = \frac{-55}{52.5} = -1.05$$

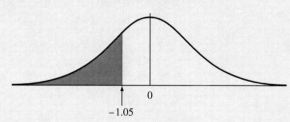

There is not enough evidence to reject the forecasting model, so we accept its recommendations.

6.13 Review and Discussion Questions

1. Examine Exhibit 6.3 and suggest which model you might use for (*a*) bathing suit demand, (*b*) demand for new houses, (*c*) electrical power usage, (*d*) new plant expansion plans.
2. What is the logic in the least squares method of linear regression analysis?
3. Explain the procedure to create a forecast using the decomposition method of least squares regression.
4. Give some very simple rules you might use to manage demand for a firm's product. (An example is "limited to stock on hand.")

5. What strategies are used by supermarkets, airlines, hospitals, banks, and cereal manufacturers to influence demand?

6. All forecasting methods using exponential smoothing, adaptive smoothing, and exponential smoothing including trend require starting values to get the equations going. How would you select the starting value for, say, F_{t-1}?

7. From the choice of simple moving average, weighted moving average, exponential smoothing, and linear regression analysis, which forecasting technique would you consider the most accurate? Why?

8. Give some examples that have a multiplicative seasonal trend relationship.

9. What is the main disadvantage of daily forecasting using regression analysis?

10. What are the main problems with using adaptive exponential smoothing in forecasting?

11. How is a seasonal index computed from a regression line analysis?

12. Discuss the basic differences between the mean absolute deviation and the standard deviation.

13. What implications do forecast errors have for the search for ultrasophisticated statistical forecasting models?

14. Causal relationships are potentially useful for which component of a time series?

6.14 Problems

1. Demand for stereo headphones and MP3 players for joggers has caused Nina Industries to grow almost 50 percent over the past year. The number of joggers continues to expand, so Nina expects demand for headsets to also expand, because, as yet, no safety laws have been passed to prevent joggers from wearing them. Demand for the stereo units for last year was as follows:

Month	Demand (Units)	Month	Demand (Units)
January	4,200	July	5,300
February	4,300	August	4,900
March	4,000	September	5,400
April	4,400	October	5,700
May	5,000	November	6,300
June	4,700	December	6,000

a. Using least squares regression analysis, what would you estimate demand to be for each month next year? Using a spreadsheet, follow the general format in Exhibit 15.5. Compare your results to those obtained by using the forecast spreadsheet function.

b. To be reasonably confident of meeting demand, Nina decides to use three standard errors of estimate for safety. How many additional units should be held to meet this level of confidence?

2. Historical demand for a product is

	Demand
January	12
February	11
March	15
April	12
May	16
June	15

a. Using a weighted moving average with weights of 0.60, 0.30, and 0.10, find the July forecast.

b. Using a simple three-month moving average, find the July forecast.

c. Using single exponential smoothing with $\alpha = 0.2$ and a June forecast $= 13$, find the July forecast. Make whatever assumptions you wish.

d. Using simple linear regression analysis, calculate the regression equation for the preceding demand data.

e. Using the regression equation in *d*, calculate the forecast for July.

3. The following tabulations are actual sales of units for six months and a starting forecast in January.

a. Calculate forecasts for the remaining five months using simple exponential smoothing with $\alpha = 0.2$.

b. Calculate MAD for the forecasts.

	Actual	Forecast
January	100	80
February	94	
March	106	
April	80	
May	68	
June	94	

4. Zeus Computer Chips, Inc., used to have major contracts to produce the Centrino-type chips. The market has been declining during the past three years because of the dual-core chips, which it cannot produce, so Zeus has the unpleasant task of forecasting next year. The task is unpleasant because the firm has not been able to find replacement chips for its product lines. Here is demand over the past 12 quarters:

2007		2008		2009	
I	4,800	I	3,500	I	3,200
II	3,500	II	2,700	II	2,100
III	4,300	III	3,500	III	2,700
IV	3,000	IV	2,400	IV	1,700

Use the decomposition technique to forecast the four quarters of 2010.

5. Sales data for two years are as follows. Data are aggregated with two months of sales in each "period."

Months	Sales	Months	Sales
January–February	109	January–February	115
March–April	104	March–April	112
May–June	150	May–June	159
July–August	170	July–August	182
September–October	120	September–October	126
November–December	100	November–December	106

a. Plot the data.

b. Fit a simple linear regression model to the sales data.

c. In addition to the regression model, determine multiplicative seasonal index factors. A full cycle is assumed to be a full year.

d. Using the results from parts *b* and *c*, prepare a forecast for the next year.

6. The tracking signals computed using past demand history for three different products are as follows. Each product used the same forecasting technique.

	TS 1	TS 2	TS 3
1	-2.70	1.54	0.10
2	-2.32	-0.64	0.43
3	-1.70	2.05	1.08
4	-1.10	2.58	1.74
5	-0.87	-0.95	1.94
6	-0.05	-1.23	2.24
7	0.10	0.75	2.96
8	0.40	-1.59	3.02
9	1.50	0.47	3.54
10	2.20	2.74	3.75

Discuss the tracking signals for each and what the implications are.

7. The following table shows the past two years of quarterly sales information. Assume that there are both trend and seasonal factors and that the seasonal cycle is one year. Use time series decomposition to forecast quarterly sales for the next year.

Quarter	Sales	Quarter	Sales
1	160	5	215
2	195	6	240
3	150	7	205
4	140	8	190

8. Tucson Machinery, Inc., manufactures numerically controlled machines, which sell for an average price of $0.5 million each. Sales for these NCMs for the past two years were as follows:

Quarter	Quantity (Units)	Quarter	Quantity (Units)
2008		2009	
I	12	I	16
II	18	II	24
III	26	III	28
IV	16	IV	18

a. Hand fit a line (or do a regression using Excel).
b. Find the trend and seasonal factors.
c. Forecast sales for 2010.

9. Not all the items in your office supply store are evenly distributed as far as demand is concerned, so you decide to forecast demand to help plan your stock. Past data for legal-sized yellow tablets for the month of August are

Week 1	300	Week 3	600
Week 2	400	Week 4	700

a. Using a three-week moving average, what would you forecast the next week to be?
b. Using exponential smoothing with $\alpha = 0.20$, if the exponential forecast for week 3 was estimated as the average of the first two weeks $[(300 + 400)/2 = 350]$, what would you forecast week 5 to be?

10. Given the following history, use focus forecasting to forecast the third quarter of this year. Use three focus forecasting strategies.

	Jan	Feb	Mar	Apr	May	Jun	Jul	Aug	Sep	Oct	Nov	Dec
Last year	100	125	135	175	185	200	150	140	130	200	225	250
This year	125	135	135	190	200	190						

11. Here are the actual tabulated demands for an item for a nine-month period (January through September). Your supervisor wants to test two forecasting methods to see which method was better over this period.

Month	Actual	Month	Actual
January	110	June	180
February	130	July	140
March	150	August	130
April	170	September	140
May	160		

   a. Forecast April through September using a three-month moving average.
   b. Use simple exponential smoothing with an alpha of .3 to estimate April through September.
   c. Use MAD to decide which method produced the better forecast over the six-month period.

12. A particular forecasting model was used to forecast a six-month period. Here are the forecasts and actual demands that resulted:

	Forecast	Actual
April	250	200
May	325	250
June	400	325
July	350	300
August	375	325
September	450	400

   Find the tracking signal and state whether you think the model being used is giving acceptable answers.

13. Harlen Industries has a simple forecasting model: Take the actual demand for the same month last year and divide that by the number of fractional weeks in that month. This gives the average weekly demand for that month. This weekly average is used as the weekly forecast for the same month this year. This technique was used to forecast eight weeks for this year, which are shown below along with the actual demand that occurred.

Week	Forecast Demand	Actual Demand	Week	Forecast Demand	Actual Demand
1	140	137	5	140	180
2	140	133	6	150	170
3	140	150	7	150	185
4	140	160	8	150	205

   a. Compute the MAD of forecast errors.
   b. Using the RSFE, compute the tracking signal.
   c. Based on your answers to *a* and *b,* comment on Harlen's method of forecasting.

14. The following table contains the demand from the last 10 months:

Month	Actual Demand	Month	Actual Demand
1	31	6	36
2	34	7	38
3	33	8	40
4	35	9	40
5	37	10	41

   a. Calculate the single exponential smoothing forecast for these data using an α of .30 and an initial forecast (F_1) of 31.

   b. Calculate the exponential smoothing with trend forecast for these data using an α of .30, a δ of .30, an initial trend forecast (T_1) of 1, and an initial exponentially smoothed forecast (F_1) of 30.

   c. Calculate the mean absolute deviation (MAD) for each forecast. Which is best?

15. In this problem, you are to test the validity of your forecasting model. Here are the forecasts for a model you have been using and the actual demands that occurred:

Week	Forecast	Actual
1	800	900
2	850	1,000
3	950	1,050
4	950	900
5	1,000	900
6	975	1,100

Use the method stated in the text to compute the MAD and tracking signal. Then decide whether the forecasting model you have been using is giving reasonable results.

16. Assume that your stock of sales merchandise is maintained based on the forecast demand. If the distributor's sales personnel call on the first day of each month, compute your forecast sales by each of the three methods requested here.

	Actual
June	140
July	180
August	170

   a. Using a simple three-month moving average, what is the forecast for September?

   b. Using a weighted moving average, what is the forecast for September with weights of .20, .30, and .50 for June, July, and August, respectively?

   c. Using single exponential smoothing and assuming that the forecast for June had been 130, forecast sales for September with a smoothing constant alpha of .30.

17. Historical demand for a product is as follows:

	Demand
April	60
May	55
June	75
July	60
August	80
September	75

a. Using a simple four-month moving average, calculate a forecast for October.

b. Using single exponential smoothing with $\alpha = 0.2$ and a September forecast = 65, calculate a forecast for October.

c. Using simple linear regression, calculate the trend line for the historical data. Say the X axis is April = 1, May = 2, and so on, while the Y axis is demand.

d. Calculate a forecast for October.

18. Sales by quarter for last year and the first three quarters of this year were as follows:

	Quarter			
	I	II	III	IV
Last year	23,000	27,000	18,000	9,000
This year	19,000	24,000	15,000	

Using the focus forecasting procedure described in the text, forecast expected sales for the fourth quarter of this year.

19. The following table shows predicted product demand using your particular forecasting method along with the actual demand that o-ccurred:

Forecast	Actual
1,500	1,550
1,400	1,500
1,700	1,600
1,750	1,650
1,800	1,700

a. Compute the tracking signal using the mean absolute deviation and running sum of forecast errors.

b. Discuss whether your forecasting method is giving good predictions.

20. Your manager is trying to determine what forecasting method to use. Based upon the following historical data, calculate the following forecast and specify what procedure you would utilize.

Month	Actual Demand	Month	Actual Demand
1	62	7	76
2	65	8	78
3	67	9	78
4	68	10	80
5	71	11	84
6	73	12	85

a. Calculate the simple three-month moving average forecast for periods 4–12.

b. Calculate the weighted three-month moving average using weights of 0.50, 0.30, and 0.20 for periods 4–12.

c. Calculate the single exponential smoothing forecast for periods 2–12 using an initial forecast (F_1) of 61 and an α of 0.30.

d. Calculate the exponential smoothing with trend component forecast for periods 2–12 using an initial trend forecast (T_1) of 1.8, an initial exponential smoothing forecast (F_1) of 60, an α of 0.30, and a δ of 0.30.

e. Calculate the mean absolute deviation (MAD) for the forecasts made by each technique in periods 4–12. Which forecasting method do you prefer?

21. Use regression analysis on deseasonalized demand to forecast demand in summer 2010, given the following historical demand data:

Year	Season	Actual Demand
2008	Spring	205
	Summer	140
	Fall	375
	Winter	575
2009	Spring	475
	Summer	275
	Fall	685
	Winter	965

22. Here are the data for the past 21 months for actual sales of a particular product:

	2008	2009
January	300	275
February	400	375
March	425	350
April	450	425
May	400	400
June	460	350
July	400	350
August	300	275
September	375	350
October	500	
November	550	
December	500	

Develop a forecast for the fourth quarter using three different focus forecasting rules. (Note that to correctly use this procedure, the rules are first tested on the third quarter; the best-performing one is used to forecast the fourth quarter.) Do the problem using quarters, as opposed to forecasting separate months.

23. Actual demand for a product for the past three months was

Three months ago	400 units
Two months ago	350 units
Last month	325 units

a. Using a simple three-month moving average, make a forecast for this month.

b. If 300 units were actually demanded this month, what would your forecast be for next month?

c. Using simple exponential smoothing, what would your forecast be for this month if the exponentially smoothed forecast for three months ago was 450 units and the smoothing constant was 0.20?

24. After using your forecasting model for six months, you decide to test it using MAD and a tracking signal. Here are the forecast and actual demands for the six-month period:

Period	Forecast	Actual
May	450	500
June	500	550
July	550	400

Period	Forecast	Actual
August	600	500
September	650	675
October	700	600

a. Find the tracking signal.

b. Decide whether your forecasting routine is acceptable.

25. Here are earnings per share for two companies by quarter from the first quarter of 2006 through the second quarter of 2009. Forecast earnings per share for the rest of 2009 and 2010. Use exponential smoothing to forecast the third period of 2009, and the time series decomposition method to forecast the last two quarters of 2009 and all four quarters of 2010. (It is much easier to solve this problem on a computer spreadsheet so you can see what is happening.)

		Earnings per Share	
	Quarter	Company A	Company B
2006	I	$1.67	$0.17
	II	2.35	0.24
	III	1.11	0.26
	IV	1.15	0.34
2007	I	1.56	0.25
	II	2.04	0.37
	III	1.14	0.36
	IV	0.38	0.44
2008	I	0.29	0.33
	II	20.18 (loss)	0.40
	III	20.97 (loss)	0.41
	IV	0.20	0.47
2009	I	21.54 (loss)	0.30
	II	0.38	0.47

a. For the exponential smoothing method, choose the first quarter of 2006 as the beginning forecast. Make two forecasts, one with $\alpha = 0.10$ and one with $\alpha = 0.30$.

b. Using the MAD method of testing the forecasting model's performance, plus actual data from 2006 through the second quarter of 2009, how well did the model perform?

c. Using the decomposition of a time series method of forecasting, forecast earnings per share for the last two quarters of 2009 and all four quarters of 2010. Is there a seasonal factor in the earnings?

d. Using your forecasts, comment on each company.

26. The following are sales revenues for a large utility company for 1999 through 2009. Forecast revenue for 2010 through 2013. Use your own judgment, intuition, or common sense concerning which model or method to use, as well as the period of data to include.

	Revenue (millions)		Revenue (millions)
1999	$4,865.9	2005	$5,094.4
2000	5,067.4	2006	5,108.8
2001	5,515.6	2007	5,550.6
2002	5,728.8	2008	5,738.9
2003	5,497.7	2009	5,860.0
2004	5,197.7		

27. Mark Price, the new productions manager for Speakers and Company, needs to find out which variable most affects the demand for the company's line of stereo speakers. He is uncertain whether the unit price of the product or the effects of increased marketing are the main drivers in sales and wants to use regression analysis to figure out which factor drives more demand for its particular market. Pertinent information was collected by an extensive marketing project that lasted over the past 10 years and was reduced to the data that follow:

Year	Sales/Unit (Thousands)	Price/ Unit	Advertising ($000)
1998	400	280	600
1999	700	215	835
2000	900	211	1,100
2001	1,300	210	1,400
2002	1,150	215	1,200
2003	1,200	200	1,300
2004	900	225	900
2005	1,100	207	1,100
2006	980	220	700
2007	1,234	211	900
2008	925	227	700
2009	800	245	690

   a. Perform a regression analysis based on these data using Excel. Answer the following questions based on your results.
   b. Which variable, price or advertising, has a larger effect on sales and how do you know?
   c. Predict average yearly speaker sales for Speakers and Company based on the regression results if the price was $300 per unit and the amount spent on advertising (in thousands) was $900.

28. Assume an initial starting F_t of 300 units, a trend of eight units, an alpha of 0.30, and a delta of 0.40. If actual demand turned out to be 288, calculate the forecast for the next period.

29. The following table contains the number of complaints received in a department store for the first six months of operation.

Month	Complaints	Month	Complaints
January	36	April	90
February	45	May	108
March	81	June	144

   If a three-month moving average is used to smooth this series, what would have been the forecast for May?

30. The number of cases of merlot wine sold by the Connor Owen winery in an eight-year period is as follows:

Year	Cases of Merlot Wine	Year	Cases of Merlot Wine
2002	270	2006	358
2003	356	2007	500
2004	398	2008	410
2005	456	2009	376

   Using an exponential smoothing model with an alpha value of 0.20, estimate the smoothed value calculated as of the end of 2009. Use the average demand for 2002 through 2004 as your initial forecast, then smooth the forecast forward to 2009.

6.15 Case: Altavox Electronics

Altavox is a manufacturer and distributor of many different electronic instruments and devices, including digital/analog multimeters, function generators, oscilloscopes, frequency counters, and other test and measuring equipment. Altavox sells a line of test meters that are popular with professional electricians. The model VC202 is sold through five distributors to retail stores in the United States. These distributors are located in Atlanta, Boston, Chicago, Dallas, and Los Angeles and have been selected to serve different regions in the country.

The model VC202 has been a steady seller over the years due to its reliability and rugged construction. Altavox does not consider this a seasonal product, but there is some variability in demand. Demand for the product over the past 13 weeks is shown in the following table.

These data are contained in an Excel spreadsheet *Altavox Data*. The demand in the regions varies between a high of 40 units on average per week in Atlanta and 48 units in Dallas. This quarter's data are pretty close to the demand last quarter.

Management would like you to experiment with some forecasting models to determine what should be used in a new system being implemented. The new system is programmed to use one of two models: simple moving average or exponential smoothing.

Week	1	2	3	4	5	6	7	8	9	10	11	12	13	Average
Atlanta	33	45	37	38	55	30	18	58	47	37	23	55	40	40
Boston	26	35	41	40	46	48	55	18	62	44	30	45	50	42
Chicago	44	34	22	55	48	72	62	28	27	95	35	45	47	47
Dallas	27	42	35	40	51	64	70	65	55	43	38	47	42	48
LA	32	43	54	40	46	74	40	35	45	38	48	56	50	46
Total	162	199	189	213	246	288	245	204	236	257	174	248	229	222

6.16 Questions

Excel: Altavox Data

1. Consider using a simple moving average model. Experiment with models using five weeks' and three weeks' past data. The past data in each region is given below (week −1 is the week before week 1 in the table, −2 is two weeks before week 1, etc.). Evaluate the forecasts that would have been made over the 13 weeks for each distributor using the mean absolute deviation, mean absolute percent error, and tracking signal as criteria.

Week	−5	−4	−3	−2	−1
Atlanta	45	38	30	58	37
Boston	62	18	48	40	35
Chicago	62	22	72	44	48
Dallas	42	35	40	64	43
LA	43	40	54	46	35
Total	254	153	244	252	198

2. Next, consider using a simple exponential smoothing model. In your analysis, test two alpha values, .2 and .4. Use the same criteria for evaluating the model as in question 1. Assume that the initial previous forecast for the model using an alpha value of .2 is the past three-week average. For the model using an alpha of .4, assume that the previous forecast is the past five-week average.

3. Altavox is considering a new option for distributing the model VC202 where, instead of using five distributors, only a single distributor would be used. Evaluate this option by analyzing how accurate the forecast would be based on the demand aggregated across all regions. Use the model that you think is best from your analysis of questions 1 and 2. What are the advantages and disadvantages of aggregating demand from a forecasting view? Are there other things that should be considered when going from multiple distributors to a single distributor?

6.17 Super Quiz

1. This is a type of forecast used to make long-term decisions such as where to locate a warehouse or how many employees to have in a plant next year.

2. This is the type of demand that is most appropriate for using forecasting models.

3. This is a term used for actually influencing the sale of a product or service.

4. These are the six major components of demand.

5. This type of analysis is most appropriate when the past is a good predictor of the future.

6. This is identifying and separating time series data into components of demand.

7. If the demand in the current week was 102 units and we had forecast it to be 125, what would be next week's forecast using an exponential smoothing model with an alpha of 0.3?

8. Assume that you are using exponential smoothing with an adjustment for trend. Demand is increasing at a very steady rate of about five units per week. Would you expect your alpha and delta parameters to be closer to one or zero?

9. Your forecast is, on average, incorrect by about 10 percent. The average demand is 130 units. What is the MAD?

10. If the tracking signal for your forecast were consistently positive, you could then say this about your forecasting technique.

11. What would you suggest to improve the forecast described in question 10?

12. You know that sales are greatly influenced by the amount your firm advertises in the local paper. What forecasting technique would you suggest trying?

13. What forecasting tool is most appropriate when closely working with customers dependent on your products?

1. Strategic forecast 2. Independent demand 3. Demand management 4. Average demand for the period, trend, seasonal elements, cyclical elements, random variation, and autocorrelation 5. Time series analysis 6. Decomposition 7. 118 units 8. Zero 9. 13 10. Bias, consistently too low 11. Add a trend component 12. Causal relationship forecasting (using regression) 13. Collaborative Planning, Forecasting, and Replenishment (CPFR)

6.18 Selected Bibliography

Diebold, F. X. *Elements of Forecasting.* 4th ed. Mason, OH: South-Western College Publishing, 2006.

Hanke, J. E.; A. G. Reitsch; and D. W. Wichem. *Business Forecasting.* 8th ed. Upper Saddle River, NJ : Prentice Hall, 2004.

Makridakis, S; S. C. Wheelwright; and R. J. Hyndman. *Forecasting: Methods for Management.* New York: John Wiley & Sons, 1998.

6.19 Footnotes

1. In addition to dependent and independent demands, other relationships include complementary products and causal relationships where demand for one causes the demand for another.

2. An equation for the standard error that is often easier to compute is $S_{yx} = \sqrt{\dfrac{\Sigma y^2 - a\Sigma y - b\Sigma xy}{n-2}}$.

3. Some writers prefer to call F_t a smoothed average.

4. When exponential smoothing is first introduced, the initial forecast or starting point may be obtained by using a simple estimate or an average of preceding periods such as the average of the first two or three periods.

5. Special thanks to Gene Fliedner for help with this section. Gene Fliedner, "Hierarchical Forecasting: Issues and Use Guidelines," *Industrial Management & Data Systems* 101, no. 1 (2001), pp. 5–12.

6. Marshall L. Fisher, "What Is the Right Supply Chain for Your Product?" *Harvard Business Review,* March–April 1997, pp. 105–16.

Chapter 7

Inventory Control

After reading the chapter you will:

1. Explain the different purposes for keeping inventory.
2. Understand that the type of inventory system logic that is appropriate for an item depends on the type of demand for that item.
3. Calculate the appropriate order size when a one-time purchase must be made.
4. Describe what the economic order quantity is and how to calculate it.
5. Summarize fixed–order quantity and fixed–time period models, including ways to determine safety stock when there is variability in demand.
6. Discuss why inventory turn is directly related to order quantity and safety stock.

7.1 Direct to Store—The Ups Vision

Supply Chain

Logistics visionaries have talked for years about eliminating—or, at least, drastically reducing—the role of inventory in modern supply chains. The most efficient, slack-free supply chains, after all, wouldn't require any inventory buffer, because supply and demand would be in perfect sync. This vision certainly has its appeal: The death of inventory would mean dramatically reduced logistics costs and simplified fulfillment.

There's no need to write a eulogy for inventory just yet. Most companies haven't honed their networks and technologies well enough to eliminate the need for at least minimal inventory. Logistics managers have to perform a daily, delicate balancing act, balancing

- Transportation costs against fulfillment speed
- Inventory costs against the cost of stock-outs
- Customer satisfaction against cost to serve
- New capabilities against profitability

What's more, two accelerating business trends are making it even harder to synchronize supply chains.

Global

First, global sourcing is forcing supply chains to stretch farther across borders. The goods people consume are increasingly made in some other part of the world, particularly in Asia. This acceleration in global sourcing changes the logistics equation.

When goods cross borders, considerations such as fulfillment speed (these are the activities performed once an order is received) and inventory costs get more complicated. Second, powerful retailers and other end customers with clout are starting to push value-added supply chain responsibilities further up the supply chain. More customers are asking manufacturers or third-party logistics providers to label and prepare individual items so the products are ready to go directly to store shelves. With added responsibilities, of course, come added costs. Upstream suppliers are always looking for ways to squeeze more costs out of other areas of the supply chain, such as transportation and distribution.

The UPS Direct Approach

A growing number of companies are overcoming these barriers by taking a more direct approach to global fulfillment. This direct-to-store approach—also known as distribution center bypass or direct distribution—keeps inventory moving from manufacturer to end customer by eliminating stops at warehouses along the way. Because companies can shrink the fulfillment cycle and eliminate inventory costs, direct-to-store can offer a good balance between fulfillment speed and logistics costs.

What accounts for the emergence of the direct-to-store model?

Global sourcing and the upstream migration of value-added logistics services are certainly primary drivers. But other pieces of the puzzle have fallen into place in recent years to make direct-to-store shipments feasible.

Internet-enabled electronic links between supply chain partners have allowed better coordination and collaboration among the various supply chain segments. Meanwhile, at the front of the supply chain, increasingly sophisticated point-of-sale systems can capture product demand patterns. This information can then be fed up the supply chain to manufacturers and components suppliers. More accurate sales-forecasting tools take some of the guesswork out of production and reduce the need for large inventory safety stocks.

Tracking and tracing tools are also available to follow orders across borders and through the hands of different supply partners.

In short, companies no longer need as much inventory gathering dust in warehouses because they can better synchronize production and distribution with demand. Direct-to-store lets them keep inventory in motion—across borders and around the world.

See United Parcel Service of America (UPS) Supply Chain Solutions for more information about these types of services: www.ups.com.

You should visualize inventory as stacks of money sitting on forklifts, on shelves, and in trucks and planes while in transit. That's what inventory is—money. For many businesses, inventory is the largest asset on the balance sheet at any given time, even though it is often not very liquid. It is a good idea to try to get your inventory down as far as possible.

Global

A few years ago, Heineken, the Netherlands beer company, figured it could save a whole bunch of money on inventory-in-transit if it could just shorten the forecasting lead time. Management expected two things to happen. First, they expected to reduce the need for inventory in the pipeline, therefore cutting down the amount of money devoted to inventory itself. Second, they figured that with a shorter forecasting time, forecasts would be more accurate, reducing emergencies and waste. The Heineken system, called HOPS, cut overall inventory in the system from 16 to 18 weeks to 4 to 6 weeks—a huge drop in time, and a big gain in cash. Forecasts were more accurate, and there was another benefit, too.

Heineken found that its salespeople were suddenly more productive. That is because they were not dealing with all those calls where they had to check on inventory or solve bad forecasting problems, or change orders that were already in process. Instead, they could concentrate on good customer service and helping distributors do better. It was a "win" all the way around.

The key here involves doing things that decrease your inventory order cycle time and increase the accuracy of your forecast. Look for ways to use automated systems and electronic communication to substitute the rapid movement of electrons for the cumbersome movement of masses of atoms.

The economic benefit from inventory reduction is evident from the following statistics: The average cost of inventory in the United States is 30 to 35 percent of its value. For example, a firm that carries an inventory of $20 million accrues costs of more than $6 million per year mainly through obsolescence, insurance, and last opportunity. If the amount of inventory could be reduced to $10 million, for instance, the firm would save over $3 million, which goes directly to the bottom line. That is, the savings from reduced inventory results in increased profit.

**Supply
Chain**

This chapter present techniques designed to manage inventory in different supply chain settings. In this chapter, the focus is on settings where the desire is to maintain a stock of inventory that can be delivered to customers on demand. The concept of *customer order decoupling point,* which is a point where inventory is positioned to allow processes or entities in the supply chain to operate independently. For example, if a product is stocked at a retailer, the customer pulls the item from the shelf and the manufacturer never sees a customer order. In this case, inventory acts as a buffer to separate the customer from the manufacturing process. Selection of decoupling points is a strategic decision that determines customer lead times and can greatly impact inventory investment. The closer this point is to the customer, the quicker the customer can be served.

The techniques described in this chapter are suited for managing the inventory at these decoupling points. Typically, there is a trade-off where quicker response to customer demand comes at the expense of greater inventory investment. This is because finished goods inventory is more expensive than raw material inventory. In practice, the idea of a single decoupling point in a supply chain is unrealistic. There may actually be multiple points where buffering takes place.

Service

Good examples of where the models described in this chapter are used include retail stores, grocery stores, wholesale distributors, hospital suppliers, and suppliers of repair parts needed to fix or maintain equipment quickly. Situations in which it is necessary to have the item "in-stock" are ideal candidates for the models described in this chapter. A distinction that needs to be made with the models included in this chapter is whether this is a one-time purchase, for example, for a seasonal item or for use at a special event, or whether the item will be stocked on an ongoing basis.

Exhibit 7.1 depicts different types of supply chain inventories that would exist in a make-to-stock environment, typical of items directed at the consumer. In the upper echelons of the supply chain, which are supply points closer to the customer, stock usually is kept so that an item can be delivered quickly when a customer need occurs. Of course, there are many exceptions, but in general this is the case. The raw materials and manufacturing plant inventory held in the lower echelon potentially can be managed in a special way to take advantage of the planning and synchronization that are needed to efficiently operate this part of the supply chain. In this case, the models in this chapter are most appropriate for the upper echelon inventories (retail and warehouse), and the lower echelon should use the Material Requirements Planning (MRP) technique. The applicability of these models could be different for other environments such as when we produce directly to customer order as in the case of an aircraft manufacturer.

**Supply
Chain**

The techniques described here are most appropriate when demand is difficult to predict with great precision. In these models, we characterize demand by using a probability distribution and maintain stock so that the risk associated with stock out is managed. For these applications, the following three models are discussed:

1. **The single-period model.**   This is used when we are making a one-time purchase of an item. An example might be purchasing T-shirts to sell at a one-time sporting event.

2. **Fixed–order quantity model.**   This is used when we want to maintain an item "in-stock," and when we resupply the item, a certain number of units must be ordered each time. Inventory for the item is monitored until it gets down to a level where the risk of stocking out is great enough that we are compelled to order.

3. **Fixed–time period model.**   This is similar to the fixed–order quantity model; it is used when the item should be in-stock and ready to use. In this case, rather than monitoring the inventory level and ordering when the level gets down to a critical quantity, the item is ordered at certain intervals of time, for example, every Friday morning. This is often convenient when a group of items is ordered together. An example is the delivery of different types of bread to a grocery store. The bakery supplier may have 10 or more products stocked in a store, and rather than delivering each product individually at different times, it is much more efficient to deliver all 10 together at the same time and on the same schedule.

In this chapter, we want to show not only the mathematics associated with great inventory control but also the "art" of managing inventory. Ensuring accuracy in inventory records is essential to running an efficient inventory control process. Techniques such as ABC analysis and cycle counting are essential to the actual management of the system since

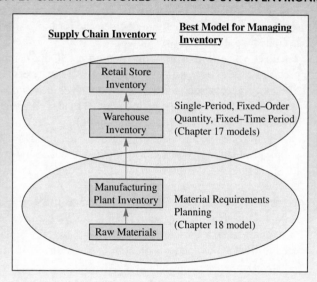

they focus attention on the high-value items and ensure the quality of the transactions that affect the tracking of inventory levels.

7.2   Definition of Inventory

Inventory

Inventory is the stock of any item or resource used in an organization. An *inventory system* is the set of policies and controls that monitor levels of inventory and determine what levels should be maintained, when stock should be replenished, and how large orders should be.

By convention, *manufacturing inventory* generally refers to items that contribute to or become part of a firm's product output. Manufacturing inventory is typically classified into *raw materials, finished products, component parts, supplies,* and *work-in-process.* In services, *inventory* generally refers to the tangible goods to be sold and the supplies necessary to administer the service.

The basic purpose of inventory analysis in manufacturing and stockkeeping services is to specify (1) when items should be ordered and (2) how large the order should be. Many firms are tending to enter into longer-term relationships with vendors to supply their needs for perhaps the entire year. This changes the "when" and "how many to order" to "when" and "how many to deliver."

7.3   Purposes of Inventory

All firms (including JIT operations) keep a supply of inventory for the following reasons:

1. **To maintain independence of operations.**   A supply of materials at a work center allows that center flexibility in operations. For example, because there are costs for making each new production setup, this inventory allows management to reduce the number of setups.

Independence of workstations is desirable on assembly lines as well. The time needed to do identical operations will naturally vary from one unit to the next. Therefore, it is desirable to have a cushion of several parts within the workstation so that shorter performance times can compensate for longer performance times. This way the average output can be fairly stable.

2. **To meet variation in product demand.** If the demand for the product is known precisely, it may be possible (though not necessarily economical) to produce the product to exactly meet the demand. Usually, however, demand is not completely known, and a safety or buffer stock must be maintained to absorb variation.

3. **To allow flexibility in production scheduling.** A stock of inventory relieves the pressure on the production system to get the goods out. This causes longer lead times, which permit production planning for smoother flow and lower-cost operation through larger lot-size production. High setup costs, for example, favor producing a larger number of units once the setup has been made.

4. **To provide a safeguard for variation in raw material delivery time.** When material is ordered from a vendor, delays can occur for a variety of reasons: a normal variation in shipping time, a shortage of material at the vendor's plant causing backlogs, an unexpected strike at the vendor's plant or at one of the shipping companies, a lost order, or a shipment of incorrect or defective material.

5. **To take advantage of economic purchase order size.** There are costs to place an order: labor, phone calls, typing, postage, and so on. Therefore, the larger each order is, the fewer the orders that need to be written. Also, shipping costs favor larger orders—the larger the shipment, the lower the per-unit cost.

For each of the preceding reasons (especially for items 3, 4, and 5), be aware that inventory is costly and large amounts are generally undesirable. Long cycle times are caused by large amounts of inventory and are undesirable as well.

7.4 Inventory Costs

In making any decision that affects inventory size, the following costs must be considered.

1. **Holding (or carrying) costs.** This broad category includes the costs for storage facilities, handling, insurance, pilferage, breakage, obsolescence, depreciation, taxes, and the opportunity cost of capital. Obviously, high holding costs tend to favor low inventory levels and frequent replenishment.

2. **Setup (or production change) costs.** To make each different product involves obtaining the necessary materials, arranging specific equipment setups, filling out the required papers, appropriately charging time and materials, and moving out the previous stock of material.

   If there were no costs or loss of time in changing from one product to another, many small lots would be produced. This would reduce inventory levels, with a resulting savings in cost. One challenge today is to try to reduce these setup costs to permit smaller lot sizes. (This is the goal of a JIT system.)

3. **Ordering costs.** These costs refer to the managerial and clerical costs to prepare the purchase or production order. Ordering costs include all the details, such as counting items and calculating order quantities. The costs associated with maintaining the system needed to track orders are also included in ordering costs.

4. **Shortage costs.** When the stock of an item is depleted, an order for that item must either wait until the stock is replenished or be canceled. There is a trade-off between

Toyota priuses and other vehicles clad in protective covering await shipment to U.S. dealers at the Long Beach, CA, Port. In 2008 the value of the company's inventory totaled about ¥1.83 trillion and the cost of goods sold was ¥21.5 trillion. So Toyota's inventory turned over about 11.7 times per year, or roughly 31 days of inventory on hand.

Global

carrying stock to satisfy demand and the costs resulting from stockout. This balance is sometimes difficult to obtain, because it may not be possible to estimate lost profits, the effects of lost customers, or lateness penalties. Frequently, the assumed shortage cost is little more than a guess, although it is usually possible to specify a range of such costs.

Establishing the correct quantity to order from vendors or the size of lots submitted to the firm's production facilities involves a search for the minimum total cost resulting from the combined effects of four individual costs: holding costs, setup costs, ordering costs, and shortage costs. Of course, the timing of these orders is a critical factor that may impact inventory cost.

7.5   Independent Versus Dependent Demand

In inventory management, it is important to understand the trade-offs involved in using different types of inventory control logic. Exhibit 7.2 is a framework that shows how characteristics of demand, transaction cost, and the risk of obsolete inventory map into different types of systems. The systems in the upper left of the exhibit are described in this chapter.

Transaction cost is dependent on the level of integration and automation incorporated in the system. Manual systems such as simple *two-bin* logic depend on human posting of the transactions to replenish inventory, which is relatively expensive compared to using a computer to automatically detect when an item needs to be ordered. Integration relates

INVENTORY CONTROL-SYSTEM DESIGN MATRIX: FRAMEWORK DESCRIBING INVENTORY CONTROL LOGIC

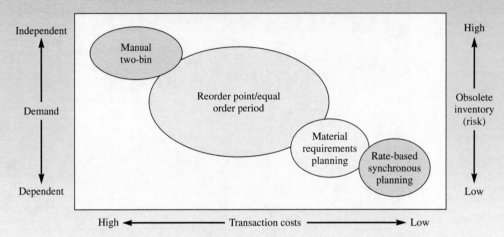

to how connected systems are. For example, it is common for orders for material to be automatically transferred to suppliers electronically and for these orders to be automatically captured by the supplier inventory control system. This type of integration greatly reduces transaction cost.

The risk of obsolescence is also an important consideration. If an item is used infrequently or only for a specific purpose, there is considerable risk in using inventory control logic that does not track the specific source of demand for the item. Further, items that are sensitive to technical obsolescence, such as computer memory chips, and processors, need to be managed carefully based on actual need to reduce the risk of getting stuck with inventory that is outdated.

An important characteristic of demand relates to whether demand is derived from an end item or is related to the item itself. We use the terms **independent and dependent demand** to describe this characteristic. Briefly, the distinction between independent and dependent demand is this. In independent demand, the demands for various items are unrelated to each other. For example, a workstation may produce many parts that are unrelated but meet some external demand requirement. In dependent demand, the need for any one item is a direct result of the need for some other item, usually a higher-level item of which it is part.

In concept, dependent demand is a relatively straightforward computational problem. Needed quantities of a dependent-demand item are simply computed, based on the number needed in each higher-level item in which it is used. For example, if an automobile company plans on producing 500 cars per day, then obviously it will need 2,000 wheels and tires (plus spares). The number of wheels and tires needed is *dependent* on the production levels and is not derived separately. The demand for cars, on the other hand, is *independent*—it comes from many sources external to the automobile firm and is not a part of other products; it is unrelated to the demand for other products.

To determine the quantities of independent items that must be produced, firms usually turn to their sales and market research departments. They use a variety of techniques, including customer surveys, forecasting techniques, and economic and sociological trends,

Independent and dependent demand

as we discussed in Chapter 8 on forecasting. Because independent demand is uncertain, extra units must be carried in inventory. This chapter presents models to determine how many units need to be ordered, and how many extra units should be carried to reduce the risk of stocking out.

7.6   Inventory Systems

An inventory system provides the organizational structure and the operating policies for maintaining and controlling goods to be stocked. The system is responsible for ordering and receipt of goods: timing the order placement and keeping track of what has been ordered, how much, and from whom. The system also must follow up to answer such questions as, Has the supplier received the order? Has it been shipped? Are the dates correct? Are the procedures established for reordering or returning undesirable merchandise?

This section divides systems into single-period systems and multiple-period systems. The classification is based on whether the decision is just a one-time purchasing decision where the purchase is designed to cover a fixed period of time and the item will not be reordered, or the decision involves an item that will be purchased periodically where inventory should be kept in stock to be used on demand. We begin with a look at the one-time purchasing decision and the single-period inventory model.

**Tutorial:
Inventory**

Service

A Single-Period Inventory Model

Certainly, an easy example to think about is the classic single-period "newsperson" problem. For example, consider the problem that the newsperson has in deciding how many newspapers to put in the sales stand outside a hotel lobby each morning. If the person does not put enough papers in the stand, some customers will not be able to purchase a paper and the newsperson will lose the profit associated with these sales. On the other hand, if too many papers are placed in the stand, the newsperson will have paid for papers that were not sold during the day, lowering profit for the day.

Actually, this is a very common type of problem. Consider the person selling T-shirts promoting a championship basketball or football game. This is especially difficult, since the person must wait to learn what teams will be playing. The shirts can then be printed with the proper team logos. Of course, the person must estimate how many people will actually want the shirts. The shirts sold prior to the game can probably be sold at a premium price, whereas those sold after the game will need to be steeply discounted.

A simple way to think about this is to consider how much risk we are willing to take for running out of inventory. Let's consider that the newsperson selling papers in the sales stand had collected data over a few months and had found that on average each Monday 90 papers were sold with a standard deviation of 10 papers (assume that during this time the papers were purposefully overstocked in order not to run out, so the newsperson would know what "real" demand was). With these data, our newsperson could simply state a service rate that is felt to be acceptable. For example, the newsperson might want to be 80 percent sure of not running out of papers each Monday.

Recall from your study of statistics, assuming that the probability distribution associated with the sales of the paper is normal, then if we stocked exactly 90 papers each Monday morning, the risk of stocking out would be 50 percent, since 50 percent of the time we expect demand to be less than 90 papers and 50 percent of the time we expect demand to be greater than 90. To be 80 percent sure of not stocking out, we need to carry a few more papers. From the "cumulative standard normal distribution" table given in Appendix A, we see that we need approximately 0.85 standard deviation of extra papers to be 80 percent sure of not stocking out. A quick way to find the exact number of standard deviations needed for a given probability of stocking out is with the NORMSINV(probability) function in Microsoft Excel (NORMSINV(0.8) = 0.84162). Given our result from Excel, which is more accurate than what we can get from the tables, the number of extra papers would be $0.84162 \times 10 = 8.416$, or 9 papers (there is no way to sell 0.4 paper!).

To make this more useful, it would be good to actually consider the potential profit and loss associated with stocking either too many or too few papers on the stand. Let's say that our newspaper person pays \$0.20 for each paper and sells the papers for \$0.50. In this case the marginal cost associated with underestimating demand is \$0.30, the lost profit. Similarly, the marginal cost of overestimating demand is \$0.20, the cost of buying too many papers. The optimal stocking level, using marginal analysis, occurs at the point where the expected benefits derived from carrying the next unit are less than the expected costs for that unit. Keep in mind that the specific benefits and costs depend on the problem.

In symbolic terms, define

$$C_o = \text{Cost per unit of demand overestimated}$$
$$C_u = \text{Cost per unit of demand underestimated}$$

By introducing probabilities, the expected marginal cost equation becomes

$$P(C_o) \leq (1 - P)C_u$$

where P is the probability that the unit will not be sold and $1 - P$ is the probability of it being sold, because one or the other must occur. (The unit is sold or is not sold.)[1]

Then, solving for P, we obtain

$$P \leq \frac{C_u}{C_o + C_u} \qquad \text{[7.1]}$$

This equation states that we should continue to increase the size of the order so long as the probability of selling what we order is equal to or less than the ratio $C_u/(C_o + C_u)$.

Returning to our newspaper problem, our cost of overestimating demand (C_o) is \$0.20 per paper and the cost of underestimating demand (C_u) is \$0.30. The probability therefore is $0.3/(0.2 + 0.3) = 0.6$. Now, we need to find the point on our demand distribution that corresponds to the cumulative probability of 0.6. Using the NORMSINV function to get the number of standard deviations (commonly referred to as the Z-score) of extra newspapers to carry, we get 0.253, which means that we should stock $0.253(10) = 2.53$ or 3 extra papers. The total number of papers for the stand each Monday morning, therefore, should be 93 papers.

7.1 Example

Hotel Reservations

Step by Step

A hotel near the university always fills up on the evening before football games. History has shown that when the hotel is fully booked, the number of last-minute cancellations has a mean of 5 and standard deviation of 3. The average room rate is \$80. When the hotel is overbooked, policy is to find a room in a nearby hotel and to pay for the room for the customer. This usually costs the hotel approximately \$200 since rooms booked on such late notice are expensive. How many rooms should the hotel overbook?

Solution

Service

The cost of underestimating the number of cancellations is $80 and the cost of overestimating cancellations is $200.

$$P \leq \frac{C_u}{C_o + C_u} = \frac{\$80}{\$200 + \$80} = 0.2857$$

Using NORMSINV(.2857) from Excel gives a Z-score of −0.56599. The negative value indicates that we should overbook by a value less than the average of 5. The actual value should be −0.56599(3) = −1.69797, or 2 reservations less than 5. The hotel should overbook three reservations on the evening prior to a football game.

Another common method for analyzing this type of problem is with a discrete probability distribution found using actual data and marginal analysis. For our hotel, consider that we have collected data and our distribution of no-shows is as follows:

Number of No-Shows	Probability	Cumulative Probability
0	0.05	0.05
1	0.08	0.13
2	0.10	0.23
3	0.15	0.38
4	0.20	0.58
5	0.15	0.73
6	0.11	0.84
7	0.06	0.90
8	0.05	0.95
9	0.04	0.99
10	0.01	1.00

Excel: Inventory Control

Using these data, a table showing the impact of overbooking is created. Total expected cost of each overbooking option is then calculated by multiplying each possible outcome by its probability and summing the weighted costs. The best overbooking strategy is the one with minimum cost.

		Number of Reservations Overbooked										
No-Shows	Probability	0	1	2	3	4	5	6	7	8	9	10
0	0.05	0	200	400	600	800	1,000	1,200	1,400	1,600	1,800	2,000
1	0.08	80	0	200	400	600	800	1,000	1,200	1,400	1,600	1,800
2	0.1	160	80	0	200	400	600	800	1,000	1,200	1,400	1,600
3	0.15	240	160	80	0	200	400	600	800	1,000	1,200	1,400
4	0.2	320	240	160	80	0	200	400	600	800	1,000	1,200
5	0.15	400	320	240	160	80	0	200	400	600	800	1,000
6	0.11	480	400	320	240	160	80	0	200	400	600	800
7	0.06	560	480	400	320	240	160	80	0	200	400	600
8	0.05	640	560	480	400	320	240	160	80	0	200	400
9	0.04	720	640	560	480	400	320	240	160	80	0	200
10	0.01	800	720	640	560	480	400	320	240	160	80	0
Total cost		337.6	271.6	228	212.4	238.8	321.2	445.6	600.8	772.8	958.8	1,156

From the table, the minimum total cost is when three extra reservations are taken. This approach using discrete probability is useful when valid historic data are available. ●

Single-period inventory models are useful for a wide variety of service and manufacturing applications. Consider the following:

Service

1. **Overbooking of airline flights.** It is common for customers to cancel flight reservations for a variety of reasons. Here the cost of underestimating the number of cancellations is the revenue lost due to an empty seat on a flight. The cost of overestimating cancellations is the awards, such as free flights or cash payments, that are given to customers unable to board the flight.

2. **Ordering of fashion items.** A problem for a retailer selling fashion items is that often only a single order can be placed for the entire season. This is often caused by long lead times and limited life of the merchandise. The cost of underestimating demand is the lost profit due to sales not made. The cost of overestimating demand is the cost that results when it is discounted.

3. **Any type of one-time order.** Two examples are ordering T-shirts for a sporting event and printing maps that become obsolete after a certain period of time.

Multiperiod Inventory Systems

Fixed–order quantity models (Q-model)

Fixed–time period models (P-model)

There are two general types of multiperiod inventory systems: **fixed–order quantity models** (also called the *economic order quantity*, EOQ, and **Q-model**) and **fixed–time period models** (also referred to variously as the *periodic* system, *periodic review* system, *fixed-order interval* system, and **P-model**). Multiperiod inventory systems are designed to ensure that an item will be available on an ongoing basis throughout the year. Usually the item will be ordered multiple times throughout the year where the logic in the system dictates the actual quantity ordered and the timing of the order.

The basic distinction is that fixed–order quantity models are "event triggered" and fixed–time period models are "time triggered." That is, a fixed–order quantity model initiates an order when the event of reaching a specified reorder level occurs. This event may take place at any time, depending on the demand for the items considered. In contrast, the fixed–time period model is limited to placing orders at the end of a predetermined time period; only the passage of time triggers the model.

To use the fixed–order quantity model (which places an order when the remaining inventory drops to a predetermined order point, R), the inventory remaining must be continually monitored. Thus, the fixed–order quantity model is a *perpetual* system, which requires that every time a withdrawal from inventory or an addition to inventory is made, records must be updated to reflect whether the reorder point has been reached. In a fixed–time period model, counting takes place only at the review period. (We will discuss some variations of systems that combine features of both.)

Tutorial: Inventory

Some additional differences tend to influence the choice of systems (also see Exhibit 7.3):

- The fixed–time period model has a larger average inventory because it must also protect against stockout during the review period, T; the fixed–order quantity model has no review period.

- The fixed–order quantity model favors more expensive items because average inventory is lower.

- The fixed–order quantity model is more appropriate for important items such as critical repair parts because there is closer monitoring and therefore quicker response to potential stockout.

- The fixed–order quantity model requires more time to maintain because every addition or withdrawal is logged.

Exhibit 7.3

FIXED–ORDER QUANTITY AND FIXED–TIME PERIOD DIFFERENCES

	Q-Model	P-Model
Feature	**Fixed–Order Quantity Model**	**Fixed–Time Period Model**
Order quantity	Q—constant (the same amount ordered each time)	q—variable (varies each time order is placed)
When to place order	R—when inventory position drops to the reorder level	T—when the review period arrives
Recordkeeping	Each time a withdrawal or addition is made	Counted only at review period
Size of inventory	Less than fixed–time period model	Larger than fixed–order quantity model
Time to maintain	Higher due to perpetual recordkeeping	
Type of items	Higher-priced, critical, or important items	

Exhibit 7.4 shows what occurs when each of the two models is put into use and becomes an operating system. As we can see, the fixed–order quantity system focuses on order quantities and reorder points. Procedurally, each time a unit is taken out of stock, the withdrawal is logged and the amount remaining in inventory is immediately compared to the reorder point. If it has dropped to this point, an order for Q items is placed. If it has not, the system remains in an idle state until the next withdrawal.

In the fixed–time period system, a decision to place an order is made after the stock has been counted or reviewed. Whether an order is actually placed depends on the inventory position at that time.

7.7 Fixed–Order Quantity Models

Inventory position

Fixed–order quantity models attempt to determine the specific point, R, at which an order will be placed and the size of that order, Q. The order point, R, is always a specified number of units. An order of size Q is placed when the inventory available (currently in stock and on order) reaches the point R. **Inventory position** is defined as the on-hand plus on-order minus backordered quantities. The solution to a fixed–order quantity model may stipulate something like this: When the inventory position drops to 36, place an order for 57 more units.

The simplest models in this category occur when all aspects of the situation are known with certainty. If the annual demand for a product is 1,000 units, it is precisely 1,000—not 1,000 plus or minus 10 percent. The same is true for setup costs and holding costs. Although the assumption of complete certainty is rarely valid, it provides a good basis for our coverage of inventory models.

Exhibit 7.5 and the discussion about deriving the optimal order quantity are based on the following characteristics of the model. These assumptions are unrealistic, but they represent a starting point and allow us to use a simple example.

- Demand for the product is constant and uniform throughout the period.
- Lead time (time from ordering to receipt) is constant.

Exhibit 7.4

COMPARISON FOR FIXED–ORDER QUANTITY AND FIXED–TIME PERIOD REORDERING INVENTORY SYSTEMS

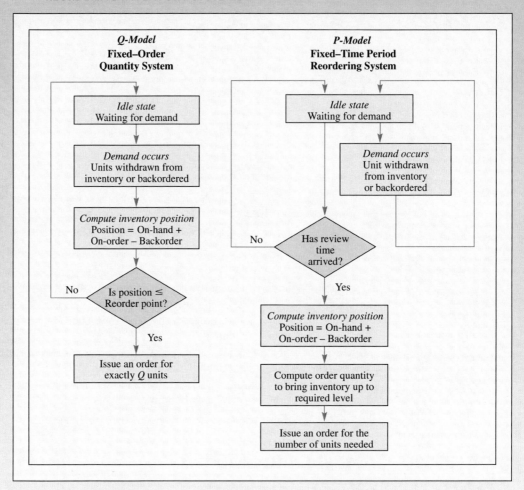

- Price per unit of product is constant.
- Inventory holding cost is based on average inventory.
- Ordering or setup costs are constant.
- All demands for the product will be satisfied. (No backorders are allowed.)

The "sawtooth effect" relating Q and R in Exhibit 7.5 shows that when the inventory position drops to point R, a reorder is placed. This order is received at the end of time period L, which does not vary in this model.

In constructing any inventory model, the first step is to develop a functional relationship between the variables of interest and the measure of effectiveness. In this case, because we are concerned with cost, the following equation pertains:

$$\begin{array}{c}\text{Total} \\ \text{annual cost}\end{array} = \begin{array}{c}\text{Annual} \\ \text{purchase cost}\end{array} + \begin{array}{c}\text{Annual} \\ \text{ordering cost}\end{array} + \begin{array}{c}\text{Annual} \\ \text{holding cost}\end{array}$$

or

BASIC FIXED–ORDER QUANTITY MODEL

**Excel:
Inventory
Control**

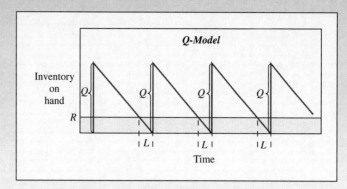

$$TC = DC + \frac{D}{Q}S + \frac{Q}{2}H \qquad \textbf{[7.2]}$$

where

TC = Total annual cost

D = Demand (annual)

C = Cost per unit

Q = Quantity to be ordered (the optimal amount is termed the *economic order quantity*—EOQ—or Q_{opt})

S = Setup cost or cost of placing an order

H = Annual holding and storage cost per unit of average inventory (often holding cost is taken as a percentage of the cost of the item, such as $H = iC$, where i is the percent carrying cost)

On the right side of the equation, DC is the annual purchase cost for the units; $(D/Q)S$ is the annual ordering cost (the actual number of orders placed, D/Q, times the cost of each order, S); and $(Q/2)H$ is the annual holding cost (the average inventory, $Q/2$, times the cost per unit for holding and storage, H). These cost relationships are graphed in Exhibit 7.6.

The second step in model development is to find that order quantity Q_{opt} at which total cost is a minimum. In Exhibit 7.5, the total cost is minimal at the point where the slope of the curve is zero. Using calculus, we take the derivative of total cost with respect to Q and set this equal to zero. For the basic model considered here, the calculations are

$$TC = DC + \frac{D}{Q}S + \frac{Q}{2}H$$

$$\frac{dTC}{dQ} = 0 + \left(\frac{-DS}{Q^2}\right) + \frac{H}{2} = 0$$

$$Q_{opt} = \sqrt{\frac{2DS}{H}} \qquad \textbf{[7.3]}$$

Because this simple model assumes constant demand and lead time, neither safety stock nor stockout cost is necessary, and the reorder point, R, is simply

$$R = \bar{d}L \qquad \textbf{[7.4]}$$

where

$\bar{d}$ = Average daily demand (constant)

L = Lead time in days (constant)

ANNUAL PRODUCT COSTS, BASED ON SIZE OF THE ORDER

**Excel:
Inventory
Control**

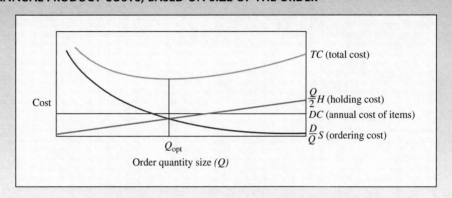

**Excel:
Inventory
Control**

Step by Step

7.2 Example

Economic Order Quantity and Reorder Point

Find the economic order quantity and the reorder point, given

Annual demand $(D) = 1,000$ units
Average daily demand $(\bar{d}) = 1,000/365$
Ordering cost $(S) = \$5$ per order
Holding cost $(H) = \$1.25$ per unit per year
Lead time $(L) = 5$ days
Cost per unit $(C) = \$12.50$

What quantity should be ordered?

Solution

The optimal order quantity is

$$Q_{opt} = \sqrt{\frac{2DS}{H}} = \sqrt{\frac{2(1,000)5}{1.25}} = \sqrt{8,000} = 89.4 \text{ units}$$

The reorder point is

$$R = \bar{d}L = \frac{1,000}{365}(5) = 13.7 \text{ units}$$

Rounding to the nearest unit, the inventory policy is as follows: When the inventory position drops to 14, place an order for 89 more.

The total annual cost will be

$$TC = DC + \frac{D}{Q}S + \frac{Q}{2}H$$

$$= 1,000(12.50) + \frac{1,000}{89}(5) + \frac{89}{2}(1.25)$$

$$= \$12,611.81$$

Note that in this example, the purchase cost of the units was not required to determine the order quantity and the reorder point because the cost was constant and unrelated to order size. ●

Establishing Safety Stock Levels

Safety stock

The previous model assumed that demand was constant and known. In the majority of cases, though, demand is not constant but varies from day to day. Safety stock must therefore be maintained to provide some level of protection against stockouts. **Safety stock** can be defined as the amount of inventory carried in addition to the expected demand. In a normal distribution, this would be the mean. For example, if our average monthly demand is 100 units and we expect next month to be the same, if we carry 120 units, then we have 20 units of safety stock.

Safety stock can be determined based on many different criteria. Frequently a company simply states that a certain number of weeks of supply must be kept in safety stock. It is better, though, to use an approach that captures the variability in demand. For example, an objective may be something like "set the safety stock level so that there will only be a 5 percent chance of stocking out if demand exceeds 300 units." We call this approach to setting safety stock the probability approach.

The Probability Approach Using the probability criterion to determine safety stock is pretty simple. With the models described in this chapter, we assume that the demand over a period of time is normally distributed with a mean and a standard deviation. *Again, remember that this approach considers only the probability of running out of stock, not how many units we are short.* To determine the probability of stocking out over the time period, we can simply plot a normal distribution for the expected demand and note where the amount we have on hand lies on the curve.

Let's take a few simple examples to illustrate this. Say we expect demand to be 100 units over the next month, and we know that the standard deviation is 20 units. If we go into the month with just 100 units, we know that our probability of stocking out is 50 percent. Half of the months we would expect demand to be greater than 100 units; half of the months we would expect it to be less than 100 units. Taking this further, if we ordered a month's worth of inventory of 100 units at a time and received it at the beginning of the month, over the long run we would expect to run out of inventory in six months of the year.

If running out this often was not acceptable, we would want to carry extra inventory to reduce this risk of stocking out. One idea might be to carry an extra 20 units of inventory for the item. In this case, we would still order a month's worth of inventory at a time, but we would schedule delivery to arrive when we still have 20 units remaining in inventory. This would give us that little cushion of safety stock to reduce the probability of stocking out. If the standard deviation associated with our demand was 20 units, we would then be carrying one standard deviation worth of safety stock. Looking at the cumulative standard normal distribution (Appendix A), and moving one standard deviation to the right of the mean, gives a probability of 0.8413. So approximately 84 percent of the time we would not expect to stock out, and 16 percent of the time we would. Now if we order every month, we would expect to stock out approximately two months per year ($0.16 \times 12 = 1.92$). For those using Excel, given a z value, the probability can be obtained with the NORMSDIST function.

Companies using this approach generally set the probability of not stocking out at 95 percent. This means we would carry about 1.64 standard deviations of safety stock, or 33 units ($1.64 \times 20 = 32.8$) for our example. Once again, keep in mind that this does not mean that we

Netflix is the world's largest online movie rental service, providing access to more than 100,000 DVD titles plus a growing library of over 12,000 movies available for instant watching on PC or Mac. On average, Netflix ships 1.9 million DVDs to customers each day from 58 distribution centers.

would order 33 units extra each month. Rather, it means that we would still order a month's worth each time, but we would schedule the receipt so that we could expect to have 33 units in inventory when the order arrives. In this case, we would expect to stock out approximately 0.6 month per year, or that stockouts would occur in 1 of every 20 months.

Fixed–Order Quantity Model with Safety Stock

A fixed–order quantity system perpetually monitors the inventory level and places a new order when stock reaches some level, R. The danger of stockout in this model occurs only during the lead time, between the time an order is placed and the time it is received. As shown in Exhibit 7.7, an order is placed when the inventory position drops to the reorder point, R. During this lead time L, a range of demands is possible. This range is determined either from an analysis of past demand data or from an estimate (if past data are not available).

The amount of safety stock depends on the service level desired, as previously discussed. The quantity to be ordered, Q, is calculated in the usual way considering the demand, shortage cost, ordering cost, holding cost, and so forth. A fixed–order quantity model can be used to compute Q, such as the simple Q_{opt} model previously discussed. The reorder point is then set to cover the expected demand during the lead time plus a safety stock determined by the desired service level. Thus, *the key difference between a fixed–order quantity model where demand is known and one where demand is uncertain is in computing the reorder point. The order quantity is the same in both cases.* The uncertainty element is taken into account in the safety stock.

The reorder point is

$$R = \bar{d}L + z\sigma_L \qquad [7.5]$$

where

R = Reorder point in units
$\bar{d}$ = Average daily demand
L = Lead time in days (time between placing an order and receiving the items)
z = Number of standard deviations for a specified service probability
σ_L = Standard deviation of usage during lead time

The term $z\sigma_L$ is the amount of safety stock. Note that if safety stock is positive, the effect is to place a reorder sooner. That is, R without safety stock is simply the average demand during the lead time. If lead time usage was expected to be 20, for example, and safety stock was computed to be 5 units, then the order would be placed sooner, when 25 units remained. The greater the safety stock, the sooner the order is placed.

Computing $\bar{d}$, σ_L, and z   Demand during the replenishment lead time is really an estimate or forecast of expected use of inventory from the time an order is placed to when it is received. It may be a single number (for example, if the lead time is a month, the demand may be taken as the previous year's demand divided by 12), or it may be a summation of expected demands over the lead time (such as the sum of daily demands over a 30-day lead time). For the daily demand situation, d can be a forecast demand using any of the models in Chapter 6 on forecasting. For example, if a 30-day period was used to calculate d, then a simple average would be

$$\bar{d} = \frac{\sum_{i=1}^{n} d_i}{n} \qquad [7.6]$$

$$= \frac{\sum_{i=1}^{30} d_i}{30}$$

where n is the number of days.

Exhibit 7.7

FIXED–ORDER QUALITY MODEL

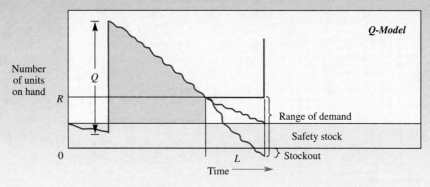

The standard deviation of the daily demand is

$$\sigma_d = \sqrt{\frac{\sum_{i=1}^{n}(d_i - \bar{d})^2}{n}} \qquad \text{[7.7]}$$

$$= \sqrt{\frac{\sum_{i=1}^{30}(d_i - \bar{d})^2}{30}}$$

Because σ_d refers to one day, if lead time extends over several days, we can use the statistical premise that the standard deviation of a series of independent occurrences is equal to the square root of the sum of the variances. That is, in general,

$$\sigma_L = \sqrt{\sigma_1^2 + \sigma_2^2 + \cdots + \sigma_L^2} \qquad \text{[7.8]}$$

For example, suppose we computed the standard deviation of demand to be 10 units per day. If our lead time to get an order is five days, the standard deviation for the five-day period, assuming each day can be considered independent, is

$$\sigma_5 = \sqrt{(10)^2 + (10)^2 + (10)^2 + (10)^2 + (10)^2} = 22.36$$

Next we need to find z, the number of standard deviations of safety stock.

Suppose we wanted our probability of not stocking out during the lead time to be 0.95. The z value associated with a 95 percent probability of not stocking out is 1.64 (see Appendix A or use the Excel NORMSINV function). Given this, safety stock is calculated as follows:

$$\begin{aligned} SS &= z\sigma_L \qquad \text{[7.9]} \\ &= 1.64 \times 22.36 \\ &= 36.67 \end{aligned}$$

We now compare two examples. The difference between them is that in the first, the variation in demand is stated in terms of standard deviation over the entire lead time, while in the second, it is stated in terms of standard deviation per day.

7.3 Example

Reorder Point

Step by Step

Consider an economic order quantity case where annual demand $D = 1,000$ units, economic order quantity $Q = 200$ units, the desired probability of not stocking out $P = 0.95$, the standard deviation of demand during lead time $\sigma_L = 25$ units, and lead time $L = 15$ days. Determine the reorder point. Assume that demand is over a 250-workday year.

Solution

In our example, $\bar{d} = \dfrac{1000}{250} = 4$, and lead time is 15 days. We use the equation

$$R = \bar{d}L + z\sigma_L$$
$$= 4(15) + z(25)$$

In this case z is 1.64.

Completing the solution for R, we have

$$R = 4(15) + 1.64(25) = 60 + 41 = 101 \text{ units}$$

This says that when the stock on hand gets down to 101 units, order 200 more. ●

7.4 Example

Order Quantity and Reorder Point

Step by Step

Excel: Inventory Control

Daily demand for a certain product is normally distributed with a mean of 60 and standard deviation of 7. The source of supply is reliable and maintains a constant lead time of six days. The cost of placing the order is $10 and annual holding costs are $0.50 per unit. There are no stockout costs, and unfilled orders are filled as soon as the order arrives. Assume sales occur over the entire 365 days of the year. Find the order quantity and reorder point to satisfy a 95 percent probability of not stocking out during the lead time.

Solution

In this problem we need to calculate the order quantity Q as well as the reorder point R.

$$\bar{d} = 60 \qquad S = \$10$$
$$\sigma_d = 7 \qquad H = \$0.50$$
$$D = 60(365) \qquad L = 6$$

The optimal order quantity is

$$Q_{opt} = \sqrt{\frac{2DS}{H}} = \sqrt{\frac{2(60)365(10)}{0.50}} = \sqrt{876,000} = 936 \text{ units}$$

To compute the reorder point, we need to calculate the amount of product used during the lead time and add this to the safety stock.

The standard deviation of demand during the lead time of six days is calculated from the variance of the individual days. Because each day's demand is independent[2]

$$\sigma_L = \sqrt{\sum_{i=1}^{L} \sigma_d^2} = \sqrt{6(7)^2} = 17.15$$

Once again, z is 1.64.

$$R = \bar{d}L + z\sigma_L = 60(6) + 1.64(17.15) = 388 \text{ units}$$

To summarize the policy derived in this example, an order for 936 units is placed whenever the number of units remaining in inventory drops to 388. ●

7.8 Fixed–Time Period Models

In a fixed–time period system, inventory is counted only at particular times, such as every week or every month. Counting inventory and placing orders periodically is desirable in situations such as when vendors make routine visits to customers and take orders for their complete line of products, or when buyers want to combine orders to save transportation costs. Other firms operate on a fixed time period to facilitate planning their inventory count; for example, Distributor X calls every two weeks and employees know that all Distributor X's product must be counted.

Fixed–time period models generate order quantities that vary from period to period, depending on the usage rates. These generally require a higher level of safety stock than a fixed–order quantity system. The fixed–order quantity system assumes continual tracking of inventory on hand, with an order immediately placed when the reorder point is reached. In contrast, the standard fixed–time period models assume that inventory is counted only at the time specified for review. It is possible that some large demand will draw the stock down to zero right after an order is placed. This condition could go unnoticed until the next review period. Then the new order, when placed, still takes time to arrive. Thus, it is possible to be out of stock throughout the entire review period, T, and order lead time, L. Safety stock, therefore, must protect against stockouts during the review period itself as well as during the lead time from order placement to order receipt.

Fixed–Time Period Model with Safety Stock

In a fixed–time period system, reorders are placed at the time of review (T), and the safety stock that must be reordered is

$$\text{Safety stock} = z\sigma_{T+L} \qquad \textbf{[7.10]}$$

Exhibit 7.8 shows a fixed–time period system with a review cycle of T and a constant lead time of L. In this case, demand is randomly distributed about a mean d. The quantity to order, q, is

Tutorials

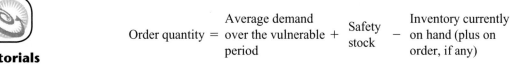

$$\text{Order quantity} = \begin{array}{c}\text{Average demand}\\\text{over the vulnerable}\\\text{period}\end{array} + \begin{array}{c}\text{Safety}\\\text{stock}\end{array} - \begin{array}{c}\text{Inventory currently}\\\text{on hand (plus on}\\\text{order, if any)}\end{array} \qquad \textbf{[7.11]}$$

$$q \quad = \quad \bar{d}(T+L) \quad + \quad z\sigma_{T+L} \quad - \quad I$$

where

q = Quantity to be ordered

T = The number of days between reviews

L = Lead time in days (time between placing an order and receiving it)

$\bar{d}$ = Forecast average daily demand

z = Number of standard deviations for a specified service probability

σ_{T+L} = Standard deviation of demand over the review and lead time

I = Current inventory level (includes items on order)

Note: The demand, lead time, review period, and so forth can be any time units such as days, weeks, or years so long as they are consistent throughout the equation.

In this model, demand ($\bar{d}$) can be forecast and revised each review period if desired or the yearly average may be used if appropriate. We assume that demand is normally distributed.

Exhibit 7.8

FIXED–TIME PERIOD INVENTORY MODEL

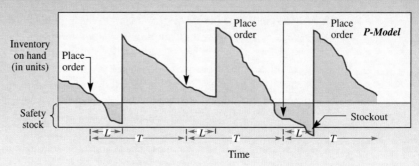

The value of z is dependent on the probability of stocking out and can be found using Appendix A or by using the Excel NORMSINV function.

7.5 Example

Quantity to Order

Step by Step

Daily demand for a product is 10 units with a standard deviation of 3 units. The review period is 30 days, and lead time is 14 days. Management has set a policy of satisfying 98 percent of demand from items in stock. At the beginning of this review period, there are 150 units in inventory.
How many units should be ordered?

**Excel:
Inventory
Control**

Solution

The quantity to order is

$$q = \bar{d}(T + L) + z\sigma_{T+L} - I$$
$$= 10(30 + 14) + z\sigma_{T+L} - 150$$

Before we can complete the solution, we need to find σ_{T+L} and z. To find σ_{T+L}, we use the notion, as before, that the standard deviation of a sequence of independent random variables equals the square root of the sum of the variances. Therefore, the standard deviation during the period $T + L$ is the square root of the sum of the variances for each day:

$$\sigma_{T+L} = \sqrt{\sum_{i=1}^{T+L} \sigma_d^2} \qquad \text{[7.12]}$$

Because each day is independent and σ_d is constant,

$$\sigma_{T+L} = \sqrt{(T + L)\sigma_d^2} = \sqrt{(30 + 14)(3)^2} = 19.90$$

The z value for $P = 0.98$ is 2.05.
The quantity to order, then, is

$$q = \bar{d}(T + L) + z\sigma_{T+L} - I = 10(30 + 14) + 2.05(19.90) - 150 = 331 \text{ units}$$

To ensure a 98 percent probability of not stocking out, order 331 units at this review period. ●

7.9   Inventory Control and Supply Chain Management

Supply Chain

It is important for managers to realize that how they run items using inventory control logic relates directly to the financial performance of the firm. A key measure that relates to company performance is inventory turn. Recall that inventory turn is calculated as follows:

$$\text{Inventory turn} = \frac{\text{Cost of goods sold}}{\text{Average inventory value}}$$

So what is the relationship between how we manage an item and the inventory turn for that item? Here, let us simplify things and consider just the inventory turn for an individual item or a group of items. First, if we look at the numerator, the cost of goods sold for an individual item relates directly to the expected yearly demand (D) for the item. Given a cost per unit (C) for the item, the cost of goods sold is just D times C. Recall this is the same as what was used in our EOQ equation. Next, consider average inventory value. Recall from EOQ that the average inventory is $Q/2$, which is true if we assume that demand is constant. When we bring uncertainty into the equation, safety stock is needed to manage the risk created by demand variability. The fixed–order quantity model and fixed–time period model both have equations for calculating the safety stock required for a given probability of stocking out. In both models, we assume that when going through an order cycle, half the time we need to use the safety stock and half the time we do not. So on average, we expect the safety stock (SS) to be on hand. Given this, the average inventory is equal to the following:

$$\text{Average inventory value} = (Q/2 + SS)C \qquad \textbf{[7.13]}$$

The inventory turn for an individual item then is

$$\text{Inventory turn} = \frac{DC}{(Q/2 + SS)C} = \frac{D}{Q/2 + SS} \qquad \textbf{[7.14]}$$

Step by Step

7.6 Example

Average Inventory Calculation—Fixed–Order Quantity Model

Suppose the following item is being managed using a fixed–order quantity model with safety stock.

Annual demand (D) = 1,000 units
Order quantity (Q) = 300 units
Safety stock (SS) = 40 units

What are the average inventory level and inventory turn for the item?

Solution

$$\text{Average inventory} = Q/2 + SS = 300/2 + 40 = 190 \text{ units}$$

$$\text{Inventory turn} = \frac{D}{Q/2 + SS} = \frac{1{,}000}{190} = 5.263 \text{ turns per year} \; \bullet$$

Step by Step

7.7 Example

Average Inventory Calculation—Fixed–Time Period Model

Consider the following item that is being managed using a fixed–time period model with safety stock.

$$\text{Weekly demand } (d) = 50 \text{ units}$$
$$\text{Review cycle } (T) = 3 \text{ weeks}$$
$$\text{Safety stock } (SS) = 30 \text{ units}$$

Solution

What are the average inventory level and inventory turn for the item?
Here we need to determine how many units we expect to order each cycle. If we assume that demand is fairly steady, then we would expect to order the number of units that we expect demand to be during the review cycle. This expected demand is equal to dT if we assume that there is no trend or seasonality in the demand pattern.

$$\text{Average inventory} = dT/2 + SS = 50(3)/2 + 30 = 105 \text{ units}$$

$$\text{Inventory turn} = \frac{52d}{dT/2 + SS} = \frac{52(50)}{105} = 24.8 \text{ turns per year}$$

assuming there are 52 weeks in the year. ●

7.10 Price-Break Models

Price-break models deal with the fact that, generally, the selling price of an item varies with the order size. This is a discrete or step change rather than a per-unit change. For example, wood screws may cost $0.02 each for 1 to 99 screws, $1.60 per 100, and $13.50 per 1,000. To determine the optimal quantity of any item to order, we simply solve for the economic order quantity for each price and at the point of price change. But not all of the economic order quantities determined by the formula are feasible. In the wood screw example, the Q_{opt} formula might tell us that the optimal decision at the price of 1.6 cents is to order 75 screws. This would be impossible, however, because 75 screws would cost 2 cents each.

In general, to find the lowest-cost order quantity, we need to calculate the economic order quantity for each possible price and check to see whether the quantity is feasible. It is possible that the economic order quantity that is calculated is either higher or lower than the range to which the price corresponds. Any feasible quantity is a potential candidate order quantity. We also need to calculate the cost at each of the price-break quantities, since we know that price is feasible at these points and the total cost may be lowest at one of these values.

The calculations can be simplified a little if holding cost is based on a percentage of unit price (they will be in all the examples and problems given in this book). In this case, we only need to look at a subset of the price-break quantities. The following two-step procedure can be used:

Step 1. Sort the prices from lowest to highest and then, beginning with the lowest price, calculate the economic order quantity for each price level until a feasible economic order

Step by Step

7.8 Example

Price Break

Consider the following case, where

D = 10,000 units (annual demand)
S = $20 to place each order
i = 20 percent of cost (annual carrying cost, storage, interest, obsolescence, etc.)
C = Cost per unit (according to the order size; orders of 0 to 499 units, $5.00 per unit; 500 to 999, $4.50 per unit; 1,000 and up, $3.90 per unit)

What quantity should be ordered?

Solution

The appropriate equations from the basic fixed–order quantity case are

$$TC = DC + \frac{D}{Q}S + \frac{Q}{2}iC$$

and

$$Q = \sqrt{\frac{2DS}{iC}} \qquad\qquad [7.15]$$

Solving for the economic order size, we obtain

@C = $3.90,	Q = 716	Not feasible
@C = $4.50,	Q = 667	Feasible, cost = $45,600
Check Q = 1,000,	Cost = $39,590	Optimal solution

In Exhibit 7.10, which displays the cost relationship and order quantity range, note that most of the order quantity–cost relationships lie outside the feasible range and that only a single, continuous range results. This should be readily apparent because, for example, the first order quantity specifies buying 633 units at $5.00 per unit. However, if 633 units are ordered, the price is $4.50, not $5.00. The same holds true for the third order quantity, which specifies an order of 716 units at $3.90 each. This $3.90 price is not available on orders of fewer than 1,000 units.

Exhibit 7.10 itemizes the total costs at the economic order quantities and at the price breaks. The optimal order quantity is shown to be 1,000 units. ●

quantity is found. By feasible, we mean that the price is in the correct corresponding range.

Step 2. If the first feasible economic order quantity is for the lowest price, this quantity is best and you are finished. Otherwise, calculate the total cost for the first feasible economic order quantity (you did these from lowest to highest price) and also calculate the total cost at each price break lower than the price associated with the first feasible economic order quantity. This is the lowest order quantity at which you can take advantage of the price break. The optimal Q is the one with the lowest cost.

Looking at Exhibit 7.9, we see that order quantities are solved from right to left, or from the lowest unit price to the highest, until a valid Q is obtained. Then the order quantity at each *price break* above this Q is used to find which order quantity has the least cost—the computed Q or the Q at one of the price breaks.

CURVES FOR THREE SEPARATE ORDER QUANTITY MODELS IN A THREE-PRICE-BREAK SITUATION (RED LINE DEPICTS FEASIBLE RANGE OF PURCHASES)

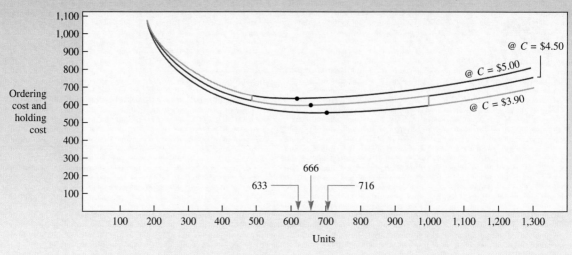

One practical consideration in price-break problems is that the price reduction from volume purchases frequently makes it seemingly economical to order amounts larger than the Q_{opt}. Thus, when applying the model, we must be particularly careful to obtain a valid estimate of product obsolescence and warehousing costs.

7.11 ABC Inventory Planning

Maintaining inventory through counting, placing orders, receiving stock, and so on, takes personnel time and costs money. When there are limits on these resources, the logical move is to try to use the available resources to control inventory in the best way. In other words, focus on the most important items in inventory.

In the nineteenth century Vilfredo Pareto, in a study of the distribution of wealth in Milan, found that 20 percent of the people controlled 80 percent of the wealth. This logic of the few having the greatest importance and the many having little importance has been broadened to include many situations and is termed the *Pareto principle*.[3] This is true in our everyday lives (most of our decisions are relatively unimportant, but a few shape our future) and is certainly true in inventory systems (where a few items account for the bulk of our investment).

Any inventory system must specify when an order is to be placed for an item and how many units to order. Most inventory control situations involve so many items that it is not practical to model and give thorough treatment to each item. To get around this problem, the ABC classification scheme divides inventory items into three groupings: high dollar volume (A), moderate dollar volume (B), and low dollar volume (C). Dollar volume is a measure of importance; an item low in cost but high in volume can be more important than a high-cost item with low volume.

	Q = 633 where	Q = 667 where	Q = 716 where	Price Break
	$c = \$5$	$c = \$4.50$	$c = \$3.90$	1,000
Holding cost $\left(\dfrac{Q}{2}ic\right)$		$\dfrac{667}{2}(0.20)4.50$ $= \$300.15$		$\dfrac{1,000}{2}(0.20)3.90$ $= \$390$
Ordering cost $\left(\dfrac{D}{Q}s\right)$	Not feasible	$\dfrac{10,000(20)}{667}$ $= \$299.85$	Not feasible	$\dfrac{10,000(20)}{1,000}$ $= \$200$
Holding and ordering cost		$600.00		$590
Item cost (DC)		10,000(4.50)		10,000(3.90)
Total cost		$45,600		$39,590

ABC Classification

If the annual usage of items in inventory is listed according to dollar volume, generally, the list shows that a small number of items account for a large dollar volume and that a large number of items account for a small dollar volume. Exhibit 7.11A illustrates the relationship.

The ABC approach divides this list into three groupings by value: A items constitute roughly the top 15 percent of the items, B items the next 35 percent, and C items the last 50 percent. From observation, it appears that the list in Exhibit 7.11A can be meaningfully grouped with A including 20 percent (2 of the 10), B including 30 percent, and C including 50 percent. These points show clear delineations between sections. The result of this segmentation is shown in Exhibit 7.11B and plotted in Exhibit 7.11C.

Segmentation may not always occur so neatly. The objective, though, is to try to separate the important from the unimportant. Where the lines actually break depends on the particular inventory under question and on how much personnel time is available. (With more time, a firm could define larger A or B categories.)

The purpose of classifying items into groups is to establish the appropriate degree of control over each item. On a periodic basis, for example, class A items may be more clearly controlled with weekly ordering, B items may be ordered biweekly, and C items may be ordered monthly or bimonthly. Note that the unit cost of items is not related to their classification. An A item may have a high dollar volume through a combination of either low cost and high usage or high cost and low usage. Similarly, C items may have a low dollar volume because of either low demand or low cost. In an automobile service station, gasoline would be an A item with daily or weekly replenishment; tires, batteries, oil, grease, and transmission fluid may be B items and ordered every two to four weeks; and C items would consist of valve stems, windshield wiper blades, radiator caps, hoses, fan belts, oil and gas additives, car wax, and so forth. C items may be ordered every two or three months or even be allowed to run out before reordering because the penalty for stockout is not serious.

Item Number	Annual Dollar Usage	Percentage of Total Value
22	$95,000	40.69%
68	75,000	32.13
27	25,000	10.71
03	15,000	6.43
82	13,000	5.57
54	7,500	3.21
36	1,500	0.64
19	800	0.34
23	425	0.18
41	225	0.10
	$233,450	100.0%

B. ABC Grouping of Inventory Items

Classification	Item Number	Annual Dollar Usage	Percentage of Total
A	22, 68	$170,000	72.9%
B	27, 03, 82	53,000	22.7
C	54, 36, 19, 23, 41	10,450	4.4
		$233,450	100.0%

C. ABC Inventory Classification (inventory value for each group versus the group's portion of the total list)

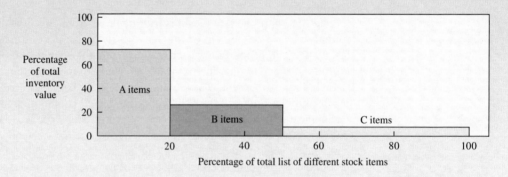

Sometimes an item may be critical to a system if its absence creates a sizable loss. In this case, regardless of the item's classification, sufficiently large stocks should be kept on hand to prevent runout. One way to ensure closer control is to designate this item an A or a B, forcing it into the category even if its dollar volume does not warrant such inclusion.

7.12 Inventory Accuracy and Cycle Counting

Inventory records usually differ from the actual physical count; inventory accuracy refers to how well the two agree. Companies such as Walmart understand the importance of inventory accuracy and expend considerable effort ensuring it. The question is, How much error is acceptable? If the record shows a balance of 683 of part X and an actual count shows 652, is this within reason? Suppose the actual count shows 750, an excess of 67 over the record; is this any better?

Every production system must have agreement, within some specified range, between what the record says is in inventory and what actually is in inventory. There are many reasons why records and inventory may not agree. For example, an open stockroom area allows items to be removed for both legitimate and unauthorized purposes. The legitimate removal may have been done in a hurry and simply not recorded. Sometimes parts are misplaced, turning up months later. Parts are often stored in several locations, but records may be lost or the location recorded incorrectly. Sometimes stock replenishment orders

A sales clerk at Tokyo's Mitsukoshi department store reads an RFID tag on jeans to check stock. Mitsukoshi and Japan's electronic giant Fujitsu partnered to use RFID to improve stock control and customer service.

are recorded as received, when in fact they never were. Occasionally, a group of parts is recorded as removed from inventory, but the customer order is canceled and the parts are replaced in inventory without canceling the record. To keep the production system flowing smoothly without parts shortages and efficiently without excess balances, records must be accurate.

How can a firm keep accurate, up-to-date records? Using bar codes and RFID tags is important to minimizing errors caused by inputting wrong numbers in the system. It is also important to keep the storeroom locked. If only storeroom personnel have access, and one of their measures of performance for personnel evaluation and merit increases is record accuracy, there is a strong motivation to comply. Every location of inventory storage, whether in a locked storeroom or on the production floor, should have a recordkeeping mechanism. A second way is to convey the importance of accurate records to all personnel and depend on them to assist in this effort. (This all boils down to this: Put a fence that goes all the way to the ceiling around the storage area so that workers cannot climb over to get parts; put a lock on the gate and give one person the key. Nobody can pull parts without having the transaction authorized and recorded.)

Another way to ensure accuracy is to count inventory frequently and match this against records. A widely used method is called *cycle counting.*

Cycle counting

Cycle counting is a physical inventory-taking technique in which inventory is counted frequently rather than once or twice a year. The key to effective cycle counting and, therefore, to accurate records lies in deciding which items are to be counted, when, and by whom.

Virtually all inventory systems these days are computerized. The computer can be programmed to produce a cycle count notice in the following cases:

1. When the record shows a low or zero balance on hand. (It is easier to count fewer items.)
2. When the record shows a positive balance but a backorder was written (indicating a discrepancy).
3. After some specified level of activity.
4. To signal a review based on the importance of the item (as in the ABC system) such as in the following table:

Annual Dollar Usage	Review Period
$10,000 or more	30 days or less
$3,000–$10,000	45 days or less
$250–$3,000	90 days or less
Less than $250	180 days or less

The easiest time for stock to be counted is when there is no activity in the stockroom or on the production floor. This means on the weekends or during the second or third shift, when the facility is less busy. If this is not possible, more careful logging and separation of items are required to count inventory while production is going on and transactions are occurring.

The counting cycle depends on the available personnel. Some firms schedule regular stockroom personnel to do the counting during lulls in the regular working day. Other companies hire private firms that come in and count inventory. Still other firms use full-time cycle counters who do nothing but count inventory and resolve differences with the records. Although this last method sounds expensive, many firms believe that it is actually less costly than the usual hectic annual inventory count generally performed during the two- or three-week annual vacation shutdown.

The question of how much error is tolerable between physical inventory and records has been much debated. Some firms strive for 100 percent accuracy, whereas others accept 1, 2, or 3 percent error. The accuracy level often recommended by experts is ±0.2 percent for A items, ±1 percent for B items, and ±5 percent for C items. Regardless of the specific accuracy decided on, the important point is that the level be dependable so that safety stocks may be provided as a cushion. Accuracy is important for a smooth production process so that customer orders can be processed as scheduled and not held up because of unavailable parts.

7.13 Summary

This chapter introduced the two main classes of demand: (1) independent demand, referring to the external demand for a firm's end product, and (2) dependent demand, usually referring—within the firm—to the demand for items created because of the demand for more complex items of which they are a part. Most industries have items in both classes. In manufacturing, for example, independent demand is common for finished products, service and repair parts, and operating supplies; and dependent demand is common for those parts and materials needed to produce the end product. In wholesale and retail sales of consumer goods, most demand is independent—each item is an end item, with the wholesaler or retailer doing no further assembly or fabrication.

Independent demand, the focus of this chapter, is based on statistics. In the fixed–order quantity and fixed–time period models, the influence of service level was shown on safety stock and reorder point determinations. One special-purpose model—the single-period model—was also presented.

To distinguish among item categories for analysis and control, the ABC method was offered. The importance of inventory accuracy was also noted, and cycle counting was described.

In this chapter, we also pointed out that inventory reduction requires a knowledge of the operating system. It is not simply a case of selecting an inventory model off the shelf and plugging in some numbers. In the first place, a model might not even be appropriate. In the second case, the numbers might be full of errors or even based on erroneous data. Determining order quantities is often referred to as a trade-off problem; that is, trading off holding costs for setup costs. Note that companies really want to reduce both.

The simple fact is that firms have very large investments in inventory, and the cost to carry this inventory runs from 25 to 35 percent of the inventory's worth annually. Therefore, a major goal of most firms today is to reduce inventory.

A caution is in order, though. The formulas in this chapter try to minimize cost. Bear in mind that a firm's objective should be something like "making money"—so be sure that reducing inventory cost does, in fact, support this. Usually, correctly reducing inventory lowers cost, improves quality and performance, and enhances profit.

7.14 Key Terms

Inventory The stock of any item or resource used in an organization.

Independent demand The demands for various items are unrelated to each other.

Dependent demand The need for any one item is a direct result of the need for some other item, usually an item of which it is a part.

Fixed–order quantity model (or Q-model) An inventory control model where the amount requisitioned is fixed and the actual ordering is triggered by inventory dropping to a specified level of inventory.

Fixed–time period model (or P-model) An inventory control model that specifies inventory is ordered at the end of a predetermined time period. The interval of time between orders is fixed and the order quantity varies.

Inventory position The amount on-hand plus on-order minus backordered quantities. In the case where inventory has been allocated for special purposes, the inventory position is reduced by these allocated amounts.

Safety stock The amount of inventory carried in addition to the expected demand.

Cycle counting A physical inventory-taking technique in which inventory is counted on a frequent basis rather than once or twice a year.

7.15
Formula
Review

Single-period model. Cumulative probability of not selling the last unit. Ratio of marginal cost of underestimating demand and marginal cost of overestimating demand.

$$P \le \frac{C_u}{C_o + C_u}$$

[7.1]

Q-model. Total annual cost for an order Q, a per-unit cost C, setup cost S, and per-unit holding cost H.

$$TC = DC + \frac{D}{Q}S + \frac{Q}{2}H$$

[7.2]

Q-model. Optimal (or economic) order quantity.

$$Q_{opt} = \sqrt{\frac{2DS}{H}}$$

[7.3]

Q-model. Reorder point R based on average daily demand $\bar{d}$ and lead time L in days.

$$R = \bar{d}L$$

[7.4]

Q-model. Reorder point providing a safety stock of $z\sigma_L$.

$$R = \bar{d}L + z\sigma_L$$

[7.5]

Average daily demand over a period of n days.

$$\bar{d} = \frac{\sum_{i=1}^{n} d_i}{n}$$

[7.6]

Standard deviation of demand over a period of n days.

$$\sigma_d = \sqrt{\frac{\sum_{i=1}^{n}(d_i - \bar{d})^2}{n}}$$

[7.7]

Standard deviation of a series of independent demands.

$$\sigma_L = \sqrt{\sigma_1^2 + \sigma_2^2 + \cdots + \sigma_L^2}$$

[7.8]

Q-model. Safety stock calculation.

$$SS = z\sigma_L$$

[7.9]

P-model. Safety stock calculation.

$$SS = z\sigma_{T+L}$$

[7.10]

P-model. Optimal order quantity in a fixed-period system with a review period of T days and lead time of L days.

$$q = \bar{d}(T + L) + z\sigma_{T+L} - I$$

[7.11]

P-model. Standard deviation of a series of independent demands over the review period T and lead time L.

$$\sigma_{T+L} = \sqrt{\sum_{i=1}^{T+L} \sigma_d^2}$$

[7.12]

Average inventory.

$$\text{Average inventory value} = (Q/2 + SS)C \qquad \textbf{[7.13]}$$

Inventory turn.

$$\text{Inventory turn} = \frac{DC}{(Q/2 + SS)C} = \frac{D}{Q/2 + SS} \qquad \textbf{[7.14]}$$

Economic order quantity (with carrying cost percentage).

$$Q = \sqrt{\frac{2DS}{iC}} \qquad \textbf{[7.15]}$$

7.16 Solved Problems

Solved Problem 1

A product is priced to sell at $100 per unit, and its cost is constant at $70 per unit. Each unsold unit has a salvage value of $20. Demand is expected to range between 35 and 40 units for the period; 35 definitely can be sold and no units over 40 will be sold. The demand probabilities and the associated cumulative probability distribution (P) for this situation are shown below.

Number of Units Demanded	Probability of This Demand	Cumulative Probability
35	0.10	0.10
36	0.15	0.25
37	0.25	0.50
38	0.25	0.75
39	0.15	0.90
40	0.10	1.00

Excel: Inventory Control

How many units should be ordered?

Solution

The cost of underestimating demand is the loss of profit, or $C_u = \$100 - \$70 = \$30$ per unit. The cost of overestimating demand is the loss incurred when the unit must be sold at salvage value, $C_o = \$70 - \$20 = \$50$.

The optimal probability of not being sold is

$$P \le \frac{C_u}{C_o + C_u} = \frac{30}{50 + 30} = 0.375$$

From the distribution data above, this corresponds to the 37th unit.

The following is a full marginal analysis for the problem. Note that the minimum cost is when 37 units are purchased.

Units Demanded	Probability	Number of Units Purchased					
		35	36	37	38	39	40
35	0.1	0	50	100	150	200	250
36	0.15	30	0	50	100	150	200
37	0.25	60	30	0	50	100	150
38	0.25	90	60	30	0	50	100
39	0.15	120	90	60	30	0	50
40	0.1	150	120	90	60	30	0
Total cost		75	53	43	53	83	125

Solved Problem 2

Items purchased from a vendor cost $20 each, and the forecast for next year's demand is 1,000 units. If it costs $5 every time an order is placed for more units and the storage cost is $4 per unit per year, what quantity should be ordered each time?
a. What is the total ordering cost for a year?
b. What is the total storage cost for a year?

Solution

The quantity to be ordered each time is

$$Q = \sqrt{\frac{2DS}{H}} = \sqrt{\frac{2(1,000)5}{4}} = 50 \text{ units}$$

a. The total ordering cost for a year is

$$\frac{D}{Q}S = \frac{1,000}{50}(\$5) = \$100$$

b. The storage cost for a year is

$$\frac{Q}{2}H = \frac{50}{2}(\$4) = \$100$$

Solved Problem 3

Daily demand for a product is 120 units, with a standard deviation of 30 units. The review period is 14 days and the lead time is 7 days. At the time of review, 130 units are in stock. If only a 1 percent risk of stocking out is acceptable, how many units should be ordered?

Solution

$$\sigma_{T+L} = \sqrt{(14 + 7)(30)^2} = \sqrt{18,900} = 137.5$$
$$z = 2.33$$
$$q = \bar{d}(T + L) + z\sigma_{T+L} - I$$
$$= 120(14 + 7) + 2.33(137.5) - 130$$
$$= 2,710 \text{ units}$$

Excel: Inventory Control

Solved Problem 4

A company currently has 200 units of a product on hand that it orders every two weeks when the salesperson visits the premises. Demand for the product averages 20 units per day with a standard deviation of 5 units. Lead time for the product to arrive is seven days. Management has a goal of a 95 percent probability of not stocking out for this product.

The salesperson is due to come in late this afternoon when 180 units are left in stock (assuming that 20 are sold today). How many units should be ordered?

Excel: Inventory Control

Solution

Given $I = 180, T = 14, L = 7, d = 20$
$$\sigma_{T+L} = \sqrt{21(5)^2} = 23$$
$$z = 1.64$$
$$q = \bar{d}(T + L) + z\sigma_{T+L} - I$$
$$= 20(14 + 7) + 1.64(23) - 180$$
$$q = 278 \text{ units}$$

7.17 Review and Discussion Questions

1. Distinguish between dependent and independent demand in a McDonald's restaurant, in an integrated manufacturer of personal copiers, and in a pharmaceutical supply house.
2. Distinguish between in-process inventory, safety stock inventory, and seasonal inventory.
3. Discuss the nature of the costs that affect inventory size.
4. Under which conditions would a plant manager elect to use a fixed–order quantity model as opposed to a fixed–time period model? What are the disadvantages of using a fixed–time period ordering system?
5. What two basic questions must be answered by an inventory-control decision rule?
6. Discuss the assumptions that are inherent in production setup cost, ordering cost, and carrying costs. How valid are they?
7. "The nice thing about inventory models is that you can pull one off the shelf and apply it so long as your cost estimates are accurate." Comment.
8. Which type of inventory system would you use in the following situations?
   a. Supplying your kitchen with fresh food.
   b. Obtaining a daily newspaper.
   c. Buying gas for your car.
   To which of these items do you impute the highest stockout cost?
9. Why is it desirable to classify items into groups, as the ABC classification does?

7.18 Problems

1. The local supermarket buys lettuce each day to ensure really fresh produce. Each morning any lettuce that is left from the previous day is sold to a dealer that resells it to farmers who use it to feed their animals. This week the supermarket can buy fresh lettuce for $4.00 a box. The lettuce is sold for $10.00 a box and the dealer that sells old lettuce is willing to pay $1.50 a box. Past history says that tomorrow's demand for lettuce averages 250 boxes with a standard deviation of 34 boxes. How many boxes of lettuce should the supermarket purchase tomorrow?
2. Next week, Super Discount Airlines has a flight from New York to Los Angeles that will be booked to capacity. The airline knows from past history that an average of 25 customers (with a standard deviation of 15) cancel their reservation or do not show for the flight. Revenue from a ticket on the flight is $125. If the flight is overbooked, the airline has a policy of getting the customer on the next available flight and giving the person a free round-trip ticket on a future flight. The cost of this free round-trip ticket averages $250. Super Discount considers the cost of flying the plane from New York to Los Angeles a sunk cost. By how many seats should Super Discount overbook the flight?
3. Ray's Satellite Emporium wishes to determine the best order size for its best-selling satellite dish (model TS111). Ray has estimated the annual demand for this model at 1,000 units. His cost to carry one unit is $100 per year per unit, and he has estimated that each order costs $25 to place. Using the EOQ model, how many should Ray order each time?
4. Dunstreet's Department Store would like to develop an inventory ordering policy of a 95 percent probability of not stocking out. To illustrate your recommended procedure, use as an example the ordering policy for white percale sheets.

   Demand for white percale sheets is 5,000 per year. The store is open 365 days per year. Every two weeks (14 days) inventory is counted and a new order is placed. It takes 10 days for the sheets to be delivered. Standard deviation of demand for the sheets is five per day. There are currently 150 sheets on hand.

   How many sheets should you order?
5. Charlie's Pizza orders all of its pepperoni, olives, anchovies, and mozzarella cheese to be shipped directly from Italy. An American distributor stops by every four weeks to take orders. Because the orders are shipped directly from Italy, they take three weeks to arrive.

   Charlie's Pizza uses an average of 150 pounds of pepperoni each week, with a standard deviation of 30 pounds. Charlie's prides itself on offering only the best-quality ingredients and a high level of service, so it wants to ensure a 98 percent probability of not stocking out on pepperoni.

Assume that the sales representative just walked in the door and there are currently 500 pounds of pepperoni in the walk-in cooler. How many pounds of pepperoni would you order?

6. Given the following information, formulate an inventory management system. The item is demanded 50 weeks a year.

Item cost	$10.00	Standard deviation of weekly demand	25 per week
Order cost	$250.00	Lead time	1 week
Annual holding cost (%)	33% of item cost	Service probability	95%
Annual demand	25,750		
Average demand	515 per week		

a. State the order quantity and reorder point.

b. Determine the annual holding and order costs.

c. If a price break of $50 per order was offered for purchase quantities of over 2,000, would you take advantage of it? How much would you save annually?

7. Lieutenant Commander Data is planning to make his monthly (every 30 days) trek to Gamma Hydra City to pick up a supply of isolinear chips. The trip will take Data about two days. Before he leaves, he calls in the order to the GHC Supply Store. He uses chips at an average rate of five per day (seven days per week) with a standard deviation of demand of one per day. He needs a 98 percent service probability. If he currently has 35 chips in inventory, how many should he order? What is the most he will ever have to order?

8. Jill's Job Shop buys two parts (Tegdiws and Widgets) for use in its production system from two different suppliers. The parts are needed throughout the entire 52-week year. Tegdiws are used at a relatively constant rate and are ordered whenever the remaining quantity drops to the reorder level. Widgets are ordered from a supplier who stops by every three weeks. Data for both products are as follows:

Item	Tegdiw	Widget
Annual demand	10,000	5,000
Holding cost (% of item cost)	20%	20%
Setup or order cost	$150.00	$25.00
Lead time	4 weeks	1 week
Safety stock	55 units	5 units
Item cost	$10.00	$2.00

a. What is the inventory control system for Tegdiws? That is, what is the reorder quantity and what is the reorder point?

b. What is the inventory control system for Widgets?

9. Demand for an item is 1,000 units per year. Each order placed costs $10; the annual cost to carry items in inventory is $2 each. In what quantities should the item be ordered?

10. The annual demand for a product is 15,600 units. The weekly demand is 300 units with a standard deviation of 90 units. The cost to place an order is $31.20, and the time from ordering to receipt is four weeks. The annual inventory carrying cost is $0.10 per unit. Find the reorder point necessary to provide a 98 percent service probability.

Suppose the production manager is asked to reduce the safety stock of this item by 50 percent. If she does so, what will the new service probability be?

11. Daily demand for a product is 100 units, with a standard deviation of 25 units. The review period is 10 days and the lead time is 6 days. At the time of review there are 50 units in stock. If 98 percent service probability is desired, how many units should be ordered?

12. Item X is a standard item stocked in a company's inventory of component parts. Each year the firm, on a random basis, uses about 2,000 of item X, which costs $25 each. Storage costs, which include insurance and cost of capital, amount to $5 per unit of average inventory. Every time an order is placed for more item X, it costs $10.

   a. Whenever item X is ordered, what should the order size be?

   b. What is the annual cost for ordering item X?

   c. What is the annual cost for storing item X?

13. Annual demand for a product is 13,000 units; weekly demand is 250 units with a standard deviation of 40 units. The cost of placing an order is $100, and the time from ordering to receipt is four weeks. The annual inventory carrying cost is $0.65 per unit. To provide a 98 percent service probability, what must the reorder point be?

   Suppose the production manager is told to reduce the safety stock of this item by 100 units. If this is done, what will the new service probability be?

14. In the past, Taylor Industries has used a fixed–time period inventory system that involved taking a complete inventory count of all items each month. However, increasing labor costs are forcing Taylor Industries to examine alternative ways to reduce the amount of labor involved in inventory stockrooms, yet without increasing other costs, such as shortage costs. Here is a random sample of 20 of Taylor's items.

Item Number	Annual Usage	Item Number	Annual Usage
1	$1,500	11	$13,000
2	12,000	12	600
3	2,200	13	42,000
4	50,000	14	9,900
5	9,600	15	1,200
6	750	16	10,200
7	2,000	17	4,000
8	11,000	18	61,000
9	800	19	3,500
10	15,000	20	2,900

   a. What would you recommend Taylor do to cut back its labor cost? (Illustrate using an ABC plan.)

   b. Item 15 is critical to continued operations. How would you recommend it be classified?

15. Gentle Ben's Bar and Restaurant uses 5,000 quart bottles of an imported wine each year. The effervescent wine costs $3 per bottle and is served only in whole bottles because it loses its bubbles quickly. Ben figures that it costs $10 each time an order is placed, and holding costs are 20 percent of the purchase price. It takes three weeks for an order to arrive. Weekly demand is 100 bottles (closed two weeks per year) with a standard deviation of 30 bottles.

   Ben would like to use an inventory system that minimizes inventory cost and will provide a 95 percent service probability.

   a. What is the economic quantity for Ben to order?

   b. At what inventory level should he place an order?

16. Retailers Warehouse (RW) is an independent supplier of household items to department stores. RW attempts to stock enough items for a 98 percent service probability.

   A stainless steel knife set is one item it stocks. Demand (2,400 sets per year) is relatively stable over the entire year. Whenever new stock is ordered, a buyer must assure that numbers are correct for stock on hand and then phone in a new order. The total cost involved to place an order is about $5. RW figures that holding inventory in stock and paying for interest on borrowed capital, insurance, and so on, adds up to about $4 holding cost per unit per year.

Analysis of the past data shows that the standard deviation of demand from retailers is about four units per day for a 365-day year. Lead time to get the order is seven days.

a. What is the economic order quantity?

b. What is the reorder point?

17. Daily demand for a product is 60 units with a standard deviation of 10 units. The review period is 10 days, and lead time is 2 days. At the time of review there are 100 units in stock. If 98 percent service probability is desired, how many units should be ordered?

18. University Drug Pharmaceuticals orders its antibiotics every two weeks (14 days) when a salesperson visits from one of the pharmaceutical companies. Tetracycline is one of its most prescribed antibiotics, with average daily demand of 2,000 capsules. The standard deviation of daily demand was derived from examining prescriptions filled over the past three months and was found to be 800 capsules. It takes five days for the order to arrive. University Drug would like to satisfy 99 percent of the prescriptions. The salesperson just arrived, and there are currently 25,000 capsules in stock.

How many capsules should be ordered?

19. Sally's Silk Screening produces specialty T-shirts that are primarily sold at special events. She is trying to decide how many to produce for an upcoming event. During the event itself, which lasts one day, Sally can sell T-shirts for $20 apiece. However, when the event ends, any unsold T-shirts are sold for $4 apiece. It costs Sally $8 to make a specialty T-shirt. Using Sally's estimate of demand that follows, how many T-shirts should she produce for the upcoming event?

Demand	Probability
300	0.05
400	0.10
500	0.40
600	0.30
700	0.10
800	0.05

20. Famous Albert prides himself on being the Cookie King of the West. Small, freshly baked cookies are the specialty of his shop. Famous Albert has asked for help to determine the number of cookies he should make each day. From an analysis of past demand he estimates demand for cookies as

Demand	Probability of Demand
1,800 dozen	0.05
2,000	0.10
2,200	0.20
2,400	0.30
2,600	0.20
2,800	0.10
3,000	0.05

Each dozen sells for $0.69 and costs $0.49, which includes handling and transportation. Cookies that are not sold at the end of the day are reduced to $0.29 and sold the following day as day-old merchandise.

a. Construct a table showing the profits or losses for each possible quantity.

b. What is the optimal number of cookies to make?

c. Solve this problem by using marginal analysis.

21. Sarah's Muffler Shop has one standard muffler that fits a large variety of cars. Sarah wishes to establish a reorder point system to manage inventory of this standard muffler. Use the following information to determine the best order size and the reorder point:

Annual demand	3,500 mufflers	Ordering cost	$50 per order
Standard deviation of daily demand	6 mufflers per working day	Service probability	90%
Item cost	$30 per muffler	Lead time	2 working days
Annual holding cost	25% of item value	Working days	300 per year

22. Alpha Products, Inc., is having a problem trying to control inventory. There is insufficient time to devote to all its items equally. Here is a sample of some items stocked, along with the annual usage of each item expressed in dollar volume.

Item	Annual Dollar Usage	Item	Annual Dollar Usage
a	$7,000	k	$80,000
b	1,000	l	400
c	14,000	m	1,100
d	2,000	n	30,000
e	24,000	o	1,900
f	68,000	p	800
g	17,000	q	90,000
h	900	r	12,000
i	1,700	s	3,000
j	2,300	t	32,000

   a. Can you suggest a system for allocating control time?
   b. Specify where each item from the list would be placed.

23. After graduation, you decide to go into a partnership in an office supply store that has existed for a number of years. Walking through the store and stockrooms, you find a great discrepancy in service levels. Some spaces and bins for items are completely empty; others have supplies that are covered with dust and have obviously been there a long time. You decide to take on the project of establishing consistent levels of inventory to meet customer demands. Most of your supplies are purchased from just a few distributors that call on your store once every two weeks.

   You choose, as your first item for study, computer printer paper. You examine the sales records and purchase orders and find that demand for the past 12 months was 5,000 boxes. Using your calculator you sample some days' demands and estimate that the standard deviation of daily demand is 10 boxes. You also search out these figures:

Cost per box of paper: $11.
Desired service probability: 98 percent.
Store is open every day.
Salesperson visits every two weeks.
Delivery time following visit is three days.

   Using your procedure, how many boxes of paper would be ordered if, on the day the salesperson calls, 60 boxes are on hand?

24. A distributor of large appliances needs to determine the order quantities and reorder points for the various products it carries. The following data refer to a specific refrigerator in its product line:

Cost to place an order	$100
Holding cost	20 percent of product cost per year
Cost of refrigerator	$500 each
Annual demand	500 refrigerators
Standard deviation during lead time	10 refrigerators
Lead time	7 days

Consider an even daily demand and a 365-day year.

a. What is the economic order quantity?

b. If the distributor wants a 97 percent service probability, what reorder point, R, should be used?

25. It is your responsibility, as the new head of the automotive section of Nichols Department Store, to ensure that reorder quantities for the various items have been correctly established. You decide to test one item and choose Michelin tires, XW size 185 × 14 BSW. A perpetual inventory system has been used, so you examine this as well as other records and come up with the following data:

Cost per tire	$35 each
Holding cost	20 percent of tire cost per year
Demand	1,000 per year
Ordering cost	$20 per order
Standard deviation of daily demand	3 tires
Delivery lead time	4 days

Because customers generally do not wait for tires but go elsewhere, you decide on a service probability of 98 percent. Assume the demand occurs 365 days per year.

a. Determine the order quantity.

b. Determine the reorder point.

26. UA Hamburger Hamlet (UAHH) places a daily order for its high-volume items (hamburger patties, buns, milk, and so on). UAHH counts its current inventory on hand once per day and phones in its order for delivery 24 hours later. Determine the number of hamburgers UAHH should order for the following conditions:

Average daily demand	600
Standard deviation of demand	100
Desired service probability	99%
Hamburger inventory	800

27. DAT, Inc., produces digital audiotapes to be used in the consumer audio division. DAT lacks sufficient personnel in its inventory supply section to closely control each item stocked, so it

has asked you to determine an ABC classification. Here is a sample from the inventory records:

Item	Average Monthly Demand	Price per Unit	Item	Average Monthly Demand	Price per Unit
1	700	$6.00	6	100	10.00
2	200	4.00	7	3,000	2.00
3	2,000	12.00	8	2,500	1.00
4	1,100	20.00	9	500	10.00
5	4,000	21.00	10	1,000	2.00

Develop an ABC classification for these 10 items.

28. A local service station is open 7 days per week, 365 days per year. Sales of 10W40 grade premium oil average 20 cans per day. Inventory holding costs are $0.50 per can per year. Ordering costs are $10 per order. Lead time is two weeks. Backorders are not practical—the motorist drives away.

    a. Based on these data, choose the appropriate inventory model and calculate the economic order quantity and reorder point. Describe in a sentence how the plan would work. Hint: Assume demand is deterministic.

    b. The boss is concerned about this model because demand really varies. The standard deviation of demand was determined from a data sample to be 6.15 cans per day. The manager wants a 99.5 percent service probability. Determine a new inventory plan based on this information and the data in *a*. Use Q_{opt} from *a*.

29. Dave's Auto Supply custom mixes paint for its customers. The shop performs a weekly inventory count of the main colors that are used for mixing paint. Determine the amount of white paint that should be ordered using the following information:

Average weekly demand	20 gallons
Standard deviation of demand	5 gallons/week
Desired service probability	98%
Current inventory	25 gallons
Lead time	1 week

30. A particular raw material is available to a company at three different prices, depending on the size of the order:

Less than 100 pounds	$20 per pound
100 pounds to 1,000 pounds	$19 per pound
More than 1,000 pounds	$18 per pound

The cost to place an order is $40. Annual demand is 3,000 units. Holding (or carrying) cost is 25 percent of the material price.

What is the economic order quantity to buy each time?

HP DESKJET SUPPLY CHAIN

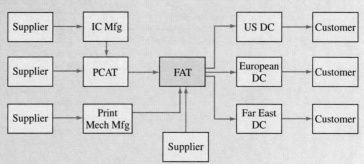

Key: IC Mfg—Integrated Circuit Manufacturing
PCAT—Printed Circuit Assembly and Test
FAT—Final Assembly and Test
Print Mech Mfg—Print Mechanism Manufacturing

31. CU, Incorporated (CUI), produces copper contacts that it uses in switches and relays. CUI needs to determine the order quantity, Q, to meet the annual demand at the lowest cost. The price of copper depends on the quantity ordered. Here are price-break and other data for the problem:

Price of copper	$0.82 per pound up to 2,499 pounds
	$0.81 per pound for orders between 2,500 and 5,000 pounds
	$0.80 per pound for orders greater than 5,000 pounds
Annual demand	50,000 pounds per year
Holding cost	20 percent per unit per year of the price of the copper
Ordering cost	$30

Which quantity should be ordered?

7.19 CASE: Hewlett-Packard—Supplying the DeskJet Printer in Europe

The DeskJet printer was introduced in 1988 and has become one of Hewlett-Packard's (HP's) most successful products. Sales have grown steadily, now reaching a level of over 600,000. Unfortunately, inventory growth has tracked sales growth closely. HP's distribution centers are filled with pallets of the DeskJet printer. Worse yet, the organization in Europe claims that inventory levels there need to be raised even further to maintain satisfactory product availability.

7.20 The DeskJet Supply Chain

The network of suppliers, manufacturing sites, distribution centers (DCs), dealers, and customers for the DeskJet product make up the DeskJet supply chain (see Exhibit 7.12). HP in Vancouver does manufacturing. There are two key stages in the manufacturing process: (1) printed circuit assembly and test (PCAT) and (2) final assembly and test (FAT). PCAT involves the assembly and testing of electronic components (like integrated circuits, read-only memories, and raw printed circuit boards)

Exhibit 7.13

HP DESKJET BILL OF MATERIALS

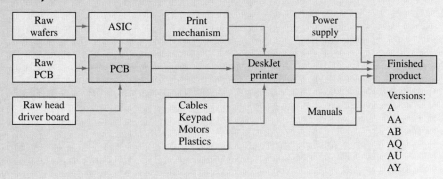

to make logic boards used in the printer. FAT involves the assembly of other subassemblies (like motors, cables, keypads, plastic chassis, gears, and the printed circuit assemblies from PCAT) to produce a working printer, as well as the final testing of the printer. The components needed for PCAT and FAT are sourced from other HP divisions as well as from external suppliers worldwide.

Selling the DeskJet in Europe requires customizing the printer to meet the language and power supply requirements of the local countries, a process known as "localization." Specifically, the localization of the DeskJet of different countries involves assembling the appropriate power supply module, which reflects the correct voltage requirements (110 or 220) and power cord plug, and packaging it with the working printer and a manual written in the appropriate language. Currently, the final test is done with the actual power supply module included with the printer. Hence, the finished products of the factory are "localized" versions of the printer destined for all the different countries. For the European Union six different versions are currently produced. These are designated A, AA, AB, AQ, AU, and AY as indicated in the Bills of Materials shown in Exhibit 7.13.

The total factory throughput time through the PCAT and FAT stages is about one week. The transportation time from Vancouver to the European DC is five weeks. The long shipment time to Europe is due to ocean transit and the time to clear customs and duties at port of entry. The plant sends a weekly shipment of printers to the DC in Europe.

The printer industry is highly competitive. Resellers want to carry as little inventory as possible. Consequently there has been increasing pressure for HP as a manufacturer to provide high levels of availability at the DC. In response, management has decided to stock the DCs so that a high level of availability is maintained.

Global

Supply Chain

7.21 The Inventory Service Crisis

To limit the amount of inventory throughout the DeskJet supply chain and at the same time provide the high level of service needed has been quite a challenge to Vancouver's management. The manufacturing group has been very successful in reducing the uncertainties caused by delivery to the European DC. Forecasting demand in Europe, though, is a significant problem. It has become common to have product shortages for model demands from some countries, while inventory of other models keeps piling up. In the past, the target inventory levels at the DCs were based on safety stocks that were a result of some judgmental rule of thumb. Specifically, target inventory levels, equal to one-month average sales, were set for each model carried in the DC. Now, however, it seems that the increasing difficulty of getting accurate forecasts means the safety stock rules should be revisited.

HP has put together a team of employees to help implement a scientifically based safety stock system that will be responsive to forecast errors and replenishment lead times. They are to recommend a method for calculating appropriate safety stock levels for the various DeskJet models carried in the European DC. The team has a good sample of demand data that can be used for developing

Exhibit 7.14

DESKJET DEMAND DATA FROM EUROPE

Europe Options	Nov.	Dec.	Jan.	Feb.	Mar.	Apr.	May	Jun.	Jul.	Aug.	Sep.	Oct.
A	80	—	60	90	21	48	—	9	20	54	84	42
AB	20,572	20,895	19,252	11,052	19,864	20,316	13,336	10,578	6,095	14,496	23,712	9,792
AU	4,564	3,207	7,485	4,908	5,295	90	—	5,004	4,385	5,103	4,302	6,153
AA	400	255	408	645	210	87	432	816	430	630	456	273
AQ	4,008	2,196	4,761	1,953	1,008	2,358	1,676	540	2,310	2,046	1,797	2,961
AY	248	450	378	306	219	204	248	484	164	363	384	234
Total	29,872	27,003	32,344	18,954	26,617	23,103	15,692	17,431	13,405	22,692	30,735	19,455

Excel: HP Deskjet

the safety stock methodology (see Exhibit 7.14). HP hopes this new methodology will solve the inventory and service problem.

One issue that continually comes up is the choice of inventory carrying cost to be used in safety stock analyses. Estimates within the company range from 12 percent (HP's cost of debt plus some warehousing expenses) to 60 percent (based on the ROI expected of new product development projects). Management has decided to use 25 percent for this study. Assume that all printers cost an average of approximately $250 each to produce and ship to Europe. Another issue is the choice of safety stock probability for the model. The company has decided to use a probability of 98 percent, a number that marketing feels is appropriate.

7.22 The Distribution Process

The DCs have traditionally envisioned their process as a simple, straight-line, standardized process. There are four process stops:

1. Receive (complete) products from various suppliers and stock them.
2. Pick the various products needed to fill a customer order.
3. Shrink-wrap the complete order and label it.
4. Ship the order via the appropriate carrier.

The DeskJet printer fits well into the standard process. In contrast, other products, such as personal computers and monitors, require special processing called "integration," which includes addition of an appropriate keyboard and manual for the destination country. Although this extra processing does not require much extra labor, it is difficult to accommodate in the standard process and disrupts the material flow. There is considerable frustration within DC management regarding the support of assembly processes. In general, DC management stresses the DCs' role as warehouses and the need to continue to do what they are best at—distribution.

Top management, though, feels that integration of the product at the warehouse is extremely valuable because it allows generic products to be sent to the DC with final configuration of the product done just prior to shipment to the customer. Rather than the factory making products specific to a country, generic products could be produced and shipped to Europe. Management is very interested in studying the value of this approach as it could be applied to the DeskJet printers.

7.23 Questions

1. Develop an inventory model for managing the DeskJet printers in Europe assuming that the Vancouver plant continues to produce the six models sold in Europe. Using the data in Exhibit 7.13, apply your model and calculate the expected yearly investment in DeskJet printer inventory in the Europe DC.

2. Compare your results from question 1 to the current policy of carrying one month's average inventory at the DC.

3. Evaluate the idea of supplying generic printers to the Europe DC and integrating the product by packaging the power supply and the instruction manual at the DC just prior to delivery to the European resellers. Focus on the impact on DC inventory investment in this analysis.

4. What is your recommendation to HP?

7.24 Super Quiz

1. Model most appropriate for making a one-time purchase of an item.

2. Model most appropriate when inventory is replenished only in fixed intervals of time, for example, on the first Monday of each month.

3. Model most appropriate when a fixed amount must be purchased each time an order is placed.

4. Based on an EOQ-type ordering criterion, what cost must be taken to zero if the desire is to have an order quantity of a single unit?

5. Term used to describe demand that can be accurately calculated to meet the need of a production schedule, for example.

6. Term used to describe demand that is uncertain and needs to be forecast.

7. We are ordering T-shirts for the spring party and are selling them for twice what we paid for them. We expect to sell 100 shirts and the standard deviation associated with our forecast is 10 shirts. How many shirts should we order?

8. We have an item that we stock in our store that has fairly steady demand. Our supplier insists that we buy 1,200 units at a time. The lead time is very short on the item, since the supplier is only a few blocks away and we can pick up another 1,200 units when we run out. How many units do you expect to have in inventory on average?

9. For the item described in question 8, if we expect to sell approximately 15,600 units next year, how many trips will we need to make to the supplier over the year?

10. If we decide to carry 10 units of safety stock for the item described in questions 8 and 9, and we implemented this by going to our supplier when we had 10 units left, how much inventory would you expect to have on average now?

11. We are being evaluated based on the percentage of total demand met in a year (not the probability of stocking out as used in the chapter). Consider an item that we are managing using a fixed-order quantity model with safety stock. We decide to double the order quantity, but leave the reorder point the same. Would you expect the percent of total demand met next year to go up or down? Why?

12. Consider an item that we have 120 units currently in inventory. The average demand for the item is 60 units per week. The lead time for the item is exactly 2 weeks and we carry 16 units for safety stock. What is the probability of running out of the item if we order right now?

13. If we take advantage of a quantity discount, would you expect your average inventory to go up or down? Assume that the probability of stocking out criterion stays the same.

14. This is an inventory auditing technique where inventory levels are checked more frequently than one time a year.

1. Single-period model 2. Fixed–time period model 3. Fixed–order quantity model 4. Setup or ordering cost 5. Dependent demand 6. Independent demand 7. 100 shirts 8. 600 units 9. 13 trips 10. 610 units 11. Go up (we are taking fewer chances of running out) 12. 50 percent 13. Will probably go up if the probability of stocking out stays the same 14. Cycle counting

7.25
Selected
Bibliography

Brooks, R. B., and L. W. Wilson. *Inventory Record Accuracy: Unleashing the Power of Cycle Counting.* Essex Junction, VT: Oliver Wight, 1993.

Silver, E.; D. Pyke; and R. Peterson. *Decision Systems for Inventory Management and Production Planning and Control.* 3rd ed. New York: Wiley, 1998.

Sipper, D., and R. L. Bulfin Jr. *Production Planning, Control, and Integration.* New York: McGraw-Hill, 1997.

Tersine, R. J. *Principles of Inventory and Materials Management.* 4th ed. New York: North-Holland, 1994.

Vollmann, T. E.; W. L. Berry; D. C. Whybark; and F. R. Jacobs. *Manufacturing Planning and Control Systems for Supply Chain Management.* 5th ed. New York: McGraw-Hill, 2004.

Wild, T. *Best Practices in Inventory Management.* New York: Wiley, 1998.

Zipkin, P. H. *Foundations of Inventory Management.* New York: Irwin/ McGraw-Hill, 2000.

7.26
Footnotes

1. P is actually a cumulative probability because the sale of the nth unit depends not only on exactly n being demanded but also on the demand for any number greater than n.

2. As previously discussed, the standard deviation of a sum of independent variables equals the square root of the sum of the variances.

3. The Pareto principle is also widely applied in quality problems through the use of Pareto charts.

Chapter 8

Global Sourcing and Procurement

After reading the chapter you will:

1. Understand how important sourcing decisions go beyond simple material purchasing decisions.
2. Demonstrate the "bullwhip effect" and how it is important to synchronize the flow of material between supply chain partners.
3. Describe how characteristics of supply and demand have an impact on structuring supply chains.
4. Know the reason for outsourcing capabilities.
5. Illustrate what "green" sourcing is.
6. Analyze the total cost of ownership.
7. Calculate inventory turnover and days of supply.

8.1 The World is Flat

Flattener 5: Outsourcing
Flattener 6: Offshoring

The owner of a fuel pump factory in Beijing posted the following African proverb, translated into Mandarin, on his factory floor:

Every morning in Africa, a gazelle wakes up.
It knows it must run faster than the fastest lion or it will be killed.
Every morning a lion wakes up.
It knows it must outrun the slowest gazelle or it will starve to death.
It doesn't matter whether you are a lion or a gazelle.
When the sun comes up, you better start running.

Global

The opening of China to the rest of the world started on December 11, 2001, when that country formally joined the World Trade Organization (WTO). Ever since China joined the WTO, both it and the rest of the world have had to run faster and faster. This is because China's membership in the WTO gave a huge boost to another form of collaboration: off-shoring. Offshoring, which has been around for decades, is different from outsourcing.

Adapted from: Thomas L. Friedman, *The World Is Flat* [updated and expanded], New York: Farrar, Straus and Giroux, 2006, p. 136.

Outsourcing means taking some specific but limited function that your company was doing in-house—such as research, call centers, or accounts receivable—and having another company perform the exact same function for you and then reintegrating its work back into your overall operation. Offshoring, by contrast, is when a company takes one of its factories that is operating in Canton, Ohio, and moves the whole factory offshore to Canton, China. There, it produces the very same product in the very same way, only with cheaper labor, lower taxes, subsidized energy, and lower health-care costs. Just as Y2K took India and the world to a whole new level of outsourcing, China's joining the WTO took Beijing and the world to a whole new level of offshoring, with more companies shifting production offshore and then integrating it into the global supply chain.

8.2   Strategic Sourcing

Strategic sourcing

Strategic sourcing is the development and management of global supplier relationships to acquire goods and services in a way that aids in achieving the immediate needs of the business. In the past the term *sourcing* was just another term for purchasing, a corporate function that financially was important but strategically was not the center of attention. Today, as a result of globalization and inexpensive communications technology, the basis for competition is changing. A firm is no longer constrained by the capabilities it owns; what matters is its ability to make the most of capabilities available globally, whether they are owned by the firm or not. Outsourcing is so sophisticated that even core functions such as engineering, research and development, manufacturing, information technology, and marketing can be moved outside the firm.

Supply Chain

Sourcing activities can vary greatly and depend on the item being purchased. Exhibit 8.1 maps different processes for sourcing or purchasing an item. The term *sourcing* implies a more complex process suitable for products that are strategically important. Purchasing processes that span from a simple "spot" or one-time purchase to a long-term strategic alliance are depicted on the diagram. The diagram positions a purchasing process according to the specificity of the item, contract duration, and intensity of transaction costs.

Specificity refers to how common the item is and, in a relative sense, how many substitutes might be available. For example, blank DVD disks are commonly available from many different vendors and would have low specificity. A custom-made envelope that is padded and specially shaped to contain a specific item that is to be shipped would be an example of a high specificity item.

THE SOURCING/PURCHASING DESIGN MATRIX

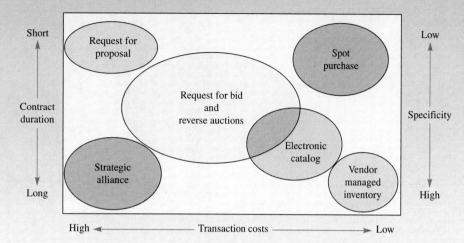

Commonly available products can be purchased using a relatively simple process. For low volume and inexpensive items purchased during the regular routine of work, a firm may order from an online catalog. Often, these online catalogs are customized for a customer. Special user identifications can be set up to authorize customer-employees to purchase certain groups of items within spending limits. Other items require a more complex process.

A request for proposal (RFP) is commonly used for purchasing items that are more complex or expensive and where there may be a number of potential vendors. A detailed information packet describing what is to be purchased is prepared and distributed to potential vendors. The vendor then responds with a detailed proposal of how the company intends to meet the terms of the RFP. A request for bid or reverse auction is similar in terms of the information packet needed. A major difference is how the bid price is negotiated. In the RFP, the bid is included in the proposal, whereas in a request for bid or reverse auction, vendors actually bid on the item in real time and often using Internet software.

Vendor managed inventory

Vendor managed inventory is when the supplier takes full responsibility to manage an item or group of items for the customer. In this case the supplier is given the freedom to replenish the item as the supplier sees fit. Typically, there are some constraints related to the maximum that the customer is willing to carry, required service levels, and other billing transaction processes. Selecting the proper process depends on minimizing the balance between the supplier's delivered costs of the item over a period of time; say a year, and the customer's costs of managing the inventory. This is discussed later in the chapter in the context of the "total cost of ownership" for a purchased item.

The Bullwhip Effect

Marshall Fisher argues that in many cases there are adversarial relations between supply chain partners as well as dysfunctional industry practices such as a reliance on price promotions.[1] Consider the common food industry practice of offering price promotions every January on a product. Retailers respond to the price cut by stocking up, in some cases buying a year's supply—a practice the industry calls *forward buying*. Nobody wins in the deal. Retailers have to pay to carry the year's supply, and the shipment bulge adds cost throughout the supplier's system. For example, the supplier plants must go on overtime starting in October to meet the bulge. Even the vendors that supply the manufacturing plants are affected because they must quickly react to the large surge in raw material requirements.

The impact of these types of practices has been studied at companies such as Procter & Gamble. Exhibit 8.2 shows typical order patterns faced by each node in a supply chain that consists of a manufacturer, a distributor, a wholesaler, and a retailer. In this case, the demand is for disposable baby diapers. The retailer's orders to the wholesaler display greater variability than the end-consumer sales; the wholesaler's orders to the manufacturer show even more oscillations; and, finally, the manufacturer's orders to its suppliers are the most volatile. This phenomenon of variability magnification as we move from the customer to the producer in the supply chain is often referred to as the **bullwhip effect**. The effect indicates a lack of synchronization among supply chain members. Even a slight change in consumer sales ripples backward in the form of magnified oscillations upstream, resembling the result of a flick of a bullwhip handle. Because the supply patterns do not match the demand patterns, inventory accumulates at various stages, and shortages and delays occur at others. This bullwhip effect has been observed by many firms in numerous industries, including Campbell Soup and Procter & Gamble in consumer products; Hewlett-Packard, IBM, and Motorola in electronics; General Motors in automobiles; and Eli Lilly in pharmaceuticals.

Bullwhip effect

Campbell Soup has a program called *continuous replenishment* that typifies what many manufacturers are doing to smooth the flow of materials through their supply chain. Here is how the program works. Campbell establishes electronic data interchange (EDI) links with retailers and offers an "everyday low price" that eliminates discounts. Every morning, retailers electronically inform the company of their demand for all Campbell products and of the level of inventories in their distribution centers. Campbell uses that information to forecast demand and to determine which products require replenishment based on upper and lower inventory limits previously established with each supplier. Trucks leave the Campbell shipping plant that afternoon and arrive at the retailers' distribution centers with the required replenishments the same day. Using this system, Campbell can cut the retailers' inventories, which under the old system averaged four weeks of supply, to about two weeks of supply.

This solves some problems for Campbell Soup, but what are the advantages for the retailer? Most retailers figure that the cost to carry the inventory of a given product for a year equals at least 25 percent of what they paid for the product. A two-week inventory reduction represents a cost savings equal to nearly 1 percent of sales. The average retailer's profits equal about 2 percent of sales, so this saving is enough to increase profits by 50 percent. Because the retailer makes more money on Campbell products delivered through continuous replenishment, it has an incentive to carry a broader line of them and to give them more shelf

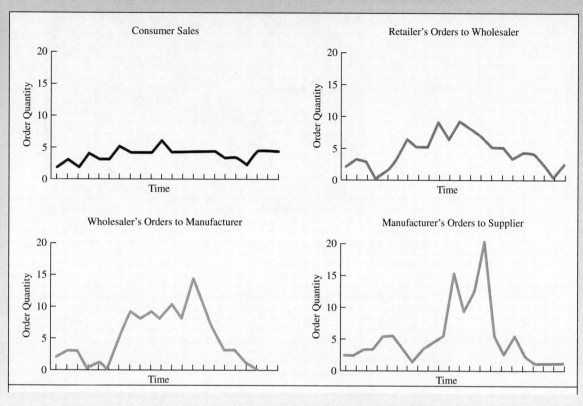

Supply Chain

space. Campbell Soup found that after it introduced the program, sales of its products grew twice as fast through participating retailers as they did through other retailers.

Fisher has developed a framework to help managers understand the nature of demand for their products and then devise the supply chain that can best satisfy that demand. Many aspects of a product's demand are important—for example, product life cycle, demand predictability, product variety, and market standards for lead times and service. Fisher has found that products can be categorized as either primarily functional or primarily innovative. Because each category requires a distinct kind of supply chain, the root cause of supply chain problems is a mismatch between the type of product and type of supply chain.

Functional products

Functional products include the staples that people buy in a wide range of retail outlets, such as grocery stores and gas stations. Because such products satisfy basic needs, which do not change much over time, they have stable, predictable demand and long life cycles. But their stability invites competition, which often leads to low profit margins. Specific criteria suggested by Fisher for identifying functional products include the following: product life cycle of more than two years, contribution margin of 5 to 20 percent, only 10 to 20 product variations, an average forecast error at time of production of only 10 percent, and a lead time for make-to-order products of from six months to one year.

To avoid low margins, many companies introduce innovations in fashion or technology to give customers an additional reason to buy their products. Fashionable clothes and personal computers are good examples. Although innovation can enable a company to achieve higher profit margins, the very newness of the innovative products makes demand for them

Innovative
products

unpredictable. These **innovative products** typically have a life cycle of just a few months. Imitators quickly erode the competitive advantage that innovative products enjoy, and companies are forced to introduce a steady stream of newer innovations. The short life cycles and the great variety typical of these products further increase unpredictability. Exhibit 8.3 summarizes the differences between functional and innovative products.

Hau Lee expands on Fisher's ideas by focusing on the "supply" side of the supply chain.[2] While Fisher has captured important demand characteristics, Lee points out that there are uncertainties revolving around the supply side that are equally important drivers for the right supply chain strategy.

Lee defines a *stable supply process* as one where the manufacturing process and the underlying technology are mature and the supply base is well established. In contrast, an *evolving supply process* is where the manufacturing process and the underlying technology are still under early development and are rapidly changing. As a result the supply base may be limited in both size and experience. In a stable supply process, manufacturing complexity tends to be low or manageable. Stable manufacturing processes tend to be highly automated, and long-term supply contracts are prevalent. In an evolving supply process, the manufacturing process requires a lot of fine-tuning and is often subject to breakdowns and uncertain yields. The supply base may not be reliable, as the suppliers themselves are going through process innovations. Exhibit 8.3 summarizes some of the differences between stable and evolving supply processes.

Lee argues that while functional products tend to have a more mature and stable supply process, that is not always the case. For example, the annual demand for electricity and other utility products in a locality tend to be stable and predictable, but the supply of hydroelectric power, which relies on rainfall in a region, can be erratic year by year. Some food products also have a very stable demand, but the supply (both quantity and quality) of the products depends on yearly weather conditions. Similarly, there are also innovative products with a stable supply process. Fashion apparel products have a short selling season and their demand is highly unpredictable. However, the supply process is very stable, with a reliable supply base and a mature manufacturing process technology. Exhibit 8.4 gives some examples of products that have different demand and supply uncertainties.

According to Lee, it is more challenging to operate a supply chain that is in the right column of Exhibit 8.4 than in the left column, and similarly it is more challenging to operate a supply chain that is in the lower row of Exhibit 8.4 than in the upper row. Before

Demand Characteristics		Supply Characteristics	
Functional	**Innovative**	**Stable**	**Evolving**
Low demand uncertainty	High demand uncertainty	Less breakdowns	Vulnerable to breakdowns
More predictable demand	Difficult to forecast	Stable and higher yields	Variable and lower yields
Long product life	Short selling season	Fewer quality problems	Potential quality problems
Low inventory cost	High inventory cost	More supply sources	Limited supply sources
Low profit margin	High profit margin	Reliable suppliers	Unreliable suppliers
Low product variety	High product variety	Fewer process changes	More process changes
Higher volume	Low volume	Fewer capacity constraints	Potential capacity constrained
Low stockout cost	High stockout cost	Easier to change over	Difficult to change over
Low obsolescence	High obsolescence	Dependable lead times	Variable lead time

setting up a supply chain strategy, it is necessary to understand the sources of the underlying uncertainties and explore ways to reduce these uncertainties. If the uncertainty characteristics of the product can be moved from the right column to the left or from the lower row to the upper; then the supply chain performance will improve.

Lee characterizes four types of supply chain strategies as shown in Exhibit 8.4. Information technologies play an important role in shaping such strategies.

Supply Chain

- **Efficient supply chains.**   These are supply chains that utilize strategies aimed at creating the highest cost efficiency. For such efficiencies to be achieved, non-value-added activities should be eliminated, scale economies should be pursued, optimization techniques should be deployed to get the best capacity utilization in production and distribution, and information linkages should be established to ensure the most efficient, accurate, and cost-effective transmission of information across the supply chain.

- **Risk-hedging supply chains.**   These are supply chains that utilize strategies aimed at pooling and sharing resources in a supply chain so that the risks in supply disruption can be shared. A single entity in a supply chain can be vulnerable to supply disruptions, but if there is more than one supply source or if alternative supply resources are available, then the risk of disruption is reduced. A company may, for example, increase the safety stock of its key component to hedge against the risk of supply disruption, and by sharing the safety stock with other companies that also need this key component, the cost of maintaining this safety stock can be shared. This type of strategy is common in retailing, where different retail stores or dealerships share inventory. Information technology is important for the success of these strategies since real-time information on inventory and demand allows the most cost-effective management and transshipment of goods between partners sharing the inventory.

- **Responsive supply chains.**   These are supply chains that utilize strategies aimed at being responsive and flexible to the changing and diverse needs of the customers. To be responsive, companies use build-to-order and mass customization processes as a means to meet the specific requirements of customers.

		Demand Uncertainty	
		Low (Functional Products)	**High (Innovative Products)**
Supply Uncertainty	Low (Stable Process)	Grocery, basic apparel, food, oil and gas Efficient supply chain	Fashion apparel, computers, popular music Responsive supply chain
	High (Evolving Process)	Hydroelectric power, some food produce Risk-hedging supply chain	Telecom, high-end computers, semiconductor Agile supply chain

- **Agile supply chains.** These are supply chains that utilize strategies aimed at being responsive and flexible to customer needs, while the risks of supply shortages or disruptions are hedged by pooling inventory and other capacity resources. These supply chains essentially have strategies in place that combine the strengths of "hedged" and "responsive" supply chains. They are agile because they have the ability to be responsive to the changing, diverse, and unpredictable demands of customers on the front end, while minimizing the back-end risks of supply disruptions.

Demand and supply uncertainty is a good framework for understanding supply chain strategy. Innovative products with unpredictable demand and an evolving supply process face a major challenge. Because of shorter and shorter product life cycles, the pressure for dynamically adjusting and adopting a company's supply chain strategy is great. In the following we explore the concepts of outsourcing, green sourcing, and total cost of ownership. These are important tools for coping with demand and supply uncertainty.

8.3   Outsourcing

Outsourcing

Outsourcing is the act of moving some of a firm's internal activities and decision responsibility to outside providers. The terms of the agreement are established in a contract. Outsourcing goes beyond the more common purchasing and consulting contracts because not only are the activities transferred, but resources that make the activities occur, including people, facilities, equipment, technology, and other assets, are also transferred. The responsibilities for making decisions over certain elements of the activities are also transferred as well. Taking complete responsibility for this is a specialty of contract manufacturers such as Flextronics.[3]

The reasons why a company decides to outsource can vary greatly. Exhibit 8.5 lists examples of reasons to outsource and the accompanying benefits. Outsourcing allows a firm to focus on activities that represent its core competencies. Thus, the company can create a competitive advantage while reducing cost. An entire function may be outsourced, or some elements of an activity may be outsourced, with the rest kept in-house. For example, some of the elements of information technology may be strategic, some may be critical, and some may be performed less expensively by a third party. Identifying a function as a potential outsourcing target, and then breaking that function into its components, allows decision makers to determine which activities are strategic or critical and should remain in-house and which can be outsourced like commodities. As an example, outsourcing the logistics function will be discussed.

REASONS TO OUTSOURCE AND THE RESULTING BENEFITS

Financially Driven Reasons

Improve return on assets by reducing inventory and selling unnecessary assets.
Generate cash by selling low-return entities.
Gain access to new markets, particularly in developing countries.
Reduce costs through a lower cost structure.
Turn fixed costs into variable costs.

Improvement-Driven Reasons

Improve quality and productivity.
Shorten cycle time.
Obtain expertise, skills, and technologies that are not otherwise available.
Improve risk management.
Improve credibility and image by associating with superior providers.

Organizationally Driven Reasons

Improve effectiveness by focusing on what the firm does best.
Increase flexibility to meet changing demand for products and services.
Increase product and service value by improving response to customer needs.

Logistics

There has been dramatic growth in outsourcing in the logistics area. **Logistics** is a term that refers to the management functions that support the complete cycle of material flow: from the purchase and internal control of production materials; to the planning and control of work-in-process; to the purchasing, shipping, and distribution of the finished product. The emphasis on lean inventory means there is less room for error in deliveries. Trucking companies such as Ryder have started adding the logistics aspect to their businesses—changing from merely moving goods from point A to point B, to managing all or part of all shipments over a longer period, typically three years, and replacing the shipper's employees with their own. Logistics companies now have complex computer tracking technology that reduces the risk in transportation and allows the logistics company to add more value to the firm than it could if the function were performed in-house. Third-party logistics providers track freight using electronic data interchange technology and a satellite system to tell customers exactly where its drivers are and when deliveries will be made. Such technology is critical in some environments where the delivery window may be only 30 minutes long.

Federal Express has one of the most advanced systems available for tracking items being sent through its services. The system is available to all customers over the Internet. It tells the exact status of each item currently being carried by the company. Information on the exact time a package is picked up, when it is transferred between hubs in the company's network, and when it is delivered is available on the system. You can access this system at the FedEx Web site (www.fedex.com). Select your country on the initial screen and then select "Track Shipments" in the Track box in the lower part of the page. Of course, you will need the actual tracking number for an item currently in the system to get information. Federal Express has integrated its tracking system with many of its customers' in-house information systems.

Another example of innovative outsourcing in logistics involves Hewlett-Packard. Hewlett-Packard turned over its inbound raw materials warehousing in Vancouver, Washington, to Roadway Logistics. Roadway's 140 employees operate the warehouse 24 hours a day, seven days a week, coordinating the delivery of parts to the warehouse and

DHL SmartTrucks use a type of route planning software which navigates away from inner city traffic jams and calculates the best route to deliver packages. This reduces time and costs but also fuel consumption and CO_2 emissions. Transported mail items use radio frequency identification (RFID) smart tags attached to them to monitor vehicle loads.

managing storage. Hewlett-Packard's 250 employees were transferred to other company activities. Hewlett-Packard reports savings of 10 percent in warehousing operating costs.

One of the drawbacks to outsourcing is the layoffs that often result. Even in cases where the outsourcing partner hires former employees, they are often hired back at lower wages with fewer benefits. Outsourcing is perceived by many unions as an effort to circumvent union contracts.

In theory, outsourcing is a no-brainer. Companies can unload noncore activities, shed balance sheet assets, and boost their return on capital by using third-party service providers. But in reality, things are more complicated. "It's really hard to figure out what's core and what's noncore today," says Jane Linder, senior research fellow and associate director of Accenture's Institute for Strategic Change in Cambridge, Massachusetts. "When you take another look tomorrow, things may have changed. On September 9, 2001, airport security workers were noncore; on September 12, 2001, they were core to the federal government's ability to provide security to the nation. It happens every day in companies as well."[4]

Exhibit 8.6 is a useful framework to help managers make appropriate choices for the structure of supplier relationships. The decision goes beyond the notion that "core competencies" should be maintained under the direct control of management of the firm and that other activities should be outsourced. In this framework, a continuum that ranges from vertical integration to arm's-length relationships forms the basis for the decision.

An activity can be evaluated using the following characteristics: required coordination, strategic control, and intellectual property. Required coordination refers to how difficult it is to ensure that the activity will integrate well with the overall process. Uncertain activities that require much back-and-forth exchange of information should not be outsourced whereas activities that are well understood and highly standardized can easily move to business partners who specialize in the activity. Strategic control refers to the degree of loss that would be incurred if the relationship with the partner were severed. There could be many types of losses that would be important to consider including specialized

Exhibit 8.6

A FRAMEWORK FOR STRUCTURING SUPPLIER RELATIONSHIPS

	Vertical Integration (do not outsource)	Arm's-Length Relationships (outsource)
Coordination	"Messy" interfaces; adjacent tasks involve a high degree of mutual adaptation, exchange of implicit knowledge, and learning-by-doing. Requisite information is highly particular to the task.	Standardized interfaces between adjacent tasks; requisite information is highly codified and standardized (prices, quantities, delivery schedules, etc.).
Strategic control	Very high: significant investments in highly durable relationship-specific assets needed for optimal execution of tasks. Investments cannot be recovered if relationship terminates: • Co-location of specialized facilities • Investment in brand equity • Large proprietary learning curves • Long-term investments in specialized R&D programs	Very low: assets applicable to businesses with a large number of other potential customers or suppliers.
Intellectual property	Unclear or weak intellectual property protection Easy-to-imitate technology "Messy" interfaces between different technological components	Strong intellectual property protection Difficult-to-imitate technology "Clean" boundaries between different techno logical components

Source: Robert Hayes, Gary Pisano, David Upton, and Steven Wheelwright, *Operations Strategy and Technology: Pursuing the Competitive Edge* (New York: John Wiley & Sons, 2005), p. 137. Copyright © 2005 John Wiley & Sons. Reprinted by Permission.

facilities, knowledge of major customer relationships, and investment in research and development. A final consideration is the potential loss of intellectual property through the partnership.

Global

Intel is an excellent example of a company that recognized the importance of this type of decision framework in the mid-1980s. During the early 1980s, Intel found itself being squeezed out of the market for the memory chips that it had invented by Japanese competitors such as Hitachi, Fujitsu, and NEC. These companies had developed stronger capabilities to develop and rapidly scale up complex semiconductor manufacturing processes. It was clear by 1985 that a major Intel competency was its ability to design complex integrated circuits, not in manufacturing or developing processes for more standardized chips. As a result, faced with growing financial losses, Intel was forced to exit the memory chip market.

Learning a lesson from the memory market, Intel shifted its focus to the microprocessor market, a device that it had invented in the late 1960s. To keep from repeating the mistake with memory chips, Intel felt it was essential to develop strong capabilities in process development and manufacturing. A pure "core competency" strategy would have suggested that Intel focus on the design of microprocessors and use outside partners to manufacture them. Given the close connection between semiconductor product development and process development, however, relying on outside parties for manufacturing would likely have created costs in terms of longer development lead times. Over the late 1980s Intel invested heavily in building world-class capabilities in process development and manufacturing. These capabilities are one of the chief reasons it has been able to maintain approximately 90 percent of the personal computer microprocessor market, despite the ability of competitors like AMD to "clone" Intel designs relatively quickly. Expanding its capabilities beyond its original core capability of product design has been a critical ingredient in Intel's sustained success.

The following chart shows how 7-Eleven has structured key partnerships:

Activity	Outsourcing Strategy
Gasoline	Outsourced distribution of fuel products. Maintains control over pricing and promotion. These are activities that can differentiate its stores.
Snack foods	Frito-Lay distributes its products directly to the stores. 7-Eleven makes critical decisions about order quantities and shelf placement. 7-Eleven mines extensive data on local customer purchase patterns to make these decisions at each store.
Prepared foods	Joint venture with E.A. Sween: Combined Distribution Centers (CDC), a direct-store delivery operation that supplies 7-Eleven stores with sandwiches and other fresh goods two times a day.
Specialty products	Many are developed specially for 7-Eleven customers. For example, 7-Eleven worked with Hershey to develop an edible straw used with the popular Twizzler treat. Worked with Anheuser-Bush on special NASCAR and Major League Baseball promotions.
Data analysis	7-Eleven relies on an outside vendor, IRI, to maintain and format purchasing data while keeping the data proprietary. Only 7-Eleven can see the actual mix of products its customers purchase at each location.
New capabilities	American Express supplies automated teller machines. Western Union handles money wire transfers. CashWorks furnishes check-cashing capabilities. Electronic Data Systems (EDS) maintains network functions.

8.5 Green Sourcing

Being environmentally responsible has become a business imperative and many firms are looking to their supply chains to deliver "green" results. A significant area of focus relates to how a firm works with suppliers where the opportunity to save money and benefit the environment might not be a strict trade-off proposition. Financial results can often be improved through both cost reductions and boosting revenues.

Deloitte (www.deloitte.com) has developed a green strategic sourcing process that can be used with conventional sourcing techniques to enhance sourcing savings by taking advantage of environmental factors. Before looking at this six-step process, it is worth considering the long-term benefits of this type of approach. Green sourcing is not just about finding new environmentally friendly technologies or increasing the use of recyclable materials. It can also help drive cost reductions in a variety of ways including product content substitution, waste reduction, and lower usage.

SIX-STEP PROCESS FOR GREEN SOURCING

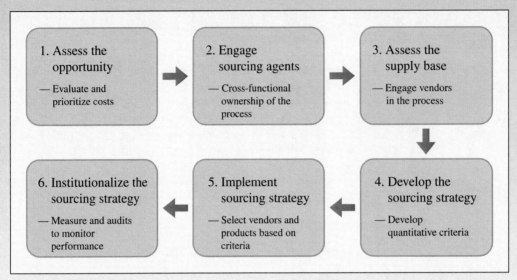

Source: Adapted from www.deloite.com.

A comprehensive green sourcing effort should assess how a company uses items that are purchased internally, in its own operations, or in its products and services. As costs of commodity items like steel, electricity, and fossil fuels continue to increase, properly designed green sourcing efforts should find ways to significantly reduce and possibly eliminate the need for these types of commodities. As an example, consider retrofitting internal lighting in a large office building to a modern energy efficient technology. Electricity cost savings of 10 to 12 percent per square foot can easily translate into millions of dollars in associated electricity cost savings.

Another important cost area in green sourcing is waste reduction opportunities. This includes everything from energy and water to packaging and transportation. A great example of this is the redesigned milk jug introduced recently by leading grocery retailers. Using the new jug, with more rectangular dimensions and a square base, cuts the associated water consumption of the jugs by 60 to 70 percent compared to earlier jug designs because the new design does not require the use of milk crates. Milk crates typically become filthy during use due to spillage and other natural factors; thus, they are usually hosed down before reuse, consuming thousands of gallons of water. The new design also reduces fuel costs. Since crates are no longer used, they also do not have to be transported back to the dairy plant or farm distribution point for future shipments. Furthermore, the new jugs have the unexpected benefit of fitting better in modern home refrigerator doors and allow retailers to fit more of them in their in-store coolers. Breakthrough results like the new milk jug can result from comprehensive partnerships between users and their suppliers working to find innovative solutions.

A recent supply chain survey by Florida International University (see business.fiu.edu/greensupplychain) revealed that working with suppliers can result in opportunities that improve revenue. They can be the opportunity to turn waste products into sources of revenue. For example, a leading beverage manufacturer operates a recycling subsidiary that sources used aluminum cans from a large number of suppliers. The subsidiary actually processes more aluminum cans than are used in the company's own products, consequently developing a strong secondary revenue stream for the company.

In other cases, green sourcing can help establish entirely new lines of business to serve environmentally conscious customers. In the cleaning products aisle of a super-market shoppers will find numerous options of "green" cleaning products from a variety of consumer products companies. These products typically use natural ingredients in lieu of chemicals, and many are in concentrated amounts to reduce overall packaging costs.

Green sourcing can also be essential for companies interested in winning high-profile deals. Being green can be the "order winner" for selection when many sourcing options are available. For example, the organizers of the 2008 U.S. Democratic National Convention (DNC) stipulated very stringent green procurement regulations for the convention's food suppliers. Suppliers that could source food from local and organic farms won the majority of the DNC's business.

Logistics suppliers could find business opportunities coming directly to them as a result of the green trend. A large automobile manufacturer completed a project to green its logistics/distribution network. The automaker analyzed the shipping carriers, locations, and overall efficiency of its distribution network for both parts and finished automobiles. By increasing the use of rail transportation for parts, consolidating shipments in fewer ports, and partnering with its logistics providers to increase fuel efficiency for both marine and road transportation, the company reduced its overall distribution-related carbon dioxide emissions by several thousand tons per year.

The following is an outline of a six-step process (see Exhibit 8.7) designed to transform a traditional process to a green sourcing process:

1. **Assess the opportunity.** For a given category of expense, all relevant costs need to be taken into account. The five most common areas include electricity and other energy costs; disposal and recycling; packaging; commodity substitution (alternative materials to replace materials such as steel or plastic); and water (or other related resources). These costs are identified and incorporated into an analysis of total cost (sometimes referred to as "spend" cost analysis) at this step. From this analysis it is possible to prioritize the different costs based on the highest potential savings and criticality to the organization. This is important to directing effort to where it will likely have the most impact on the firm's financial position and cost reduction goals.

Supply Chain

2. **Engage internal supply chain sourcing agents.** Internal sourcing agents are those within the firm that purchase items and have direct knowledge of business require-ments, product specifications, and other internal perspectives inherent in the sup-ply chain. These individuals and groups need to be "on-board" and partners in the improvement process to help set realistic green goals. The goal of generating no waste, for example, becomes a cross-functional supply chain effort that relies heavily on finding and developing the right suppliers. These internal managers need to identify the most significant opportunities. They can develop a robust baseline model of what should be possible for reducing current and ongoing costs. In the case of procuring new equipment, for example, the baseline model would include not just the initial price of the equipment as in traditional sourcing, but also energy, disposal, recycling, and maintenance costs.

3. **Assess the supply base.** A sustainable sourcing process requires engaging new and existing vendors. As in traditional sourcing, the firm needs to understand vendor capabilities, constraints, and product offering. The green process needs to be aug-mented with formal requirements that relate to green opportunities, including possible commodity substitutions and new manufacturing processes. These requirements need to be incorporated in vendor bid documents or the request for proposals (RFPs).

Fly ash is generally stored at coal power plants or placed in landfills as shown here. About 43 percent is recycled reducing the harmful impact on the environment from landfills.

A good example is concrete that uses fly ash, a by-product from coal-fired power plants. Fly ash can be substituted for Portland cement in ready-mix concrete or in concrete block to produce a stronger and lighter product with reduced water consumption. Fly ash substitution helped a company reduce its exposure to volatile and rapidly increasing prices for cement. At the same time, the reduced weight of the block lowered transportation costs to the company's new facilities. The company was also able to establish a specification incorporating fly ash for all new construction sites to follow. Finally, the substitution also helped the power plant, by providing a new market for the fly ash, which previously had to be discarded.

4. **Develop the sourcing strategy.** The main goal of this step is to develop quantitative and qualitative criteria that will be used to evaluate the sourcing process. These are needed to properly analyze associated costs and benefits. These criteria need to be clearly articulated in bid documents and RFP when working with potential suppliers so that their proposals will address relevant goals related to sustainability.

5. **Implement the sourcing strategy.** The evaluation criteria developed in step 4 should help in the selection of vendors and products for each business requirement. The evaluation process should consider initial cost and the total cost of ownership for the items in the bid. So, for example, energy-efficient equipment that is proposed with a higher initial cost may, over its productive life, actually result in a lower total cost due to energy savings and a related lower carbon footprint. Relevant green opportunities such as energy efficiency and waste reduction need to be modeled and then incorporated into the sourcing analysis to make it as comprehensive as possible and to facilitate an effective vendor selection process that supports the firm's needs.

6. **Institutionalize the sourcing strategy.** Once the vendor is selected and contracts finalized, the procurement process begins. Here the sourcing and procurement department needs to define a set of metrics against which the supplier will be measured for the contract's duration. These metrics should be based on performance, delivery, compliance with pricing guidelines, and similar factors. It is vital that metrics that relate to the company's sustainability goals are considered as well. Periodic audits may also need to be incorporated in the process to directly observe practices that relate to these metrics to ensure honest reporting of data.

A key aspect of green sourcing, compared to a traditional process, is the expanded view of the sourcing decision. This expanded view requires the incorporation of new criteria for evaluating alternatives. Further, it requires a wider range of internal integration such as designers, engineers, and marketers. Finally, visualizing and capturing the green sourcing savings often involves greater complexity and longer payback periods compared to a traditional process.

8.6   Total Cost of Ownership

Total cost of ownership

The **total cost of ownership** (TCO) is an estimate of the cost of an item that includes all the costs related to the procurement and use of an item, including any related costs in disposing of the item after it is no longer useful. The concept can be applied to a company's internal costs or it can be viewed more broadly to consider costs throughout the supply chain. To fully appreciate the cost of purchasing an item from a particular vendor, an approach that captures the costs of the activities associated with purchasing and actually using the item should be considered. Depending on the complexity of the purchasing process, activities such as pre-bid conferences, visits by potential suppliers, and even visits to potential suppliers can significantly impact the total cost of the item.

A TCO analysis is highly dependent on the actual situation, although, in general, the costs outlined in Exhibit 8.8 should be considered. The costs can be categorized into three broad areas: acquisition costs, ownership costs, and post-ownership costs.[5] Acquisition costs are the initial costs associated with the purchase of materials, products, and services. They are not long-term costs of ownership but represent an immediate cash outflow. Acquisition costs include the prepurchase costs associated with preparing documents to distribute to potential suppliers, identifying suppliers and evaluating suppliers, and other costs associated with procuring the item. The actual purchase prices, including taxes and transportation costs, are also included.

Ownership costs are incurred after the initial purchase and are associated with the ongoing use of the product or material. Examples of costs that are quantifiable include energy usage, scheduled maintenance, repair, and financing (leasing situation). There can also be qualitative costs such as aesthetic factors (e.g., the item is psychologically pleasing to the eye), and ergonomic factors (e.g., productivity improvement or reducing fatigue). These ownership costs can often exceed the initial purchase price and have an impact on cash flow, profitability, and even employee morale and productivity.

Major costs associated with post-ownership include salvage value and disposal costs. For many purchases, there are established markets that provide data to help estimate reasonable future values, such as the *Kelley Blue Book* for used automobiles. Other areas that can be included are the long-term environment impact (particularly when the firm has sustainability goals), warranty and product liabilities, and the negative marketing impact of low customer satisfaction with the item.

Exhibit 8.8

TOTAL COST OF OWNERSHIP

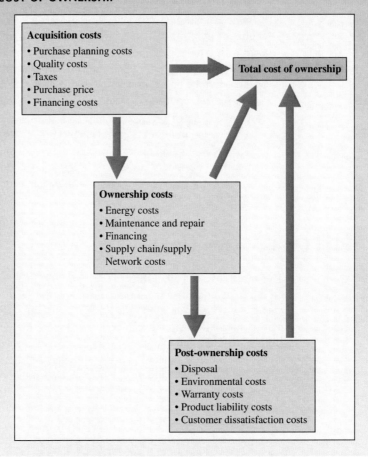

Overemphasis on acquisition cost or purchase price frequently results in failure to address other significant ownership and post-ownership costs. TCO is a philosophy for understanding all relevant costs of doing business with a particular supplier for a good or service. It is not only relevant for a business that wants to reduce its cost of doing business but also for a firm that aims to design products or services that provide the lowest total cost of ownership to customers. For example, some automobile manufacturers have extended the tune-up interval on many models to 100,000 miles, thereby reducing vehicle operating cost for car owners. Viewing TCO in this way can lead to an increased value of the product to existing and potential customers.

These costs can be estimated as cash inflows (the sale of used equipment, etc.) or outflows (purchase prices, demolition of an obsolete facility, etc.). The following example shows how this analysis can be organized using a spreadsheet. Keep in mind that the costs considered need to be adapted to the decision being made. Costs that do not vary based on the decision need not be considered, but relevant costs that vary depending on the decision should be included in the analysis.

Exhibit 8.9

Exhibit 8.9

ANALYSIS OF THE PURCHASE OF AN OFFICE COPIER

Year	Now	1	2	3	4	5	6
Cost of copier including installation	−$120,000						
Manufacturer required overhaul				$−9,000			
Cash inflows from using the machine		$ 40,000	$ 40,000	$ 40,000	$ 40,000	$ 40,000	$ 40,000
Supplies needed to use the machine		$−7,000	$−7,000	$−7,000	$−7,000	$−7,000	$−7,000
Salvage value							$ 7,500
Total of annual streams	−$120,000	$ 33,000	$ 33,000	$ 24,000	$ 33,000	$ 33,000	$ 40,500
Discount factor $(1 + .2)^{-\text{Year}}$	1.000	0.833	0.694	0.579	0.482	0.402	0.335
Present value − yearly	−$120,000	$ 27,500	$ 22,917	$ 13,889	$ 15,914	$ 13,262	$ 13,563
Present value	$−12,955						

Discount factor = 20%.
Note: These calculations were done using the full precision of a spreadsheet.

Step by Step

8.1 Example

Total Cost of Ownership Analysis

Consider the analysis of the purchase of a copy machine that might be used in a copy center. The machine has an initial cost of $120,000 and is expected to generate income of $40,000 per year.[6] Supplies are expected to be $7,000 per year and the machine needs to be overhauled during year 3 at a cost of $9,000. It has a salvage value of $7,500 when we plan to sell it at year 6.

Solution

Laying these costs out over time can lead to the use of net present value analysis to evaluate the decision. Consider Exhibit 8.9. Are the present values of each yearly stream discounted to now? As we can see, the present value in this analysis shows that the present value cost of the copier is $12,955. ●

TCO actually draws on many areas for a thorough analysis. These include finance (net present value), accounting (product pricing and costing), operations management (reliability, quality, need and inventory planning), marketing (demand), and information technology (systems integration). It is probably best to approach this using a cross-functional team representing the key functional areas.

8.7 Measuring Sourcing Performance

One view of sourcing is centered on the inventories that are positioned in the system. Exhibit 8.10 shows how hamburger meat and potatoes are stored in various locations in a typical fast-food restaurant chain. Here we see the steps that the beef and potatoes move through on their way to the local retail store and then to the customer. At each step inventory is carried, and this inventory has a particular cost to the company. Inventory serves as a buffer, thus allowing each stage to operate independently of the others. For example, the distribution

Exhibit 8.10

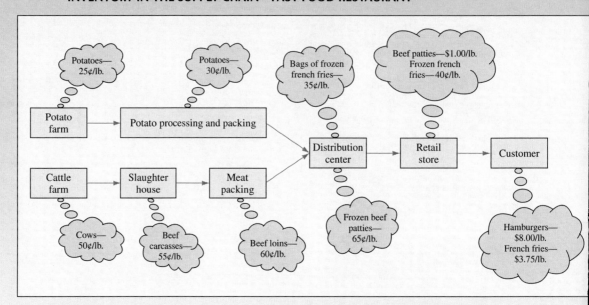

Service

Tutorials: Strategic Sourcing

Inventory turnover

Cost of goods

Average aggregate inventory value

Weeks of supply

center inventory allows the system that supplies the retail stores to operate independently of the meat and potato packing operations. Because the inventory at each stage ties up money, it is important that the operations at each stage are synchronized to minimize the size of these buffer inventories. The efficiency of the supply chain can be measured based on the size of the inventory investment in the supply chain. The inventory investment is measured relative to the total cost of the goods that are provided through the supply chain.

Two common measures to evaluate supply chain efficiency are *inventory turnover* and *weeks of supply*. These essentially measure the same thing and mathematically are the inverse of one another. **Inventory turnover** is calculated as follows:

$$\text{Inventory turnover} = \frac{\text{Cost of goods sold}}{\text{Average aggregate inventory value}} \qquad \textbf{[8.1]}$$

The **cost of goods** sold is the annual cost for a company to produce the goods or services provided to customers; it is sometimes referred to as the *cost of revenue*. This does not include the selling and administrative expenses of the company. The **average aggregate inventory value** is the total value of all items held in inventory for the firm valued at cost. It includes the raw material, work-in-process, finished goods, and distribution inventory considered owned by the company.

Good inventory turnover values vary by industry and the type of products being handled. At one extreme, a grocery store chain may turn inventory over 100 times per year. Values of six to seven are typical for manufacturing firms.

In many situations, particularly when distribution inventory is dominant, **weeks of supply** is the preferred measure. This is a measure of how many weeks' worth of inventory is in the system at a particular point in time. The calculation is as follows:

$$\text{Weeks of supply} = \left(\frac{\text{Average aggregate inventory value}}{\text{Cost of goods sold}}\right) \times 52 \text{ weeks} \qquad \textbf{[8.2]}$$

When company financial reports cite inventory turnover and weeks of supply, we can assume that the measures are being calculated firmwide. This type of calculation is shown in the example that follows using Dell Computer data. These calculations, though, can be done on individual entities within the organization. For example, we might be interested in the production raw materials inventory turnover or the weeks of supply associated with the warehousing operation of a firm. In these cases, the cost would be that associated with the total amount of inventory that runs through the specific inventory. In some very-low-inventory operations, days or even hours are a better unit of time for measuring supply.

A firm considers inventory an investment because the intent is for it to be used in the future. Inventory ties up funds that could be used for other purposes, and a firm may have to borrow money to finance the inventory investment. The objective is to have the proper amount of inventory and to have it in the correct locations in the supply chain. Determining the correct amount of inventory to have in each position requires a thorough analysis of the supply chain coupled with the competitive priorities that define the market for the company's products.

8.2 Example

Inventory Turnover Calculation

Step by Step

Dell Computer reported the following information in its 2005 annual report (all dollar amounts are expressed in millions):

Net revenue (fiscal year 2005)	$49,205
Cost of revenue (fiscal year 2005)	$40,190
Production materials on hand (28 January 2005)	$ 228
Work-in-process and finished goods on hand (28 January 2005)	$ 231
Days of supply in inventory	4 days

The cost of revenue corresponds to what we call cost of goods sold. One might think that U.S. companies, at least, would use a common accounting terminology, but this is not true. The inventory turnover calculation is

$$\text{Inventory turnover} = \frac{40,190}{228 + 231} = 87.56 \text{ turns per year}$$

This is amazing performance for a high-tech company, but it explains much of why the company is such a financial success.

The corresponding weeks of supply calculation is

$$\text{Weeks of supply} = \left(\frac{228 + 231}{40,190} \right) \times 52 = .59 \text{ week} \quad \bullet$$

8.8 Summary

Strategic sourcing is important in business today. Outsourcing is an important way to reduce cost while improving the strategic focus of a firm. Many companies have enjoyed significant success as a result of the unique ways in which they work with their suppliers. Many firms have adopted sourcing strategies that incorporate criteria that consider sustainable goals related to the environment and people.

Measures of sourcing efficiency are inventory turnover and weeks of supply. Efficient processes should be used for functional products, and responsive processes for innovative products. This alignment of sourcing strategy and product demand characteristics is extremely important to the operational success of a company.

Companies that face diverse sourcing, production, and distribution decisions need to weigh the costs associated with materials, transportation, production, warehousing, and distribution to develop a comprehensive network designed to minimize costs and preserve the environments.

8.9 Key Terms

Strategic sourcing The development and management of supplier relationships to acquire goods and services in a way that aids in achieving the immediate needs of a business.

Vendor managed inventory When a customer allows the supplier to manage an item or group of items.

Bullwhip effect The variability in demand is magnified as we move from the customer to the producer in the supply chain.

Functional products Staples that people buy in a wide range of retail outlets, such as grocery stores and gas stations.

Innovative products Products such as fashionable clothes and personal computers that typically have a life cycle of just a few months.

Outsourcing Moving some of a firm's internal activities and decision responsibility to outside providers.

Logistics Management functions that support the complete cycle of material flow: from the purchase and internal control of production materials; to the planning and control of work-in-process; to the purchasing, shipping, and distribution of the finished product.

Total cost of ownership (TCO) Estimate of the cost of an item that includes all the costs related to the procurement and use of the item including disposing of the item after its useful life.

Inventory turnover and weeks of supply Measures of supply chain efficiency that are mathematically the inverse of one another.

Cost of goods sold The annual cost for a company to produce the goods or services provided to customers.

Average aggregate inventory value The total value of all items held in inventory for the firm, valued at cost.

Weeks of supply A measure of how many weeks' worth of inventory is in the system at a particular point in time.

8.10 Formula Review

$$\text{Inventory turnover} = \frac{\text{Cost of goods sold}}{\text{Average aggregate inventory value}} \qquad \textbf{[8.1]}$$

$$\text{Weeks of supply} = \left(\frac{\text{Average aggregate inventory value}}{\text{Cost of goods sold}} \right) \times 52 \text{ weeks} \qquad \textbf{[8.2]}$$

8.11 Review and Discussion Questions

1. What recent changes have caused supply chain management to gain importance?
2. With so much productive capacity and room for expansion in the United States, why would a company based in the United States choose to purchase items from a foreign firm? Discuss the pros and cons.
3. Describe the differences between functional and innovative products.
4. What are characteristics of efficient, responsive, risk-hedging, and agile supply chains? Can a supply chain be both efficient and responsive? Risk-hedging and agile? Why or why not?
5. As a supplier, which factors about a buyer (your potential customer) would you consider to be important in setting up a long-term relationship?
6. Describe how outsourcing works. Why would a firm want to outsource?

8.12
Problems

1. One of your Taiwanese suppliers has bid on a new line of molded plastic parts that is currently being assembled at your plant. The supplier has bid $0.10 per part, given a forecasted demand of 200,000 parts in year 1; 300,000 in year 2; and 500,000 in year 3. Shipping and handling of parts from the supplier's factory is estimated at $0.01 per unit. Additional inventory handling charges should amount to $0.005 per unit. Finally, administrative costs are estimated at $20 per month.

   Although your plant is able to continue producing the part, the plant would need to invest in another molding machine, which would cost $10,000. Direct materials can be purchased for $0.05 per unit. Direct labor is estimated at $0.03 per unit plus a 50 percent surcharge for benefits; indirect labor is estimated at $0.011 per unit plus 50 percent benefits. Up-front engineering and design costs will amount to $30,000. Finally, management has insisted that overhead be allocated if the parts are made in-house at a rate of 100 percent of direct labor cost. The firm uses a cost of capital of 15 percent per year.

   What should you do, continue to produce in-house or accept the bid from your Taiwanese supplier?

2. Your company assembles five different models of a motor scooter that is sold in specialty stores in the United States. The company uses the same engine for all five models. You have been given the assignment of choosing a supplier for these engines for the coming year. Due to the size of your warehouse and other administrative restrictions, you must order the engines in lot sizes of 1,000 each. Because of the unique characteristics of the engine, special tooling is needed during the manufacturing process, for which you agree to reimburse the supplier. Your assistant has obtained quotes from two reliable engine suppliers and you need to decide which to use. The following data have been collected:

Requirements (annual forecast)	12,000 units
Weight per engine	22 pounds
Order processing cost	$125 per order
Inventory carry cost	20 percent of the average value of inventory per year

   Note: Assume that half of lot size is in inventory on average (1,000/2 = 500 units).

   Two qualified suppliers have submitted the following quotations:

Unit Price	Supplier 1	Supplier 2
1 to 999 units/order	$ 510.00	$ 505.00
1,000 to 2,999 units/order	500.00	498.00
3,000 + units/order	490.00	488.00
Tooling costs	$ 22,000	$ 20,000
Distance	125 miles	100 miles

   Your assistant has obtained the following freight rates from your carrier:

Truckload (40,000 each load):	$ 0.80 per ton-mile
Less-than-truckload:	$ 1.20 per ton-mile

   Note: Per ton-mile = 2,000 lbs. per mile

   a. Perform a total cost of ownership analysis and select a supplier.

   b. If you could move the lot size up to ship in truckload quantities, would your supplier selection change?

3. The McDonald's fast-food restaurant on campus sells an average of 4,000 quarter-pound hamburgers each week. Hamburger patties are resupplied twice a week, and on average the store has 350 pounds of hamburger in stock. Assume that the hamburger costs $1.00 a pound. What is the inventory turnover for the hamburger patties? On average, how many days of supply are on hand?

Excel: U.S. Airfilter

4. The U.S. Airfilter company has hired you as a supply chain consultant. The company makes air filters for residential heating and air-conditioning systems. These filters are made in a single plant located in Louisville, Kentucky, in the United States. They are distributed to retailers through wholesale centers in 100 locations in the United States, Canada, and Europe. You have collected the following data relating to the value of inventory in the U.S. Airfilter supply chain:

	Quarter 1 (January through March)	Quarter 2 (April through June)	Quarter 3 (July through September)	Quarter 4 (October through December)
Sales (Total Quarter):				
United States	300	350	405	375
Canada	75	60	75	70
Europe	30	33	20	15
Cost of goods sold (total quarter)	280	295	340	350
Raw materials at the Louisville plant (end-of-quarter)	50	40	55	60
Work-in-process and finished goods at the Louisville plant (end-of-quarter)	100	105	120	150
Distribution center inventory (end-of-quarter):				
United States	25	27	23	30
Canada	10	11	15	16
Europe	5	4	5	5

All amounts in millions of U.S. dollars

a. What is the average inventory turnover for the firm?

b. If you were given the assignment to increase inventory turnover, what would you focus on? Why?

c. The company reported that it used $500M worth of raw material during the year. On average, how many weeks of supply of raw material are on hand at the factory?

8.13 Case: Pepe Jeans

Pepe began to produce and sell denim jeans in the early 1970s in the United Kingdom and has achieved enormous growth. Pepe's success was the result of a unique approach in a product market dominated by strong brands and limited variety. Pepe presented a range of jeans styles that offered a better fit than traditional five-pocket Western jeans (such as those made by Levi Strauss in the United States)—particularly for female customers. The Pepe range of basic styles is modified each season, but each style keeps its identity with a slightly whimsical name featured prominently on the jeans and on the point- of-sale material. Variations such as modified washes, leather trim, and even designer wear marks are applied to respond to changing fashion trends. To learn more about Pepe and its products, visit its Web site at http://www.pepejeans.com.

Pepe's brand strength is such that the company can demand a retail price that averages about £45 (£1 = $1.8) for its standard products. A high percentage of Pepe sales are through about 1,500 independent outlets throughout the United Kingdom. The company maintains contact with its independent retailers via a group of approximately 10 agents, who are self-employed and work exclusively for Pepe. Each agent is responsible for retailers in a particular area of the country.

Pepe is convinced that a good relationship with the independent retailers is vital to its success. The agent meets with each independent retailer three to four times each year in order to present the new collections and to take sales orders. Because the number of accounts for each agent is so large, contact is often achieved by holding a presentation in a hotel for several retailers. Agents take orders from retailers for six-month delivery. After Pepe receives an order, the retailer has only one week in which to cancel because of the need to place immediate firm orders in Hong Kong to meet the delivery date. The company has had a long-standing policy of not holding any inventory of jeans in the United Kingdom.

After an order is taken and confirmed, the rest of the process up to delivery is administered from the Pepe office in Willesden. The status of orders can be checked from a Web site maintained by Pepe. The actual orders are sent to a sourcing agent in Hong Kong who arranges for manufacturing the jeans. The sourcing agent handles all the details associated with materials, fabrication, and shipping the completed jeans to the retailer. Pepe has an outstanding team of young in-house designers who are responsible for developing new styles and the accompanying point-of-sale material. Jeans are made to specifications provided by this team. The team works closely with the Hong Kong sourcing agent to ensure that the jeans are made properly and that the material used is of the highest quality.

A recent survey of the independent retailers indicated some growing problems. The independents praised the fit, quality, and variety of Pepe's jeans, although many thought that they had become much less of a trendsetter than in their early days. It was felt that Pepe's variety of styles and quality were the company's key advantage over the competition. However, the independents were unhappy with Pepe's requirements to place firm orders six months in advance with no possibility of amendment, cancellation, or repeat ordering. Some claimed that the inflexible order system forced them to order less, resulting in stockouts of particular sizes and styles. The retailers estimated that Pepe's sales would increase by about 10 percent with a more flexible ordering system.

The retailers expected to have some slow-moving inventory, but the six-month order lead time made it difficult to accurately order and worsened the problem. Because the fashion market was so impulsive, the current favorites were often not in vogue six months in the future. On the other hand, when demand exceeded expectations, it took a long time to fill the gap. What the retailers wanted was some method of limited returns, exchange, or reordering to overcome the worst of these problems. Pepe was feeling some pressure to respond to these complaints because some of Pepe's smaller competitors offered delivery in only a few days.

Pepe has enjoyed considerable financial success with its current business model. Sales last year were approximately £200M. Cost of sales was approximately 40 percent, operating expenses 28 percent, and profit before taxes nearly 32 percent of sales. The company has no long-term debt and has a very healthy cash position.

Pepe was feeling considerable pressure and felt that a change was going to be needed soon. In evaluating alternatives the company found that the easiest would be to work with the Hong Kong sourcing agent to reduce the lead time associated with orders. The agent agreed that the lead time could be shortened, possibly to as little as six weeks, but costs would increase significantly. Currently, the agent collects orders over a period of time and about every two weeks puts these orders out on bid to about 1,000 potential suppliers. The sourcing agent estimated that costs might go up 30 percent if the lead time were shortened to six weeks. Even with the significant increase in cost, consistent delivery schedules would be difficult to keep.

The sourcing agent suggested that Pepe consider building a finishing operation in the United Kingdom. The agent indicated that a major retail chain in the United States had moved to this type of structure with considerable success. Basically, all the finishing operation did for the U.S. retail chain was apply different washes to the jeans to give them different "worn" looks. The U.S. operation also took orders for the retail stores and shipped the orders. The U.S. firm found that it could give two-day response time to the retail stores.

The sourcing agent indicated that costs for the basic jeans (jeans where the wash has not been applied) could probably be reduced by 10 percent because the volumes would be higher. In addition, lead time for the basic jeans could be reduced to approximately three months because the finishing step would be eliminated and the orders would be larger.

The Pepe designers found this an interesting idea, so they visited the U.S. operation to see how the system worked. They found that they would have to keep about six weeks' supply of basic jeans on hand in the United Kingdom and that they would have to invest in about £1,000,000 worth of equipment. They estimated that it would cost about £500,000 to operate the facility each year. They could locate the facility in the basement of the current Willesden office building, and the renovations would cost about £300,000.

8.14 Questions

1. Acting as an outside consultant, what would you recommend that Pepe do? Given the data in the case, perform a financial analysis to evaluate the alternatives that you have identified. (Assume that the new inventory could be valued at six weeks' worth of the yearly cost of sales. Use a 30 percent inventory carrying cost rate.) Calculate a payback period for each alternative.

2. Are there other alternatives that Pepe should consider?

Source: The idea for this case came from a case titled "pepe jeans" written by D. Bramley and C. John of the London Business School. Pepe Jeans is a real company, but the data given in the case do not represent actual company data.

8.15 Super Quiz

1. Refers to how common an item is or how many substitutes might be available.

2. When a customer allows the supplier to manage an item or group of items.

3. A phenomenon characterized by increased variation in ordering as we move from the customer to the manufacturer in the supply chain.

4. Products that satisfy basic needs and do not change much over time.

5. Products with short life cycles and typically high profit margins.

6. A supply chain that must deal with high levels of both supply and demand uncertainty.

7. In order to cope with high levels of supply uncertainty a firm would use this strategy to reduce risk.

8. Used to describe functions related to the flow of material in a supply chain.

9. When a firm works with suppliers to look for opportunities to save money and benefit the environment.

10. Refers to an estimate of the cost of an item that includes all costs related to the procurement and use of an item, including the costs of disposing after its useful life.

1. Specificity 2. Vendor managed inventory 3. Bullwhip effect 4. Functional products 5. Innovative products 6. Agile supply chain 7. Multiple sources of supply (pooling) 8. Logistics 9. Green sourcing 10. Total cost of ownership.

8.16 Selected Bibliography

Bowersox, D. J.; D. J. Closs; and M. B. Cooper. *Supply Chain and Logistics Management.* New York: Irwin/McGraw-Hill, 2002.

Burt, D. N.; D. W. Dobler; and S. L. Starling. *World Class Supply Management*[SM]*: The Key to Supply Chain Management.* 7th ed. New York: McGraw-Hill/Irwin, 2003.

Chopra, S., and P. Meindl. *Supply Chain Management: Strategy, Planning, and Operations.* 2nd ed. Upper Saddle River, NJ: Prentice Hall, 2003.

Greaver II, M. F. *Strategic Outsourcing: A Structured Approach to Outsourcing Decisions and Initiatives.* New York: American Management Association, 1999.

Hayes, R.; G. Pisano; D. Upton; and S. Wheelwright. *Operations Strategy and Technology: Pursuing the Competitive Edge.* New York: John Wiley & Sons, 2005.

Simchi-Levi, D.; P. Kaminski; and E. Simchi-Levi. *Supply Chain Management.* 2nd ed. New York: McGraw-Hill, 2003.

Vollmann, T.; W. L. Berry; D. C. Whybark; and F. R. Jacobs. *Manufacturing Planning and Control Systems for Supply Chain Management: The Definitive Guide for Professionals.* New York: McGraw-Hill/Irwin, 2004.

8.17 Footnotes

1. M. L. Fisher, "What Is the Right Supply Chain for Your Product?" *Harvard Business Review,* March–April 1997, pp. 105–16.

2. Hau L. Lee, "Aligning Supply Chain Strategies with Product Uncertainties," *California Management Review* 44, no. 3 (Spring 2002), pp. 105–19. Copyright © 2002 by the Regents of the University of California. By permission of the Regents.

3. "Have Factory Will Travel," *The Economist,* February 12–18, 2000, pp. 61–62.

4. Adapted from Martha Craumer, "How to Think Strategically about Outsourcing," *Harvard Management Update,* May 2002, p. 4.

5. See David Burt et al., *Supply Management,* 8th ed. (McGraw-Hill/Irwin, 2010), pp. 306–10.

6. Example is from Burt et al., *Supply Management,* p. 311.

Chapter

9

Projects

After reading this chapter you will:

1. Explain what project management is and why it is important.
2. Identify the different ways projects can be structured.
3. Describe how projects are organized into major subprojects.
4. Understand what a project milestone is.
5. Determine the "critical path" for a project.
6. Demonstrate how to "crash," or reduce the length of, a project.

9.1 National Aeronautics and Space Administration's Constellation Program May Land Men on the Moon by 2020

Source: NASA 2010 Budget request. http://www.nasa.gov.

It has been over 40 years since United States astronaut Neil Armstrong set foot on the Moon on July 20, 1969. Today the United States Space Exploration Policy calls ". . . *for a sustained and affordable exploration program to explore the solar system, including a return to the Moon by the end of the next decade, to establish a human presence there, and to open the path to other destinations including Mars.*"

NASA's exploration activity is now in a period of transition, as the Agency works to complete the International Space Station and retire the Shuttle fleet by 2010, while developing the next generation of spacecraft to support human space flight.

To complete the goal of returning to the Moon, NASA has initiated the Constellation Program to accomplish the feat. The Constellation Program is developing and testing a set of space exploration systems that include the Orion crew exploration vehicle, the Ares I launch vehicle that is intended to propel Orion to low Earth orbit, and the Ares V, which is

Implementation Schedule

Project	Schedule by Fiscal Year															Phase	Beg	End	
	Prior	08	09	10	11	12	13	14	15	16	17	18	19	20	21	22			
Orion																	Tech		
																	Form	Nov-04	Feb-10
																	Dev	Feb-10	Sep-15
																	Ops	Oct-15	Sep-20
																	Res		
Ares I Crew Launch Vehicle (under review)																	Tech		
																	Form	Nov-04	Dec-08
																	Dev	Jan-09	Sep-15
																	Ops	Oct-15	Sep-20
																	Res		
Ares V Cargo Launch Vehicle (preliminary dates)																	Tech		
																	Form	Oct-07	Apr-13
																	Dev	May-13	Apr-20
																	Ops	May-20	
																	Res		

- Tech & Adv Concepts (Tech)
- Formulation (Form)
- Development (Dev)
- Operations (Ops)
- Research (Res)
- Represents a period of no activity for the Project

intended to carry a lunar lander to low Earth orbit to dock with Orion and deliver the crew and cargo to the Moon.

The implementation schedule shows the timeline for each of the major projects within the program. The Orion, Ares I, and Ares V projects are each divided into major phases starting with Technology and Advanced concepts, Formulation, Development and Operations. NASA uses the techniques described in this chapter to organize the Constellation Program and to manage the projects within the program. It will be exciting to track this nearly trillion dollar program where man will once again have the opportunity to explore our galaxy for real.

> *"The high-impact project is the gem . . . the fundamental nugget . . . the fundamental atomic particle from which the new white collar world will be constructed and/or reconstructed. Projects should be, well WOW!"*
>
> —Tom Peters

Although most of the material in this chapter focuses on the technical aspects of project management (structuring project networks and calculating the critical path), as we see in the opening vignette, the management aspects are certainly equally important. Success in project management is very much an activity that requires careful control of critical resources. We spend much of the time in this book focused on the management of nonhuman resources such as machines and material; for projects, however, the key resource is often our employees' time. Human resources are often the most expensive and those people involved in the projects critical to the success of the firm are often the most valuable managers, consultants, and engineers.

At the highest levels in an organization, management often involves juggling a portfolio of projects. There are many different types of projects ranging from the development of

Exhibit 9.1

TYPES OF DEVELOPMENT PROJECTS

	Breakthrough Projects	Platform Projects	Derivative Projects
	More ◄——— Change ———► Less		
Product Change	New core product	Additional to product family	Product enhancement
Process Change	New core process	Process upgrade	Incremental change
Research & Development	New core technology	Technology upgrade	Incremental change
Alliance & Partnership	Outsource major activity	Select new partner	Incremental change

totally new products, revisions to old products, new marketing plans, and a vast array of projects for better serving customers and reducing costs.

Most companies deal with projects individually—pushing each through the pipeline as quickly and cost-effectively as possible. Many of these same companies are very good at applying the techniques described in this chapter in a manner where the myriad of tasks are executed flawlessly, but the projects just do not deliver the expected results. Worse, what often happens is the projects consuming the most resources have the least connection to the firm's strategy.

The vital big-picture decision is what mix of projects is best for the organization. A firm should have the right mix of projects that best support a company's strategy. Projects should be selected from the following types: derivative (incremental changes such as new product packaging or no-frills versions), breakthrough (major changes that create entirely new markets), platform (fundamental improvements to existing products). Projects can be categorized in four major areas: product change, process change, research and development, and alliance and partnership (see Exhibit 9.1).

In this chapter we only scratch the surface in our introduction to the topic of project management. Professional project managers are individuals skilled at not only the technical aspects of calculating such things as early start and early finish time but, just as important, the people skills related to motivation. In addition, the ability to resolve conflicts as key decision points occur in the project is a critical skill. Without a doubt, leading successful projects is the best way to prove your promotability to the people who make promotion decisions. Virtually all project work is teamwork and leading a project involves leading a team. Your success at leading a project will spread quickly through the individuals on the team. As organizations flatten (through reengineering, downsizing, outsourcing), more will depend on projects and project leaders to get work done, work that previously was handled within departments.

9.2   What is Project Management?

Project
Project
management

A **project** may be defined as a series of related jobs usually directed toward some major output and requiring a significant period of time to perform. **Project management** can be defined as planning, directing, and controlling resources (people, equipment, material) to meet the technical, cost, and time constraints of the project.

Although projects are often thought to be one-time occurrences, the fact is that many projects can be repeated or transferred to other settings or products. The result will be another project output. A contractor building houses or a firm producing low-volume products such as supercomputers, locomotives, or linear accelerators can effectively consider these as projects.

9.3   Structuring Projects

Before the project starts, senior management must decide which of three organizational structures will be used to tie the project to the parent firm: pure project, functional project, or matrix project. We next discuss the strengths and weaknesses of the three main forms.

Pure Project

Pure project

Tom Peters predicts that most of the world's work will be "brainwork," done in semipermanent networks of small project-oriented teams, each one an autonomous, entrepreneurial center of opportunity, where the necessity for speed and flexibility dooms the hierarchical management structures we and our ancestors grew up with. Thus, out of the three basic project organizational structures, Peters favors the **pure project** (nicknamed *skunkworks*), where a self-contained team works full time on the project.

Advantages

- The project manager has full authority over the project.
- Team members report to one boss. They do not have to worry about dividing loyalty with a functional-area manager.
- Lines of communication are shortened. Decisions are made quickly.
- Team pride, motivation, and commitment are high.

Disadvantages

- Duplication of resources. Equipment and people are not shared across projects.
- Organizational goals and policies are ignored, as team members are often both physically and psychologically removed from headquarters.
- The organization falls behind in its knowledge of new technology due to weakened functional divisions.
- Because team members have no functional area home, they worry about life-after-project, and project termination is delayed.

Functional Project

Functional project

At the other end of the project organization spectrum is the **functional project**, housing the project within a functional division.

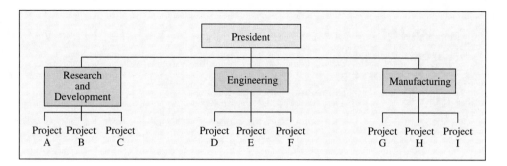

Advantages

- A team member can work on several projects.
- Technical expertise is maintained within the functional area even if individuals leave the project or organization.
- The functional area is a home after the project is completed. Functional specialists can advance vertically.
- A critical mass of specialized functional-area experts creates synergystic solutions to a project's technical problems.

Disadvantages

- Aspects of the project that are not directly related to the functional area get short-changed.
- Motivation of team members is often weak.
- Needs of the client are secondary and are responded to slowly.

Matrix Project

Matrix project

The classic specialized organizational form, "the **matrix project**," attempts to blend properties of functional and pure project structures. Each project utilizes people from different functional areas. The project manager (PM) decides what tasks and when they will be performed, but the functional managers control which people and technologies are used. If the matrix form is chosen, different projects (rows of the matrix) borrow resources from functional areas (columns). Senior management must then decide whether a weak, balanced, or strong form of a matrix is to be used. This establishes whether project managers have little, equal, or more authority than the functional managers with whom they negotiate for resources.

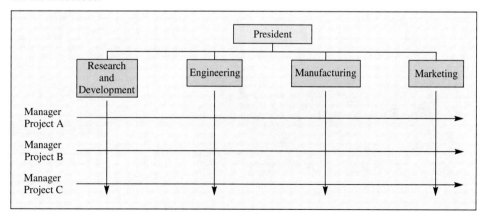

9.4 The World's Biggest Construction Projects

Think redoing your kitchen is a headache? Imagine supervising one of these megaprojects.

South-to-North Water Transfer Project, China

Who's building it: The Chinese government.
Budget: $62 billion (445 billion yuan).
Estimated completion date: 2050.
What it takes: 400,000 relocated citizens and a very thirsty northern China. Economic development in the North China Plain is booming, but its water supplies are falling short, far short. Desperate farming communities are digging wells as deep as 600 feet to find clean water, but the Chinese government has much more digging in mind. Drawing on an unimple-

mented proposal from Mao himself, the Communist Party has decided to divert water from the Yangtze—a southern river known for its rising tides—to the dry rivers of the north. If it is completed, 12 trillion gallons of water will flow northward yearly through three man-made channels whose combined construction is expected to displace almost 400,000 people. Construction is well under way for the east and central canals, but environmental concerns have kept the western route at the planning stage. The project's $62 billion price tag also makes the South-to-North project by far the most expensive construction project ever in China. But having finished the Three Gorges Dam—a $25 billion project that has forced the relocation of more than 1 million people—China is no stranger to pricey megaprojects.

Panama Canal Expansion

Who's building it: The Panamanian government.
Budget: $5.2 billion.
Estimated completion date: 2014.
What it takes: 123 million cubic meters of excavated material and 3,000 ships that just don't fit. Once a marvel of engineering, today's Panama Canal is too narrow to fit 92 percent of the world's shipping fleet through its passage. More than a quarter of the goods that are transported through its locks are carried on Panamax-size vessels—ships that are the maximum size that can fit through the canal. But in a project that broke ground—or canal bed—in the fall of 2007, the Panama Canal will soon be equipped with the world's biggest locks, capable of handling most shipping vessels that are over Panamax size. Also, by adding a wider, deeper, and longer third lock lane to the existing two, the project will more than double the canal's current effective capacity of 15,000 transits per year.

Crystal Island, Moscow

Who's building it: Shalva Chigirinsky, oil and real estate mogul.
Budget: $4 billion (98 billion rubles).
Estimated completion date: 2014.
What it takes: 27 million square feet of floor space in the middle of the Moscow River and an eye for the extreme. In a city booming with petro-wealth projects, Crystal Island—designed to be the largest building in the world—is sure to grab most of the attention. Planned as a "city in microcosm," this tentlike structure of steel and glass will, if completed, stand at almost 1,500 feet and house

900 apartments, 3,000 hotel rooms, shopping spaces, offices, an international school for 500 students, a major sports complex, an IMAX theater, and a system of solar panels, wind turbines, and naturally insulating winter gardens designed for energy efficiency. Throw in a few onion domes, and Crystal Island could replace Moscow altogether. Filling one of the few large-scale sites left near the city's center, Crystal Island will sit on the Nagatinskaya, a large peninsula that juts into the Moscow River, less than 5 miles from the Kremlin.

Source: http://www.foreignpolicy.com/

Advantages

- Communication between functional divisions is enhanced.
- A project manager is held responsible for successful completion of the project.
- Duplication of resources is minimized.
- Team members have a functional "home" after project completion, so they are less worried about life-after-project than if they were a pure project organization.
- Policies of the parent organization are followed. This increases support for the project.

Disadvantages

- There are two bosses. Often the functional manager will be listened to before the project manager. After all, who can promote you or give you a raise?
- It is doomed to failure unless the PM has strong negotiating skills.
- Suboptimization is a danger, as PMs hoard resources for their own project, thus harming other projects.

Note that regardless of which of the three major organizational forms is used, the project manager is the primary contact point with the customer. Communication and flexibility are greatly enhanced because one person is responsible for successful completion of the project.

9.5 Work Breakdown Structure

A project starts out as a *statement of work* (SOW). The SOW may be a written description of the objectives to be achieved, with a brief statement of the work to be done and a proposed schedule specifying the start and completion dates. It also could contain performance measures in terms of budget and completion steps (milestones) and the written reports to be supplied.

A *task* is a further subdivision of a project. It is usually not longer than several months in duration and is performed by one group or organization. A *subtask* may be used if needed to further subdivide the project into more meaningful pieces.

A *work package* is a group of activities combined to be assignable to a single organizational unit. It still falls into the format of all project management; the package provides a description of what is to be done, when it is to be started and completed, the budget, measures of performance, and specific events to be reached at points in time. These specific events are called **project milestones**. Typical milestones might be the completion of the design, the production of a prototype, the completed testing of the prototype, and the approval of a pilot run.

Project milestone

The **work breakdown structure** (WBS) defines the hierarchy of project tasks, subtasks, and work packages. Completion of one or more work packages results in the completion of a subtask; completion of one or more subtasks results in the completion of a task; and finally, the completion of all tasks is required to complete the project. A representation of this structure is shown in Exhibit 9.2.

Work breakdown structure

AN EXAMPLE OF A WORK BREAKDOWN STRUCTURE

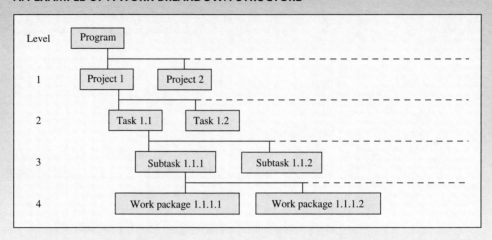

Exhibit 9.3 shows the WBS for an optical scanner project. The WBS is important in organizing a project because it breaks the project down into manageable pieces. The number of levels will vary depending on the project. How much detail or how many levels to use depends on the following:

- The level at which a single individual or organization can be assigned responsibility and accountability for accomplishing the work package.
- The level at which budget and cost data will be collected during the project.

There is not a single correct WBS for any project, and two different project teams might develop different WBSs for the same project. Some experts have referred to project management as an art rather than a science, because there are so many different ways that a project can be approached. Finding the correct way to organize a project depends on experience with the particular task.

Activities

Activities are defined within the context of the work breakdown structure and are pieces of work that consume time. Activities do not necessarily require the expenditure of effort by people, although they often do. For example, waiting for paint to dry may be an activity in a project. Activities are identified as part of the WBS. From our sample project in Exhibit 9.3, activities would include telescope design and fabrication (1.1.1), telescope/simulator optical interface (1.1.2), and data recording (1.2.4). Activities need to be defined in such a way that when they are all completed, the project is done.

9.6 Project Control Charts

The U.S. Department of Defense (one of the earliest large users of project management) has published a variety of helpful standard forms. Many are used directly or have been modified by firms engaged in project management. Computer programs are available to quickly generate the charts described in this section. Charts are useful because their visual presentation is easily understood. Exhibit 9.4 shows a sample of the available charts.

Gantt chart

Exhibit 9.4A is a sample **Gantt chart**, sometimes referred to as a *bar chart*, showing both the amount of time involved and the sequence in which activities can be performed.

Exhibit 9.3

WORK BREAKDOWN STRUCTURE, LARGE OPTICAL SCANNER DESIGN

Level 1	2	3	4		
x				1	Optical simulator design
	x			1.1	Optical design
		x		1.1.1	Telescope design/fab
		x		1.1.2	Telescope/simulator optical interface
		x		1.1.3	Simulator zoom system design
		x		1.1.4	Ancillary simulator optical component specification
	x			1.2	System performance analysis
		x		1.2.1	Overall system firmware and software control
			x	1.2.1.1	Logic flow diagram generation and analysis
			x	1.2.1.2	Basic control algorithm design
		x		1.2.2	Far beam analyzer
		x		1.2.3	System inter- and intra-alignment method design
		x		1.2.4	Data recording and reduction requirements
	x			1.3	System integration
	x			1.4	Cost analysis
		x		1.4.1	Cost/system schedule analysis
		x		1.4.2	Cost/system performance analysis
	x			1.5	Management
		x		1.5.1	System design/engineering management
		x		1.5.2	Program management
	x			1.6	Long lead item procurement
		x		1.6.1	Large optics
		x		1.6.2	Target components
		x		1.6.3	Detectors

The chart is named after Henry L. Gantt, who won a presidential citation for his application of this type of chart to shipbuilding during World War I. In the example in Exhibit 9.4A, "long lead procurement" and "manufacturing schedules" are independent activities and can occur simultaneously. All other activities must be done in the sequence from top to bottom. Exhibit 9.4B graphs the amounts of money spent on labor, material, and overhead. Its value is its clarity in identifying sources and amounts of cost.

Exhibit 9.4C shows the percentage of the project's labor hours that comes from the various areas of manufacturing, finance, and so on. These labor hours are related to the proportion of the project's total labor cost. For example, manufacturing is responsible for 50 percent of the project's labor hours, but this 50 percent has been allocated just 40 percent of the total labor dollars charged.

The top half of Exhibit 9.4D shows the degree of completion of these projects. The dashed vertical line signifies today. Project 1, therefore, is already late because it still has work to be done. Project 2 is not being worked on temporarily, so there is a space before the projected work. Project 3 continues to be worked on without interruption. The bottom of Exhibit 9.4D compares actual total costs and projected costs. As we see, two cost overruns occurred, and the current cumulative costs are over projected cumulative costs.

Exhibit 9.4E is a milestone chart. The three milestones mark specific points in the project where checks can be made to see if the project is on time and where it should be. The best place to locate milestones is at the completion of a major activity. In this exhibit, the major activities completed were "purchase order release," "invoices received," and "material received."

Other standard reports can be used for a more detailed presentation comparing cost to progress (such as cost schedule status report—CSSR) or reports providing the basis for partial payment (such as the earned value report, which we discuss next).

Exhibit 9.4

SAMPLE OF GRAPHIC PROJECT REPORTS

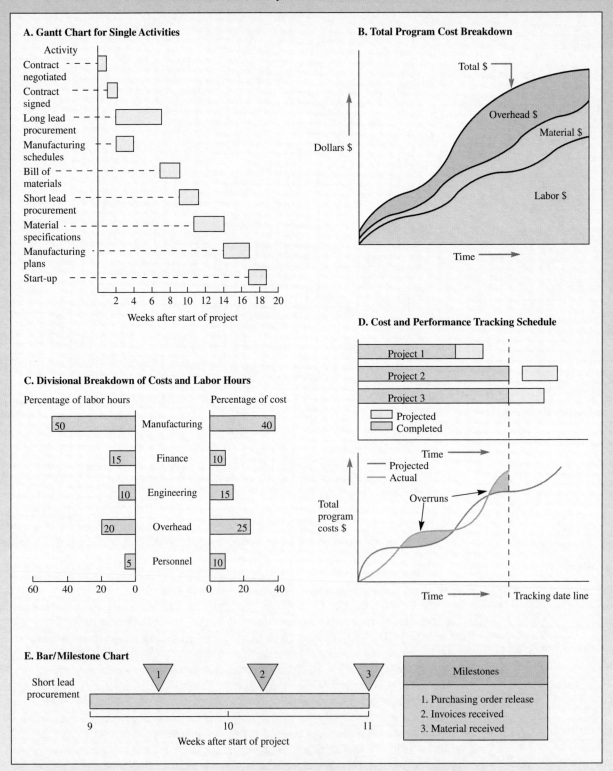

A. Gantt Chart for Single Activities

Activity
Contract negotiated
Contract signed
Long lead procurement
Manufacturing schedules
Bill of materials
Short lead procurement
Material specifications
Manufacturing plans
Start-up

Weeks after start of project

B. Total Program Cost Breakdown

Dollars $

Total $
Overhead $
Material $
Labor $

Time

C. Divisional Breakdown of Costs and Labor Hours

Percentage of labor hours		Percentage of cost
50	Manufacturing	40
15	Finance	10
10	Engineering	15
20	Overhead	25
5	Personnel	10

D. Cost and Performance Tracking Schedule

Project 1
Project 2
Project 3

Projected
Completed

Time

Total program costs $

Projected
Actual
Overruns

Time — Tracking date line

E. Bar/Milestone Chart

Short lead procurement

1   2   3

9   10   11

Weeks after start of project

Milestones

1. Purchasing order release
2. Invoices received
3. Material received

Earned Value Management (EVM)

EVM is a technique for measuring project progress in an objective manner. EVM has the ability to combine measurements of scope, schedule, and cost in a project. When properly applied, EVM provides a method for evaluating the relative success of a project at a point in time. The measures can be applied to projects focused on either "revenue generation" or "cost" depending on the type of project.

Essential features of any EVM implementation include

1. a project plan that identifies the activities to be accomplished,
2. a valuation of each activity work. In the case of a project that generates revenue this is called the planned value (PV) of the activity. In the case where a project is evaluated based on cost, this is called the budgeted cost of work scheduled (BCWS) for the activity, and
3. predefined "earning or costing rules" (also called metrics) to quantify the accomplishment of work, called earned value (EV) or budgeted cost of work performed (BCWP).

The terminology used in the features is general since the valuations could be based on either a value measure (revenue or profit) or a cost measure. EVM implementations for large or complex projects include many more features, such as indicators and forecasts of cost performance (over budget or under budget) and schedule performance (behind schedule or ahead of schedule). However, the most basic requirement of an EVM system is that it quantifies progress using PV (or BCWS) and EV (or BCWP).

Project Tracking without EVM   It is helpful to see an example of project tracking that does not include earned value performance management. Consider a project that has been planned in detail, including a time-phased spend plan for all elements of work. This is a case where the project is evaluated based on cost. Exhibit 9.5A shows the cumulative cost budget for this project as a function of time (the orange line, labeled BCWS). It also shows the cumulative actual cost of the project (green line) through week 8. To those unfamiliar with EVM, it might appear that this project was over budget through week 4 and then under budget from week 6 through week 8. However, what is missing from this chart is any understanding of how much work has been accomplished during the project. If the project was actually completed at week 8, then the project would actually be well under budget and well ahead of schedule. If, on the other hand, the project is only 10 percent complete at week 8, the project is significantly over budget and behind schedule. A method is needed to measure technical performance objectively and quantitatively, and that is what EVM accomplishes.

Project Tracking with EVM   Consider the same project, except this time the project plan includes predefined methods of quantifying the accomplishment of work. At the end of each week, the project manager identifies every detailed element of work that has been completed, and sums the Budgeted Cost of Work Performed for each of these completed elements by estimating the percent complete of the activity and multiplying by the activity budgeted cost. Budgeted Cost of Work Performed (BCWP) may be accumulated monthly, weekly, or as progress is made.

Exhibit 9.5B shows the BCWP curve (in blue) along with the BCWS curve from chart A. The chart indicates that technical performance (i.e., progress) started more rapidly than planned, but slowed significantly and fell behind schedule at week 7 and 8. This chart illustrates the schedule performance aspect of EVM. It is complementary to critical path schedule management (described in the next section).

Exhibit 9.5C shows the same BCWP curve (blue) with the actual cost data from Chart A (in green). It can be seen that the project was actually under budget, relative to the amount of work accomplished, since the start of the project. This is a much better conclusion than might be derived from Chart A.

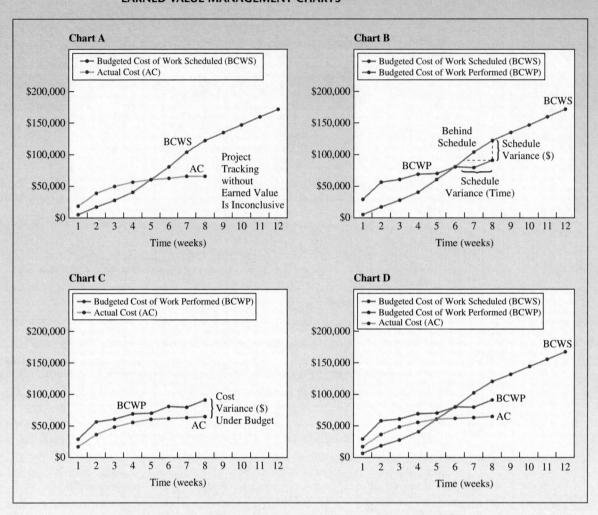

Exhibit 9.5D shows all three curves together—which is a typical EVM line chart. The best way to read these three-line charts is to identify the BCWS curve first, then compare it to BCWP (for schedule performance) and AC (for cost performance). It can be seen from this illustration that a true understanding of cost performance and schedule performance *relies first on measuring technical performance objectively*. This is the *foundational principle* of EVM.

9.1 Example

Earned Value Management

The figure above illustrates how to determine the Budgeted Cost of Work Scheduled by summing the dollar values (in $1,000s of the work scheduled for accomplishment at the end of period X. The Budgeted Cost of Work Performed is determined by summing the earned value for the work actually accomplished, shown in red shading.

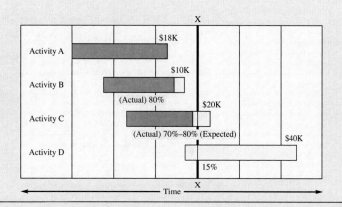

Step by Step

Solution

From the diagram the budgeted cost of all the project work is the following: Activity A — $18K, B — $10K, C — $20K, D — $40K. This is the cost of each activity when they are 100% completed.

The project is currently at day X and from the diagram 100% of activity A should be completed, and it is; 100% of activity B should be completed, but only 80% is; 80% of activity C should be completed, but only 70% is; and 15% of activity D, but it has not started.

Step 1: Calculate the Budgeted Cost of Work Scheduled (BCWS) given the current state of the project. This is the value or cost of the project that is expected, given the project is at time X:

Activity A — 100% of $18K = $18K
Activity B — 100% of $10K = $10K
Activity C — 80% of $20K = $16K
Activity D — 15% of $40K = $6K

BCWS = $18K + $10K + $16K + $6K = $50K

Step 2: Calculate the Budgeted Cost of Work Performed (BCWP) given the current state of the project. This is the actual value or cost of the project to date, given the project is at time X:

Activity A — 100% of $18K = $18K
Activity B — 80% of $10K = $8K
Activity C — 70% of $20K = $14K
Activity D — 0% of $40K = $0

BCWP = $18K + $8K + $14K + $0K = $40K

Step 3: Obtain the Actual Cost (AC) of the work performed. This would need to be obtained from accounting records for the project. Assume that the actual cost for this project to date is $45K.

AC = $45K (Data from Acct. System)

Step 4: Calculate key performance measures for the project:

Schedule Variance: This is the difference between the Budgeted Cost of Work Performed (BCWP) and the Budgeted Cost of Work Scheduled (BCWS) for the project:

Schedule Variance = BCWP − BCWS
Schedule Variance = $40K − $50K = 2$10K

Greater than 0 is generally good as it implies the project is ahead of schedule.

Schedule Performance Index: This is the ratio of the BCWP versus the BCWS for the project:

Schedule Performance Index = BCWP/BCWS
Schedule Performance Index = $40K/$50K = 0.8

Greater than 1 is generally good as it implies the project is ahead of schedule.

Cost Variance: This is the difference between BCWP and the Actual Cost (AC):

Cost Variance = BCWP − AC

Cost Variance = \$40K − \$45K = −\$5K

Greater than zero is generally good as it implies under budget.

Cost Performance Index: This is the ratio of the BCWP versus the AC for the project to date:

Cost Performance Index = BCWP/AC

Cost Performance Index = \$40K/\$45K = 0.89

< 1 means the cost of completing the work is higher than planned, which is bad;

= 1 means the cost of completing the work is right on plan, which is good;

> 1 means the cost of completing the work is lower than planned, which is usually good.

That means the project is spending about \$1.13 for every \$1.00 of budgeted work accomplished. This is not very good as the project is over budget and tasks are not being completed on time or on budget. A Schedule Performance Index and a Cost Performance Index greater than one are desirable. ●

9.7   Network-Planning Models

New Zealand's Te Apiti Wind Farm Project constructed the largest wind farm in the southern hemisphere, within one year from commission to completion, on-time and within budget. Employing effective project management and using the correct tools and techniques, the Meridian Energy company provided a viable option for renewable energy in New Zealand, and acts as benchmark for later wind farm projects.

The two best-known network-planning models were developed in the 1950s. The Critical Path Method (CPM) was developed for scheduling maintenance shutdowns at chemical processing plants owned by Du Pont. Since maintenance projects are performed often in this industry, reasonably accurate time estimates for activities are available. CPM is based on the assumptions that project activity times can be estimated accurately and that they do not vary. The Program Evaluation and Review Technique (PERT) was developed for the U.S. Navy's Polaris missile project. This was a massive project involving over 3,000 contractors. Because most of the activities had never been done before, PERT was developed to handle uncertain time estimates. As years passed, features that distinguished CPM from PERT have diminished, so in our treatment here we just use the term CPM.

In a sense, the CPM techniques illustrated here owe their development to the widely used predecessor, the Gantt chart. Although the Gantt chart is able to relate activities to time in a usable fashion for small projects, the interrelationship of activities, when displayed in this form, becomes extremely difficult to visualize and to work with for projects that include more than 25 activities. Also, the Gantt chart provides no direct procedure for determining more than 25 activities, nor does the Gantt chart provide any direct procedure for determining the critical path, which is of great practical value to identify.

Critical path   The **critical path** of activities in a project is the sequence of activities that form the longest chain in terms of their time to complete. If any one of the activities in the critical path is delayed, then the entire project is delayed. It is possible and it often happens that there are multiple paths of the same length through the network so there are multiple critical paths. Determining scheduling information about each activity in the project is the major goal of CPM techniques. The techniques calculate when an activity must start and end, together with whether the activity is part of the critical path.

Critical Path Method (CPM)

Here is a procedure for scheduling a project. In this case, a single time estimate is used because we are assuming that the activity times are known. A very simple project will be scheduled to demonstrate the basic approach.

Consider that you have a group assignment that requires a decision on whether you should invest in a company. Your instructor has suggested that you perform the analysis in the following four steps:

a. Select a company.
b. Obtain the company's annual report and perform a ratio analysis.
c. Collect technical stock price data and construct charts.
d. Individually review the data and make a team decision on whether to buy the stock.

Your group of four people decides that the project can be divided into four activities as suggested by the instructor. You decide that all the team members should be involved in selecting the company and that it should take one week to complete this activity. You will meet at the end of the week to decide what company the group will consider. During this meeting you will divide your group: two people will be responsible for the annual report and ratio analysis, and the other two will collect the technical data and construct the charts. Your group expects to take two weeks to get the annual report and perform the ratio analysis, and a week to collect the stock price data and generate the charts. You agree that the two groups can work independently. Finally, you agree to meet as a team to make the purchase decision. Before you meet, you want to allow one week for each team member to review all the data.

This is a simple project, but it will serve to demonstrate the approach. The following are the appropriate steps.

1. **Identify each activity to be done in the project and estimate how long it will take to complete each activity.** This is simple, given the information from your instructor. We identify the activities as follows: A(1), B(2), C(1), D(1). The number is the expected duration of the activity.

2. **Determine the required sequence of activities and construct a network reflecting the precedence relationships.** An easy way to do this is to first identify the **immediate predecessors** associated with an activity. The immediate predecessors are the activities that need to be completed immediately before an activity. Activity A needs to be completed before activities B and C can start. B and C need to be completed before D can start. The following table reflects what we know so far:

Immediate predecessors

Activity	Designation	Immediate Predecessors	Time (weeks)
Select company	A	None	1
Obtain annual report and perform ratio analysis	B	A	2
Collect stock price data and perform technical analysis	C	A	1
Review data and make a decision	D	B and C	1

Here is a diagram that depicts these precedence relationships:

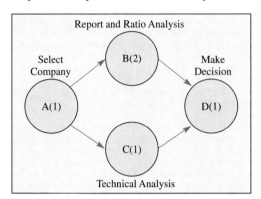

3. **Determine the critical path.** Consider each sequence of activities that runs from the beginning to the end of the project. For our simple project there are two paths: A–B–D and A–C–D. The critical path is the path where the sum of the activity times is the longest. A–B–D has a duration of four weeks and A–C–D, a duration of three weeks. The critical path, therefore, is A–B–D. If any activity along the critical path is delayed, then the entire project will be delayed.

4. **Determine the early start/finish and late start/finish schedule.** To schedule the project, find when each activity needs to start and when it needs to finish. For some activities in a project there may be some leeway in when an activity can start and finish. This is called the **slack time** in an activity. For each activity in the project, we calculate four points in time: the early start, early finish, late start, and late finish times. The early start and early finish are the earliest times that the activity can start and be finished. Similarly, the late start and late finish are the latest times the activities can start and finish. The difference between the late start time and early start time is the slack time. To help keep all of this straight, we place these numbers in special places around the nodes that represent each activity in our network diagram, as shown here.

Slack time

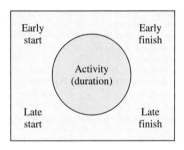

To calculate numbers, start from the beginning of the network and work to the end, calculating the early start and early finish numbers. Start counting with the current period, designated as period 0. Activity A has an early start of 0 and an early finish of 1. Activity B's early start is A's early finish, or 1. Similarly, C's early start is 1. The early finish for B is 3, and the early finish for C is 2. Now consider activity D. D cannot start until both B and C are done. Because B cannot be done until 3, D cannot start until that time. The early start for D, therefore, is 3, and the early finish is 4. Our diagram now looks like this.

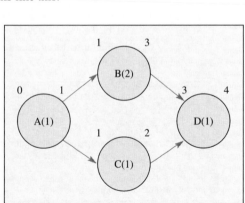

9.2 Example

Critical Path Method

Excel: Project Management

Step by Step

Many firms that have tried to enter the notebook computer market have failed. Suppose your firm believes that there is a big demand in this market because existing products have not been designed correctly. They are too heavy, too large, or too small to have standard-size keyboards. Your intended computer will be small enough to carry inside a jacket pocket if need be. The ideal size will be no larger than 5 inches × 9½ inches × 1 inch with a folding keyboard. It should weigh no more than 15 ounces and have an LCD display, a micro disk drive, and a wireless connection. This should appeal to traveling businesspeople, but it could have a much wider market, including students. It should be priced in the $175–$200 range.

The project, then, is to design, develop, and produce a prototype of this small computer. In the rapidly changing computer industry, it is crucial to hit the market with a product of this sort in less than a year. Therefore, the project team has been allowed approximately eight months (35 weeks) to produce the prototype.

Solution

The first charge of the project team is to develop a project network chart and determine if the prototype computer can be completed within the 35-week target. Let's follow the steps in the development of the network.

1. **Activity identification.** The project team decides that the following activities are the major components of the project: design of the computer, prototype construction, prototype testing, methods specification (summarized in a report), evaluation studies of automatic assembly equipment, an assembly equipment study report, and a final report summarizing all aspects of the design, equipment, and methods.

2. **Activity sequencing and network construction.** On the basis of discussion with staff, the project manager develops the precedence table and sequence network shown in Exhibit 9.6. When constructing a network, take care to ensure that the activities are in the proper order and that the logic of their relationships is maintained. For example, it would be illogical to have a situation where Event A precedes Event B, B precedes C, and C precedes A.

3. **Determine the critical path.** The critical path is the longest sequence of connected activities through the network and is defined as the path with zero slack time. This network has four different paths: A–C–F–G, A–C–E–G, A–B–D–F–G, and A–B–D–E–G. The lengths of these paths are 38, 35, 38, and 35 weeks. Note that this project has two different critical paths; this might indicate that this would be a fairly difficult project to manage. Calculating the early start and late start schedules gives additional insight into how difficult this project might be to complete on time. ●

To calculate the late finish and late start times, start from the end of the network and work toward the front. Consider activity D. The earliest that it can be done is at time 4; and if we do not want to delay the completion of the project, the late finish needs to be set to 4. With a duration of 1, the latest that D can start is 3. Now consider activity C. C must be done by time 3 so that D can start, so C's late finish time is 3 and its late start time is 2. Notice the difference between the early and late start and finish times: This activity has one week of slack time. Activity B must be done by time 3 so that D can start, so its late finish time is 3 and late start time is 1. There is no slack in B. Finally, activity A must be done so that B and C can start. Because B must start earlier than C, and A must get done in time for B to start, the late finish time for A is 1. Finally, the late start time for A is 0. Notice there is no slack in activities A, B, and D. The final network looks like this. (Hopefully the stock your investment team has chosen is a winner!)

CPM NETWORK FOR COMPUTER DESIGN PROJECT

	CPM Activity Designations and Time Estimates		
Activity	Designation	Immediate Predecessors	Time (Weeks)
Design	A	—	21
Build prototype	B	A	5
Evaluate equipment	C	A	7
Test prototype	D	B	2
Write equipment report	E	C, D	5
Write methods report	F	C, D	8
Write final report	G	E, F	2

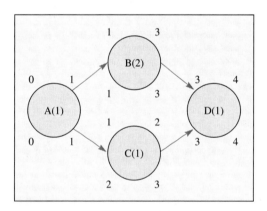

Early start schedule

Late start schedule

Early Start and Late Start Schedules An **early start schedule** is one that lists all of the activities by their early start times. For activities not on the critical path, there is slack time between the completion of each activity and the start of the next activity. The early start schedule completes the project and all its activities as soon as possible.

A **late start schedule** lists the activities to start as late as possible without delaying the completion date of the project. One motivation for using a late start schedule is that savings are realized by postponing purchases of materials, the use of labor, and other costs until necessary. These calculations are shown in Exhibit 9.7. From this we see that the only activity that has slack is activity E. This certainly would be a fairly difficult project to complete on time.

CPM with Three Activity Time Estimates

If a single estimate of the time required to complete an activity is not reliable, the best procedure is to use three time estimates. These three times not only allow us to estimate the activity time but also let us obtain a probability estimate for completion time for the

CPM NETWORK FOR COMPUTER DESIGN PROJECT

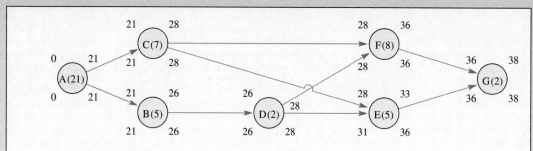

SLACK CALCULATIONS AND CRITICAL PATH DETERMINATIONS

ACTIVITY	LS−ES	SLACK	ON CRITICAL PATH
A	0−0	0	✔
B	21−21	0	✔
C	21−21	0	✔
D	26−26	0	✔
E	31−28	3	
F	28−28	0	✔
G	36−36	0	✔

entire network. Briefly, the procedure is as follows: The estimated activity time is calculated using a weighted average of a minimum, maximum, and most likely time estimate. The expected completion time of the network is computed using the procedure described above. Using estimates of variability for the activities on the critical path, the probability of completing the project by particular times can be estimated. (Note that the probability calculations are a distinguishing feature of the classic PERT approach.)

Step by Step

9.3 Example

Three Times Estimates

We use the same information as in Example 9.2 with the exception that activities have three time estimates.

Solution

1. Identify each activity to be done in the project.

2. Determine the sequence of activities and construct a network reflecting the precedence relationships.

3. The three estimates for an activity time are

   a = Optimistic time: the minimum reasonable period of time in which the activity can be completed. (There is only a small probability, typically assumed to be 1 percent, that the activity can be completed in less time.)

   m = Most likely time: the best guess of the time required. Since m would be the time thought most likely to appear, it is also the mode of the beta distribution discussed in step 4.

   b = Pessimistic time: the maximum reasonable period of time the activity would take to be completed. (There is only a small probability, typically assumed to be 1 percent, that it would take longer.)

Typically, this information is gathered from those people who are to perform the activity.

4. Calculate the expected time (ET) for each activity. The formula for this calculation is

$$ET = \frac{a + 4m + b}{6} \qquad \textbf{[9.1]}$$

This is based on the beta statistical distribution and weights the most likely time (m) four times more than either the optimistic time (a) or the pessimistic time (b). The beta distribution is extremely flexible. It can take on the variety of forms that typically arise; it has finite end points (which limit the possible activity times to the area between a and b); and, in the simplified version, it permits straightforward computation of the activity mean and standard deviation.

5. Determine the critical path. Using the expected times, a critical path is calculated in the same way as the single time case.

6. Calculate the variances (σ^2) of the activity times. Specifically, this is the variance, σ^2, associated with each ET and is computed as follows:

$$\sigma^2 = \left(\frac{b - a}{6}\right)^2 \qquad \textbf{[9.2]}$$

As you can see, the variance is the square of one-sixth the difference between the two extreme time estimates. Of course, the greater this difference, the larger the variance.

7. Determine the probability of completing the project on a given date, based on the application of the standard normal distribution. A valuable feature of using three time estimates is that it enables the analyst to assess the effect of uncertainty on project completion time. (If you are not familiar with this type of analysis, see the box titled "Probability Analysis.") The mechanics of deriving this probability are as follows:

   a. Sum the variance values associated with each activity on the critical path.

   b. Substitute this figure, along with the project due date and the project expected completion time, into the Z transformation formula. This formula is

$$Z = \frac{D - T_{\text{E}}}{\sqrt{\Sigma \, \sigma_{cp}^2}} \qquad \textbf{[9.3]}$$

where

$$D = \text{Desired completion date for the project}$$
$$T_{\text{E}} = \text{Expected completion time for the project}$$
$$\Sigma \, \sigma_{cp}^2 = \text{Sum of the variances along the critical path}$$

   c. Calculate the value of Z, which is the number of standard deviations (of a standard normal distribution) that the project due date is from the expected completion time.

   d. Using the value of Z, find the probability of meeting the project due date (using a table of normal probabilities such as Appendix A). The *expected completion time* is the starting time plus the sum of the activity times on the critical path.

Following the steps just outlined, we developed Exhibit 9.8 showing expected times and variances. The project network was created the same as we did previously. The only difference is that the activity times are weighted averages. We determine the critical path as before, using these values as if they were single numbers. The difference between the single time estimate and the three times (optimistic, most likely, and pessimistic) is in computing probabilities of completion. Exhibit 9.9 shows the network and critical path.

Because there are two critical paths in the network, we must decide which variances to use in arriving at the probability of meeting the project due date. A conservative approach dictates using the path with the largest total variance to focus management's attention on the activities most likely to exhibit broad variations. On this basis, the variances associated with activities A, C, F, and G would

ACTIVITY EXPECTED TIMES AND VARIANCES

Excel: Project Management

Activity	Activity Designation	Time Estimates			Expected Times (ET) $\dfrac{a + 4m + b}{6}$	Activity Variances (σ^2) $\left(\dfrac{b - a}{6}\right)^2$
		a	m	b		
Design	A	10	22	28	21	9
Build prototype	B	4	4	10	5	1
Evaluate equipment	C	4	6	14	7	$2\frac{7}{9}$
Test prototype	D	1	2	3	2	$\frac{1}{9}$
Write report	E	1	5	9	5	$1\frac{7}{9}$
Write methods report	F	7	8	9	8	$\frac{1}{9}$
Write final report	G	2	2	2	2	0

be used to find the probability of completion. Thus $\Sigma\sigma_{cp}^2 = 9 + 2\frac{7}{9} + \frac{1}{9} + 0 = 11.89$. Suppose management asks for the probability of completing the project in 35 weeks. D, then, is 35. The expected completion time was found to be 38. Substituting into the Z equation and solving, we obtain

$$Z = \frac{D - T_E}{\sqrt{\Sigma\,\sigma_{cp}^2}} = \frac{35 - 38}{\sqrt{11.89}} = -0.87$$

Looking at Appendix A, we see that a Z value of -0.87 yields a probability of 0.1922, which means that the project manager has only about a 19 percent chance of completing the project in 35 weeks. Note that this probability is really the probability of completing the critical path A–C–F–G. Because there is another critical path and other paths that might become critical, the probability of completing the project in 35 weeks is actually less than 0.19. ●

Exhibit 9.9

COMPUTER DESIGN PROJECT WITH THREE TIME ESTIMATES

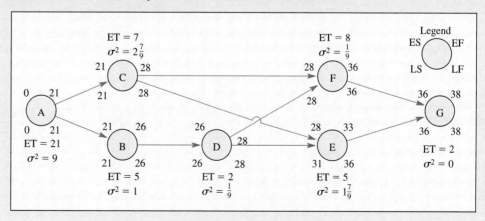

9.8 Probability Analysis

The three-time-estimate approach introduces the ability to consider the probability that a project will be completed within a particular amount of time. The assumption needed to make this probability estimate is that the activity duration times are independent random variables. If this is true, the central limit theorem can be used to find the mean and the variance of the sequence of activities that form the critical path. The central limit theorem says that the sum of a group of independent, identically distributed random variables approaches a normal distribution as the number of random variables increases. In the case of project management problems, the random variables are the actual times for the activities in the project. (Recall that the time for each activity is assumed to be independent of other activities, and to follow a beta statistical distribution.) For this

the expected time to complete the critical path activities is the sum of the activity times.

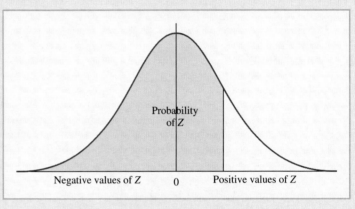

Likewise, because of the assumption of activity time independence, the sum of the variances of the activities along the critical path is the variance of the expected time to complete the path.

Recall that the standard deviation is equal to the square root of the variance.

To determine the actual probability of completing the critical path activities within a certain amount of time, we need to find where on our probability distribution the time falls. Appendix A shows the areas of the cumulative standard normal distribution for different values of Z. Z measures the number of standard deviations either to the right or to the left of zero in the distribution. The values correspond to the cumulative probability associated with each value of Z. For example, the first value in the table, -4.00, has a $G(z)$ equal to .00003. This means that the probability associated with a Z value of -4.0 is only .003 percent. Similarly, a Z value of 1.50 has a $G(z)$ equal to .93319 or 93.319 percent. The Z values are calculated using equation (9.3) given in Step 7b of the "Three Time Estimates" example solution. These cumulative probabilities also can be obtained by using the NORMSDIST (Z) function built into Microsoft Excel.

Time–Cost Models and Project Crashing

Time–cost models

In practice, project managers are as much concerned with the cost to complete a project as with the time to complete the project. For this reason, **time–cost models** have been devised. These models—extensions of the basic critical path method—attempt to develop a minimum-cost schedule for an entire project and to control expenditures during the project.

Minimum-Cost Scheduling (Time–Cost Trade-Off)   The basic assumption in minimum-cost scheduling, also known as "Crashing," is that there is a relationship between activity completion time and the cost of a project. Crashing refers to the compression or shortening of the time to complete the project. On one hand, it costs money to expedite an activity; on the other, it costs money to sustain (or lengthen) the project. The costs associated with expediting activities are termed *activity direct costs* and add to the project direct cost. Some may be worker-related, such as overtime work, hiring more workers, and transferring workers from other jobs; others are resource-related, such as buying or leasing additional or more efficient equipment and drawing on additional support facilities.

The costs associated with sustaining the project are termed *project indirect costs:* overhead, facilities, and resource opportunity costs, and, under certain contractual situations, penalty costs or lost incentive payments. Because *activity direct costs and project indirect costs* are opposing costs dependent on time, the scheduling problem is essentially one of finding the project duration that minimizes their sum, or in other words, finding the optimum point in a time–cost trade-off.

The procedure for project crashing consists of the following five steps. It is explained by using the simple four-activity network shown in Exhibit 9.10. Assume that the indirect costs remain constant for eight days and then increase at the rate of $5 per day.

1. **Prepare a CPM-type network diagram.** For each activity this diagram should list
   a. Normal cost (NC): the lowest expected activity costs. (These are the lesser of the cost figures shown under each node in Exhibit 9.10.)
   b. Normal time (NT): the time associated with each normal cost.
   c. Crash time (CT): the shortest possible activity time.
   d. Crash cost (CC): the cost associated with each crash time.

2. **Determine the cost per unit of time (assume days) to expedite each activity.** The relationship between activity time and cost may be shown graphically by plotting CC and CT coordinates and connecting them to the NC and NT coordinates by a concave, convex, or straight line—or some other form, depending on the actual cost structure of activity performance, as in Exhibit 9.10. For activity A, we assume a linear relationship between time and cost. This assumption is common in practice and helps us derive the cost per day to expedite because this value may be found directly by taking the slope of the line using the formula Slope = (CC − NC) ÷ (NT − CT). (When the assumption of linearity cannot be made, the cost of expediting must be determined graphically for each day the activity may be shortened.)

   The calculations needed to obtain the cost of expediting the remaining activities are shown in Exhibit 9.11.

3. **Compute the critical path.** For the simple network we have been using, this schedule would take 10 days. The critical path is A–B–D.

4. **Shorten the critical path at the least cost.** The easiest way to proceed is to start with the normal schedule, find the critical path, and reduce the path time by one day using the lowest-cost activity. Then recompute and find the new critical path and reduce it by one day also. Repeat this procedure until the time of completion is satisfactory, or until there can be no further reduction in the project completion time. Exhibit 9.12 shows the reduction of the network one day at a time.

Working though Exhibit 9.12 might initially seem difficult. In the first line, all activities are at their normal time and costs are at their lowest value. The critical path is A–B–D, cost for completing the project is $26, and the project completion time is 10 days.

The goal in line two is to reduce the project completion time by one day. We know it is necessary to reduce the time for one or more of the activities on the critical path. In the second column we note that activity A can be reduced one day (from two to one day), activity B can be reduced three days (from five to two days), and activity D can be reduced two days (from three to one day). The next column tracks the cost to reduce

EXAMPLE OF TIME–COST TRADE-OFF PROCEDURE

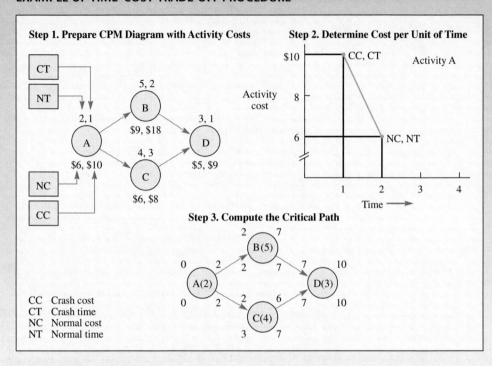

Step 1. Prepare CPM Diagram with Activity Costs

Step 2. Determine Cost per Unit of Time

Step 3. Compute the Critical Path

CC Crash cost
CT Crash time
NC Normal cost
NT Normal time

Excel: Project Management

each of the activities by a single day. For example, for activity A, it normally costs $6 to complete in two days. It could be completed in one day at a cost of $10, a $4 increase. So we indicate the cost to expedite activity A by one day is $4. For activity B, it normally costs $9 to complete in five days. It could be completed in two days at a cost of $18. Our cost to reduce B by three days is $9, or $3 per day. For C, it normally costs $5 to complete in three days. It could be completed in one day at a cost of $9; a two-day reduction would cost $4 ($2 per day). The least expensive alternative for a one-day reduction in time is to expedite activity D at a cost of $2. Total cost for the network goes up to $28 and the project completion time is reduced to nine days.

Our next iteration starts in line three, where the goal is to reduce the project completion time to eight days. The nine-day critical path is A–B–D. We could shorten activity A by one day, B by three days, and D by one day (note D has already been reduced from three to two days). Cost to reduce each activity by one day is the same as in line two. Again, the least expensive activity to reduce is D. Reducing activity D from two to one day results in the total cost for all activities in the network going up to $30 and the project completion time coming down to eight days.

Line four is similar to line three, but now only A and B are on the critical path and can be reduced. B is reduced, which takes our cost up $3 to $33 and reduces the project completion time to seven days.

In line five (actually our fifth iteration in solving the problem), activities A, B, C, and D are all critical. D cannot be reduced, so our only options are activities A, B, and C. Note that B and C are in parallel, so it does not help to reduce B without reducing C. Our options are to reduce A alone at a cost of $4 or B and C together at a cost of $5 ($3 for B and $2 for C), so we reduce A in this iteration.

Exhibit 9.11

CALCULATION OF COST PER DAY TO EXPEDITE EACH ACTIVITY

Activity	CC − NC	NT − CT	$\dfrac{CC - NC}{NT - CT}$	Cost Per Day to Expedite	Number of Days Activity may be Shortened
A	$10 − $6	2 − 1	$\dfrac{\$10 - \$6}{2 - 1}$	$4	1
B	$18 − $9	5 − 2	$\dfrac{\$18 - \$9}{5 - 2}$	$3	3
C	$8 − $6	4 − 3	$\dfrac{\$8 - \$6}{4 - 3}$	$2	1
D	$9 − $5	3 − 1	$\dfrac{\$9 - \$5}{3 - 1}$	$2	2

In line six, we take the B and C option that was considered in line five. Finally, in line seven, our only option is to reduce activity B. Since B and C are in parallel and we cannot reduce C, there is no value in reducing B alone. We can reduce the project completion time no further.

5. **Plot project direct, indirect, and total-cost curves and find the minimum-cost schedule.** Exhibit 9.13 shows the indirect cost plotted as a constant $10 per day for up to eight days and increasing $5 per day thereafter. The direct costs are plotted from Exhibit 9.12, and the total project cost is shown as the total of the two costs.

Summing the values for direct and indirect costs for each day yields the project total cost curve. As you can see, this curve is at its minimum with an eight-day schedule, which costs $40 ($30 direct + $10 indirect).

9.9 Managing Resources

In addition to scheduling each task, we must assign resources. Modern software quickly highlights overallocations—situations in which allocations exceed resources.

To resolve overallocations manually, you can either add resources or reschedule. Moving a task within its slack can free up resources.

Mid- to high-level project management information systems (PMIS) software can resolve overallocations through a "leveling" feature. Several rules of thumb can be used. You can specify that low-priority tasks should be delayed until higher-priority onces are complete. or that the project should end before or after the original deadline.

Tracking Progress

The real action starts after the project gets under way. Actual progress will differ from your original, or baseline, planned progress. Software can hold several different baseline plans, so you can compare monthly snapshots.

A *tracking Gantt chart* superimposes the current schedule onto a baseline plan so deviations are easily noticed. If you prefer, a spreadsheet view of the same information could be output. Deviations between planned start/finish and newly scheduled start/finish also appear, and a "slipping filter" can be applied to highlight or output only those tasks that are scheduled to finish at a later date than the planned baseline.

Exhibit 9.12

REDUCING THE PROJECT COMPLETION TIME ONE DAY AT A TIME

Current Critical Path(s)	Remaining Number of Days Activity May Be Shortened	Cost per Day to Expedite Each Activity	Least-Cost Activity to Expedite	Total Cost of All Activities in Network	Project Completion Time
ABD	All activity times and costs are normal.			$26	10
ABD	A–1, B–3, D–2	A–4, B–3, D–2	D	28	9
ABD	A–1, B–3, D–1	A–4, B–3, D–2	D	30	8
ABD	A–1, B–3	A–4, B–3	B	33	7
ABD ACD	A–1, B–2, C–1	A–4, B–3, C–2	A*	37	6
ABD ACD	B–2, C–1	B–3, C–2	B&C†	42	5
ABD ACD	B–1	B–3	B+	45	5

*To reduce the critical path by one day, reduce either A alone or B and C together at the same time (either B or C by itself just modifies the critical path without shortening it).

†B&C must be crashed together to reduce the path by one day.

+Crashing activity B does not reduce the length of the project, so this additional cost would not be incurred.

Exhibit 9.13

PLOT OF COSTS AND MINIMUM-COST SCHEDULE

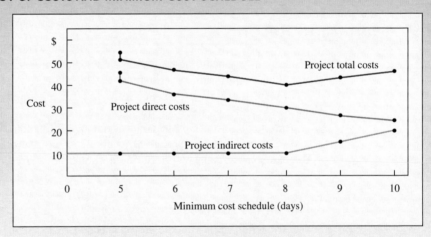

Management by exception also can be applied to find deviations between budgeted costs and actual costs. (See the box titled "Project Management Information Systems.")

9.10 Project Management Information Systems

Interest in the techniques and concepts of project management has exploded in the past 10 years. This has resulted in a parallel increase in project management software offerings. Now there are over 100 companies offering project management software. For the most up-to-date information about software available, check out the Web site of the Project Management Institute (www.pmi.org). Two of the leading companies are Microsoft, with Microsoft Project, and Primavera, with Primavera Project Planner. The following is a brief review of these two programs:

The Microsoft Project program comes with an excellent online tutorial, which is one reason for its overwhelming popularity with project managers tracking midsized projects. This package is compatible with the Microsoft Office Suite, which opens all the communications and Internet integration capability that Microsoft offers. The program includes features for scheduling, allocating, and leveling resources, as well as controlling costs and producing presentation-quality graphics and reports.

Finally, for managing very large projects or programs having several projects, Primavera Project Planner is often the choice. Primavera was the first major vendor of this type of software and has possibly the most sophisticated capability.

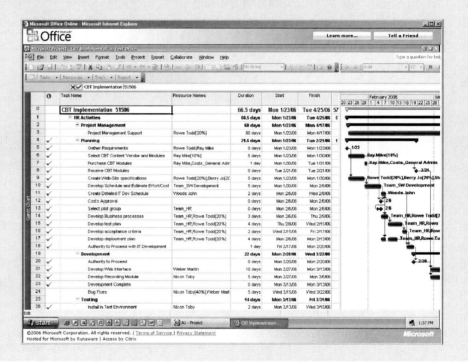

9.11 Summary

This chapter provides a description of the basics of managing projects. The chapter first describes how the people involved with a project are organized from a management viewpoint. The scope of the project will help define the organization. This organization spans the use of a dedicated team to a largely undedicated matrix structure. Next, the chapter considers how project activities are organized into subprojects by using the work breakdown structure. Following this, the technical details of calculating the shortest time it should take to complete a project are covered. Finally, the chapter considers how projects can be shortened through the use of "crashing" concepts.

9.12
Key Terms

Project A series of related jobs usually directed toward some major output and requiring a significant period of time to perform.

Project management Planning, directing, and controlling resources (people, equipment, material) to meet the technical, cost, and time constraints of a project.

Pure project A structure for organizing a project where a self-contained team works full time on the project.

Functional project A structure where team members are assigned from the functional units of the organization. The team members remain a part of their functional units and typically are not dedicated to the project.

Matrix project A structure that blends the functional and pure project structures. Each project uses people from different functional areas. A dedicated project manager decides what tasks need to be performed and when, but the functional managers control which people to use.

Project milestone A specific event in a project.

Work breakdown structure The hierarchy of project tasks, subtasks, and work packages.

Activities Pieces of work within a project that consume time. The completion of all the activities of a project marks the end of the project.

Gantt chart Shows in a graphic manner the amount of time involved and the sequence in which activities can be performed. Often referred to as a *bar chart*.

Earned value management Technique that combines measures of scope, schedule, and cost for evaluating project progress.

Critical path The sequence of activities in a project that forms the longest chain in terms of their time to complete. This path contains zero slack time. It is possible for there to be multiple critical paths in a project. Techniques used to find the critical path are called CPM or Critical Path Method techniques.

Immediate predecessor Activity that needs to be completed immediately before another activity.

Slack time The time that an activity can be delayed; the difference between the late and early start times of an activity.

Early start schedule A project schedule that lists all activities by their early start times.

Late start schedule A project schedule that lists all activities by their late start times. This schedule may create savings by postponing purchases of material and other costs associated with the project.

Time–cost models Extension of the critical path models that considers the trade-off between the time required to complete an activity and cost. This is often referred to as "crashing" the project.

9.13
Formula
Review

Expected Time

$$ET = \frac{a + 4m + b}{6}$$ [9.1]

Variance (σ^2) of the activity times

$$\sigma^2 = \left(\frac{b - a}{6}\right)^2$$ [9.2]

Z transformation formula

$$Z = \frac{D - T_E}{\sqrt{\Sigma s_{cp}^2}}$$

[9.3]

9.14 Solved Problems

Solved Problem 1

You have been asked to calculate the Cost Performance Index for a project using Earned Value Management techniques. It is currently day 20 of the project and the following summarizes the current status of the project:

Activity	Expected Cost	Activity Duration	Expected Start Date	Expected Completion Date	Expected % Complete	Actual % Complete	Actual Cost to Date
Startup	$100,000	10 days	0	10	100%	100%	$105,000
Construction	$325,000	14 days	8	22	12/14 = 85.7%	90%	$280,000
Finishing	$50,000	12 days	18	30	2/12 = 16.7%	25%	$2,500

Calculate the Schedule Variance, Schedule Performance Index, and the Cost Performance Index for the project.

Solution

Step 1: Calculate budgeted cost of the work scheduled to date:

Startup is 100% complete and we are beyond the expected completion date, so budgeted cost is $100,000 for this activity.

Would expect Construction to be 85.7% complete and cost $278,200 to date.
Would expect Finishing to be 16.7% complete at a cost of $8,333 to date.

Budgeted cost of work scheduled = $100,000 + 278,200 + 8,333 = $386,533

Step 2: Calculate the budgeted cost of the work performed to date:

Startup is 100% complete, so budgeted cost is $100,000.
Construction is actually only 90% complete, so budget cost for this much of the activity is $(325,000 \times .9) = $292,500$.

Finishing is now 25% complete, so budgeted cost is $(50,000 \times .25) = $12,500$.

Budgeted cost of work performed = 100,000 + 292,500 + 12,500 = $405,000

Step 3: Actual cost of the project to date is 105,000 + 280,000 + 2,500 = $387,500.

Step 4: Calculate performance measures:

Schedule variance = $405,000 − $386,533 = $18,467
Schedule Performance Index = $405,000/$386,533 = 1.047
Cost Performance Index = $405,000/$387,500 = 1.045

The project looks good since it is both ahead of schedule and ahead of budgeted cost.

Solved Problem 2

A project has been defined to contain the following list of activities, along with their required times for completion.

Activity	Time (days)	Immediate Predecessors
A	1	—
B	4	A
C	3	A
D	7	A
E	6	B
F	2	C, D
G	7	E, F
H	9	D
I	4	G, H

   a. Draw the critical path diagram.

   b. Show the early start, early finish, late start, and late finish times.

   c. Show the critical path.

   d. What would happen if activity F was revised to take four days instead of two?

Solution

The answers to *a*, *b*, and *c* are shown in the following diagram.

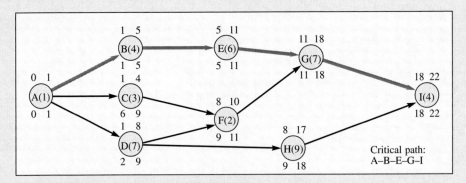

   a. New critical path: A–D–F–G–I. Time of completion is 23 days.

Solved Problem 3

A project has been defined to contain the following activities, along with their time estimates for completion:

Activity	Time Estimates (wk)			Immediate Predecessor
	a	*m*	*b*	
A	1	4	7	—
B	2	6	7	A
C	3	4	6	A, D
D	6	12	14	A
E	3	6	12	D
F	6	8	16	B, C
G	1	5	6	E, F

a. Calculate the expected time and the variance for each activity.

b. Draw the critical path diagram.

c. Show the early start, early finish times and late start, late finish times.

d. Show the critical path.

e. What is the probability that the project can be completed in 34 weeks?

Solution

a.

Activity	Expected Time $\dfrac{a + 4m + b}{6}$	Activity Variance $\left(\dfrac{b - a}{6}\right)^2$
A	4.00	1
B	5.50	$\frac{25}{36}$
C	4.17	$\frac{1}{4}$
D	11.33	$1\frac{7}{9}$
E	6.50	$2\frac{1}{4}$
F	9.00	$2\frac{7}{9}$
G	4.50	$\frac{25}{36}$

b.

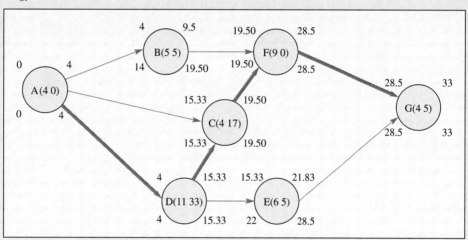

c. Shown on diagram.

d. Shown on diagram.

e. $Z = \dfrac{D - T_E}{\sqrt{\Sigma \sigma_{cp}^2}} = \dfrac{34 - 33}{\sqrt{1 + 1\frac{7}{9} + \frac{1}{4} + 2\frac{7}{9} + \frac{25}{36}}} = \dfrac{1}{2.5495} = .3922$

Look up that value in Appendix A and we see that there is about a 65 percent chance of completing the project by that date.

Solved Problem 4

Here are the precedence requirements, normal and crash activity times, and normal and crash costs for a construction project:

Excel: PM_Solved Problems

Activity	Preceding Activities	Required Time (weeks)		Cost	
		Normal	Crash	Normal	Crash
A	—	4	2	$10,000	$11,000
B	A	3	2	6,000	9,000
C	A	2	1	4,000	6,000
D	B	5	3	14,000	18,000
E	B, C	1	1	9,000	9,000
F	C	3	2	7,000	8,000
G	E, F	4	2	13,000	25,000
H	D, E	4	1	11,000	18,000
I	H, G	6	5	20,000	29,000

a. What are the critical path and the estimated completion time?

b. To shorten the project by three weeks, which tasks would be shortened and what would the final total project cost be?

Solution

The construction project network is shown below:

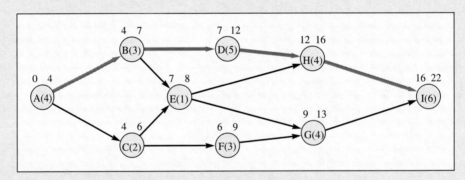

a. Critical path A–B–D–H–I.

Normal completion time is 22 weeks.

b.

Activity	Crash Cost	Normal Cost	Normal Time	Crash Time	Cost Per Week	Weeks
A	$11,000	$10,000	4	2	$500	2
B	9,000	6,000	3	2	3,000	1
C	6,000	4,000	2	1	2,000	1
D	18,000	14,000	5	3	2,000	2
E	9,000	9,000	1	1		0
F	8,000	7,000	3	2	1,000	1
G	25,000	13,000	4	2	6,000	2
H	18,000	11,000	4	1	2,333	3
I	29,000	20,000	6	5	9,000	1

(1) 1st week: CP = A–B–D–H–I. Cheapest is A at $500. Critical path stays the same.

(2) 2nd week: A is still the cheapest at $500. Critical path stays the same.

(3) 3rd week: Because A is no longer available, the choices are B (at $3,000), D (at $2,000), H (at $2,333), or I (at $9,000). Therefore, choose D at $2,000.

Total Project cost shortened there week is

A	$11,000
B	6,000
C	4,000
D	16,000
E	9,000
F	7,000
G	13,000
H	11,000
I	20,000
	$97,000

9.15 Review and Discussion Questions

1. What was the most complex project that you have been involved in? Give examples of the following as they pertain to the project: the work breakdown structure, tasks, subtasks, and work package. Were you on the critical path? Did it have a good project manager?

2. What are some reasons project scheduling is not done well?

3. Discuss the graphic presentations in Exhibit 9.4. Are there any other graphic outputs you would like to see if you were project manager?

4. Which characteristics must a project have for critical path scheduling to be applicable? What types of projects have been subjected to critical path analysis?

5. What are the underlying assumptions of minimum-cost scheduling? Are they equally realistic?

6. "Project control should always focus on the critical path." Comment.

7. Why would subcontractors for a government project want their activities on the critical path? Under what conditions would they try to avoid being on the critical path?

9.16 Problems

1. Your project to obtain charitable donations is now 30 days into a planned 40-day project. The project is divided into three activities. The first activity is designed to solicit individual donations. It is scheduled to run the first 25 days of the project and to bring in $25,000. Even though we are 30 days into the project, we still see that we have only 90% of this activity complete. The second activity relates to company donations and is scheduled to run for 30 days starting on day 5 and extending through day 35. We estimate that even though we should have (25/30) 83% of this activity complete, it is actually only 50% complete. This part of the project was scheduled to bring in $150,000 in donations. The final activity is for matching funds. This activity is scheduled to run the last 10 days of the project and has not started. It is scheduled to bring in an additional $50,000. So far $175,000 has actually been brought in on the project.

   Calculate the schedule variance, schedule performance index, and cost (actually value in this case) performance index. How is the project going? Hint: Note that this problem is different since revenue rather than cost is the relevant measure. Use care in how the measures are interpreted.

2. A project to build a new bridge seems to be going very well since the project is well ahead of schedule and costs seem to be running very low. A major milestone has been reached where the first two activities have been totally completed and the third activity is 60% complete. The planners were only expecting to be 50% through the third activity at this time. The first activity involves prepping the site for the bridge. It was expected that this would cost $1,420,000 and it was done for only $1,300,000. The second activity was the pouring of concrete for the bridge. This was expected to cost $10,500,000 but was actually done for $9,000,000. The third and final activity is the actual construction of the bridge superstructure. This was expected to cost a total of $8,500,000. To date they have spent $5,000,000 on the superstructure.

Calculate the schedule variance, schedule performance index, and the cost index for the project to date. How is the project going?

3. The following activities are part of a project to be scheduled using CPM:

Activity	Immediate Predecessor	Time (weeks)
A	—	6
B	A	3
C	A	7
D	C	2
E	B, D	4
F	D	3
G	E, F	7

a. Draw the network.
b. What is the critical path?
c. How many weeks will it take to complete the project?
d. How much slack does activity B have?

4. Schedule the following activities using CPM:

Activity	Immediate Predecessor	Time (weeks)
A	—	1
B	A	4
C	A	3
D	B	2
E	C, D	5
F	D	2
G	F	2
H	E, G	3

a. Draw the network.
b. What is the critical path?
c. How many weeks will it take to complete the project?
d. Which activities have slack, and how much?

5. The R&D department is planning to bid on a large project for the development of a new communication system for commercial planes. The accompanying table shows the activities, times, and sequences required:

Activity	Immediate Predecessor	Time (weeks)
A	—	3
B	A	2
C	A	4
D	A	4
E	B	6
F	C, D	6
G	D, F	2
H	D	3
I	E, G, H	3

a. Draw the network diagram.

b. What is the critical path?

c. Suppose you want to shorten the completion time as much as possible, and you have the option of shortening any or all of B, C, D, and G each one week. Which would you shorten?

d. What is the new critical path and earliest completion time?

6. The following represents a project that should be scheduled using CPM

Activity	Immediate Predecessors	Times (days)		
		a	m	b
A	—	1	3	5
B	—	1	2	3
C	A	1	2	3
D	A	2	3	4
E	B	3	4	11
F	C, D	3	4	5
G	D, E	1	4	6
H	F, G	2	4	5

a. Draw the network.

b. What is the critical path?

c. What is the expected project completion time?

d. What is the probability of completing this project within 16 days?

7. There is an 82% chance the project below can be completed in *X* weeks or less. What is *X*?

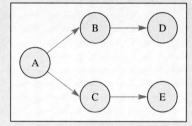

Activity	Most optimistic	Most Likely	Most Pessimistic
A	2	5	11
B	3	3	3
C	1	3	5
D	6	8	10
E	4	7	10

8. The following table represents a plan for a project:

Job No.	Predecessor Job(s)	Times (days)		
		a	m	b
1	—	2	3	4
2	1	1	2	3
3	1	4	5	12
4	1	3	4	11
5	2	1	3	5
6	3	1	2	3
7	4	1	8	9
8	5, 6	2	4	6
9	8	2	4	12
10	7	3	4	5
11	9, 10	5	7	8

a. Construct the appropriate network diagram.

b. Indicate the critical path.

c. What is the expected completion time for the project?

d. You can accomplish any one of the following at an additional cost of $1,500:

   (1) Reduce job 5 by two days.
   (2) Reduce job 3 by two days.
   (3) Reduce job 7 by two days.

   If you will save $1,000 for each day that the earliest completion time is reduced, which action, if any, would you choose?

e. What is the probability that the project will take more than 30 days to complete?

9. A construction project is broken down into the following 10 activities:

Activity	Immediate Predecessor	Time (weeks)
1	—	4
2	1	2
3	1	4
4	1	3
5	2, 3	5
6	3	6
7	4	2
8	5	3
9	6, 7	5
10	8, 9	7

a. Draw the network diagram.
b. Find the critical path.
c. If activities 1 and 10 cannot be shortened, but activities 2 through 9 can be shortened to a minimum of one week each at a cost of $10,000 per week, which activities would you shorten to cut the project by four weeks?

10. Here is a CPM network with activity times in weeks:

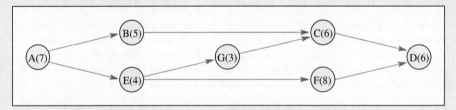

a. Determine the critical path.
b. How many weeks will the project take to complete?
c. Suppose F could be shortened by two weeks and B by one week. How would this affect the completion date?

11. Here is a network with the activity times shown in days:

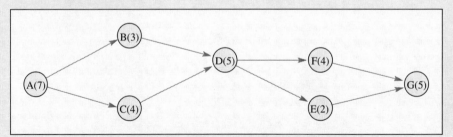

a. Find the critical path.
b. The following table shows the normal times and the crash times, along with the associated costs for each activity.

Activity	Normal Time	Crash Time	Normal Cost	Crash Cost
A	7	6	$7,000	$8,000
B	3	2	5,000	7,000
C	4	3	9,000	10,200
D	5	4	3,000	4,500
E	2	1	2,000	3,000
F	4	2	4,000	7,000
G	5	4	5,000	8,000

If the project is to be shortened by four days, show which activities, in order of reduction, would be shortened and the resulting cost.

12. The home office billing department of a chain of department stores prepares monthly inventory reports for use by the stores' purchasing agents. Given the following information, use the critical path method to determine:

a. How long the total process will take.

b. Which jobs can be delayed without delaying the early start of any subsequent activity.

Job and Description		Immediate Predecessors	Time (hours)
a	Start	—	0
b	Get computer printouts of customer purchases	a	10
c	Get stock records for the month	a	20
d	Reconcile purchase printouts and stock records	b, c	30
e	Total stock records by department	b, c	20
f	Determine reorder quantities for coming period	e	40
g	Prepare stock reports for purchasing agents	d, f	20
h	Finish	g	0

13. For the network shown:

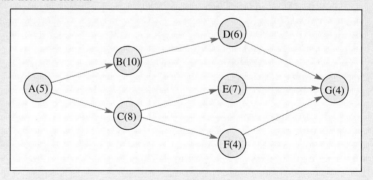

a. Determine the critical path and the early completion time in weeks for the project.

b. For the data shown, reduce the project completion time by three weeks. Assume a linear cost per week shortened, and show, step by step, how you arrived at your schedule.

Activity	Normal Time	Normal Cost	Crash Time	Crash Cost
A	5	$ 7,000	3	$13,000
B	10	12,000	7	18,000
C	8	5,000	7	7,000
D	6	4,000	5	5,000
E	7	3,000	6	6,000
F	4	6,000	3	7,000
G	4	7,000	3	9,000

14. The following CPM network has estimates of the normal time in weeks listed for the activities:

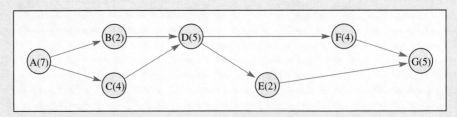

a. Identify the critical path.
b. What is the length of time to complete the project?
c. Which activities have slack, and how much?
d. Here is a table of normal and crash times and costs. Which activities would you shorten to cut two weeks from the schedule in a rational fashion? What would be the incremental cost? Is the critical path changed?

Activity	Normal Time	Crash Time	Normal Cost	Crash Cost
A	7	6	$7,000	$8,000
B	2	1	5,000	7,000
C	4	3	9,000	10,200
D	5	4	3,000	4,500
E	2	1	2,000	3,000
F	4	2	4,000	7,000
G	5	4	5,000	8,000

15. Bragg's Bakery is building a new automated bakery in downtown Sandusky. Here are the activities that need to be completed to get the new bakery built and the equipment installed.

Activity	Predecessor	Normal Time (Weeks)	Crash Time (Weeks)	Expediting Cost/Week
A	—	9	6	$3,000
B	A	8	5	$3,500
C	A	15	10	$4,000
D	B, C	5	3	$2,000
E	C	10	6	$2,500
F	D, E	2	1	$5,000

a. Draw the project diagram.
b. What is the normal project length?
c. What is the project length if all activities are crashed to their minimum?
d. Bragg's loses $3,500 in profit per week for every week the bakery is not completed. How many weeks will the project take if we are willing to pay crashing cost as long as it is less than $3,500?

Advanced Problem

16. Assume the network and data that follow:

Activity	Normal Time (weeks)	Normal Cost	Crash Time (weeks)	Crash Cost	Immediate Predecessors
A	2	$50	1	$70	—
B	4	80	2	160	A
C	8	70	4	110	A
D	6	60	5	80	A
E	7	100	6	130	B
F	4	40	3	100	D
G	5	100	4	150	C, E, F

a. Construct the network diagram.

b. Indicate the critical path when normal activity times are used.

c. Compute the minimum total direct cost for each project duration based on the cost associated with each activity. Consider durations of 13, 14, 15, 16, 17, and 18 weeks.

d. If the indirect costs for each project duration are $400 (18 weeks), $350 (17 weeks), $300 (16 weeks), $250 (15 weeks), $200 (14 weeks), and $150 (13 weeks), what is the total project cost for each duration? Indicate the minimum total project cost duration.

9.17 Case: Cell Phone Design Project

You work for Motorola in its global cell phone group. You have been made project manager for the design of a new cell phone model. Your supervisors have already scoped the project so you have a list showing the work breakdown structure and this includes major project activities. You must plan the project schedule and calculate project duration and project costs. Your boss wants the schedule and costs on his desk tomorrow morning!

You have been given the information in Exhibit 9.14. It includes all the activities required in the project and the duration of each activity. Also, dependencies between the activities have been identified. Remember that the preceding activity must be fully completed before work on the following activity can be started.

Your project is divided into five major tasks. Task P involves developing specifications for the new cell phone. Here decisions related to such things as battery life, size of the phone, and features need to be determined. These details are based on how a customer uses the cell phone. These user specifications are redefined in terms that have meaning to the subcontractors that will actually make the new cell phone in Task S, supplier specifications. These involve engineering details for how the product will perform. The individual components that make up the product are the focus of Task D. Task I brings all the components together and a working prototype is built and tested. Finally in Task V, vendors are selected and contracts are negotiated.

1. Draw a project network that includes all the activities.

2. Calculate the start and finish times for each activity and determine the minimum number of weeks for completing the project. Find the critical set of activities for the project.

3. Identify slack in the activities not on the project critical path.

4. Your boss would like you to suggest changes that could be made to the project that would significantly shorten it. What would you suggest?

WORK BREAKDOWN STRUCTURE AND ACTIVITIES FOR THE CELL PHONE DESIGN PROJECT

Major Project Tasks/ Activities	Activity Identification	Dependency	Duration (weeks)
Product specifications (P)			
Overall product specifications	P1	—	4
Hardware specifications	P2	P1	5
Software specifications	P3	P1	5
Market research	P4	P2, P3	2
Supplier specifications (S)			
Hardware	S1	P2	5
Software	S2	P3	6
Market research	S3	P4	1
Product design (D)			
Circuits	D1	S1, D7	8
Battery	D2	S1	1
Display	D3	S1	2
Outer cover	D4	S3	4
User interface	D5	S2	4
Camera	D6	S1, S2, S3	1
Functionality	D7	D5, D6	4
Product integration (I)			
Hardware	I1	D1, D2, D3, D4, D6	3
Software	I2	D7	5
Prototype testing	I3	I1, I2	5
Subcontracting (V)			
Vendor selection	V1	D7	10
Contract negotiation	V2	I3, V1	2

**Excel:
Cell_Phone
Design**

9.18
Case: The Campus Wedding (A)

On March 31 of last year, Mary Jackson burst into the family living room and announced that she and Larry Adams (her college boyfriend) were going to be married. After recovering from the shock, her mother hugged her and asked, "When?" The following conversation resulted:

Mary: April 22.

Mother: What!

Father: The Adams–Jackson wedding will be the social hit of the year. Why so soon?

Mary: Because on April 22 the cherry blossoms on campus are always in full bloom! The wedding pictures will be beautiful.

Mother: But honey, we can't possibly finish all the things that need to be done by then. Remember all the details that were involved in your sister's wedding? Even if we start tomorrow, it takes a day to reserve the church and reception hall, and they need at least 17 days' notice. That has to be done before we can start decorating the church, which takes three days. An extra $100 contribution on Sunday would probably cut that 17-day notice to 10 days, though.

Father: Ugh!

Mary: I want Jane Summers to be my maid of honor.

Father: But she's in the Peace Corps, in Guatemala, isn't she? It would take her 10 days to get ready and drive up here.

Mary: But we could fly her up in two days, and it would cost only $500. She would have to be here in time to have her dress fitted.

Father:	Ugh!
Mother:	And catering! It takes two days to choose the cake and table decorations, and Jack's Catering wants at least 10 days' notice prior to the rehearsal dinner (the night before the wedding).
Mary:	Can I wear your wedding dress, Mom?
Mother:	Well, we'd have to replace some lace, but you could wear it, yes. We could order the lace from New York when we order the material for the bridesmaids' dresses. It takes eight days to order and receive the material. The pattern needs to be chosen first, and that would take three days.
Father:	We could get the material here in five days if we paid an extra $25 to airfreight it.
Mary:	I want Mrs. Watson to work on the dresses.
Father:	But she charges $120 a day!
Mother:	If we did all the sewing, we could finish the dresses in 11 days. If Mrs. Watson helped, we could cut that down to six days, at a cost of $120 for each day less than 11 days.
Mary:	I don't want anyone but her.
Mother:	It would take another two days to do the final fitting. It normally takes two days to clean and press the dresses, but that new cleaner downtown could do them in one day if we pay the $30 charge for express service.
Father:	Everything should be completed by rehearsal night, and that's only 21 days from now. I bet that will be a busy day.
Mother:	We've forgotten something. The invitations.
Father:	We should order the invitations from Bob's Printing Shop, and that usually takes 12 days. I'll bet he would do it in five days if we slipped him an extra $35.
Mother:	It would take us three days to choose the invitation style before we could order them, and we want the envelopes printed with our return address.
Mary:	Oh! That will be elegant.
Mother:	The invitations should go out at least 10 days before the wedding. If we let them go any later, some of the relatives would get theirs too late to come, and that would make them mad. I'll bet that if we didn't get them out until eight days before the wedding, Aunt Ethel couldn't make it, and she would reduce her wedding gift by $200.
Father:	Ugh!
Mother:	We'll have to take them to the post office to mail them, and that takes a day. Addressing would take four days unless we hired some part-time help, and we can't start until the printer is finished. If we hired someone, we could probably save two days by spending $25 for each day saved.
Mary:	We need to get gifts to give to the bridesmaids at the rehearsal dinner. I can spend a day and do that.
Mother:	Before we can even start to write out those invitations, we need a guest list. Heavens, that will take four days to get in order, and only I can understand our address file.
Mary:	Oh, Mother, I'm so excited. We can start each of the relatives on a different job.
Mother:	Honey, I don't see how we can do it. Why, we've got to choose the invitations and patterns and reserve the church and . . .
Father:	Why don't you just take $1,500 and elope. Your sister's wedding cost me $1,200, and she didn't have to fly people up from Guatemala, hire extra people, use airfreight, or anything like that.

9.19 Questions

1. Given the activities and precedence relationships described in the (A) case, develop a network diagram for the wedding plans.
2. Identify the paths. Which are critical?
3. What is the minimum-cost plan that meets the April 22 date?

9.20 Case: The Campus Wedding (B)

Several complications arose during the course of trying to meet the deadline of April 21 for the Adams–Jackson wedding rehearsal. Because Mary Jackson was adamant about having the wedding on April 22 (as was Larry Adams, because he wanted her to be happy), the implications of each of these complications had to be assessed.

1. On April 1 the chairman of the Vestry Committee at the church was left unimpressed by the added donation and said he wouldn't reduce the notice period from 17 to 10 days.
2. A call to Guatemala revealed that the potential bridesmaid had several commitments and could not possibly leave the country until April 10.
3. Mother came down with the four-day flu just as she started on the guest list.
4. The lace and dress materials were lost in transit. Notice of the loss was delivered to the Jackson home early on April 10.
5. There was a small fire at the caterer's shop on April 8. It was estimated that the shop would be closed two or three days for repairs.

 Mary Jackson's father, in particular, was concerned about expenses and kept offering $1,500 to Mary and Larry for them to elope.

9.21 Question

1. Given your answers to the (A) case, describe the effects on the wedding plans of each incident noted in the (B) case.

Source: Adapted from a case originally written by Professor D. C. Whybank, University of North Carolina, Chapel Hill, North Carolina.

9.22 Super Quiz

1. A project structured where a self-contained team works full time on the project.
2. Specific events that upon completion mark important progress toward completing a project.
3. This defines the hierarchy of project tasks, subtasks, and work packages.
4. Pieces of work in a project that consume time to complete.
5. A chart that shows both the time and sequence for completing the activities in a project.
6. Activities that in sequence form the longest chain in a project.
7. The difference between the late and early start time for an activity.
8. When activities are scheduled with probabilistic task times.
9. The procedure used to reduce project completion time by trading off time versus cost.
10. A key assumption related to the resources needed to complete activities when using the critical path method.

 1. Pure project or skunkworks 2. Milestones 3. Work breakdown structure 4. Activities 5. Gantt chart 6. Critical path(s) 7. Slack 8. The Program Evaluation and Review Technique (PERT) 9. Crashing 10. Resources are always available

9.23 Selected Bibliography

Gray, C. *Agile Project Management: How to Succeed in the Face of Changing Project Requirements.* New York: American Management Association, 2004.

Gray, C. F., and E. W. Larson. Project Management: The Managerial Process. New York: Irwin/McGraw-Hill, 2002.

Kerzner, H. *Project Management: A Systems Approach to Planning, Scheduling, and Controlling.* 8th ed. New York: Wiley, 2002.

Lewis, James P. *The Project Manager's Desk Reference.* New York: McGraw-Hill Professional Publishing, 1999.

Chapter 10

Risk-Pooling Strategies to Reduce and Hedge Uncertainty[1]

Uncertainty is the bane of operations. No matter in what form—for example, uncertain demand, uncertain supply, or uncertain quality—operational performance never benefits from the presence of uncertainty. Previous chapters have discussed models for coping with uncertainty (e.g., queuing, newsvendor, and order-up-to) and have emphasized the need to quantify uncertainty. Some strategies for reducing and hedging uncertainty have already been suggested: combine servers in a queuing system; reduce uncertainty by collecting data to ensure that the best demand forecast is always implemented (Chapter 8); establish make-to-order production and invest in reactive capacity to better respond to demand.

This chapter explores several additional strategies based on the concept of risk pooling. The idea behind risk pooling is to redesign the supply chain, the production process, or the product to either reduce the uncertainty the firm faces or hedge uncertainty so that the firm is in a better position to mitigate the consequence of uncertainty. Several types of risk pooling are presented (location pooling, virtual pooling, product pooling, lead time pooling, and capacity pooling), but these are just different names to describe the same basic phenomenon. With each strategy, we work through a numerical example to illustrate its effectiveness and to highlight the situations in which the strategy is most appropriate.

10.1 Location Pooling

The newsvendor and the order-up-to inventory models are tools for deciding how much inventory to put at a single location to serve demand. An equally important decision, and one that we have ignored so far, is in how many different locations should the firm store inventory to serve demand. To explain, consider the Medtronic supply chain. In that supply chain, each sales representative in the field manages a cache of inventory to serve the rep's territory and there is a single distribution center to serve the entire U.S. market. Should there be one stockpile of inventory per sales representative or should the demands from

[1] Data in this chapter have been disguised to protect confidentiality.

multiple territories be served from a single location? Should there be a single distribution center or should the U.S. market demand be divided among multiple distribution centers? We explore those questions in this section.

Pooling Medtronic's Field Inventory

Let's begin with where to locate Medtronic's field inventory. Instead of the current system in which each sales representative manages his or her own inventory, maybe the representatives in adjacent territories could share inventory. For example, Medtronic could rent a small space in a centrally located and easily accessible location (e.g., a back room in a strip mall off the interchange of two major highways) and two to five representatives could pool their inventory at that location. Sharing inventory means that each representative would only carry inventory needed for immediate use; that is, each representative's trunk and consignment inventory would be moved to this shared location. Control of the pooled inventory would be guided by an automatic replenishment system based on the order-up-to model. What impact would this new strategy have on inventory performance?

Recall that average daily demand for Medtronic's InSync pacemaker in Susan Magnotto's Madison, Wisconsin, territory is represented with a Poisson distribution with mean 0.29 unit per day. For the sake of argument, let's suppose there are several other territories adjacent to Susan's, each with a single sales representative and each with average daily demand of 0.29 unit for the InSync pacemaker. Instead of each representative carrying his or her own inventory, now they share a common pool of inventory. We refer to the combined territories in this new system as the *pooled territory* and the inventory there as the *pooled inventory*. In contrast, we refer to the territories in the current system as the *individual territories* and the inventory in one of those territories as the *individual inventory*. We refer to the strategy of combining the inventory from multiple territories/ locations into a single location as *location pooling*. We have already evaluated the expected inventory with the current individual territory system, so now we need to evaluate the performance of the system with pooled territories, that is, the impact of location pooling.

The order-up-to model is used to manage the inventory at the pooled territory. The same aggressive target in-stock probability is used for the pooled territory as is used at the individual territories, 99.9 percent. Furthermore, the lead time to replenish the pooled territory is also one day. (There is no reason to believe the lead time to the pooled territory should be different than to the individual territories.)

If the Poisson distribution represents demand at two different territories, then their combined demand has a Poisson distribution with a mean that equals the sum of their means. For example, suppose Susan shares inventory with two nearby sales representatives and they all have mean demand for the InSync pacemaker of 0.29 unit per day. Then total demand across the three territories is Poisson with mean $3 \times 0.29 = 0.87$ unit per day. We then can apply the order-up-to model to that pooled territory assuming a lead time of one day and a mean demand of 0.87 unit.

Table 10.1 presents data on the impact of pooling the sales representatives' territories. To achieve the 99.9 percent in-stock probability for three sales representatives requires $S = 7$, where S is the order-up-to level. If Susan's inventory is not combined with another representative's, then $S = 4$ is needed to hit the target in-stock probability. The expected inventory at the pooled location is 5.3 units, in contrast to 3.4 units for each individual location. However, the total inventory for three individual locations is $3 \times 3.4 = 10.2$ units. Hence, pooling three locations reduces expected inventory by about 48 percent $[(10.2 - 5.3)/10.2]$, without any degradation in service!

TABLE 10.1
The Impact on InSync Pacemaker Inventory from Pooling Sales Representatives' Territories
Demand at each territory is Poisson with average daily demand of 0.29 unit, the target in-stock probability is 99.9 percent, and the lead time is one day.

Number of Territories Pooled	Pooled Territory's Expected Demand per Day (a)	S	Expected Inventory		Pipeline Inventory	
			Units (b)	Days-of-Demand (b/a)	Units (c)	Days-of-Demand (c/a)
1	0.29	4	3.4	11.7	0.29	1.0
2	0.58	6	4.8	8.3	0.58	1.0
3	0.87	7	5.3	6.1	0.87	1.0
4	1.16	8	5.7	4.9	1.16	1.0
5	1.45	9	6.1	4.2	1.45	1.0
6	1.74	10	6.5	3.7	1.74	1.0
7	2.03	12	7.9	3.9	2.03	1.0
8	2.32	13	8.4	3.6	2.32	1.0

There is another approach to make the comparison between pooled territories and individual territories: Evaluate each inventory quantity relative to the demand it serves, that is, calculate expected inventory measured in days-of-demand rather than units:

$$\text{Expected inventory in days-of-demand} = \frac{\text{Expected inventory in units}}{\text{Expected daily demand}}$$

Table 10.1 also provides that measure of expected inventory. We see that inventory at each individual territory equals 3.4/0.29 = 11.7 days-of-demand whereas inventory at three pooled territories equals only 5.3/0.87 = 6.1 days-of-demand. Using our days-of-demand measure, we see that pooling three territories results in a 48 percent [(11.7 − 6.1)/11.7] reduction in inventory investment. We obtain the same inventory reduction (48 percent) because the two measures of inventory, units and days-of-demand, only differ by a constant factor (the expected daily demand). Hence, we can work with either measure.

While pooling two or three territories has a dramatic impact on inventory, Table 10.1 indicates that there are decreasing marginal returns to pooling territories; that is, each new territory added to the pool brings a smaller reduction in inventory than the previous territory added to the pool. For example, adding two more territories to a pool of six (to make a total of eight combined territories) has very little impact on the inventory investment (3.6 days-of-demand versus 3.7 days-of-demand), whereas adding two more territories to a pool of one (to make a total of three combined territories) has a dramatic impact in inventory (6.1 days-of-demand versus 11.7 days-of-demand). This is good news: the majority of the benefit of pooling territories comes from the first couple of territories combined, so there is little value in trying to combine many territories together.

Although location pooling generally reduces inventory, a careful observer of the data in Table 10.1 would discover that this is not always so: adding the seventh location to the pool slightly increases inventory (3.9 days-of-demand versus 3.7 days-of-demand). This is due to the restriction that the order-up-to level must be an integer (0, 1, 2, . . .) quantity. As a result, the in-stock probability might be even higher than the target: the in-stock probability with six pooled territories is 99.90 percent, whereas it is 99.97 percent with seven pooled territories. Overall, this issue does not invalidate the general trend that location pooling reduces inventory.

This discussion obviously leads to the question of why does location pooling reduce the required inventory investment? We'll find a good answer by looking at how demand variability changes as locations are added to the pooled location. And, as we have already discussed, the coefficient of variation (the ratio of the standard deviation to the mean) is our choice for measuring demand variability.

Recall that the standard deviation of a Poisson distribution equals the square root of its mean. Therefore,

$$\text{Coefficient of variation of a Poisson distribution} =$$

$$\frac{\text{Standard deviation}}{\text{Mean}} = \frac{\sqrt{\text{Mean}}}{\text{Mean}} = \frac{1}{\sqrt{\text{Mean}}} \qquad \textbf{(10.1)}$$

As the mean of a Poisson distribution increases, its coefficient of variation decreases, that is, the Poisson distribution becomes less variable. Less variable demand leads to less inventory for any given service level. Hence, combining locations with Poisson demand reduces the required inventory investment because a higher demand rate implies less variable demand. However, because the coefficient of variation decreases with the square root of the mean, it decreases at a decreasing rate. In other words, each incremental increase in the mean has a proportionally smaller impact on the coefficient of variation, and, hence, on the expected inventory investment.

Figure 10.1 displays the relationship between inventory and the coefficient of variation for the data in Table 10.1. Notice that the decreasing pattern in inventory closely mimics the decreasing pattern in the coefficient of variation.

In addition to the total expected inventory in the field, we also are interested in the total pipeline inventory (inventory on order between the distribution center and the field). Table 10.1 provides the pipeline inventory in terms of units and in terms of days-of-demand. While location pooling decreases the expected inventory in days-of-demand, it has absolutely no impact on the pipeline inventory in terms of days-of-demand! Why? Little's Law governs pipeline inventory, and Little's Law depends on averages, not variability.

FIGURE 10.1

The Relationship between Expected Inventory (circles) and the Coefficient of Variation (squares) as Territories Are Pooled

Demand in each territory is Poisson with mean 0.29 unit per day, the target in-stock probability is 99.9 percent, and the lead time is one day.

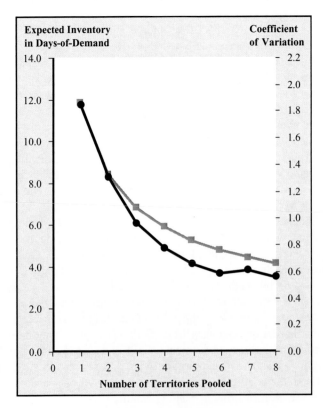

TABLE 10.2
Using Location Pooling to Raise the In-Stock Probability While Maintaining the Same Inventory Investment
Demand at each territory is Poisson with average daily demand of 0.29 unit, and the lead time is one day.

Number of Territories Pooled	Pooled Territory's Expected Demand per Day	S	Expected Inventory		
			Units	Days-of-Demand	In-Stock Probability
1	0.29	4	3.4	11.7	99.96615%
2	0.58	8	6.8	11.7	99.99963
3	0.87	12	10.3	11.8	100.00000

Hence, because pooling territories reduces the variability of demand, it reduces expected inventory in the field, but it has no impact on the pipeline inventory. As we mentioned before, the only way to reduce pipeline inventory is to get a faster lead time. (Reducing demand reduces pipeline inventory in terms of units but does not change pipeline inventory measured in days-of-demand.)

While we can exploit location pooling to reduce inventory while maintaining a service level, we also can use location pooling to increase our service level. For example, we could choose an order-up-to level in the pooled territory that generates the same inventory investment as the individual territories (measured in days-of-demand) and see how much higher our in-stock could be. Table 10.2 presents those data for pooling up to three territories; beyond three territories we can raise the in-stock to essentially 100 percent with the same inventory investment as the individual territories.

Because the in-stock probability target with individual territories is so high (99.9 percent), it probably makes better sense to use location pooling to reduce the inventory investment rather than to increase the service level. However, in other settings it may be more desirable to increase the service level, especially if the target service level is deemed to be too low.

Figure 10.2 provides another perspective on this issue. It displays the inventory–service trade-off curves with four different degrees of location pooling: individual territories, two territories pooled, four territories pooled, and eight territories pooled. As displayed in the figure, pooling territories shifts the inventory–service trade-off curve down and to the right. Hence, location pooling gives us many options: we can choose to (1) maintain the same service with less inventory, (2) maintain the same inventory with a higher service, or (3) reduce inventory and increase service simultaneously (i.e., "we can have our cake and eat it too"). We saw a similar effect when pooling servers in a queuing environment. There you can use pooling to reduce waiting time without having to staff extra workers, or you can reduce workers while maintaining the same responsiveness, or a combination of both. Furthermore, we should note that these results are not specific to the order-up-to model or Poisson demand; they are quite general and we use this model and demand only to illustrate our point.

Although our analysis highlights the potential dramatic benefit of location pooling, this does not imply that Medtronic should pool territories without further thought. There will be an explicit storage cost for the space to house the pooled inventory, whereas the current system does not have a storage cost for trunk and consignment inventory. However, location pooling might reduce theft and spoilage costs because inventory is stored in fewer locations. Furthermore, location pooling probably would reduce shipping costs because the number of items per delivery is likely to increase.

The greatest concern with location pooling is the impact on the efficiency of the sales representatives. Even if only a few territories are pooled, it is likely that the pooled location would not be as convenient to each sales representative as their own individual inventory.

FIGURE 10.2

The Inventory–Service Trade-off Curve for Different Levels of Location Pooling

The curves represent, from highest to lowest, individual territories, two pooled territories, four pooled territories, and eight pooled territories. Demand in each territory is Poisson with mean 0.29 unit per day and the lead time is one day.

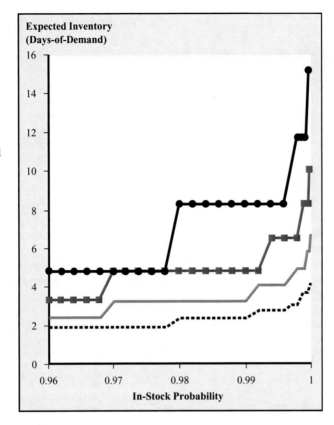

As a result, the savings in inventory is offset by the extra time sales representatives spend pulling inventory from the pooled location instead of their own trunk or consignment closet. If that time penalty is sufficient, then the sales representatives might choose to still maintain their own trunk inventory. In a worst-case scenario, the sale's representatives continue to hold the same amount of inventory in their individual territories in addition to the inventory at the pooled location. To avoid this worst-case scenario, Medtronic should involve the sales representatives in the design of the pooled territories to ensure that they have "bought into the idea." Imposing a new supply chain structure without the cooperation of all interested parties can lead to unintended consequences, especially when human behavior is at work.

The physical separation between user and inventory can be mitigated via *virtual pooling:* Representatives maintain control of their inventory, but inventory information is shared among all representatives so that each rep can obtain inventory from the central distribution center and any other rep that has excess inventory. Although virtual pooling has its own challenges (e.g., the additional cost of maintaining the necessary information systems, the added expense of transshipping inventory among territories, and the sticky design issue of how to decide when inventory can be taken from one rep to be given to another rep), it can still be better than the current system that has isolated pockets of inventory.

Medtronic's Distribution Center(s)

Now let's turn our attention to the distribution center. For the U.S. market, Medtronic currently operates a single distribution center in Mounds View, Minnesota. Suppose Medtronic were to subdivide the United States into two or more regions, with each region

TABLE 10.3
The Increase in Inventory Investment as More Distribution Centers Are Operated
Assume demand is equally divided among the DCs, demands across DCs are independent, total demand is normally distributed with mean 80.6 and standard deviation 58.8, and the lead time is three weeks in all situations.

Number of DCs	Weekly Demand Parameters at Each DC			Expected Inventory at Each DC	
	Mean	Standard Deviation	Coefficient of Variation	Units	Weeks-of-Demand
1	80.6	58.8	0.73	364	4.5
2	40.3	41.6	1.03	257	6.4
3	26.9	34.0	1.26	210	7.8
4	20.2	29.4	1.46	182	9.0
5	16.1	26.3	1.63	163	10.1
6	13.4	24.0	1.79	148	11.0
7	11.5	22.2	1.93	137	11.9
8	10.1	20.8	2.06	127	12.8

assigned a single distribution center. This idea is location pooling in reverse. Hence, the total inventory investment is likely to increase. Let's see by how much.

Recall that weekly demand of the InSync Pacemaker at the Mounds View DC is normally distributed with mean 80.6 and standard deviation 58.81. There is a three-week lead time and the target in-stock probability is 99.9 percent. Table 10.3 provides data on the expected inventory required given the number of DCs Medtronic operates.

Table 10.3 reveals that it is indeed costly to subdivide the U.S. market among multiple distribution centers: eight DCs require nearly three times more inventory to achieve the same service level as a single DC! (To be precise, it requires 12.8/4.5 = 2.84 times more inventory.)

In this situation, the connection between the coefficient of variation and the expected inventory savings from location pooling (or "dissavings" from location disintegration, as in this case) is even stronger than we saw with field inventory, as displayed in Figure 10.3.

FIGURE 10.3
The Expected Inventory in Units (circles) and the Coefficient of Variation (squares) Depending on the Number of Distribution Centers Medtronic Operates
Demand is assumed to be equally divided and independent across distribution centers. The target in-stock probability is 99.9 percent and the lead time is three weeks in all cases.

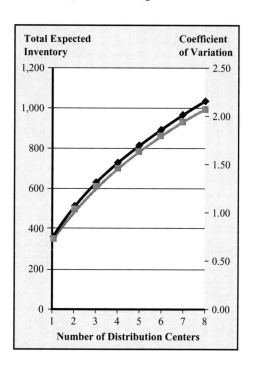

In fact, expected inventory and the coefficient of variation in this setting are proportional to one another (i.e., their ratio is a constant no matter the number of distribution centers).

To summarize, we have seen that location pooling dramatically reduces demand variability (measured with the coefficient of variation) and, in turn, dramatically reduces the expected inventory investment needed to achieve a target service level. By storing inventory in fewer locations, location pooling is also likely to lead to lower storage costs. However, there are drawbacks to location pooling as well.

The key drawback with location pooling is that inventory moves further away from demand. For example, Medtronic could really reduce the needed inventory investment of InSync pacemakers if it were to require that inventory be stored only in one location per state. That might work for the Delaware representatives, but it is silly even for Wisconsin for two reasons. First, we saw that there are declining returns from location pooling, that is, pooling two to three locations gives most of the "bang for the buck," so there is no need to pool many locations. Second, Medtronic does not want to save on inventory at the expense of sales representatives spending too much time driving to and from the pooled inventory location. Thus, Medtronic may be able to use some location pooling of field inventory, but they should not get carried away with this idea.

The physical separation between inventory and customer is also a relevant issue at the distribution-center level of the supply chain. For example, we investigated the consequence of dividing the U.S. market into multiple regions, each served with a single distribution center. This "reverse location pooling" increases inventory investment, but it does put inventory closer to customers (i.e., sales representatives). The question is whether there is any value in having DC inventory closer to the field. Given that Medtronic uses an overnight carrier for all of its shipments, it is unlikely that the lead time to the field representatives would decrease (which would reduce field inventory). Furthermore, it is unlikely that the overnight carriers would charge Medtronic less per shipment, so Medtronic's shipping costs probably would not decrease. Finally, Medtronic's storage facility cost would increase with more DCs, so there really does not appear to be any justification for Medtronic to operate more than its one DC. Nevertheless, the outcome of this analysis could be different for other firms.

While we have concluded that Medtronic should operate with no more than one distribution center in the United States, we can now speculate on whether Medtronic should operate with only one distribution center worldwide. While consolidating down to one worldwide distribution center would further reduce the required inventory investment, it is unlikely that a single distribution center for the entire world market could provide a one-day lead time to replenish field inventory in all regions of the world. Therefore, while consolidating DCs would reduce inventory at the distribution-center level of the supply chain, it would also increase field inventory. While we have not done the analysis formally, the extra field inventory needed to compensate for the longer lead time almost surely would be greater than the inventory savings at the DCs. This idea is probably a "nonstarter."

Electronic Commerce

No discussion on location pooling is complete without discussing electronic commerce. One of the well-known advantages to the e-commerce model, especially with respect to e-tailers, is the ability to operate with substantially lower inventory. As our analysis suggests, keeping inventory in fewer locations should allow an e-tailer to turn inventory much faster than a comparable brick-and-mortar retailer. However, there are extra costs to position inventory in a warehouse rather than in a neighborhood store: shipping individual items to consumers is far more expensive than shipping in bulk to retail stores and, while physical stores need not be constructed, an e-tailer needs to invest in the technology to create an electronic store (i.e., user interface, logistics management, etc.).

We also saw that there are declining returns to location pooling. Not surprisingly, while many e-tailers, such as Amazon.com, started with a single distribution center, they now operate several distribution centers in the United States. This requires that some products are stored in multiple locations, but it also means that the average customer is located closer to a distribution center, which accelerates the average delivery time and reduces shipping costs.

The ability to offer customers a huge product selection is another advantage of the e-commerce model, possibly the most important advantage. While we have focused on using location pooling to reduce inventory, location pooling also can enable a broad product assortment. Consider an item that sells but is a rather slow seller. Unfortunately for most businesses, the majority of products fall into that category. To include this item in the product assortment requires at least one unit. Placing one unit in hundreds of locations may not be economical, but it may be economical to place a few units in a single location.

To illustrate this point, consider a slow-moving product that could be sold by a retailer with 200 stores. The product would sell at each store at the average rate of 0.01 unit per week. Consequently, the retailer's total demand across all stores is $0.01 \times 200 = 2$ per week. You may think this is ridiculously slow, but in fact there are many products that sell at this pace. For example, Brynjolfsson, Hu, and Smith (2003) estimated that 40 percent of Amazon's sales came from items that sold no more than 1.5 units per week. Returning to our example, suppose this retailer must stock at least one unit in each store (the product must be available at the store). Given each store's sales rate, the retailer will stock only one unit and each item will spend nearly two years ($1/0.01 = 100$ weeks) on the shelf. That sales rate implies a measly 0.5 inventory turn (inventory is turned over once every two years). To finalize this analysis, if inventory cost 20 percent per year to hold (capital cost and, more importantly, the cost of shelf space), then this item will incur $2 \times 20\% = 40$ percent in holding costs. Most retailers do not have anywhere near a 40 percent gross margin, so it is unlikely that this product is profitable—the retailer cannot carry this item profitably because it just doesn't turn fast enough. Now contrast those economics with an e-tailer with one warehouse. If the e-tailer's demand is Poisson with mean two per week, replenishment lead time is two weeks, and the target in-stock is 99 percent, we can use the order-up-to model to determine that the retailer will have on average about six units of inventory. If total yearly demand is about 104 units (52 weeks at 2 per week), then our e-tailer turns inventory $104/6 = 17.3$ times per year. The e-tailer stands a chance to make money stocking this item, whereas the brick-and-mortar retailer does not. To summarize, there are many slow selling products in this world (which can sum up to a lot of sales, as evidenced by Amazon.com), but location pooling may be necessary for a retailer to profitably include them in the assortment.

If a firm does not want to establish a central warehouse to use location pooling to broaden its product assortment, then it can hire another firm to do that job. That practice is called *drop shipping*. For example, Circuit City hired Alliance Entertainment to hold the inventory of the approximately 55,000 video and DVD titles Circuit City wanted to offer online (Sechler 2002). Customers would browse and purchase items on Circuit City's Web site, but then the order would be transmitted to Alliance Entertainment to be shipped to the customer. Circuit City surely would not be able to provide economically that assortment at its physical stores, which currently carry 500 to 3,000 titles, and it may not have been economical to carry that many titles even if Circuit City operated a single warehouse. Alliance Entertainment makes it feasible by applying location pooling across many different retailers.

10.2   Product Pooling

The previous section considered serving demand with fewer inventory locations. A closely related idea is to serve demand with fewer products. To explain, consider O'Neill's Hammer 3/2 wetsuit discussed in Chapter 8. The Hammer 3/2 we studied is targeted to the market for surfers, but O'Neill sells another Hammer 3/2 that serves the market for recreational divers. The two wetsuits are identical with the exception that the surf Hammer has the "wave" logo (see Figure 8.1) silk screened on the chest, while the dive Hammer has O'Neill's dive logo, displayed in Figure 10.4. O'Neill's current product line has two products to serve demand for a Hammer 3/2 wetsuit, some of it from surfers, the other portion from divers. An alternative is to combine these products into a single product to serve all Hammer 3/2 wetsuit demand, that is, a *universal design*. The strategy of using a universal design is called *product pooling*. This section focuses on the merits of the product-pooling strategy with a universal design.

Recall that demand for the surf Hammer is normally distributed with mean 3,192 and standard deviation 1,181. For the sake of simplicity, let's assume demand for the dive Hammer is also normally distributed with the same mean and standard deviation. Both wetsuits sell for $180, are purchased from O'Neill's supplier for $110, and are liquidated at the end of the season for $90.

We have already evaluated the optimal order quantity and expected profit for the surf Hammer: ordering 4,101 units earns an expected profit of $191,760. Because the dive Hammer is identical to the surf Hammer, it has the same optimal order quantity and expected profit. Therefore, the total profit from both Hammer wetsuits is $383,520 (2 × $191,760).

Now let's consider what O'Neill should do if it sold a single Hammer wetsuit, which we call the universal Hammer. We need a distribution to represent demand for the universal Hammer and then we need an order quantity. Expected demand for the universal Hammer is 3,192 × 2 = 6,384 units. If demand in the dive market is independent of demand in the surf market, then the standard deviation for the universal Hammer is $1,181 \times \sqrt{2} = 1,670$. The underage cost for the universal Hammer is still $C_u = 180 - 110 = 70$ and the overage cost is still $C_o = 110 - 90 = 20$. Hence, the critical ratio has not changed:

$$\frac{C_u}{C_o + C_u} = \frac{70}{20 + 70} = 0.7778$$

The corresponding z-statistic is still 0.77, and so the optimal order quantity is

$$Q = \mu + \sigma \times z = 6,384 + 1,670 \times 0.77 = 7,670$$

FIGURE 10.4
O'Neill's Logo for Dive Wetsuits

The expected profit with the universal Hammer is

$$\text{Expected profit} = (C_u \times \text{Expected sales}) - (C_o \times \text{Expected leftover inventory})$$
$$= (70 \times 6{,}172.4) - (20 \times 1{,}497.6)$$
$$= \$402{,}116$$

Therefore, pooling the surf and dive Hammers together can potentially increase profit by 4.85 percent [(402,116 − 383,520)/383,520]. This profit increase is 1.45 percent of the expected revenue when O'Neill sells two wetsuits. Given that net profit in this industry ranges from 2 to 5 percent of revenue, this potential improvement is not trivial.

As with the location pooling examples at Medtronic, the potential benefit O'Neill receives from product pooling occurs because of a reduction in the variability of demand. With two Hammer wetsuits, O'Neill faces a coefficient of variation of about 0.37 with each suit. With a universal Hammer, the coefficient of variation is about $1{,}670/6{,}384 = 0.26$. The mismatch cost in the newsvendor model is directly proportional to the coefficient of variation, hence the connection between a lower coefficient of variation and higher expected profit.

Given this link between the coefficient of variation and the benefit of product pooling, it is important for us to understand how product pooling influences the coefficient of variation. In this example, as well as the Medtronic examples in the previous two sections, we make a key assumption that the demands we are combining are independent. Recall that independence means that the outcome of one demand provides no information about the outcome of the other demand. There are many settings in which demands are indeed independent. But there are also situations in which demands are not independent.

The link between two random events can be measured by their correlation, which ranges from −1 to 1. Independent random events have zero correlation. Positive correlation means two random events tend to move in lock step; that is, when one is high, the other tends to be high as well, and when one is low, the other tends to be low as well. In contrast, negative correlation means two random events tend to move in opposite directions; that is, when one is high, the other tends to be low, and when one is low, the other tends to be high.

We can illustrate the effect of correlation graphically with two products. Figure 10.5 displays the outcome of 100 random demand realizations for two products in three scenarios. (For example, if the random demands of the two products are five and seven respectively, then a point is plotted at {5,7}.) In the first scenario, the products' demands are negatively correlated, in the second they are independent, and in the third they are positively correlated. In the independent scenario (scenario two), we see that the outcomes form a "cloud" that roughly fits into a circle; that is, the outcome of one demand says nothing about the outcome of the other demand. In the negative correlation scenario (scenario one), the outcome cloud is a downward-sloping ellipse: high demand with one product suggests low demand with the other product. The positive correlation scenario (scenario three) also has an outcome cloud shaped like an ellipse, but now it is upward sloping: high demand with one product suggests high demand with the other product.

Many different demand outcomes lead to the same total demand. For example, in the graphs in Figure 10.5, the total demand is 20 units if the products' demands are {0,20}, {1,19}, . . . , {19,1}, {20,0}. In other words, all of the points along the dashed line in each graph have total demand of 20 units. In general, all points along the same downward-sloping 45° line have the same total demand. Because the outcome ellipse in the negative correlation scenario is downward sloping along a 45° line, the total demands of those outcomes are nearly the same. In contrast, because the outcome ellipse in the

FIGURE 10.5
Random Demand for Two Products
In the graphs, x-axis is product 1 and y-axis is product 2. In scenario 1 (upper-left graph), the correlation is −0.90; in scenario 2 (upper-right graph), the correlation is 0; and in scenario 3 (the lower graph), the correlation is 0.90. In all scenarios, demand is normally distributed for each product with mean 10 and standard deviation 3.

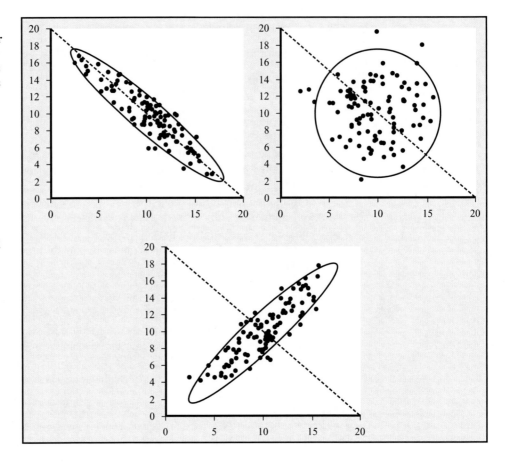

positive correlation scenario is *upward* sloping, those outcomes generally sum to different total demands. In other words, we expect to see more variability in the total demand with positive correlation than with negative correlation.

We can now be more precise about the impact of correlation. If we combine two demands with the same mean μ and standard deviation σ, then the pooled demand has the following parameters:

$$\text{Expected pooled demand} = 2 \times \mu$$
$$\text{Standard deviation of pooled demand} = \sqrt{2 \times (1 + \text{Correlation})} \times \sigma$$

Notice that the correlation has no impact on the expected demand, but it does influence the standard deviation. Furthermore, the above equations are equivalent to the ones we have been using when the correlation is zero, that is, when the two demands are independent.

The coefficient of variation for the pooled demand is then

$$\text{Coefficient of variation of pooled demand} = \sqrt{\frac{1}{2}(1 + \text{Correlation})} \times \left(\frac{\sigma}{\mu}\right)$$

As the correlation increases, the coefficient of variation of pooled demand increases as well, just as the graphs in Figure 10.5 suggest.

FIGURE 10.6
**The Inventory/
Stockout Outcome
Given the Order
Quantities for Surf
and Dive Suits,
Q_{surf} and Q_{dive}**

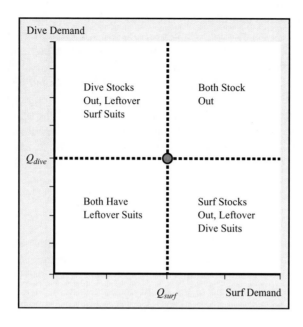

Now let's visualize what happens when we choose quantities for both the dive and the surf suits. Figure 10.6 displays the result of our quantity choices for different demand outcomes. For example, if the demand outcome is in the lower-left-hand "square" of the graph, then we have leftover surf and dive suits. The ideal outcome is if demand for each suit happens to equal its order quantity, an outcome labeled with a circle in the graph. The demand–supply mismatch penalty increases as the demand outcome moves further away from that ideal point in any direction.

The comparable graph for the universal Hammer is different, as is shown in Figure 10.7. Now any demand outcome along the downward-sloping 45° line (circles) is an ideal outcome because total demand equals the quantity of universal suits. In other words, the number of ideal demand outcomes with the universal suit has expanded considerably relative to the single ideal demand outcome with two suits. How likely are we to be close to

FIGURE 10.7
**Outcomes for the
Universal Hammer
Given Q Units
Purchased**
Outcomes on the
diagonal line with
circles are ideal; there
is no leftover inventory
and no stockouts.
Outcomes below and
to the left of that line
have leftover suits;
outcomes to the right
and above that line
result in stockouts.
Ellipses identify
likely outcomes under
different correlations.

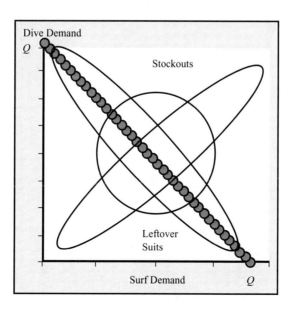

one of those ideal points? Figure 10.7 also superimposes the three "outcome clouds" from Figure 10.5. Clearly, with negative correlation we are more likely to be close to an ideal point (the downward-sloping ellipse) and with positive correlation we are least likely to be near an ideal point.

We can confirm the intuition developed with the graph in Figure 10.7 by actually evaluating O'Neill's optimal order quantity for the universal Hammer 3/2 and its expected profit for the entire range of correlations. We first notice that the optimal order quantity for the Hammer 3/2 is generally *not* the sum of the optimal order quantities of the two suits. For example, O'Neill's total order with two wetsuits is 4,101 × 2 = 8,202 units, but with correlation 0.2 the optimal order for the universal Hammer is 7,793 units and with correlation −0.7 the optimal order is 7,088.

The results with respect to expected profit are displayed in Figure 10.8: We indeed see that the expected profit of the universal Hammer declines as surf and dive demand become more positively correlated.

The extreme ends in Figure 10.8 are interesting. With perfectly positive correlation (i.e., correlation = 1), there is absolutely no benefit from inventory pooling: The expected profit with the universal Hammer is $383,520, and that is also the profit with two Hammer wetsuits! At the other end of the spectrum, correlation = −1, the coefficient of variation of total Hammer demand is 0, and so the maximum profit is achieved, $446,880! In fact, in that situation, the optimal order quantity for universal suits is just 6,384 units, which also happens to be the expected demand for universal suits. (This makes sense; we only earn the maximum profit if we sell on average the expected demand and we never have leftover inventory.)

While we have been discussing the impact of demand correlation on the efficacy of product pooling, this issue applies even with location pooling. If the demands at two locations are negatively correlated, then location pooling is even more effective than if

FIGURE 10.8

The Correlation between Surf and Dive Demand for the Hammer 3/2 and the Expected Profit of the Universal Hammer Wetsuit (decreasing curve) and the Coefficient of Variation of Total Demand (increasing curve)

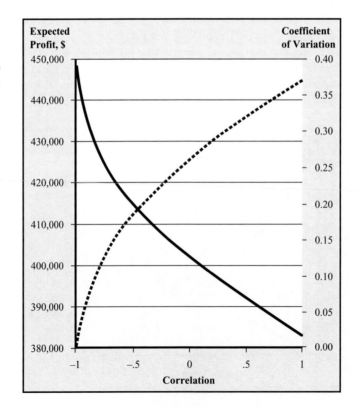

the demands were merely independent. And if demands are positively correlated across locations, then location pooling is less effective than we evaluated, given our assumption of independence.

We also should discuss the conditions that we can expect when demand has a particular type of correlation. Positive correlation can occur if the products are linked to some common source of uncertainty, for example, general economic conditions. For example, positive correlation is likely to be present if all of a firm's products tend to perform poorly in a depressed economy and perform well in a robust economy. Negative correlation is present when there is relatively little uncertainty with respect to total category sales but substantial uncertainty with respect to the allocation of those sales across the product line. For example, a firm selling fashionable jackets may know pretty well how many jackets will sell in total but have considerable uncertainty over which colors will be hot this season.

To summarize, a key benefit of a universal design is the reduction in demand variability, which leads to better performance in terms of matching supply and demand (e.g., higher profit or lower inventory for a targeted service level). But there are drawbacks to a universal design strategy as well:

• A universal design may not provide the needed functionality to consumers with special needs. For example, most bicycle manufacturers produce road bikes designed for fast touring on well-paved roads and mountain bikes for tearing through rugged trails. They even sell hybrid bikes that have some of the features of a road bike as well as some of the features of a mountain bike. But it is not sufficient to just sell a hybrid bike because it would not satisfy the high-performance portions of the road and mountain bike segments. The lower functionality of a universal design for some segments implies that it might not capture the same total demand as a set of focused designs.

• A universal design may be more expensive or it may be cheaper to produce than focused products. Because a universal design is targeted to many different uses, either it has components that are not necessary to some consumers or it has components that are of better quality than needed by certain consumers. These extra components or the extra quality increases a universal design's cost relative to focused designs. However, it is often cheaper to manufacture or procure a large quantity of a single component than small quantities of a bunch of components; that is, there are economies of scale in production and procurement. In that sense, a universal design may be cheaper.

• A universal design may eliminate some brand/price segmentation opportunities. By definition, a universal design has a single brand/price, but a firm may wish to maintain distinct brands/prices. As with the concern regarding functionality, a single brand/price may not be able to capture the same demand as multiple brands/prices.

With respect to O'Neill's Hammer 3/2 wetsuit, it appears that the first two concerns regarding a universal design are not relevant: Given that the surf and dive Hammers are identical with the exception of the logo, their functionality should be identical as well, and there is no reason to believe their production costs should be much different. However, the universal Hammer wetsuit does eliminate the opportunity to maintain two different O'Neill logos, one geared for the surf market and one geared for the dive market. If it is important to maintain these separate identities (e.g., you might not want serious surfers to think they are purchasing the same product as recreational divers), then maybe two suits are needed. On the other hand, if you wish to portray a single image for O'Neill, then maybe it is even better to have a single logo, in which case two different wetsuits make absolutely no sense.

While we have concentrated on the benefits of serving demand with a universal design, this discussion provides a warning for firms that may be engaging in excessive product proliferation. Every firm wishes to be "customer focused" or "customer oriented," which suggests that a firm should develop products to meet all of the needs of its potential customers. Truly innovative new products that add to a firm's customer base should be incorporated into a firm's product assortment. But if extra product variety merely divides a fixed customer base into smaller pieces, then the demand–supply mismatch cost for each product will increase. Given that some of the demand–supply mismatch costs are indirect (e.g., loss of goodwill due to poor service), a firm might not even realize the additional costs it bears due to product proliferation. Every once in a while a firm realizes that its product assortment has gone amok and *product line rationalization* is sorely needed. The trick to assortment reductions is to "cut the fat, but leave the meat (and surely the bones)"; that is, products should only be dropped if they merely cannibalize demand from other products.

10.3 Lead Time Pooling: Consolidated Distribution and Delayed Differentiation

Location and product pooling, discussed in the previous two sections, have limitations: location pooling creates distance between inventory and customers and product pooling potentially degrades product functionality. This section studies two strategies that address those limitations: consolidated distribution and delayed differentiation. Both of those strategies use a form of risk pooling that we call lead time pooling.

Consolidated Distribution

The key weakness of location pooling is that inventory is moved away from customers, thereby preventing customers from physically seeing a product before purchase, thus increasing the time a customer must wait to receive a product and generally increasing the delivery cost. However, as we have learned, it also can be costly to position inventory near every customer. A major reason for this cost is the problem of having product in the wrong place. For example, with Medtronic's approximately 500 sales territories, it is highly unlikely that all 500 territories will stock out at the same time. If a stockout occurs in one territory, it is quite likely that there is some other territory that has inventory to spare, even maybe a nearby territory. This imbalance of inventory occurs because a firm faces two different kinds of uncertainty, even with a single product: uncertainty with respect to total demand (e.g., how many InSync pacemakers are demanded in the United States on a particular day) and uncertainty with respect to the allocation of that demand (e.g., how many InSync pacemakers are demanded in each territory in the United States on a particular day). The consolidated-distribution strategy attempts to keep inventory close to customers while hedging against the second form of uncertainty.

We'll demonstrate the consolidated-distribution strategy via a retail example. Imagine demand for a single product occurs in 100 stores and average weekly demand per store follows a Poisson distribution with a mean of 0.5 unit per week. Each store is replenished directly from a supplier with an eight-week lead time. To provide good customer service, the retailer uses the order-up-to model and targets a 99.5 percent in-stock probability. The top panel of Figure 10.9 displays a schematic of this supply chain. Let's evaluate the amount of inventory the retailer needs.

With an eight-week lead time and a mean demand of 0.5 unit per week, the expected demand over $l + 1$ periods is $(8 + 1) \times 0.5 = 4.5$. From the Poisson Distribution Function Table, we see that with a mean of 4.5, the order-up-to level $S = 10$ yields an in-stock probability of 99.33 percent and $S = 11$ yields an in-stock probability of 99.76 percent, so we need to choose $S = 11$ for each store. According to the Poisson Loss Function Table, with mean demand of 4.5 units over $l + 1$ periods and an order-up-to level $S = 11$, the

FIGURE 10.9

Two Retail Supply Chains, One with Direct Shipments from the Supplier, the Other with Consolidated Distribution in a Distribution Center
Expected weekly demand at each store is 0.5 unit and the target in-stock probability is 99.5 percent.

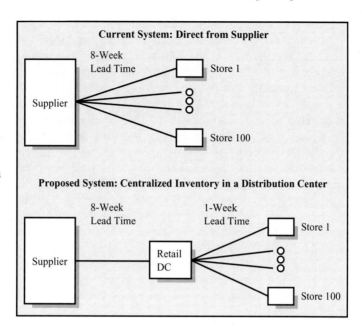

expected back order is 0.00356 unit per week. Hence, each of the 100 stores will have the following expected inventory:

$$
\begin{aligned}
\text{Expected inventory} &= S - \text{Expected demand over } l + 1 \text{ periods} \\
&\quad + \text{Expected back order} \\
&= 11 - 4.5 + 0.00356 \\
&= 6.50356
\end{aligned}
$$

The total inventory among the 100 stores is then $6.504 \times 100 = 650.4$ units.

Now suppose the retailer builds a distribution center to provide consolidated distribution. The distribution center receives all shipments from the supplier and then replenishes each of the retail stores; it allows for consolidated distribution. The lead time for the distribution center remains eight weeks from the supplier. The lead time to replenish each of the retail stores is one week. To ensure a reliable delivery to the retail stores, the distribution center operates with a high in-stock probability, 99.5 percent. The bottom panel in Figure 10.9 displays the proposed supply chain with a distribution center.

The distribution center provides the retailer with a centralized location for inventory while still allowing the retailer to position inventory close to the customer. In contrast, the location pooling strategy would just create the centralized inventory location, eliminating the 100 stores close to customers. Therefore, this centralized-inventory strategy resembles location pooling without the major drawback of location pooling. But what does it do for the total inventory investment?

We can repeat the evaluation of the inventory investment for each store, assuming a 99.5 percent in-stock probability target and now a one-week lead time. From the Poisson Distribution Function Table, given expected demand over $l + 1$ periods is 1.0 unit, the order-up-to level $S = 4$ generates an in-stock probability of 99.63 percent. The resulting expected inventory per store is 3.00 units, nearly a 54 percent reduction in inventory from the direct-supply model (3.00 versus 6.5 units)! Because each store now receives a one-week lead time instead of an eight-week lead time, the inventory at the retail stores is dramatically reduced.

Now we need to evaluate the inventory at the distribution center. The demand at the distribution center equals the orders from the retail stores. On average, the retail stores order 0.5 unit per week; that is, the average inflow (i.e., order) into a store must equal the average outflow (i.e., demand), otherwise inventory either builds up continuously (if the inflow exceeds the outflow) or dwindles down to zero (if the outflow exceeds the inflow). Because the retail stores' total demand is $100 \times 0.5 = 50$ units per week, the average demand at the distribution center also must be 50 units per week.

While we can be very sure of our estimate of the distribution center's expected demand, the distribution center's standard deviation of demand is not immediately apparent. The standard deviation of demand at each retailer is $\sqrt{0.50} = 0.707$. (Recall that with Poisson demand, the standard deviation equals the square root of the mean.) Hence, if demand were independent across all stores, then the standard deviation of total demand would be $0.707 \times \sqrt{100} = 7.07$. However, if there is positive correlation across stores, then the standard deviation would be higher, and with negative correlation the standard deviation would be lower. The only way to resolve this issue is to actually evaluate the standard deviation of total demand from historical sales data (the same data we used to estimate the demand rate of 0.5 unit per week at each store). Suppose we observe that the standard deviation of total weekly demand is 15. Hence, there is evidence of positive correlation in demand across the retail stores.

We now need to choose a distribution to represent demand at the distribution center. In this case, the Poisson is not the best choice. The standard deviation of a Poisson distribution is the square root of its mean, which in this case would be $\sqrt{50} = 7.07$. Because we have observed the standard deviation to be significantly higher, the Poisson distribution would not provide a good fit with the data. Our alternative, and a reasonable choice, is the normal distribution with mean 50 and standard deviation 15. We can determine that the distribution center's expected inventory is about 116 units if its target in-stock is 99.5 percent, the lead time is eight weeks, and weekly demand is normally distributed with mean 50 and standard deviation 15.

The only inventory that we have not counted so far is the pipeline inventory. In the direct-delivery model, there is pipeline inventory between the supplier and the retail stores. Using Little's Law, that pipeline inventory equals $0.5 \times 100 \times 8 = 400$ units. The consolidated-distribution model has the same amount of inventory between the supplier and the distribution center. However, with both models let's assume that pipeline inventory is actually owned by the supplier (e.g., the retailer does not start to pay for inventory until it is received). Hence, from the retailer's perspective, that inventory is not a concern. On the other hand, the retailer does own the inventory between the distribution center and the retail stores in the consolidated-distribution model. Again using Little's Law, there are $0.5 \times 100 \times 1 = 50$ units in that pipeline.

Table 10.4 summarizes the retailer's inventory in both supply chain structures. For comparison, the location pooling strategy is also included. With location pooling, all of the stores are eliminated and the retailer ships to customers from a central distribution center.

TABLE 10.4
Retail Inventory with Three Supply Chain Structures

	Direct Delivery Supply Chain	Consolidated-Distribution Supply Chain	Location Pooling
Expected total inventory at the stores	650	300	0
Expected inventory at the DC	0	116	116
Pipeline inventory between the DC and the stores	0	50	0
Total	650	466	116

Because that distribution center has an eight-week lead time and faces the same demand distribution as the DC in the consolidated-distribution strategy, its expected inventory is also 116 units.

We see from Table 10.4 that the consolidated-distribution strategy is able to reduce the expected inventory investment 28 percent [(650 − 466)/650] relative to the original direct-delivery structure. In fact, the advantage of the consolidated-distribution strategy is even better than this analysis suggests. The cost of holding one unit of inventory at a retail store is surely substantially higher than the cost of holding one unit in a distribution center: retail shelf space is more expensive than DC space, shrinkage is a greater concern, and so forth. Because the consolidated-distribution model reduces retail inventory by more than 50 percent, merely adding up the total inventory in the system underestimates the value of the consolidated-distribution model.

Interestingly, the consolidated-distribution model outperforms direct delivery even though the total lead time from the supplier to the retail stores is increased by one week due to the routing of all inventory through the DC. Why is inventory reduced despite the longer total lead time? As mentioned earlier, in this system there are two types of uncertainty: uncertainty with total demand in a given week and uncertainty with the allocation of that demand over the retail stores. When inventory leaves the supplier, the retailer is essentially betting on how much inventory will be needed eight weeks later. However, in the direct-delivery model, the retailer also must predict *where* that inventory is needed; that is, the retailer must gamble on a total quantity and an allocation of that quantity across the retail stores. There is uncertainty with the total inventory needed, but even more uncertainty with where that inventory is needed. The consolidated-distribution model allows the retailer to avoid that second gamble: The retailer only needs to bet on the amount of inventory needed for the central distribution center. In other words, while the retailer must commit to a unit's final destination in the direct-delivery model, in the consolidated-distribution model the retailer delays that commitment until the unit arrives at the distribution center. It is precisely because the DC allows the retailer to avoid that second source of uncertainty that the consolidated-distribution model can outperform the direct-delivery model.

The consolidated-distribution model exploits what is often called *lead time pooling*. Lead time pooling can be thought of as combining the lead times for multiple inventory locations. Actually, it is easier to explain graphically: in Figure 10.9 we see that the 100 connections between the supplier and the retail stores in the direct-delivery model (four of which are actually drawn) are pooled into a single connection between the supplier and the DC in the consolidated-distribution model.

We saw that demand correlation influenced the effectiveness of product pooling and location pooling. Not surprisingly, demand correlation has the same effect here. The greater the correlation, the higher the standard deviation of demand at the distribution center. Figure 10.10 displays supply chain inventory with the consolidated-distribution model over a range of demand variability for the distribution center. As retail demand becomes more negatively correlated, the inventory in the consolidated-distribution model declines. However, we have seen that inventory can be reduced even with some positive correlation: The consolidated-distribution model outperforms direct delivery if the DC's standard deviation is about 40 or lower.

Another factor that determines the attractiveness of the consolidated-distribution model relative to the direct-delivery model is the lead time from the supplier. Figure 10.11 displays total supply chain inventory with both models for various supplier lead times. The direct-delivery model performs better than the consolidated-distribution model if the supplier's lead time is three weeks or fewer; otherwise, the consolidated-distribution model does better. This occurs because lead time pooling is most effective as the lead time

FIGURE 10.10
Inventory with the Consolidated-Distribution Supply Chain
Diamonds = total retail store inventory, squares = retail + pipeline inventory, circles = retail + pipeline + DC inventory.

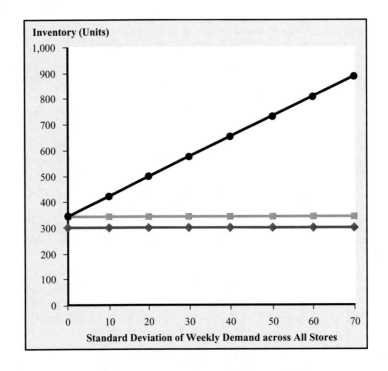

increases. In particular, the lead time before the distribution center (i.e., from the supplier) should be longer than the lead time after the distribution center (i.e., to the stores).

To summarize, a central inventory location (i.e., a distribution center) within a supply chain can exploit lead time pooling to reduce the supply chain's inventory investment while still keeping inventory close to customers. This strategy is most effective if total demand is less variable than demand at the individual stores and if the lead time before the distribution center is much longer than the lead time after the distribution center.

FIGURE 10.11
Inventory with the Consolidated-Distribution Supply Chain (squares) and the Direct-Delivery Supply Chain (circles) with Different Supplier Lead Times

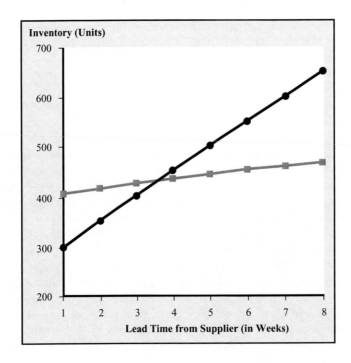

While we have concentrated on the inventory impact of the consolidated distribution strategy, that strategy has other effects on the supply chain. We have not included the extra cost of operating the distribution center, even though we did mention that the holding cost for each unit of inventory at the distribution center is likely to be lower than at the retail stores. Furthermore, we have not included the extra transportation cost from the DC to the retailer. A common critique of this kind of supply chain is that it clearly increases the distance a unit must travel from the supplier to the retailer. However, there are some additional benefits of a distribution center that we also have not included.

A DC enables a retailer to take better advantage of temporary price discounts from the supplier; that is, it is easier to store a large buy at the DC than at the retail stores. The DC also will facilitate more frequent deliveries to the retail stores. With the direct-delivery model, each store receives a shipment from each supplier. It is generally not economical to make partial truckload shipments, what is referred to as a "less-than-load" or LTL shipment. Therefore, in our example, the retailer receives weekly shipments from the supplier because the retailer would not be able to order a full truckload for each store on a more frequent basis.

But with a DC, more frequent shipments are economical. The DC allows the retailer to put products from multiple suppliers into a truck bound for a store. Because now a truck is filled with products from multiple suppliers, it can be filled more frequently. As a result, with the DC in the supply chain, each store might be able to receive a full truckload per day, whereas without the DC each store can only receive a shipment every week. (This argument also is used to justify the airlines' "hub-and-spoke" systems: It may be difficult to consistently fill a plane from Gainesville to Los Angeles on a daily basis, but Delta Airlines offers service between those two cities via its Atlanta hub because the Atlanta–Los Angeles leg can be filled with passengers flying from other southeast cities.) More frequent deliveries reduce inventory even further than our analysis suggests. Even the DC may be able to order more frequently from the supplier than weekly because the DC consolidates the orders from all of the retailers. In fact, while the lead time pooling benefit of a DC in this example is significant, it is quite possible that some of these other reasons for operating a DC are even more important.

Delayed Differentiation

Consolidated distribution is a strategy that uses lead time pooling to provide some of the benefits of location pooling without moving inventory far away from customers. Delayed differentiation is the analogous strategy with respect to product pooling; that is, delayed differentiation hedges the uncertainty associated with product variety without taking the variety away from customers. We'll illustrate delayed differentiation with our Hammer 3/2 example from O'Neill.

Recall that the Hammer 3/2 is sold by O'Neill in two versions: a surf wetsuit with the traditional wave logo silk-screened on the chest and a dive wetsuit with O'Neill's dive logo put in the same place. The product-pooling approach to this variety is to eliminate it: sell only one Hammer 3/2 suit with a single logo. However, that is an extreme solution and there may be reasons to maintain two different products.

The problem with two different products is that we might run out of surf Hammers while we have extra dive Hammers. In that situation, it would be great if we could just erase the dive logo and put on the surf logo, since the rest of the wetsuit is identical. Better yet, if we just stocked "logo-less" or generic wetsuits, then we could add the appropriate logo as demand arrives. That strategy is called *delayed differentiation* because we are delaying the differentiation of the wetsuit into its final form until after we observe demand.

Several things are necessary to make this delayed-differentiation strategy work. First, we need to be able to silk-screen the logo onto the generic wetsuit. This is a nontrivial issue. Currently the logo is silk-screened onto the chest piece before it is sewn into the suit. Silk-screening the logo onto a complete suit is substantially harder and may require some redesigning of the silk-screening process. Assuming we can overcome that technical difficulty, we still need to be able to add the silk screen quickly so that there is not much delay between the time a wetsuit is requested and when it is shipped. Hence, we'll need a sufficient amount of idle capacity in that process to ensure fast delivery even though demand may fluctuate throughout the season.

If these challenges are resolved, then we are left with deciding how many of the generic wetsuits to order and evaluating the resulting profit savings. In fact, we have already completed those steps. If we assume that we only silk-screen the logo onto wetsuits when we receive a firm demand for a surf or dive wetsuit, then we never keep finished goods inventory; that is, we only have to worry about our generic wetsuit inventory. The demand for the generic wetsuit is identical to the demand for the universal wetsuit; that is, it is the sum of surf Hammer demand and dive Hammer demand. The economics of the generic suit are the same as well: They sell for the same price, they have the same production cost, and we'll assume they have the same salvage value. (In some cases, the salvage value of the generic suit might be higher or lower than the salvage value of the finished product, but in this case it is plausibly about the same.) Therefore, as with the universal design analysis, we need to decide how many generic wetsuits to order given they are sold for $180 each, they cost $110 each, they will be salvaged for $90 each, and demand is normally distributed with mean 6,384 and standard deviation 1,670.

Using our analysis from the section on product pooling, the optimal order quantity is 7,670 units with the delayed differentiation strategy and expected profit increases to $402,116. Although product pooling and delayed differentiation result in the same numerical analysis, the two strategies are different. Delayed differentiation still offers multiple wetsuits to consumers, so their demands are not pooled together as with a universal design. Instead, delayed differentiation works like lead time pooling with consolidated distribution: a key differentiating feature of the product is delayed until after better demand information is observed; with location pooling that feature is the product's final destination (i.e., store) and with delayed differentiation that feature is the product's logo. Furthermore, product pooling does not require a significant modification to the production process, whereas delayed differentiation does require a change to the silk-screening process. In other applications, delayed differentiation may require a more dramatic change to the process and/or the product design.

In general, delayed differentiation is an ideal strategy when

1. Customers demand many versions, that is, variety is important.
2. There is less uncertainty with respect to total demand than there is for individual versions.
3. Variety is created late in the production process.
4. Variety can be added quickly and cheaply.
5. The components needed to create variety are inexpensive relative to the generic component (i.e., the main body of the product).

Let's explain further each of the five points just mentioned. (1) If variety isn't important, then the firm should offer fewer variants or just a universal design. (2) There should be less uncertainty with total demand so there will be few demand–supply mismatches with the generic component. In general, the more negative correlation across product variants the better, since negative correlation reduces uncertainty in the total demand. (3) Just as we saw that consolidated distribution works best if the supplier lead time to the distribution center is long relative to the lead time from the distribution center to the retail stores, delayed differentiation is most valuable if there is a long lead time to produce the generic component and a short lead time to convert the generic component into a finished product. (4) If adding variety to the generic component is too slow, then the waiting time for customers may be unacceptable, thereby rendering delayed differentiation unacceptable. In addition, if adding variety at the end of the process is costly, then the inventory savings from delayed differentiation may not be worth the extra production cost. (5) Finally, delayed differentiation saves inventory of the generic component (e.g., the generic wetsuit) but does not save inventory of the differentiating components. Hence, delayed differentiation is most useful if the majority of the product's value is in the generic component.

Delayed differentiation is particularly appropriate when variety is associated with the cosmetic features of a product, for example, color, labels, and packaging. For example, suppose a company such as Black and Decker sells power drills to both Home Depot and Wal-Mart. Those are two influential retailers; as a result, they may wish to have slightly different packaging, and, in particular, they might wish to have different product codes on their packages so that consumers cannot make direct price comparisons. The power drill company could store drills in the two different packages, but that creates the possibility of having Home Depot drills available while Wal-Mart drills are stocked out. Because it is relatively easy to complete the final packaging, the delayed-differentiation strategy only completes the packaging of drills after it receives firm orders from the retailers. Furthermore, packaging material is cheap compared to the drill, so while the firm doesn't want to have excessive inventory of drills, it isn't too costly to have plenty of packages available.

Retail paints provide another good example for the application of delayed differentiation. Consumers surely do not want a universal design when it comes to paint color, despite Henry Ford's famous theory of product assortment.[2] But at the same time, a store cannot afford to keep paint available in every possible shade, hue, tone, sheen, and color. One alternative is for paint to be held in a central warehouse and then shipped to customers as needed, that is, a location pooling strategy. Given the vast variety of colors, it is not clear that even a location pooling strategy can be economical. Furthermore, paint is very costly to ship directly to consumers, so that pretty much kills that idea. Instead, the paint industry has developed equipment so that a retailer can use generic materials to mix any color in their vast catalog. The final production process takes some time, but an acceptable amount of time for consumers (5 to 15 minutes). The in-store production equipment is probably more expensive than mixing paints at a factory, but again, the extra cost here is worth it. Hence, by redesigning the product to add variety at the very end of the production process (i.e., even after delivery to the retail store), paint companies are able to economically provide consumers with extensive variety.

Delayed differentiation can even be used if the "generic component" can be sold to some customers without additional processing. To explain, suppose a company sells two different quality levels of a product, for example, a fast and a slow printer or a fast and a slow microprocessor. These quality differences might allow a firm to price discriminate and thereby increase its overall margins. However, the quality difference might not imply radically different costs or designs. For example, it might be possible to design the fast and the slow printers such that a fast printer could be converted into a slow printer merely by adding a single chip or by flipping a single switch. Hence, the firm might hold only fast printers so they can serve demand for fast printers immediately. When demand for a slow printer occurs, then a fast printer is taken from inventory, the switch is flipped to make it a slow printer, and then it is shipped as a slow printer.

Delayed differentiation is indeed a powerful strategy. In fact, it bears a remarkable resemblance to another powerful strategy, make-to-order production. With make-to-order production, a firm only begins making a product after it receives a firm order from a customer.

[2] Consumers can have any Model T they want, as long as it is black.

Dell Inc. has used the make-to-order strategy with remarkable effectiveness in the personal computer industry. With delayed differentiation, a generic component is differentiated into a final product only after demand is received for that final product. So what is the difference between these two ideas? In fact, they are conceptually quite similar. Their difference is one of degree. Delayed differentiation is thought of as a strategy that stores nearly finished product and completes the remaining few production steps with essentially no delay. Make-to-order is generally thought to apply to a situation in which the remaining production steps from components to a finished unit are more substantial, therefore involving more than a trivial delay. Hence, delayed differentiation and make-to-order occupy two ends of the same spectrum with no clear boundary between them.

10.4   Capacity Pooling with Flexible Manufacturing[3]

Delayed differentiation takes advantage of completely flexible capacity at the end of the manufacturing process; that is, the final production step is capable of taking a generic component and converting it into any final product. Unfortunately, the luxury of complete flexibility is not always available or affordable to a firm, especially if one considers a larger portion of the manufacturing process. This section studies how a firm can use risk pooling with flexible capacity, but not necessarily completely flexible capacity.

To provide a context, consider the manufacturing challenge of an auto manufacturer such as General Motors. GM operates many different assembly plants and produces many different vehicles. Assembly capacity is essentially fixed in this industry over a substantial time horizon due to rigid labor contracts and the extensive capital requirements of an assembly plant. However, demand for individual vehicles can be quite variable: some products are perennially short on capacity, while others seem to always have too much capacity. To alleviate the resulting demand–supply mismatches, auto manufacturers continually strive for more manufacturing flexibility, that is, the ability to produce more than one vehicle type with the same capacity. GM could use flexible manufacturing to move capacity from slow-selling products to fast-selling products, thereby achieving higher sales and higher capacity utilization. But flexibility is not free: Tooling and assembly equipment capable of making more than one vehicle is more expensive than dedicated equipment and equipment capable of making any vehicle (complete flexibility) is extremely expensive. So how much flexibility does GM need and where should that flexibility be installed?

Let's define a specific problem that is representative of the challenge GM faces. There are 10 manufacturing plants and 10 vehicles (e.g., Chevy Malibu, GMC Yukon XL, etc.). For now each plant is assigned to produce just one vehicle, that is, there is no flexibility in the network. Capacity for each vehicle is installed before GM observes the vehicle's demand in the market. Demand is uncertain: a normal distribution represents each vehicle's demand with mean 100 and standard deviation 40. For a slight twist on the distribution, let's assume the minimum demand is 20 and the maximum demand is 180; that is, the normal distribution is truncated so that excessively extreme outcomes are not possible.[4] Even though we impose upper and lower bounds on demand, demand is still quite uncertain, a level of uncertainty that is typical in the auto industry. One last point with respect to demand: We assume the demands for each vehicle are independent; therefore, the correlation between the demands for any two vehicles is zero.

---

[3] This section is based on the research reported in Jordon and Graves (1995).

[4] In other words, any outcome of the normal distribution that is either lower than 20 or higher than 180 is ignored and additional random draws are made until an outcome is received between 20 and 180. There is only a 4.6 percent chance that an outcome of a normal distribution is greater than two standard deviations from the mean (as in this case).

FIGURE 10.12
Two Configurations, One with No Flexibility (10 links) and One with Limited Flexibility (11 links)

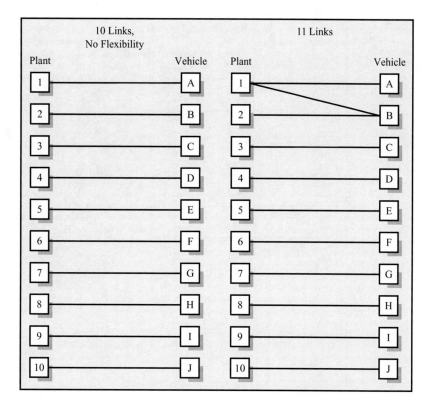

Each plant has a capacity to produce 100 units. If demand exceeds capacity for a vehicle, then the excess is lost. If demand is less than capacity, then demand is satisfied but capacity is idle. Figure 10.12 displays this situation graphically: The left-hand side of the figure represents the 10 production plants; the right-hand side represents the 10 vehicle types; and the lines are "links" that indicate which plant is capable of producing which vehicles. In the "no flexibility" situation, each plant is capable of producing only one vehicle, so there is a total of 10 links. The configuration with the smallest amount of flexibility has 11 links, an example of which is displayed on the right-hand side of Figure 10.12. With 11 links, one plant is capable of producing two different vehicles. As we add more links, we add more flexibility. Total flexibility is achieved when we have 100 links, that is, every plant is able to produce every product. Figure 10.13 displays the full flexibility configuration as well as one of the possible configurations with 20 links.

With each configuration, we are interested in evaluating the expected unit sales and expected capacity utilization. Unfortunately, for most configurations, it is quite challenging to evaluate those performance measures analytically. However, we can obtain accurate estimates of those performance measures via simulation. Each iteration of the simulation draws random demand for each product and then allocates the capacity to maximize unit sales within the constraints of the feasible links. For example, in the configuration with 11 links displayed in Figure 10.12, suppose in one of the iterations that demand for vehicle A is 85 units and vehicle B is 125 units. In that case, plant 2 uses its entire 100 units of capacity to produce vehicle B and plant 1 uses its entire 100 units of capacity to produce 85 units of vehicle A and 15 units of vehicle B, thereby only losing 10 units of potential vehicle B sales. Our estimate of each performance measure is just its average across the iterations. After many iterations, our estimates will be quite accurate.

Via simulation we find that with no flexibility, expected unit sales are 853 units and expected capacity utilization is 85.3 percent. With 11 links, the expected unit sales increase to 858 units and capacity utilization increases to 85.8 percent. We do slightly better with this

FIGURE 10.13
Flexibility
Configurations with
Approximately
Equal Capability to
Respond to Demand
Uncertainty

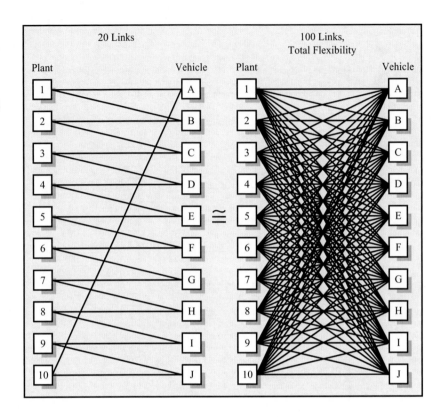

additional flexibility when demand for vehicle B exceeds plant 2's capacity and demand for vehicle A is below plant 1's capacity, because then plant 1 can use its capacity to produce both vehicles A and B (as in our previous example). Figure 10.14 provides data on the performance of configurations with 10 to 20 links and the full flexibility configuration.

Figure 10.14 reveals that total flexibility is able to increase our performance measures considerably: Capacity utilization jumps to 95.4 percent and expected sales increase to 954 units. But what is more remarkable is that adding only 10 additional links produces nearly the same outcome as full flexibility, which has an additional 90 links: capacity utilization is 94.9 percent with 20 links and expected sales are 949 units. Apparently, there is very little incremental value to the additional flexibility achieved by adding the 11th through the 90th additional links to the no-flexibility configuration. In other words, given that installing flexibility is costly, it is unlikely that total flexibility will be economically rational. This result has a similar feel to our finding that with location pooling, the majority of the benefit is captured by pooling only a few locations.

It may seem surprising that capacity pooling increases utilization, given that pooling server capacity in a queuing system has no impact on utilization. The key difference is that in a queuing system, demand is never lost; it just has to wait longer than it might want to be served. Hence, the amount of demand served is independent of how the capacity is structured. Here, demand is lost if there isn't a sufficient amount of capacity. Therefore, more flexibility increases the demand served, which increases the utilization of the capacity.

Although flexibility with 20 links can perform nearly as well as total flexibility with 100 links, not every configuration with 20 links performs that well. Figure 10.13 displays the particular 20-link configuration that nearly equals total flexibility. The effectiveness of that configuration can be explained by the concept of *chaining*. A chain is a group of plants and vehicles that are connected via links. For example, in the 11-link configuration displayed in Figure 10.12, the first two plants and vehicles form a single chain and the remaining

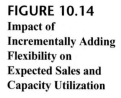

FIGURE 10.14
Impact of Incrementally Adding Flexibility on Expected Sales and Capacity Utilization

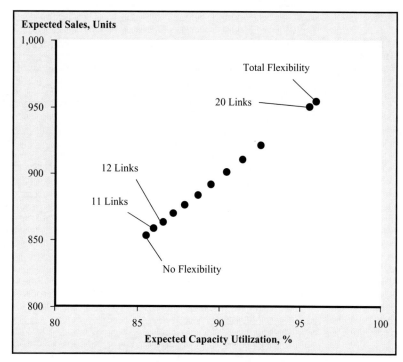

plant–vehicle pairs form eight additional chains. With the 20-link configuration displayed in Figure 10.13, there is a single chain, as there is with the total flexibility configuration.

In general, flexibility configurations with the longest and fewest chains for a given number of links perform the best. Figure 10.15 displays two 20-link configurations, one with a single chain (the same one as displayed in Figure 10.13) and the other with five chains. We already know that the single chain configuration has expected sales of 949 units. Again via simulation, we discover that the 20-link configuration with five chains generates expected sales of only 896 units, which compares to the 853 expected unit sales with no-flexibility.

Long chains are beneficial because they facilitate the reallocation of capacity to respond to demand. For example, suppose demand for vehicle A is less than expected, but demand for vehicle G is very strong. If both vehicles are in the same chain, then plant 1's idle capacity can be shifted along the chain to help fill vehicle G's demand: plant 1 produces some vehicle B, plant 2 produces some of both vehicles B and C, and so forth so that both plants 6 and 7 can produce some vehicle G. If both of those vehicles are not part of the same chain (as in our five-chain configuration), then this swapping of capacity is not possible.

In addition to how flexibility is configured, there are two additional issues worth mentioning that influence the value of flexibility: correlation and total capacity. So far we have assumed that demands across vehicles are independent. We learned with the other risk-pooling strategies that risk pooling becomes more effective as demand becomes more negatively correlated. The same holds here: With pooled capacity, the uncertainty in total demand is more important than the uncertainty with individual products; hence, negative correlation is preferred. However, this does not mean that two negatively correlated products must be produced in the same plant. Instead, it is sufficient that two negatively correlated products are produced in the same chain. This is a valuable insight if the negatively correlated products are physically quite different (e.g., a full-size truck and a compact sedan) because producing them in the same chain might be far cheaper than producing them in the same plant.

The total available capacity also influences the effectiveness of flexibility. Suppose capacity for each plant were only 20 units. In that case, each plant would always operate at

FIGURE 10.15
Flexibility Configurations with the Same Number of Links but Different Number of Chains

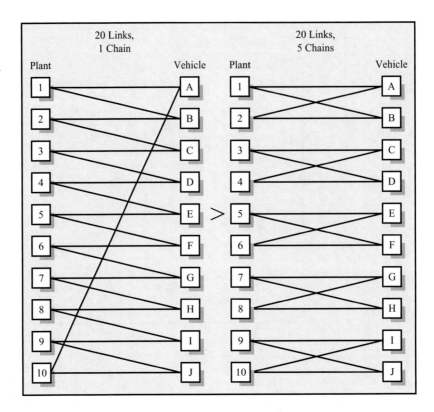

100 percent utilization, so flexibility has no value. The end result is the same with the other extreme situation. If each plant could produce 180 units, then flexibility is again not needed because every plant is sure to have idle capacity. In other words, flexibility is more valuable when capacity and demand are approximately equal, as in our numerical examples.

Figure 10.16 further emphasizes that flexibility is most valuable with intermediate amounts of capacity: The biggest gap between the no-flexibility trade-off curve and the 20-link trade-off curve occurs when total capacity equals expected total demand, 1,000 units.

Figure 10.16 illustrates another observation: flexibility and capacity are substitutes. For example, to achieve expected sales of 950 units, GM can either install total capacity of 1,250 units with no flexibility or 1,000 units of capacity with 20-link flexibility. If capacity is cheap relative to flexibility, then the high-capacity–no-flexibility option may be preferable. But if capacity is expensive relative to flexibility (especially given that we only need 10 additional links of flexibility), then the low-capacity–some-flexibility option may be better.

To summarize, this section considers the pooling of capacity via manufacturing flexibility. The main insights are

- A limited amount of flexibility can accommodate demand uncertainty nearly as well as total flexibility as long as the flexibility is configured to generate long chains.
- Flexibility should be configured so that negatively correlated products are part of the same chain but need not be produced in the same plant.
- Flexibility is most valuable when total capacity roughly equals expected demand.

Therefore, it is generally neither necessary nor economically rational for a firm to sink the huge investment needed to achieve total flexibility. Flexibility is surely valuable, but it should not be installed haphazardly. Finally, while we have used the context of automobile manufacturing to illustrate these insights, they nevertheless apply to workers in

FIGURE 10.16
Expected Sales and Capacity Utilization
Shown are seven different capacities (*C*) and two configurations, one with no flexibility (10 links) and one with 20 links and one chain (displayed in Figure 10.15). In each case, the total capacity is equally divided among the 10 products and expected total demand is 1,000 units.

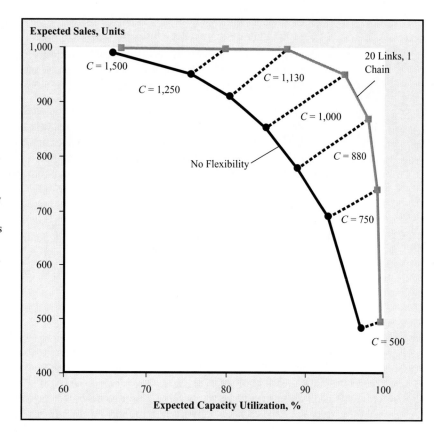

service environments. For example, it is not necessary to cross-train workers so that they can handle every task (full flexibility). Instead, it is sufficient to train workers so that long chains of skills are present in the organization.

10.5 Summary

This chapter describes and explores several different strategies that exploit risk pooling to better match supply and demand. Each has its strengths and limitations. For example, location pooling is very effective at reducing inventory but moves inventory away from customers. Consolidated distribution is not as good as location pooling at reducing inventory, but it keeps inventory near customers. Product pooling with a universal design is also quite useful but might limit the functionality of the products offered. Delayed differentiation addresses that limitation but probably requires redesigning the product/process and may introduce a slight delay to fulfill demand. Capacity pooling can increase sales and capacity utilization but requires flexible capacity, which is probably not free and may be quite expensive. Hence, these are effective strategies as long as they are applied in the appropriate settings.

Even though we considered a variety of situations and models (e.g., order-up-to and newsvendor), we have developed some consistent observations:

- A little bit of risk pooling goes a long way. With location pooling, it is usually necessary to pool only a few locations, not all of them. With capacity pooling, a little bit of flexibility, as long as it is properly designed (i.e., long chains), yields nearly the same outcome as full flexibility.

- Risk-pooling strategies are most effective when demands are negatively correlated because then the uncertainty with total demand is much less than the uncertainty with any individual item/location. It follows that these strategies become less effective as demands become more positively correlated.

- Risk-pooling strategies do not help reduce pipeline inventory. That inventory can only be reduced by moving inventory through the system more quickly.
- Risk-pooling strategies can be used to reduce inventory while maintaining the same service (fill rate or in-stock probability) or they can be used to increase service while holding the same inventory, or a combination of those improvements.

Although you are unlikely to encounter the term "risk pooling" in any discussion of modern business practice, the concept of risk pooling is often central to many recent operational innovations and strategies. The remainder of this section illustrates this point with several examples.

In the auto industry, it is estimated that 20 to 30 percent of a vehicle's cost is incurred after a vehicle leaves the factory (Simison, 1998), an amount that is unacceptably high to most manufacturers. Ford attempted to improve the efficiency of distribution by consolidating dealerships in major markets. For example, Ford consolidated the eight competing dealerships in the Salt Lake City area into a single organization (Warner, 1998). In addition to eliminating redundant advertising and back-office administration, this move was meant to provide consumers with a broader assortment for two reasons: the total number of retail locations would be reduced and inventory would be better shared across locations. In other words, by aggregating demand in fewer locations, the Salt Lake City dealer would use location pooling to reduce demand variability, thereby allowing fewer vehicles for the same service level or a broader assortment with the same inventory investment. The same consolidation strategy is being used by independent firms that have been acquiring dealerships, such as Republic Industries Inc. (Simison, 1998). However, Ford's efforts were not too successful, not due to a flaw in the theory of risk pooling, but instead because the initiative ran afoul of state franchise laws.

Cadillac also attempted to carry less inventory yet provide customers with greater variety via their XPress Delivery initiative in Florida: Instead of just holding vehicles in dealer lots, popularly configured vehicles would be kept in a central location near Orlando (Popely, 1998). Any vehicle in the central depot could be delivered to any Florida dealer within one day, thereby effectively allowing each dealer to offer customers a greater inventory than what was held on the dealers' lots. However, like most examples of location pooling, there are limitations: it moves inventory away from customers.

Chrysler uses a virtual pooling to reduce the amount of spare parts inventory needed among dealerships: Instead of physically pooling inventory in fewer locations (location pooling), Chrysler developed a system to share spare parts inventory data among dealerships (Simison, 1998). In other words, through this system, a dealer can find and quickly obtain a needed spare part at another dealership, so each dealership can improve its reliability with the same inventory investment or can maintain its reliability with lower inventory.

Several firms in the PC industry are using a form of delayed differentiation, called *channel assembly,* to try to compete against Dell (Hansell, 1998). With channel assembly a PC manufacturer such as IBM provides its distributor, such as Ingram Micron, with PC parts instead of assembled PCs. As demand occurs, the channel (Ingram), rather than the manufacturer (IBM), assembles the PCs from its parts. Relative to the traditional system in which PCs are assembled at the manufacturer and shipped to the distributor, channel assembly delays the assembly decision; hence, it is a version of delayed differentiation.

In the cell phone industry, Nokia Corp. has been quite successful, and one reason for its success has been the use of *capacity pooling* (Pringle, 2003). Unlike most of its leading competitors, Nokia owns and operates its own manufacturing facilities, some in rather high-labor-cost locations such as Finland. But that has not resulted in a competitive disadvantage because Nokia designs its handsets for manufacturing flexibility: components are shared across different models and even different components have similar geometries so that different models can be produced on the same production line without wasting setup times to switch among different models. In other words, the flexibility to switch production

FIGURE 10.17
Total Revenue of Six Leading Contract Manufacturers by Fiscal Year: Solectron Corp., Flextronics International Ltd., Sanmina-SCI, Jabil Circuit Inc., Celestica Inc., and Plexus Corp.
Note: The fiscal years of these firms vary somewhat, so total revenue in a calendar year will be slightly different.

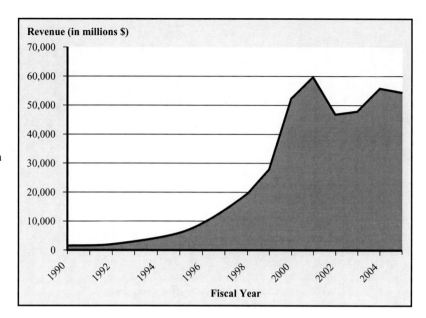

quickly and easily between different handsets effectively pools Nokia's capacity across the different models. This capability was particularly useful in the summer of 2002 when demand moved rapidly into color-screen models: Nokia took capacity that was planned for other models and reassigned it to produce the faster-selling color-screen models.

The concept of capacity pooling is a primary component of the contract manufacturing industry's value added. While certainly not household names (e.g., Solectron and Flextronics), the global contract manufacturing market has grown from almost nothing 15 years ago to an over $90 billion global industry (Thurm, 1998). Figure 10.17 displays the revenue growth from six leading firms; the sharp dip in revenue for fiscal 2002 was due to the bursting of the "tech bubble," in particular in telecommunications, from which these firms have not yet fully recovered.

Contract manufacturers produce closely related products for multiple customers. For example, in the same facility Solectron could be assembling circuit boards for IBM, Hewlett-Packard, and Cisco Systems. The same equipment and often the same components are used by these multiple manufacturers, so, instead of each one investing in its own capacity and component inventory, Solectron pools their needs. In other words, while any of these companies could produce its own circuit boards, due to capacity pooling Solectron is able to produce them with higher utilization and therefore lower cost. This added efficiency allows Solectron to charge a margin, albeit a rather thin margin, as indicated in Table 10.5.

Table 10.6 provides a summary of the key notation and equations presented in this chapter.

TABLE 10.5
Fiscal Year 2005 Results for Several Contract Manufacturers

Firm	Revenue*	Cost of Goods*	Gross Margin
Flextronics	15,288	14,090	7.8%
Sanmina-SCI	11,735	10,924	6.9%
Solectron	10,441	9,676	7.3%
Celestica	8,471	7,869	7.1%
Jabil Circuit	7,524	6,716	10.7%
Plexus	1,229	1,099	10.6%

* In millions of dollars.

TABLE 10.6
Summary of Notation and Key Equations in Chapter 10

The combination of two demands with the same mean and standard deviation yields

$$\text{Expected pooled demand} = 2 \times \mu$$

$$\text{Standard deviation of pooled demand} = \sqrt{2 \times (1 + \text{Correlation})} \times \sigma$$

$$\text{Coefficient of variation of pooled demand} = \sqrt{\frac{1}{2}(1 + \text{Correlation})} \times \left(\frac{\sigma}{\mu}\right)$$

10.6 Further Reading

In recent years, risk-pooling strategies have received considerable attention in the academic community as well as in practice.

Lee (1996) provides a technical treatment of the delayed-differentiation strategy. A more managerial description of delayed differentiation can be found in Feitzinger and Lee (1997). Brown, Lee, and Petrakian (2000) describe the application of delayed differentiation at a semiconductor firm. Simchi-Levi, Kaminsky, and Simchi-Levi (2003) and Chopra and Meindl (2004) cover risk-pooling strategies in the context of supply chain management.

Ulrich and Eppinger (2004) discuss the issues of delayed differentiation and product architecture from the perspective of a product development team.

Upton (1994, 1995) provides broad discussions on the issue of manufacturing flexibility.

10.7 Practice Problems

Q 10.1* **(Egghead)** In 1997 Egghead Computers ran a chain of 50 retail stores all over the United States. Consider one type of computer sold by Egghead. Demand for this computer at each store on any given week was independently and normally distributed with a mean demand of 200 units and a standard deviation of 30 units. Inventory at each store is replenished directly from a vendor with a 10-week lead time. At the end of 1997, Egghead decided it was time to close their retail stores, put up an Internet site, and begin filling customer orders from a single warehouse.

    a. By consolidating the demand into a single warehouse, what will be the resulting standard deviation of weekly demand for this computer faced by Egghead? Assume Egghead's demand characteristics before and after the consolidation are identical.

    b. Egghead takes physical possession of inventory when it leaves the supplier and grants possession of inventory to customers when it leaves Egghead's shipping dock. In the consolidated distribution scenario, what is the pipeline inventory?

Q 10.2* **(Two Products)** Consider two products, A and B. Demands for both products are normally distributed and have the same mean and standard deviation. The coefficient of variation of demand for each product is 0.6. The estimated correlation in demand between the two products is −0.7. What is the coefficient of variation of the total demand of the two products?

Q 10.3* **(Fancy Paints)** Fancy Paints is a small paint store. Fancy Paints stocks 200 different SKUs (stock-keeping units) and places replenishment orders weekly. The order arrives one month (let's say four weeks) later. For the sake of simplicity, let's assume weekly demand for each SKU is Poisson distributed with mean 1.25. Fancy Paints maintains a 95 percent fill rate.

    a. What is the average inventory at the store at the end of the week?

    b. Now suppose Fancy Paints purchases a color-mixing machine. This machine is expensive, but instead of stocking 200 different SKU colors, it allows Fancy Paints to stock only five basic SKUs and to obtain all the other SKUs by mixing. Weekly demand for each SKU is normally distributed with mean 50 and standard deviation 8. Suppose Fancy Paints maintains a 95 percent fill rate for each of the five colors. How much inventory on average is at the store at the end of the week?

    c. After testing the color-mixing machine for a while, the manager realizes that a 95 percent fill rate for each of the basic colors is not sufficient: Since mixing requires the presence of multiple mixing components, a higher fill rate for components is needed to maintain a 95 percent fill rate for the individual SKUs. The manager decides that a 98 percent fill rate for each of the five basic SKUs should be adequate. Suppose that each can costs $14 and

(* indicates that the solution is at the end of the book)

20 percent per year is charged for holding inventory (assume 50 weeks per year). What is the change in the store's holding cost relative to the original situation in which all paints are stocked individually?

Q 10.4* **(Burger King)** Consider the following excerpts from a *Wall Street Journal* article on Burger King (Beatty, 1996):

> Burger King intends to bring smiles to the faces of millions of parents and children this holiday season with its "Toy Story" promotion. But it has some of them up in arms because local restaurants are running out of the popular toys . . . Every Kids Meal sold every day of the year comes with a giveaway, a program that has been in place for about six years and has helped Grand Metropolitan PLC's Burger King increase its market share. Nearly all of Burger King's 7,000 U.S. stores are participating in the "Toy Story" promotion . . . Nevertheless, meeting consumer demand still remains a conundrum for the giants. That is partly because individual Burger King restaurant owners make their tricky forecasts six months before such promotions begin. "It's asking you to pull out a crystal ball and predict exactly what consumer demand is going to be," says Richard Taylor, Burger King's director of youth and family marketing. "This is simply a case of consumer demand outstripping supply." The long lead times are necessary because the toys are produced overseas to take advantage of lower costs . . . Burger King managers in Houston and Atlanta say the freebies are running out there, too . . . But Burger King, which ordered nearly 50 million of the small plastic dolls, is "nowhere near running out of toys on a national level."

Let's consider a simplified analysis of Burger King's situation. Consider a region with 200 restaurants served by a single distribution center. At the time the order must be placed with the factories in Asia, demand (units of toys) for the promotion at each restaurant is forecasted to be gamma distributed with mean 2,251 and standard deviation 1,600. A discrete version of that gamma distribution is provided in the following table, along with a graph of the density function:

Q	F(Q)	L(Q)		Q	F(Q)	L(Q)
0	0.0000	2,251.3		6,500	0.9807	31.4
500	0.1312	1,751.3		7,000	0.9865	21.7
1,000	0.3101	1,316.9		7,500	0.9906	15.0
1,500	0.4728	972.0		8,000	0.9934	10.2
2,000	0.6062	708.4		8,500	0.9954	6.9
2,500	0.7104	511.5		9,000	0.9968	4.6
3,000	0.7893	366.6		9,500	0.9978	3.0
3,500	0.8480	261.3		10,000	0.9985	1.9
4,000	0.8911	185.3		10,500	0.9989	1.2
4,500	0.9224	130.9		11,000	0.9993	0.6
5,000	0.9449	92.1		11,500	0.9995	0.3
5,500	0.9611	64.5		12,000	1.0000	0.0
6,000	0.9726	45.1				

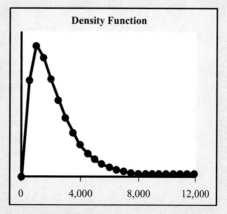

Density Function

0   4,000   8,000   12,000

(* indicates that the solution is at the end of the book)

Suppose, six months in advance of the promotion, Burger King must make a single order for each restaurant. Furthermore, Burger King wants to have an in-stock probability of at least 85 percent.

a. Given those requirements, how many toys must each restaurant order?

b. How many toys should Burger King expect to have at the end of the promotion?

Now suppose Burger King makes a single order for all 200 restaurants. The order will be delivered to the distribution center and each restaurant will receive deliveries from that stockpile as needed. If demands were independent across all restaurants, total demand would be $200 \times 2{,}251 = 450{,}200$ with a standard deviation of $\sqrt{200} \times 1{,}600 = 22{,}627$. But it is unlikely that demands will be independent across restaurants. In other words, it is likely that there is positive correlation. Nevertheless, based on historical data, Burger King estimates the coefficient of variation for the total will be half of what it is for individual stores. As a result, a normal distribution will work for the total demand forecast.

c. How many toys must Burger King order for the distribution center to have an 85 percent in-stock probability?

d. If the quantity in part c is ordered, then how many units should Burger King expect to have at the end of the promotion?

e. If Burger King ordered the quantity evaluated in part a (i.e., the amount such that each restaurant would have its own inventory and generate an 85 percent in-stock probability) but kept that entire quantity at the distribution center and delivered to each restaurant only as needed, then what would the DC's in-stock probability be?

Q 10.5* **(Livingston Tools)** Livingston Tools, a manufacturer of battery-operated, hand-held power tools for the consumer market (such as screwdrivers and drills), has a problem. Its two biggest customers are "big box" discounters. Because these customers are fiercely price competitive, each wants exclusive products, thereby preventing consumers from making price comparisons. For example, Livingston will sell the exact same power screwdriver to each retailer, but Livingston will use packing customized to each retailer (including two different product identification numbers). Suppose weekly demand of each product to each retailer is normally distributed with mean 5,200 and standard deviation 3,800. Livingston makes production decisions on a weekly basis and has a three-week replenishment lead time. Because these two retailers are quite important to Livingston, Livingston sets a target fill rate of 99.9 percent.

a. Based on the order-up-to model, what is Livingston's average inventory of each of the two versions of this power screwdriver?

b. Someone at Livingston suggests that Livingston stock power screwdrivers without putting them into their specialized packaging. As orders are received from the two retailers, Livingston would fulfill those orders from the same stockpile of inventory, since it doesn't take much time to actually package each tool. Interestingly, demands at the two retailers have a slight negative correlation, -0.20. By approximately how much would this new system reduce Livingston's inventory investment?

Q 10.6 **(Restoration Hardware)** Consider the following excerpts from a *New York Times* article (Kaufman, 2000):

> Despite its early promise . . . Restoration has had trouble becoming a mass-market player. . . . What went wrong? High on its own buzz, the company expanded at breakneck speed, more than doubling the number of stores, to 94, in the year and a half after the stock offering . . . Company managers agree, for example, that Restoration's original inventory system, which called for all furniture to be kept at stores instead of at a central warehouse, was a disaster.

Let's look at one Restoration Hardware product, a leather chair. Average weekly sales of this chair in each store is Poisson with mean 1.25 units. The replenishment lead time is 12 weeks. (This question requires using Excel to create Poisson distribution and loss function tables that are not included in the appendix.)

(* indicates that the solution is at the end of the book)

    a. If each store holds its own inventory, then what is the company's annual inventory turns if the company policy is to target a 99.25 percent in-stock probability?

    b. Suppose Restoration Hardware builds a central warehouse to serve the 94 stores. The lead time from the supplier to the central warehouse is 12 weeks. The lead time from the central warehouse to each store is one week. Suppose the warehouse operates with a 99 percent in-stock probability, but the stores maintain a 99.25 percent in-stock probability. If only inventory at the retail stores is considered, what are Restoration's annual inventory turns?

Q 10.7 **(Study Desk)** You are in charge of designing a supply chain for furniture distribution. One of your products is a study desk. This desk comes in two colors: black and cherry. Weekly demand for each desk type is normal with mean 100 and standard deviation 65 (demands for the two colors are independent). The lead time from the assembly plant to the retail store is two weeks and you order inventory replenishments weekly. There is no finished goods inventory at the plant (desks are assembled to order for delivery to the store).

    a. What is the expected on-hand inventory of desks at the store (black and cherry together) if you maintain a 97 percent in-stock probability for each desk color?

You notice that only the top part of the desk is black or cherry; the remainder (base) is made of the standard gray metal. Hence, you suggest that the store stock black and cherry tops separately from gray bases and assemble them when demand occurs. The replenishment lead time for components is still two weeks. Furthermore, you still choose an order-up-to level for each top to generate a 97 percent in-stock probability.

    b. What is the expected on-hand inventory of black tops?

    c. How much less inventory of gray bases do you have on average at the store with the new in-store assembly scheme relative to the original system in which desks are delivered fully assembled? (*Hint:* Remember that each assembled desk requires one top and one base.)

Q 10.8 **(O'Neill)** One of O'Neill's high-end wetsuits is called the Animal. Total demand for this wetsuit is normally distributed with a mean of 200 and a standard deviation of 130. In order to ensure an excellent fit, the Animal comes in 16 sizes. Furthermore, it comes in four colors, so there are actually 64 different Animal SKUs (stock-keeping units). O'Neill sells the Animal for $350 and its production cost is $269. The Animal will be redesigned this season, so at the end of the season leftover inventory will be sold off at a steep markdown. Because this is such a niche product, O'Neill expects to receive only $100 for each leftover wetsuit. Finally, to control manufacturing costs, O'Neill has a policy that at least five wetsuits of any size/color combo must be produced at a time. Total demand for the smallest size (extra small-tall) is forecasted to be Poisson with mean 2.00. Mean demand for the four colors are black = 0.90, blue = 0.50, green = 0.40, and yellow = 0.20.

    a. Suppose O'Neill already has no extra small-tall Animals in stock. What is O'Neill's expected profit if it produces one batch (five units) of extra small-tall black Animals?

    b. Suppose O'Neill announces that it will only sell the Animal in one color, black. If O'Neill suspects this move will reduce total demand by 12.5 percent, then what now is its expected profit from the black Animal?

Q 10.9* **(Consulting Services)** A small economic consulting firm has four employees, Alice, Bob, Cathy, and Doug. The firm offers services in four distinct areas, Quotas, Regulation, Strategy, and Taxes. At the current time Alice is qualified for Quotas, Bob does Regulation, and so on. But this isn't working too well: the firm often finds it cannot compete for business in one area because it has already committed to work in that area while in another area it is idle. Therefore, the firm would like to train the consultants to be qualified in more than one area. Which of the following assignments is likely to be most beneficial to the firm?

a.

	Alice	Bob	Cathy	Doug
Qualified areas:	Quotas	Regulation	Strategy	Taxes
	Regulation	Taxes	Quotas	Strategy

(* indicates that the solution is at the end of the book)

b.

	Alice	Bob	Cathy	Doug
Qualified areas:	Quotas Regulation	Regulation Quotas	Strategy Taxes	Taxes Strategy

c.

	Alice	Bob	Cathy	Doug
Qualified areas:	Quotas Regulation	Regulation Quotas	Strategy Regulation	Taxes Quotas

d.

	Alice	Bob	Cathy	Doug
Qualified areas:	Quotas Strategy	Regulation Taxes	Strategy Quotas	Taxes Regulation

e.

	Alice	Bob	Cathy	Doug
Qualified areas:	Quotas Strategy	Regulation Taxes	Strategy Quotas	Taxes Regulation

Appendix

Areas of the Cumulative Standard Normal Distribution

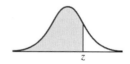

An entry in the table is the proportion under the curve cumulated from the negative tail

z	G(z)	z	G(z)	z	G(z)
−4.00	0.00003	−1.30	0.09680	1.40	0.91924
−3.95	0.00004	−1.25	0.10565	1.45	0.92647
−3.90	0.00005	−1.20	0.11507	1.50	0.93319
−3.85	0.00006	−1.15	0.12507	1.55	0.93943
−3.80	0.00007	−1.10	0.13567	1.60	0.94520
−3.75	0.00009	−1.05	0.14686	1.65	0.95053
−3.70	0.00011	−1.00	0.15866	1.70	0.95543
−3.65	0.00013	−0.95	0.17106	1.75	0.95994
−3.60	0.00016	−0.90	0.18406	1.80	0.96407
−3.55	0.00019	−0.85	0.19766	1.85	0.96784
−3.50	0.00023	−0.80	0.21186	1.90	0.97128
−3.45	0.00028	−0.75	0.22663	1.95	0.97441
−3.40	0.00034	−0.70	0.24196	2.00	0.97725
−3.35	0.00040	−0.65	0.25785	2.05	0.97982
−3.30	0.00048	−0.60	0.27425	2.10	0.98214
−3.25	0.00058	−0.55	0.29116	2.15	0.98422
−3.20	0.00069	−0.50	0.30854	2.20	0.98610
−3.15	0.00082	−0.45	0.32636	2.25	0.98778

(continued)

An entry in the table is the proportion under the curve cumulated from the negative tail   **(Concluded)**

z	G(z)	z	G(z)	z	G(z)
−3.10	0.00097	−0.40	0.34458	2.30	0.98928
−3.05	0.00114	−0.35	0.36317	2.35	0.99061
−3.00	0.00135	−0.30	0.38209	2.40	0.99180
−2.95	0.00159	−0.25	0.40129	2.45	0.99286
−2.90	0.00187	−0.20	0.42074	2.50	0.99379
−2.85	0.00219	−0.15	0.44038	2.55	0.99461
−2.80	0.00256	−0.10	0.46017	2.60	0.99534
−2.75	0.00298	−0.05	0.48006	2.65	0.99598
−2.70	0.00347	0.00	0.50000	2.70	0.99653
−2.65	0.00402	0.05	0.51994	2.75	0.99702
−2.60	0.00466	0.10	0.53983	2.80	0.99744
−2.55	0.00539	0.15	0.55962	2.85	0.99781
−2.50	0.00621	0.20	0.57926	2.90	0.99813
−2.45	0.00714	0.25	0.59871	2.95	0.99841
−2.40	0.00820	0.30	0.61791	3.00	0.99865
−2.35	0.00939	0.35	0.63683	3.05	0.99886
−2.30	0.01072	0.40	0.65542	3.10	0.99903
−2.25	0.01222	0.45	0.67364	3.15	0.99918
−2.20	0.01390	0.50	0.69146	3.20	0.99931
−2.15	0.01578	0.55	0.70884	3.25	0.99942
−2.10	0.01786	0.60	0.72575	3.30	0.99952
−2.05	0.02018	0.65	0.74215	3.35	0.99960
−2.00	0.02275	0.70	0.75804	3.40	0.99966
−1.95	0.02559	0.75	0.77337	3.45	0.99972
−1.90	0.02872	0.80	0.78814	3.50	0.99977
−1.85	0.03216	0.85	0.80234	3.55	0.99981
−1.80	0.03593	0.90	0.81594	3.60	0.99984
−1.75	0.04006	0.95	0.82894	3.65	0.99987
−1.70	0.04457	1.00	0.84134	3.70	0.99989
−1.65	0.04947	1.05	0.85314	3.75	0.99991
−1.60	0.05480	1.10	0.86433	3.80	0.99993
−1.55	0.06057	1.15	0.87493	3.85	0.99994
−1.50	0.06681	1.20	0.88493	3.90	0.99995
−1.45	0.07353	1.25	0.89435	3.95	0.99996
−1.40	0.08076	1.30	0.90320	4.00	0.99997
−1.35	0.08851	1.35	0.91149		

Using Microsoft Excel®, these probabilities are generated with the NORMSDIST(z) function.

Appendix B

ROGER BOHN

Kristen's Cookie Company (A1)[1]

You and your roommate are preparing to launch Kristen's Cookie Company in your on-campus apartment. The company will provide fresh cookies to hungry students late at night. You need to evaluate the preliminary design for the company's production process in order to make key policy decisions, including what prices to charge, what equipment to order and how many orders to accept, and to determine whether the business can be profitable.

Illustration by Jane Simon

Business Concept

Your idea is to bake fresh cookies to order, using any combination of ingredients that the buyer wants. The cookies will be ready for pickup at your apartment within an hour.

Several factors will set you apart from competing products such as store-bought cookies. First, your cookies will be completely fresh. You will not bake any cookies before receiving the order; therefore, the buyer will be getting cookies that are literally hot out of the oven.

Second, like many Boston-based area ice-cream shops, you will have a variety of ingredients available to add to the basic dough, including chocolate chips, M&M's, chopped Heath bars, coconut, walnuts, and raisins. Buyers will telephone in their orders and specify which of these ingredients they want in their cookies. You will guarantee completely fresh cookies. In short, you will have the freshest, most exotic cookies anywhere, available right on campus.

The Production Process

Baking cookies is simple: place all the ingredients in a mixing bowl and mix them; spoon the cookie dough onto a tray; put the cookies into the oven; bake them; take the tray of cookies out of the

---

[1] This case is intended to be used with "Kristen's Cookie Company (A2)," HBS No. 686-094.

Professor Roger Bohn prepared this case with the assistance of Research Associates K. Somers and G. Greenberg. HBS cases are developed solely as the basis for class discussion. Cases are not intended to serve as endorsements, sources of primary data, or illustrations of effective or ineffective management.

oven; let the cookies cool; and, finally, take the cookies off the tray and carefully pack them in a box. You and your roommate already own all the necessary capital equipment: a high-capacity professional-grade electric mixer, cookie trays, and spoons. Your apartment has a small oven that will hold one tray at a time. Your landlord pays for all the electricity. The variable costs, therefore, are merely the cost of the ingredients (estimated to be $0.60/dozen), the cost of the box in which the cookies are packed ($0.10 per box; each box holds a dozen cookies), and your time (what value do you place on your time?).

A detailed examination of the production process, which specifies how long each of the steps will take, follows. The first step is to take an order, which will be extremely fast and 100% accurate, since your roommate has devised a method using the campus e-mail system to accept orders and to inform customers when their orders will be ready for pickup. Because this runs automatically on your personal computer, it does not take any of your or your roommate's time. Therefore, this step will be ignored in further analysis.

You and your roommate have timed the necessary physical operations. The first physical production step is to wash out the electric mixer's bowl and beaters from the previous batch, add the ingredients to the bowl, and turn on the mixer to mix the ingredients. The electric mixer can hold and mix ingredients for up to three dozen cookies. You then spoon the cookies, one dozen at a time, onto a cookie tray. These activities take 6 minutes for the washing and mixing steps, regardless of how many cookies are being made in the batch. That is, to mix enough dough and ingredients for three dozen cookies takes the same 6 minutes as for one dozen cookies. However, spooning the cookies onto the tray takes 2 minutes per tray.

The next step, performed by your roommate, is to put the cookies in the oven and set the thermostat and timer, which in total takes about 1 minute. The cookies bake for the next 9 minutes. So total baking time is 10 minutes, during the first minute of which your roommate is busy setting the oven. Because the oven only holds one tray, a second dozen takes an additional 10 minutes to bake.

Your roommate also performs the last steps of the process by first removing the cookies from the oven and putting them aside to cool for 5 minutes, then carefully packing them in a box and accepting payment. Removing the cookies from the oven takes a negligible amount of time, but it must be done promptly. It takes 2 minutes to pack each dozen and about 1 minute to accept payment for the order.

This is the process you plan to use to produce cookies by the dozen at Kristen's Cookie Company. As experienced bakers know, a few simplifications were made in describing the actual cookie production process. For example, the first batch of cookies for the night requires preheating the oven. However, such complexities will be put aside for now. Begin your analysis by developing a process flow diagram of the cookie-making process.

Key Questions to Answer Before You Launch the Business

To launch the business, you need to set prices and formulate rules for accepting orders. Some issues will be resolved only after you get started and try out different ways of producing the cookies. Before you start, however, you at least want a preliminary plan, with as much as possible specified, so that you can do a careful calculation of how much time you will have to devote to this business each night, and how much money you can expect to make. For example, when you conduct a market survey to determine the likely demand, you will want to specify exactly what your order policies will be. Therefore, answering the following operational questions should help you:

1. How long will it take you to fill a rush order?

2. How many orders can you fill in a night, assuming you are open four hours each night?

3. How much of your own and your roommate's valuable time will it take to fill each order?

4. Because your baking trays can hold exactly one dozen cookies, you will produce and sell cookies by the dozen. Should you give any discount for people who order two dozen cookies, three dozen cookies, or more? If so, how much? Will it take you any longer to fill a two-dozen cookie order than a one-dozen cookie order?

5. How many electric mixers and baking trays will you need?

6. Are there any changes you can make in your production plans that will allow you to make better cookies or more cookies in less time or at lower cost? For example, is there a bottleneck operation in your production process that you can expand cheaply? What is the effect of adding another oven? How much would you be willing to pay to rent an additional oven?

Problems for Further Thought

1. What happens if you are trying to do this by yourself without your roommate?

2. Should you offer special rates for rush orders? Suppose you have just put a tray of cookies into the oven and someone calls up with a "crash priority" order for a dozen cookies of a different flavor. Can you fill the priority order while still fulfilling the order for the cookies that are already in the oven? If not, how much of a premium should you charge for filling the rush order?

3. When should you promise delivery? How can you look quickly at your order board (list of pending orders) and tell a caller when his or her order will be ready? How much of a safety margin for timing should you allow?

4. What other factors should you consider at this stage of planning your business?

5. Your product must be made to order because each order is potentially unique. If you decide to sell standard cookies instead, how should you change the production system? The order-taking process? Other policies?

BABSON

BAB034
Revised June 17, 2004

Appendix C

West Coast University Student Health Services - Primary Care Clinic

"We have a real opportunity to make some meaningful changes in the way things are done around here. With the move to the new facility, we are looking at how we can transform the process to make our patients much more satisfied with the service they are getting. Now they are seeing the doctor they have chosen for primary care more often than not, but the waiting times can be just too long. I am hoping that this new team approach will do the trick!"

Joan Carwin
Director
Primary Care Clinic
WCU Student Health Services

The West Coast University Student Health Services

The West Coast University Student Health Service (SHS) served the medical needs of the 34,700 students who attended the West Coast University (WCU). All undergraduate students (23,769) were required to be enrolled in the medical plan, while it was optional for, but usually chosen by, graduate students. Almost half of the total student population used the SHS in any given year.

The Student Health Services (SHS) offered care in a primary care clinic and several other specialty clinics. SHS had its own laboratory and performed most routine lab procedures in-house. In addition, the SHS had its own pharmacy and offered dental services, HIV testing, and a broad menu of social services.

SHS was principally funded by registration fees, so many services were available at no additional charge to registered students such as office visits, routine procedures, some lab tests, x-rays performed in SHS and fitness exams. Other services such as pharmaceuticals, immunizations, more extensive physicals or more specialized lab tests were available for a minimal fee.

David Wylie, Director of Babson College Case Publishing, worked with Professors Ashok Rao, Jay Rao and Ivor Morgan, Babson College, to prepare this case as a basis for class discussion rather than to illustrate either effective or ineffective handling of an administrative situation.

The Primary Care Clinic (PCC) served most medical needs. As elsewhere in SHS, physicians, nurses and nurse practitioners provided care. For continuity of care, patients were encouraged to choose a primary care clinician to act as a principal health care provider. In addition to meeting basic health needs, this clinician could act as an excellent resource for other health concerns.

The PCC also offered walk-in care that did not require an appointment. It was geared toward the diagnosis and treatment of minor medical problems. Because of the demand for the limited walk-in spaces, patients were sometimes asked, after having a condition assessed by a triage nurse, to return at another time especially when a particular doctor or nurse practitioner was scheduled to be on duty. Usually clinicians would set separate appointments for follow up care directly with the patient, thus circumventing triage nurses. Time was scheduled every week for clinicians to devote to such appointments. Referral appointments were also available to the specialty clinics.

Specialty Clinics provided specialized care when referred by another SHS clinician. Services included immunization, dermatology, orthopedics, surgery, internal medicine, allergy, head and neck, ophthalmology, urology and neurology.

The Primary Care Clinic

The PCC was the only walk-in clinic among the three. Patients could walk-in without appointments on a first-come-first-serve basis. The SHS was open Monday through Friday, 8 a.m. to 5 p.m. The facility was closed during noon to 1 p.m. when the clinicians would take a lunch break. Students visited the PCC for treatment of problems ranging from common colds, fever, nausea, warts to more serious problems like chest pains, hepatitis and emergencies.

The PCC was staffed, five full-time and three part-time nurse practitioners (NP), five full-time and four part-time physicians (MD), six medical assistants (MA), and support staff personnel. (See **Table 1** for information on staffing levels and cost and **Table 2** for Staffing Levels at the Walk-in Clinic). One of the NPs was always on duty as triage. However, NPs would take turns at performing this function. The staffing was assigned in cohorts of 2 MDs, 1 NP and 1 MA. Doctors were either scheduled to staff the walk-in clinic or to see appointments (see **Exhibit 1** for the staffing schedule). Nurses when not assigned to walk-in were assigned to handle appointments as well as a variety of other activities such as fitness tests and immunizations. They were helped in this by the MAs. Staffing assignments were arrived at by considering the demand during different times of the day and different days of the week, and the times clinicians felt was needed to set aside for appointments.

Table 1
Yearly Clinical Staffing Costs - Primary Care Clinic

Physicians	7.0	$722,375
Nurse Practitioners	6.5	351,661
Medical Assistants	6.0	173,343
TOTAL		$1,147,279

* Full time equivalents

Table 2
Staffing Levels in the Primary Care Clinic

Dr. Able	28	Nurse Juan	40
Dr. Babson	32	Nurse Kaplan	40
Dr. Carwin	20	Nurse Llowe	40
Dr. Davidson	40	Nurse Merlin	40
Dr. Epstein	36	Nurse Nelson	12
Dr. Franck	32	Nurse Olin	16
Dr. Good	28	Nurse Plather	40
Dr. Heather	32	Nurse Quin	24
Dr. Ito	20		
Total Hours	**268**	**Total Hours**	**252**

Note: Staff members were considered to be full time if they worked more than 30 hours per week.

Joan Carwin was director of the PCC, reporting directly to the Director of the Student Health Services. (See **Exhibit 2**, Organizational Chart). She was a doctor and held a masters degree in public health. Her responsibilities as director of the PCC, however, precluded a full-time medical practice. She split her time evenly between her role as an administrator and a physician. She had been working at the clinic for twelve years, and at her current position for six years.

In the fall of 1997, the PCC was scheduled to move out of its current location in the basement of the Student Health Center facility into a new building specifically designed for the clinic. While there was a high level of excitement coupled with the usual degree of apprehension associated with such a move, Carwin and her colleagues saw this imminent move as an opportunity to review and improve the way in which services were being delivered to the students.

Several factors had prompted this self-examination. First, the opening of the new WCU Medical Plaza within the university campus offered students easy access to qualified WCU physicians' private practices, posing a direct threat to the SHS customer base, and ultimately to its funding. Second of all, an independent study in 1995 of patient satisfaction, by a WCU student, as detailed below, suggested that there was room for improvement. Some of the students interviewed commented as follows:

> "...every time I come in I become very frustrated. I usually have to wait about 30 minutes before being seen. However, once I am seen I am very satisfied. The doctors and nurses are great - it just takes patience to get a chance to see them...."

> "...highly satisfying - excellent care and counseling from my primary care physician...the only bad thing is trying to schedule the time to see her on a student's schedule...."

"...it's just very frustrating and nerve-wracking until you've been to student health a few times and understand how it works (complicated - going to several different stations for a simple visit)...."

"...other than lengthy waiting times (45 minutes - 1 hr), the people have been very helpful, courteous, cheerful...."

"...I have used the system a lot over the past 6 years...mainly because of my physician...for many years I refused to see anyone but him because he is very thorough...."

"...I chose my doctor. He became my primary physician even though that's not how things are run here...."

The combination of the threat of decreased usage and the promise of improvement prompted an examination of the systems and procedures being used at the PCC. As the move into the new facility loomed, Carwin knew that she would have to make some definitive recommendations.

Patient Satisfaction Survey

In May of 1995, 2,100 randomly selected users of the SHS were surveyed to elicit their perceptions along ten dimensions of service, from which 775 responses were gathered (see **Table 3**). While those service dimensions that were directly related to quality of health care were rated quite highly, those related to organizational operations and procedures clearly showed room for improvement. The fact that non-users perceived the service provided by the clinic as unfavorable was of great concern to Carwin, in particular the variance between user and non-user ratings of waiting times both to get an appointment and at the walk-in clinic.

In a further study using conjoint analysis[1], it was determined that while students preferred to see particular clinicians, reducing waiting times were more important than the choice of clinician. The importance of the choice of clinician, however, increased if the patients perceived the medical condition to be more serious.

The study also revealed that there were several classes of patients at the PCC: those who preferred to have a physician as their primary care provider, those who wanted a primary care provider but were indifferent among clinicians, and finally those who did not want a primary care clinician at all. Indeed, those patients who had chosen primary care physicians and visited them regularly had significantly higher satisfaction with the PCC than the other respondents.

---

[1] Conjoint analysis is a research technique which requires respondents to make choices between competing combinations of attributes and which provides an understanding of preferences.

Table 3
Results of Student Survey

Service Dimension	Percent Favorable Ratings*		
	Non-user	**User**	**Total**
Confidentiality	93.9	93.5	93.6
Cost of Services	74.8	88.0	83.5
Quality of Medical Care	78.1	83.7	81.8
SHS Staff Attitudes	72.2	81.5	78.4
Physical Environment of SHS	73.1	77.6	76.1
SHS Hours of Operation	71.9	70.1	70.7
Campus Location	60.1	64.5	62.9
Admin. Paperwork and Procedures	46.0	63.8	57.8
Waiting Time to Get an Appointment	42.7	57.3	52.2
Waiting Time in Walk-in Clinic	29.4	52.3	44.6

* The survey was conducted using a four-point scale: very satisfied, somewhat satisfied, somewhat dissatisfied, and very dissatisfied. "Percent Favorable Ratings" referred to the percent of ratings that fell into the two positive categories. No neutral category was included.

In a follow-up study, 26.5% of the respondents noted excessive waiting times, 14% difficulty in obtaining appointments in a timely fashion, and 6.7% facility problems.

After meeting with members of her staff, Carwin formulated three broad objectives for improving the operations and service at the PCC:

- Reduce the waiting time for seeing a healthcare provider.

- Transform the perception of the clinic as an impersonal bureaucracy.

- Improve student perceptions (especially non-users) about the performance and effectiveness of the PCC.

Carwin's concern for waiting times was expressed in a recent memo to all the clinicians, "In order to accomplish PCC's objectives, we will need to use all of our skills and experience thoughtfully and in a timely manner. That includes being present and on time, especially for that first appointment of each day. Tardiness at the beginning of the day will no longer be tolerated as before. If it occurs, patients will be shifted to other staff, and the tardy staff member will be held accountable. Frequent tardiness will be dealt with in the context of the performance evaluation."

The Current System

In an effort to make SHS more personalized and pro-active, students were encouraged to choose a primary-care clinician. Doctors supported this initiative since they also wanted *their* patients to see only them. They felt strongly that it contributed to the quality of health care they could provide. In addition to being able to monitor their patients' progress several eminent doctors argued that medical care involved more than just treatment, and that personal relationships added to both the quality of health care and the patient's perception of good service. Many patients therefore had the attitude of wanting to see "my doctor".

Upon arriving at the PCC, each patient registered at the front desk and was asked to complete a short form indicating the nature of the medical problem (see **Exhibit 3**). While the student waited in a central waiting room, the staff at the front desk reviewed this form and requested that the student's medical record be pulled from the central files and given to a triage nurse. Only a few patients ever required urgent care. These patients were taken immediately to the first available nurse practitioner or doctor.

The staff at the front desk was also in charge of checking student identification, entering account information, identifying no-shows, scheduling staff, rotating nursing and medical students, and reconciling billing disputes.

Every walk-in patient who did not require emergency care had to see the triage nurse. The triage nurse would make an assessment of the patient's condition to determine if either an NP or an MD should see him or her. (See **Exhibit 4** for a list of conditions requiring the attention of a doctor). Whenever possible, the patient was scheduled to see his or her chosen primary care physician. Often, however, that clinician was not on duty in the walk-in clinic and the patient would have to return when he or she was on duty. The triage nurse therefore screened the walk-in patients and directed the patients to the clinicians. The screening was influenced by the medical condition of the patient, the patient's request to see a particular provider, if any, and each clinician's commitment for pre-scheduled appointments.

If the triage nurse determined that a clinician should see a patient, the patient took the medical file to the MA (who served three clinicians) located just outside the clinicians' office. All the full time clinicians had their own offices. The part-timers shared offices. Carwin and the head NP, who were part-time administrators and part-time clinicians, had their own offices. The clinician offices served as examination rooms as well. The PCC had 15 offices (See **Exhibit 5** for PCC Layout). The MA checked vital signs (temperature and blood pressure) and was responsible for paperwork, requesting lab tests, updating charts as noted by clinicians, returning charts to the filing area, and gathering charts for those who had appointments. They also filled out lab slips, performed various routine tests, fitted ortho devices, and washed wounds and ears. The actual attention given by the MA to each patient only took on average 3.5 minutes. Then they waited for the clinician to become available at which point they would meet in the clinician's office. Typically the clinician was with the patient for about 20 minutes. Then as the patient left the clinician would take 5 minutes to make notes and add to the patient's file.

Those patients who had come earlier but who had chosen to return when their clinician was on duty also checked in at the front desk. They then went directly to the medical assistant assigned to the clinician they wanted to see.

During the previous six months, physicians had treated 9,005 patients and nurse practitioners 6,760 patients. Sixty percent of patients were walk-ins, while the rest had appointments directly with clinicians. Twenty-one percent of all patients had a specific clinician. If a walk-in patient had a specific clinician they would request that person. If that person was not available, the patient would ask when the person would be available and plan to return at that time. Sometimes they had to wait two or even three days before their clinician would be available. If the triage nurse felt the patient should be seen earlier, he or she would try to persuade the patient to see one of the clinicians present. Usually, however, the patient would simply return when their clinician was available. On a typical day forty-five percent of the patients coming for walk-in care were returning to see their specific clinician.

Twenty-two percent of the meetings with MDs could have been treated by NPs, but were not due to patient preference for single clinician care. The mix of patients requiring MD versus NP attention did not vary meaningfully at different times of the day or the week. Overall traffic at the clinic did, however, change substantially both by the day and the day of the week. This system worked, but waiting times were excessive. (See **Exhibit 6** for process flow diagram of the current system, **Exhibit 7** for that of the new system, **Exhibit 8** for a summary of arrivals and **Exhibit 9** for the schedule of individual clinicians).

The Proposed Team System

Carwin had been working with her staff to devise a plan which she hoped would provide a suitable compromise to allow patients to still receive personalized medical attention yet avoid the long waiting times.

The basic structure of the plan was to assign all patients to teams comprised of MDs and NPs, regardless of their desire for personalized service. They would therefore no longer be able to request a certain clinician, but only a team. Patients would be assigned to teams so that each team had a patient load proportionate to its size. The teams would be scheduled so that there were always members of each team scheduled to be on hand to treat patients in their group. For example, if a team were composed of one MD and one NP, at least one clinician would always be available to see walk-ins. So, if a patient had requested the specific team, they might sometimes see the MD and on other occasions see the NP.

An incoming patient would still go to the front desk to fill out the short registration form. The form would be used to trigger pulling the medical record. The records would then be transferred to a triage nurse. The patient would wait in the front waiting area until the triage nurse could assess the need to see an MD or a NP, whether the patient should or could return for an appointment, and make an appointment if needed. The records would then be given to a "pool" of medical assistants who would take the vital signs and enter the information on the forms. Carwin estimated that at any time there could be an equivalent of up to 4 medical assistants in the pool. The records would then be put into a rack according to each patient's chosen or assigned medical team. When the appropriate clinician was free, the patient would be directed to an examination room.

The new facility was centrally located near the busy campus open-air theater. The PCC was to be on the first floor of this four-floor facility, with an attractive lobby facing the triage center and a comfortable waiting room with a full bank of windows near the central medical assistants' station. The ten examination rooms were arranged around this station, each shared by two clinicians. The remaining three upper floors housed administrative and clinicians' offices, the pharmacy, specialty clinics, a physical therapy center, and record storage. A dumb waiter would transport medical records between the fourth floor and the first floor. The clinicians would be sharing offices as well under he proposed plan, two per room, however these offices would no longer be used as examination rooms. All staff lockers would be located on the fourth floor.

Most of the NPs were enthusiastic about the move, realizing that the new facility would create a more pleasant work and treatment environment. As with any design, however, they also had some concerns. The examination rooms and clinician offices had little natural light, for example, and the only elevator seemed to be very slow. The clinicians had signed up for one or more groups to work on operational issues for the move. These relocation work groups dealt with inventory, displays, security, waste disposal, space assignments, emergency and patient flow issues. The operations coordinator, Jean Sarti, described the response from the NPs and staff to be very positive. Even though the MDs had signed up for these teams, they were described as apathetic and silent during team meetings. In fact MDs chose not to participate on 1/3 of the teams.

Reactions to the formation of the proposed clinician provider teams were not too different. The RNs and MAs were enthusiastic and up beat about the proposed changes. Some thought that the team approach was a great way to improve communications among providers and between patients and the PCC. Some noted "as long as we have to share offices, we might as well belong to teams," "I have always felt the need for a mentor," "I've heard that the team structure is working great at the WCU internal medicine division." Most of the MDs, however, were taciturn. Carwin thought that they actually were distressed but reluctant to express their opinions. She was unsure how to convince them of the benefits of the program and thus get their support.

While Carwin knew the new system would provide some improvement, she had not yet determined how many medical assistants should be assigned to the pool at various times, nor did she know the composition of the clinical teams.

She felt the composition of the clinical teams was of utmost importance. If structured properly it would reduce the waiting times as well as reduce the number of returns. The present system was effectively a team of one. So, if the clinician were not available the patient requesting that clinician would have to return. She knew that sometimes this meant the patient would have to return as much as three days later. She was also acutely aware that this contributed significantly to the poor perception of the services offered. However, if she went to the other extreme and said that everyone belonged to the same team, then in effect the patient would no longer have the choice to choose a specific clinician. She knew that this extreme would be unsatisfactory to patients. She was also well aware that many of the clinicians would criticize this approach as being too impersonal and detract from the quality of care. This was an argument to which she was sympathetic.

Guidelines

As Carwin considered the problem she realized she would need some help. Having used a WCU student before, she wondered if another would be available to help with this problem. As a first step she called some of the senior clinicians together for the purpose of outlining some concrete goals. The group came up with the following guidelines:

- Total waiting time of 20 minutes or less.

- Less than five percent of patients unable to see their specific team when they came to the walk-in clinic.

•The maximum delay for seeing a team clinician should be one day.

The ultimate goal was to improve the level of service to the patients. She also realized that one key to making the transformation smooth and effective was to gain the full support of the clinical staff.

Exhibit 1
Staffing Schedule

Walk-in Clinic[2]

	Monday			Tuesday			Wednesday			Thursday			Friday		
	MD	NP	MA	MD	NP	MA	MD	NP	MA	MD	NP	MA	MD	NP	MA
8 - 9	2	1	1	0	0	1	2	1	1	2	1	1	2	1	1
9 - 10	2	1	1	2	1	1	2	1	1	2	1	1	2	1	1
10 - 11	2	1	1	2	1	1	2	1	1	2	1	1	2	1	1
11 - 12	2	1	1	2	1	1	2	1	1	2	1	1	4	2	1
12 - 1	0	0	0	0	0	0	0	0	0	0	0	0	0	0	0
1 - 2	4	2	2	2	1	1	4	2	2	2	1	1	4	2	2
2 - 3	4	2	2	2	1	1	4	2	2	2	1	1	4	2	2
3 - 4	4	2	2	2	1	1	4	2	2	2	1	1	4	2	2
4 - 5	2	1	1	2	1	1	2	1	1	2	1	1	4	2	2

Appointment Coverage

	Monday		Tuesday		Wednesday		Thursday		Friday	
	MD	NP	MD	NP	MD	NP	MD	NP	MD	NP
8 - 9	4	4	0	0	3	1	5	3	4	4
9 - 10	4	4	4	4	5	1	5	3	4	4
10 - 11	5	6	4	4	5	3	6	5	4	4
11 - 12	5	6	4	4	5	3	6	5	2	3
12 - 1	0	0	0	0	0	0	0	0	0	0
1 - 2	4	4	4	4	1	2	5	4	4	3
2 - 3	4	4	4	4	1	2	5	4	4	3
3 - 4	4	4	4	4	1	2	5	4	4	3
4 - 5	6	5	4	4	3	2	5	4	4	3

[2] MD - Doctors, NP Nurse Practitioners, MA - Medical Assistants. The NPs took turns at the triage function so one was always on duty.

Exhibit 2
Organizational Chart

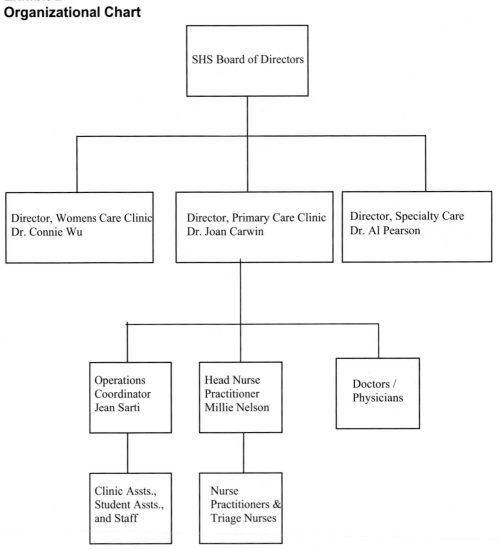

Exhibit 3
Registration Form

WCU STUDENT HEALTH SERVICE - REQUEST FOR SERVICE

Present this card with your current registration or optional health card and photo ID to the eligibility screener desk.

REGISTRATION #_____

LAST NAME   FIRST   MIDDLE

        DATE OF BIRTH

LOCAL ADDRESS, CITY, AND ZIP CODE

    PHONE NUMBER

STATE REASON FOR VISIT (YOU MAY STATE "PERSONAL PROBLEM")

SHS 800 Revised 11/87   1-OUTCARD   2-ACCOMPANY
RECORD

Exhibit 4
Conditions Requiring the Attention of a Doctor
(add those for NPs, adding frequency for each kind of condition)

Accident check
Acute body pain
Acute or chronic fatigue
Back pain
Blacking out or dizziness
Blood in stools, urine, or cough
Blurred vision, change in vision, double vision
Changing scar
Chest pain
Heart murmur
Hepatitis exposure
High blood pressure or rapid heart beat
Hypoglycemia
Inability to urinate
Irregular menstruation
Joint pains
Migraine headaches
Pneumonia
Testicular pain
Thyroid problems
Tremors or shaking
Trouble breathing or swallowing
Yellow skin coloration

Exhibit 5
PCC Layout

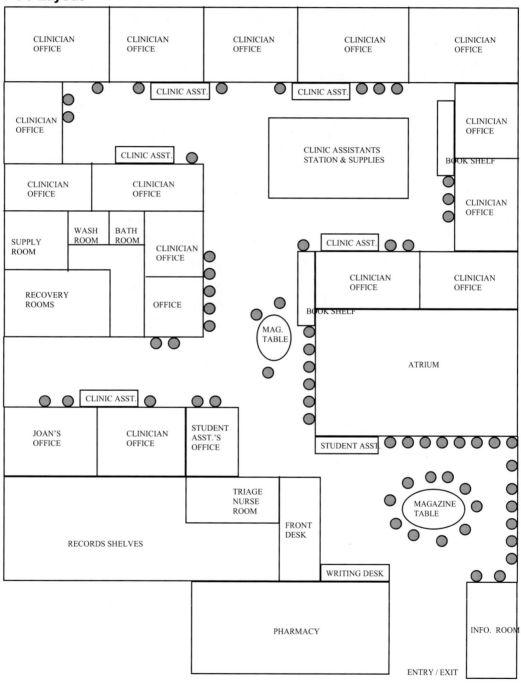

Exhibit 6
Process Flow Diagram - Current System

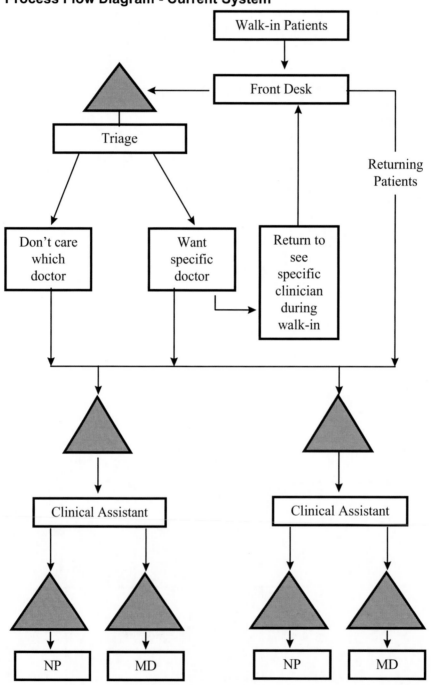

Exhibit 7
Process Flow Diagram - New System

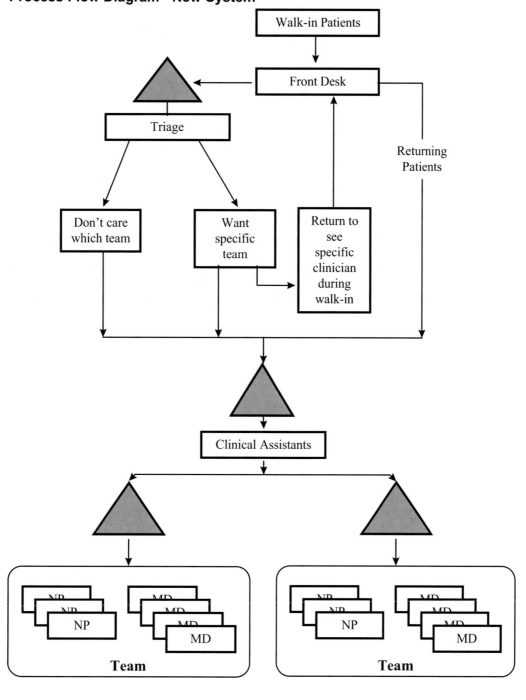

Exhibit 8
Summary of Arrival and Waiting Times

Average Patient Arrival Times for Walk-in Clinic

8 - 9	13	13	12	11	10
9 - 10	12	12	11	10	9
10 - 11	12	12	10	9	8
11 - 12	12	12	11	10	9
12 - 1	Closed	Closed	Closed	Closed	Closed
1 - 2	13	12	11	10	10
2 - 3	12	12	10	10	9
3 - 4	8	8	7	7	7
4 - 5	3	3	3	2	2
Total	85	84	75	69	64

Exhibit 9 - Schedule of Individual Clinicians

Mon	8-9	9-10	10-11	11-12	1-2	2-3	3-4	4-5
A-MD	--	--	--	--	A	A	A	A
B-MD	A	A	A	A	W	W	W	A
C-MD	W	W	W	W	W	W	W	W
D-MD	W	W	W	W	A	A	A	A
E-MD	E	E	A	A	A	A	A	A
F-MD	--	--	--	--	--	--	--	--
G-MD	A	A	A	A	W	W	W	A
H-MD	A	A	A	A	W	W	W	W
I-MD	A	A	A	A	A	A	A	A
J-NP	A	A	A	A	A	A	A	A
K-NP	W	W	W	W	A	A	A	A
L-NP	A	A	A	A	W	W	W	W
M-NP	A	A	A	A	A	A	A	A
N-NP	H	H	A	A	W	W	W	A
O-NP	E	E	A	A	--	--	--	--
P-NP	A	A	A	A	A	A	A	A
Q-NP	T	T	T	T	T	T	T	T

Thur	8-9	9-10	10-11	11-12	1-2	2-3	3-4	4-5
A-MD	A	A	A	A	W	W	W	W
B-MD	A	A	A	A	--	--	--	--
C-MD	A	A	A	A	--	--	--	--
D-MD	H	H	A	A	W	W	W	W
E-MD	--	--	--	--	A	A	A	A
F-MD	A	A	A	A	A	A	A	A
G-MD	A	A	A	A	A	A	A	A
H-MD	W	W	W	W	A	A	A	A
I-MD	W	W	W	W	A	A	A	A
J-NP	H	H	A	A	A	A	A	A
K-NP	A	A	A	A	A	A	A	A
L-NP	W	W	W	W	A	A	A	A
M-NP	A	A	A	A	A	A	A	A
N-NP	--	--	--	--	--	--	--	--
O-NP	A	A	A	A	--	--	--	--
P-NP	H	H	A	A	W	W	W	W
Q-NP	T	T	T	T	T	T	T	T

Tue	8-9	9-10	10-11	11-12	1-2	2-3	3-4	4-5
A-MD	--	--	--	--	--	--	--	--
B-MD	--	A	A	A	W	W	W	W
C-MD	--	--	--	--	--	--	--	--
D-MD	--	A	A	A	W	W	W	W
E-MD	--	A	A	A	A	A	A	A
F-MD	--	W	W	W	A	A	A	A
G-MD	--	A	A	A	A	A	A	A
H-MD	--	W	W	W	A	A	A	A
I-MD	--	--	--	--	--	--	--	--
J-NP	--	A	A	A	A	A	A	A
K-NP	--	A	A	A	A	A	A	A
L-NP	--	A	A	A	A	A	A	A
M-NP	--	W	W	W	A	A	A	A
N-NP	--	--	--	--	--	--	--	--
O-NP	--	T	T	T	--	--	--	--
P-NP	--	A	A	A	W	W	W	W
Q-NP	--	H	H	H	T	T	T	T

Fri	8-9	9-10	10-11	11-12	1-2	2-3	3-4	4-5
A-MD	A	A	A	W	W	W	W	W
B-MD	A	A	A	W	W	W	W	W
C-MD	--	--	--	--	A	A	A	A
D-MD	W	W	W	W	W	W	W	W
E-MD	W	W	W	W	W	W	W	W
F-MD	A	A	A	A	A	A	A	A
G-MD	--	--	--	--	A	A	A	A
H-MD	A	A	A	A	A	A	A	A
I-MD	--	--	--	--	--	--	--	--
J-NP	T	T	T	T	A	A	A	A
K-NP	W	W	W	W	A	A	A	A
L-NP	A	A	A	A	W	W	W	W
M-NP	A	A	A	W	W	W	W	W
N-NP	--	--	--	--	A	A	A	A
O-NP	A	A	A	A	--	--	--	--
P-NP	A	A	A	A	T	T	T	T
Q-NP	--	--	--	--	--	--	--	--

Wed	8-9	9-10	10-11	11-12	1-2	2-3	3-4	4-5
A-MD	P	A	A	A	W	W	W	W
B-MD	A	A	A	A	A	A	A	A
C-MD	P	A	A	A	--	--	--	--
D-MD	A	A	A	A	W	W	W	A
E-MD	W	W	W	W	W	W	W	A
F-MD	A	A	A	A	W	W	W	W
G-MD	--	--	--	--	--	--	--	--
H-MD	--	--	--	--	--	--	--	--
I-MD	W	W	W	W	--	--	--	--
J-NP	W	W	W	W	A	A	A	A
K-NP	P	P	A	A	W	W	W	A
L-NP	P	P	A	A	W	W	W	W
M-NP	T	T	T	T	A	A	A	A
N-NP	--	--	--	--	--	--	--	--
O-NP	--	--	--	--	--	--	--	--
P-NP	A	A	A	A	T	T	T	T
Q-NP	--	--	--	--	--	--	--	--

P - Physical
W - Walk-in
A - Appointments
T - Triage

Index